THE GREAT GURUS OF THE SIKHS SERIES

GURU TEGH BAHADUR AND GOVIND SINGH

Editor-in-Chief

O. P. RALHAN

ANMOL PUBLICATIONS PVT. LTD.
NEW DELHI-110002 (INDIA)

ANMOL PUBLICATIONS PVT. LTD.
4374/4B, Ansari Road, Daryaganj
New Delhi-110 002

Guru Tegh Bahadur & Govind Singh

First Edition 1998

ISBN 81-7488-696-6

PRINTED IN INDIA

Published by J. L. Kumar for Anmol Publications Pvt. Ltd., New Delhi-110 002 and Printed at Mehra Offset Press, Delhi.

Preface

'Great Gurus of the Sikhs' in six volumes is a monumental work by the editor drawing every succinct information on each of the ten Gurus from unapproachable historical and religious sources.

These volumes should not be treated simply in biographical sketches of their lives or travelogue of their lives, but an account of their teachings, philosophies, travelogue, their sufferings and sacrifices for the country, their mythological and theological aspects, socio-economic reforms, their political contention and wars with the autocracy at their times and many more touching incidents of their lives, miracles which they manifested on several occasions—all have been contained in them. These volumes are treasures of religious wealth enshrined in their sacred *Vanis*—viz. Guru Granth Sahib and on political scenario of their times.

The sufferings of the Gurus were immense during Mughal period. Guru Arjun Dev, Guru Teg Bahadur and Guru Gobind Singh sacrificed every thing for the sake of their sincere love for humanity and reforming zeal. Repressive policies and numerous maneuvre could not bend them, instead. The rulers have to bow before them for their unparallelled and unmatched chivalry shown by them in spite of great emotional hurdles.

These volumes are faithful and sincere narration of the political conditions, social conditions, religious fanaticity of the rulers, prevailing at that times and how all those Great Gurus not only fought against heavy odds but simultaneously never allowed to fade away the spiritual lamp lighted by them which even today imparts eternal peace to thousands of people not only of Sikh people but all other religions.

These volumes on Great Gurus of the Sikhs advocate tenaciously a superb, enchanting study for each and every one. Highly recommended for teachers, students, social reformers, historians. A useful and worthy of acquisition for each library. Section of Sikh history in each library remain incomplete without such a marvellous set.

Contents

GURU TEGH BAHADUR

1

Early Life

An event which took place just three hundred years ago like a ripple on the shore, is now rolling and roaring as a strong wave across the seven seas and is echoing throughout the world in hallowed memory of a man, the influence of whose life has never ceased, and who has left a permanent place in the world of religion. The man was Guru Tegh Bahadur, and the event was his martyrdom.

Tegh Bahadur was the youngest and sixth child of the sixth Guru, Hargobind and was born on Sunday, April 1, 1621 at Guru Ke Mahal at Amritsar. Gurditta was the eldest son, born in 1613. He was followed by his only daughter named Vire in 1615. Suraj Mal was born in 1617. The remaining three sons were Ani Rai, born in 1618, Atal Rai in 1619. The last three sons were born of Guru Hargobind's second wife, Nanaki, daughter of Hari Chand Khatri of Bakala, a village situated 40 km East of Amritsar and 4 km North of the modern Beas railway station near the river.

The child was brought up with great care and attention by his mother. The father made excellent arrangements for his education and training. The best teachers were engaged to givc him lessons in reading, writing, arithmetic, religion, music, physical exercises, riding and shooting. Bhai Buddha was given general charge of the child's upbringing in all directions.

Tegh Bahadur was administered *charan pahul* or baptism at the age of eight. Hargobind's life routine of hunting, meeting the congregations, visiting free masses, praying at the Hari Mandir and holding court at the Akal Takht deeply influenced the growing mind of the lad. On the death of his brothers he became so sad and serious that he avoided worldly pleasures and turned to meditation and prayers.

In 1632 A.D. Guru Hargobind was staying at Kartarpur, 15 km West of Jullundur. The future Guru was then eleven years old. Lal Chand Khatri of this place offered his daughter Gujari in marriage to the blooming lad. Mother Nanaki approved of the match and the nuptial ceremony was performed with the great splendour and solemnity.

Hakim Alim-ud-din, generally known as Wazir Khan, a native of Chiniot in the district of Jhang, now in Pakistan, was appointed Governor of Lahore in 1628 by the Emperor Shah Jahan. In 1633 he was transferred to Agra, where he died the next year. According to Dr. Trilochan Singh, "Wazir Khan was respected by the Sikh Gurus for his liberal views, deep scholarship and love of truth", and after Prime Minister Asaf Khan, "he was the most trusted official in Shah Jahan's regime." Besides, the celebrated Sufi saint, Mian Mir, a resident of Lahore, is stated to have been on the best of terms with the Sikh Gurus. He was highly venerated both by Shah Jahan and the Crown Prince Dara Shukoh. The contemporary author, Mohsin Fani states that Hargobind offered his formal allegience to Shah Jahan and made friends with the local Faujdar, Yar Khan.

Thus, in the circumstances no warfare between the Guru and the Government could have taken place during the years from 1628 to 1633, as is alleged by some writers. Dr. Trilochan Singh observes:

"The Emperor was now at Lahore. It was difficult to influence him as long as Wazir Khan was the Viceroy, but now that WAzir Khan had been transferred to Agra, it seemed easier to get military aid from Lahore," by officials who were jealous of the Guru. This writer further states:

"Both Wazir Khan and Mian Mir were the silver and golden bonds bridging the gulf between the aggressive and bigoted forces of Mughal Imperialism and the progressive and resurgent forces of Sikh faith."

Hence a cleavage between the Guru and the Mughal authorities could take place after the transfer of Wazir Khan and death of Mian Mir, both of which took place in 1633 A.D. The battles of Jallo and Sangrana seem to have taken place in 1633; the battle of Amritsar in 1634; the battle of Hargobindpur in 1635, the battles of Lahara and Gurusar in 1637, and the last battle of Kartarpur in 1638. The last expedition was sent from Lahore under the command of Mir Badehra and Paindah Khan. They were joined by the Jullundur troops. The Guru had only 5,000 soldiers with him. In a hard fought battle at Kartarpur, both the enemy commanders were killed. In this battle the future Guru Tegh Bahadur displayed such remarkable skill and spiritedness that his father conferred the title of Tegh Bahadur on him by which name he came to be known in history.

Tegh Bahadur means Lord of the Sword or prizefighter. General Sir John J.H. Gordon says that Tegh Bahadur preferred to be called Deg Bahadur, Lord of Hospitality or the support of the poor and cherisher of the hungry. Tegh Bahadur was at this time 17 years old. His remarks led to the following saying :

Jis ki deg
Us ki tegh
(One who is charitable commands the sword).

From Kartarpur the Guru went to Phagwara. There he stayed for some time. Mohsin Fani says as the place was situated on the highway from Delhi to Lahore, 16 km East of Jullundur, it was not safe to reside there for long. Hence Guru Hargobind decided to settle at Kiratpur. Nanaki had already lost her two elder sons, Ani Rai and Atal Rai. She did not like to go there with her only son and young daughter-in-law owing to family, jealousies. She obtained the Guru's permission to go to Bakala, her home town, and there she went and settled with her parents Hari Chand and Hardevi. Tegh Bahadur was present at Kiratpur on the occasion of Guru Hargobind's death in February 1644 together with his mother, wife and brother-in-law Kripal Chand, and after the funeral rites all of them returned to Bakala.

Tegh Bahadur lived at Bakala for nearly 26 years. Some lands of Hargobindpur had been assigned to Tegh Bahadur and the family led a comfortable life on the share received from the cultivators. To avoid the burning heat of summer every well-to-do family had a basement dug into the floor where the members of the household retired in the afternoon. Tegh Bahadur got such a cell erected for himself to meditate in solitude and peace of soul. Such a cell was generally called Bhra. His wife Gujari also devoted a good deal of her time to prayer, reflection and contemplation.

Guru Hari Rai, 1644-1661

Of Guru Hargobind's five sons, two had survived him. The elder was Suraj Mal and the youngest Tegh Bahadur. The Guru could nominate either of them as his successor, but he preferred the second son of his deceased eldest son Gurditta, named Hari Rai. His elder brother was Dhir Mal. Hari Rai was a lad of fourteen years, born at Kiratpur on January 30, 1630. Shah Jahan's eldest son Dara Shukoh was the crown prince, and Punjab was his fife. He believed in saints, whether Muslim Hindu or Sikh, and he maintained cordial relations with Guru Hari Rai.

Shah Jahan fell ill in September, 1658, and a civil war began among his sons for the throne. Dara was defeated by Aurangzeb in May, 1658. Dara fled towards the Punjab. Guru Hari Rai joined him at Rupar at the head of 2,000 troops. The Prince and the Guru reached Lahore on July 3, 1658. "But Dara was utterly broken down in body and spirit." Finding the Prince in an indecisive mood and Aurangzeb in hot pursuit of him, Guru Hari Rai returned to Kiratpur.

After firmly establishing himself on the throne. Aurangzeb summoned Guru Hari Rai to his Court. The Guru sent his 14-year old eldest son Ram Rai. He was instructed to concentrate on God and reply to the Emperor carefully and resolutely. He was advised to keep in view Guru Arjan's conduct, when Jahangir ordered him to modify the hymns in the holy Granth. He was warned to avoid flattery and to behave with grace and dignity.

The lad being over-zealous and ambitious, and perhaps out of fear for his life, tried to win over the Emperor and his courtiers. He was asked to explain why the following verse in the holy Granth abused the Musalmans:

> "Matti Musalman ki pere pai kumhar,
> Ghar bhande ittan kian jalti kare pukar."

(The dust of a Musalman is kneaded by a potter into a dough and he converts it into pots and bricks, which cry out as they burn.)

The hymn expressed Guru Nanak's vision that cremation and burial differed little. Ram Rai was overawed by the splendour of the court. In order not to offend the Emperor, Ram Rai, just in his early teens, replied that Guru Nanak's actual word was *'Beiman'* or an atheist, and not *'Musalman'* which appeared in the text by the mistake of the scribe. His answer naturally pleased the Emperor, but offended the Sikhs of Delhi who reported the matter to the Guru at Kiratpur.

Guru Hari Rai was deeply distressed at his son's behaviour in having insulted Guru Nanak and the Granth Sahib. The Guru declared Ram Rai unfit for Guruship and immediately excommunicated and excluded him from succession. Hari Rai observed:

> "The Guruship is like a tiger's milk which can only be contained in a golden cup. Only he who is ready to devote his life thereto is worthy of it. Let Ram Rai not look on my face again."

His decision was conveyed to Ram Rai as well as to the Sikhs at Delhi. Ram Rai could not come to Kiratpur and stayed at the Mughal Court from September, 1661 to 1666 A.D., where he conducted himself as a faithful courtier. Shortly afterwards Guru Hari Rai passed away at Kiratpur on October 6, 1661 at the young age of 31.

Guru Hari Krishan, 1661-1664

Guru Hari Rai had nominated his younger son Hari Krishan to be his successor. He was born on July 7, 1656. Thus he became Guru at the age of five, and was called the 'Child Saint.' Ram Rai was living at Delhi. He pressed his claim for Guruship. Aurangzeb was fully occupied in settling state affairs and had no time to turn his attention to a matter which had no urgency. Besides, he wanted the family feud to develop into an unbridgeable gulf. In 1662 he fell seriously ill, and next year went to Kashmir to recoup his health. He returned to Delhi on January 18, 1664. Ram Rai complained against his supersession, and sought the Emperor's help in getting him the Guruship. Aurangzeb was a pastmaster in the art of diplomacy. He wanted to take full advantage of the rift which had grown between the two brothers. He was keen to use Ram Rai for weakening the Sikh movement. He summoned Hari Krishan to Delhi to justify his claim to Guruship. Mirza Raja Jai Singh of Amber (Jaipur) was asked to call the Guru to Delhi. Jai Singh sent his agent Diwan Paras Ram, with suitable presents, requesting the Guru to come to Delhi on the Raja's surety. The Guru's mother was terribly afraid of the machinations of Ram Rai and the stern character of the Emperor, who had destroyed all his male relatives in the most brutal manner. But nobody could dare disobey Aurangzeb.

Hari Krishan came to Delhi and put up in the house of Mirza Raja Jai Singh at the village of Raesina in the Raja's estate called Jaisinghpura in the suburbs of the capital, 6 km distant from the Red Fort. Shortly afterwards, the Guru had an attack of smallpox with high fever, and he became delirious. Owing to this infectious disease the Guru was shifted to a house in village Bhogal near the present Nizam-ud-din railway station.

The Sikhs who were attending on him realized that the Guru might succumb to the fatal disease. They were anxious to secure from him nomination of a successor according to old tradition. They placed a coconut and five paise in a golden dish before him and pressed him to name his successor. As a rule a child would never call his ancestors by name out of respect, and would address them as *chacha, tau, baba* or *dada*. If they were living away from him, their place of residence would also be mentioned. The child placed his right hand on the dish and the articles, and uttered 'Baba Bakale', obviously referring to Tegh Bahadur, his grand-uncle, who had been living at village Bakala for the past 26 years. He closed his eyes, became unconscious, and expired on March 30, 1664, the Baisakhi day, at the age of eight. He was cremated on the bank of the river Jamuna where now stands Gurudwara Bala Sahib. A big Gurudwara was later on constructed at Raesina, called Bangla Sahib, at the site of the bungalow of Mirza Raja Jai Singh in which Guru Hari Krishan had stayed.

Tegh Bahadur becomes Guru — August, 1664

Guru Hari Krishan was accompanied by about twenty trusted followers. They included Diwan Dargaha Mal who was in charge of the Guru's finances, his nephews Mati Das and Sati Das, Gurditta the high priest, a descendant of Bhai Buddha and Dyal Das of Alipur in Multan district. These five men represented the panchayat and cabinet of the Guru's court. They discussed the matter and came to the conclusion that the obvious reference of Baba Bakale implied Tegh Bahadur who was the only Baba (grandfather) of Guru Hari Krishan then living and who was at Bakala. All other sons of Guru Hargobind had died. They first escorted Guru Hari Krishan's mother, Sulakhani, to Kiratpur towards the end of April 1664 A.D. They stayed there for a few months to console the grief-stricken lady, and set the Guru's household in order.

Meanwhile Guru Hari Krishan's nomination of 'Baba Bakale' had spread among the Sodhis of Kiratpur, Kartarpur and other places. Twenty-two of them set up their posts in village Bakala to claim Guruship. Eleven of them were Sodhis and the remaining eleven were *masands* or Sikh bishops. The most rebellious of them was Dhir Mal, the elder son of Guruditta, the eldest son of Guru Hargobind. He had shifted from Kartarpur to Bakala on hearing the news of Guru Hari Krishan's death. He based his claim on the principle of primogeniture or seniority by birth, although this principle was never accepted by the Sikh Gurus, nor even by the Mughal rulers. Further, he possessed the original copy of the holy Granth prepared by Guru Arjan which had been deposited in the Gurudwara of Kartarpur for safety. He also employed many touts to proclaim his succession as the ninth Guru.

Tegh Bahadur remained undisturbed and unruffled by the uproar of impostors. By the divine light he knew that the call was for him, and he firmly believed that if he deserved it, it would come to him automatically without any effort on his part. So he did not change his way of living and kept busy in meditation and prayer as usual. His mother and wife also knew from intuition that the great hour in their lives had struck. But the violent activities of Dhir Mal greatly alarmed the ladies. Mother Nanaki invited Dwarka Das, a scion of the house of Guru Amar Das, from Goindwal to come to Bakala for the protection of Tegh Bahadur. He called the five members of the Guru's Panchayat from Kiratpur to announce their decision and offer the sacred articles of nomination to the new Guru on behalf of the deceased Guru. All of them reached Bakala about the month of August, 1664.

They went to Mother Nanaki's house and gave a brief account of Guru Hari Krishan's death and his nomination of Tegh Bahadur as the ninth Guru. A meeting of prominent persons of Bakala was called. Then the high priest Gurditta placed the sacred coconut and five copper coins before Tegh Bahadur, bowed before him and declared him the ninth Guru. Tegh Bahadur accepted the sacred articles in all reverence and humility and declared that he would remain ever loyal to the house of Nanak. It happened in August, 1664.

The impostors were still holding on, carrying on propaganda in their favour. In October, at the end of the rains Makhan Shah, a rich Banjara merchant, accompanied by numerous bullocks, horses, hounds and armed retainers, being a follower of the Sikh Gurus, arrived at Bakala, to pay homage to the true Guru. To avert a calamity befalling him on a previous occasion, he had prayed to the Guru to save him, vowing in his heart to make an offering of 500 gold coins, by way of thanksgiving. It was to fulfil this vow that he had gone there. Finding a multitude of Gurus and visiting all the twenty-two beaters of drums somebody suggested that he should visit a recluse named Tegh Bahadur. Makhan Shah had been deeply disgusted and disappointed with all these pretenders to Guruship, as none demanded the full amount of his dedication. He did not mind calling on Tegh Bahadur and laid two coins before him. Tegh Bahadur closed his eyes for a moment and then said that his vow was for 500 and not for two coins. Makhan Shah prostrated himself before the Guru and told the congregation that he was the true Guru.

Dhir Mal's men deeply resented Makhan Shah's intervention. The sixth, seventh and eighth Gurus had lived at Kiratpur. Dhir Mal was living during this period at Kartarpur. As he possessed the original copy of the holy Granth, he had established his influence in the Amritsar and Jullundur areas. He was afraid that Tegh Bahadur from Bakala might oust him from power. He, therefore, decided to kill Tegh Bahadur. About a hundred of his armed followers attacked the house of the Guru at a time when it was unguarded. A shot was fired at the Guru, and the bullet grazed his shoulder. The Guru's house was plundered of everything of value. Then Makhan Shah appeared on the scene. His men fell upon Dhir Mal's camp and seized the Guru's property along with some articles belonging to Dhir Mal, including his copy of the holy Granth.

When Tegh Bahadur heard about it, he declared:

> To exercise forgiveness is a great act,
> To exercise forgiveness is to give alms.
> Forgiveness is equal to ablutions at all places of pilgrimage.

Forgiveness ensureth man's salvation.
There is no virtue equal to forgiveness.

He ordered that everything brought from Dhir Mal's house, whether it belonged to the Guru or to the culprit, must be restored at once. The order was partially obeyed, as the copy of the holy Granth was retained without the knowledge of the Guru. This too was returned afterwards.

Guru Tegh Bahadur at Amritsar

Guru Tegh Bahadur left for Amritsar on February 30, 1665 and called at Hari Mandir. He was accompanied by his mother Nanaki, wife Gujari, her brother Kripal Chand, Makhan Shah and a few followers. The priests would not admit him and closed the doors of the holy Temple against him. The Temple was under the control of Prithi Chand's descendants, who was the eldest brother of Guru Arjan. Prithi Chand had been passed over from succession by Guru Ram Das. Prithi Chand called himself the sixth Guru, his son Meharban dubbed himself the seventh Guru, and his son Harji took the title of the eighth Guru. Guru Hargobind's houses and property were in his possession. Guru Tegh Bahadur and his party rested under a tree only a few metres to the North of Akal Takht. This place is termed Thara Sahib or the holy platform. A Gurudwara marks that site. Makhan Shah was strictly forbidden to take any action against the culprits. A peasant woman, Hariyan, of village Walla, 7 km from Amritsar, offered her house as shelter for the Guru and his family. Tegh Bahadur retired there in the evening to spend the night. In honour of the Guru's visit a fair is held at Walla called Kothe da Mela on the full moon day of Magh (January-February). In the Guru's absence Makhan Shah entered the Hari Mandir, and Guru Tegh Bahadur was admitted to the Temple where he worshipped for a while, and then left for Khadur, the place dedicated to Guru Angad and Goindwal, the seat of the third Guru, Amar Das. He then returned to Bakala.

Gurus Travels

The Guru lived at Bakala again upto the end of the rainy season, October 1665. "Here too he was not allowed to abide in peace, for the old jealousy and enmity of the Sodhis had revived." He later visited Kiratpur. "There again he was plagued with the jealousy of the Sodhis." Guru Tegh Bahadur made up his mind to go on a pilgrimage to the East. The reasons were plain. He did not find the atmosphere in the Punjab congenial for his work. He wished to follow the example of Guru Nanak by visiting holy places. He was desirous of meeting the Sikhs living outside the Punjab at many places in Northern India. He was keen to propagate the new religion to give consolation to suffering humanity. He left Punjab in November, 1665, accompanied by his mother, wife, her brother Kripal Chand, Dyal Das, Mati Das, Sati Das, and a few other devoted followers. He had his own tents, horses carriages, bullocks, camels and necessary equipment to meet his requirements on the journey. He usually halted outside a village or town in a garden or on the bank of a river.

Visiting Pehowa and Kurukshetra, Guru Tegh Bahadur reached Delhi. Ram Rai got him arrested, as he still claimed Guruship for himself. George Forster who wrote his book about one hundred years later, says that the Guru remained in gaol for two years. It seems that he was there only for two months. Mirza Raja Jai Singh was at this time in the Deccan carrying on a campaign against Shivaji. His son Raja Ram Singh represented him at the Mughal Court, and pleaded the Guru's innocence. He said that the Guru was on his way to visit the sacred places of pilgrimage and he stood surety for his conduct. From Delhi the Guru went to Mathura, Brindaban, Agra, Etawah, Kanpur and reached Allahabad about February 1666. At the last place he stayed for six months. Guru Gobind Singh says in the *Bachitar Natak:*

> Mur pit purab kin payana
> Bhant bhant ke tirath nana
> Jab eh Jat tribaini bhaye
> Pun dan karat bitaye.
>
> (My father went to the east,
> He visited all sorts of places of pilgrimage;
> When he reached Tribaini (Prayag),
> He spent his time in alms-giving).

It was at this sacred place in the divine atmosphere and celestial environment when Guru Tegh Bahadur was busy in giving away his spiritual and material wealth that Mata Gujari conceived for the first time in thirty-four years of her married life. Passing Mirzapur, Benares and Sasaram the Guru reached Gaya where he stayed a little longer. There he was joined by Raja Ram Singh of Amber. He arrived at Patna in November, 1666.

Shortly after the Guru's departure from Delhi, Raja Ram Singh was involved in a serious trouble. On the solemn pledge given by Mirza Raja Jai Singh as a Rajput for his safety and honour, Shivaji with his elder son called on Aurangzeb at Agra on May 12, 1666. He was placed under the custody of Raja Ram Singh. Finding their lives in danger, Shivaji and his son Shambhuji escaped from Agra by a stratagem on August 19, 1666. Sir Jadunath Sarkar writes: "The Emperor suspected that Shivaji had fled with the connivance of Ram Singh. The Rajput prince was punished first by being forbidden the court and then by being deprived of his rank and pay." Aurangzeb then ordered the prince to lead an expedition for the conquest of Assam. In reality he was sent there either to die of malaria, which was rampant in those parts and of which Aurangzeb's great general Mir Jumla, had died on March 31, 1663 or to be killed in fighting. In the event of Ram Singh's death, his state of Amber (Jaipur) was to be confiscated. The base of Ram Singh's operations was to be Dacca which was the capital of Bengal, and Shaista Khan, the Emperor's maternal uncle was its governor. A Mughal army formerly under Mir Jumla was already there. Ram Singh was required to take charge of this force along with his own troops. To begin with, he was to make a preliminary survey of the situation, while the formal order of his appointment accompanied by a *khilat* was issued later.

Ram Singh did not wish to stay at the court in an atmosphere of disgrace, humiliation and suspicion. He wanted to study the situation, and then call his armed force to join him. The young prince thought of one remedy to secure his safety in the unhealthy climate and hostile jungles, hills, wild elephants, and a determined foe aided as reputed, by sorcery. This was to keep Guru Tegh Bahadur with him. He set out in pursuit of Tegh Bahadur and met him at Gaya. He implored the Guru to keep him company during the operations. He said: "It was certain death to command the invading army, and it would be equally fatal for me to disobey the Emperor's orders. Hence I have come from distant Rajputana to seek the protection of thy holy feet." The Raja did not like to stay at Patna, a stronghold of the Mughals in the east and he wanted to be at his post without any delay. The Guru would not disappoint a true devotee. He could not take his family with him owing to the approaching confinement of his wife. So he left the family at Patna without making suitable arrangements for their residence. He exhorted the local Sikhs to help Kripal Chand and Dyal Das in looking after his family, and himself with Mati Das and Sati Das followed the prince to Dacca. From Monghyr the Guru wrote a letter to the Sikhs of Patna:

> "We are accompanying Raja Ji and have left our family at Patna. It is time for the congregation to serve the Guru." He added:
>
> "Bhai Dyal Das kahe
> Sangat Guru ka hukam kar mannana."

(Whatever Bhai Dyal Das says, the *Sangat* should accept it as Guru's command).

They reached Dacca in the beginning of 1667. There Tegh Bahadur got the happy news of the birth of his son, Gobind Rai, on December 22, 1666. Ram Singh spent two years in making preparations for the war, conducting negotiations at the same time for the submission of Ahoms of Assam without fighting, if possible. The Mughal troops were already there. His Rajput forces joined him long after his arrival at Dacca. The prince was accompanied on this journey only by a suitable contingent as bodyguard. Guru Tegh Bahadur also stayed here with the prince, and visited many places in the neighbourhood to meet his followers.

Ram Singh and Guru Tegh Bahadur left Dacca in December, 1668 and reached Dhubari in Assam, about 300 km distant, in February 1669. Ram Singh's expeditionary force consisted of 4,000 Rajputs, 18,000 Mughals, all horsemen, 30,000 infantry, and 15,000 local archers.

The Guru remained busy in meditation and prayers, giving his blessings to the Rajputs and other visitors. His fame spread far and wide. A prince of some state in Assam, named Raja Ram, heard about the Guru. He had no son, and earnestly desired to have a successor. He came with his two wives to pay homage to the Guru and requested for the boon of a son. The Guru blessed him.

Guru Returns

Guru Tegh Bahadur stayed with Raja Ram Singh in Assam for about two years and a half. Meanwhile reports of Aurangzeb's fanaticism and determination to convert the Hindu population to Islam, and to make Hindu India a purely Muslim state began to pour into Ram Singh's camp. Muhammad said Mustid Khan in *Maasir-e-Alamgiri* says that in April, 1669, "the Director of the Faith issued orders to all the Governors of provinces to destroy with a willing hand the schools and temples of the infidels; and they were strictly enjoined upon to put an entire stop to the teaching and practising of idolatrous forms of worship." Leaving aside what was happening to the Hindus, we refer only to the Emperor's doings with regard to the Sikhs. The contemporary historian, Khafi Khan, writes:

> "There is a sect of infidels called Guru, more commonly known as Sikhs. Their chief, who dresses as a fakir, has fixed residence near Lahore. From old times he has built temples in all the towns and populous places and has appointed one of his followers to preside in each temple as his deputy. When anyone of the sect brought presents or offerings for the Guru to the temple, the deputy had to collect them, and after deducting sufficient for his own food and expenses, his duty was to send the balance faithfully to the Guru. This sect consists principally of Jats and Khatris of the Punjab and of other tribes of infidels. When Aurangzeb got knowledge of these matters, he ordered these deputy Gurus to be removed and temples to be pulled down."

Kalimat-e-Tayyibat says, "a Sikh temple in a village in the Sarhind Division was turned into a mosque. Mirza Inayatullah Khan in his book *Ahkam-e-Alamgiri,* on pages, 12-13, states that under Aurangzeb's orders a Gurudwara of the Sikhs (*Butkhana-e-Nanakparastan*) in the town of Buriya, Parganah Khizarabad, Sarkar Sarhind, was pulled down by the Qazi and a mosque was built in its place. Sayyid Zafer Darvesh was appointed to be in charge of that mosque to guide prayers and benedictions. Some Sikhs attacked the mosque and killed the Darvesh. The Emperor suspended the Qazi and the Superintendent of Police (*Mohtaib*). Alimullah was appointed Qazi and his father head of the Police. Such incidents had become common.

When Guru Tegh Bahadur heard of these things, he decided to return to the Punjab immediately. He took leave of Raja Ram Singh in October 1671 and came to Patna where he stayed for a while. He showed his determination to proceed to the Punjab without delay. His Sikhs and supporters suggested that the Guru should leave his family at Patna for the present and recall them if he found the situation favourable in the Punjab. The Guru agreed. Having travelled for a few days, he changed his mind. He did not like to leave the family a thousand miles away from Kiratpur. He stopped and sent his trusted men to escort the family. In a fortnight they left Patna and joined Guru Tegh Bahadur at the place of his halting. Stopping on the way at prominent places like Kashi, Ayodhya, Lucknow,

Shahjahanpur, Bareilly, Moradabad, Hardwar, Saharanpur, the party arrived at Lakhnaur, 15 km from Ambala City, about February, 1672. The Guru left his family there under the protection of Bhikhan Shah, an influential Muslim chief of Ghuram, situated nearby and the Nawab of Saifabad, a town 6 km East of Patiala now called Bahadurgarh. He himself went to Kiratpur to study the attitude of his relatives.

Guru Tegh Bahadur did not like to stay at Kiratpur which was still rife with conspiracies and intrigues. But he was fascinated with the panoramic landscape of the region lying in the outer parts of the Shivalik Hills. At a distance of 8 km to the North below the hill of Naina Devi situated 13 km distant, close to the village of Makhowal, on the left bank of the Satluj, the Guru purchased a piece of fallow land from the Raja of Bilaspur for a sum of Rs. 500/- in March, 1672. The site acquired was named Chak Nanaki after his mother. The Guru had been supplied by Raja Ram Singh and his Rajputs with a sum of seven lakhs of rupees on the occasion of his departure from Assam, mostly in the form of *Darshni Hundis* (bearer cheques) issued by Jagat Seths on the bankers of important town and cities. Their credit existed not only in India, but also all over Asia, especially in Central and Western Asia which were closely connected by trade with India. With this money the Guru started construction of buildings at Nanaki Chak, and called his family from Lakhnaur after seven months on the sacred day of Dushera, October, 1672.

The Guru felt extremely happy at having a place of his own to reside, like the previous Gurus. Guru Nanak had lived at Kartarpur on the Ravi, Guru Angad at Khadur, Guru Amar Das at Goindwal, Guru Ram Das and Guru Arjan at Amritsar, Guru Hargobind, Guru Hari Rai and Guru Hari Krishan at Kiratpur. The sight of the Dhaula Dhar Range covered with snow in December, the hill of Naina Devi in front and the river Satluj flowing nearby, fascinated him. The joy of having a loving mother, a happy wife and a gifted son inspired him. He took strolls on the open high ground now marked by a cluster of buildings lying around the Gurudwara Sis Ganj. He named that area Anandpur or the Abode of Bliss. Sir George Campbell who served as deputy commissioner around here in 1844, calls this place "Anandpore-Makhowal."

About this time the sky began to darken. In 1672 the Afridis of the Khyber Pass revolted and inflicted terrible losses on the Mughals. "Ten thousand men fell under the enemy's sword in the field, and about two crores of Rupees in cash and kind was looted by the enemy. They captured twenty thousand men and women and sent them to Central Asia for sale." The Afridis were then joined by the Khataks. Their chieftain Khushal Khan, a great poet and warrior, inspired the tribesmen in their defiance of the Mughals both by pen and poniard. The situation grew so serious that Aurangzeb had to take the direction of operations in his own hands. He remained at Hasan Abdal near Rawalpindi, also called Panja Sahib, from June, 1674 to December, 1675.

During Aurangzeb's stay in the Punjab, local officials persecuted the Hindu population and converted them to Islam in large numbers in order to win the appreciation of the Emperor, in whose mind the spread of Islam was uppermost. Syed Muhammad Latif writes: "The Emperor had in those days thrown hundreds of Brahmans into jail, in the hope that if they first embraced the religion of the Prophet, the rest of the Hindus would readily follow their example." In Kashmir, thousands of Pandits were forced to embrace Islam. The Hindus were terror-stricken. Guru Tegh Bahadur realized the imperative necessity to encourage the Hindus and Sikhs to face the situation calmly and boldly and not to yield to despair and despondency. He decided to tour from village to village first in Malwa, the land lying between the rivers Ghaggar and the Satluj.

In this region the influence of the Gurus had been firmly established since the time of Guru Hargobind. Next he was to travel in the Jullundur and Upper Bari Doabs. He left Anandpur after the Diwali festival, in November, 1674. The main theme of his sermons was:

(i) Bhay Kahun ko det nah
Nahin bhay manat an
(Neither to terrorize others nor to fear anyone)

(ii) Gun Gobind gaiyo nahin
Janam akarath kin
Kah Nanak Har bhaj mana
Jeh bidh jal ko min
(You did not sing the praise of God,
And wasted your life in vain;
Nanak says, remember God,
As a fish remembers water.)

(iii) Dhan dara, sampat sagal
Jin apni kari man
In men kachnu sangi nahin
Nanak sachi jan.
(Wealth, family, property, all of which
you consider your own;
None of these shall abide with you,
Says Nanak, this is the truth).

(iv) Sab sukh data Ram hai
Dusar nahin koi,
Keh Nanak, sun re mana
Tah simrat gat hoi.
(God is the giver of all happiness, none else.
Says Nanak, hark my mind,
You will succeed by meditating on His Name).

As the Guru was meeting his disciples after eight or nine years, many men followed him during Tegh Bahadur's tours to listen to his sermons and to get his benediction. To serve the congregation the residents of the villages voluntarily collected foodstuffs, milk and clarified butter for the Guru's *langar*. The area was backward. Rain was scarce. It was almost a desert in the absence of any irrigation facilities. The poor and ignorant but hardy and tough people, were cowed down by Muslim officials, particularly at this time when the Emperor was present in Punjab.

The Guru tried to ameliorate the condition of the inhabitants with the money he had brought from Assam. He sunk wells at places where there was scarcity of drinking water. Tanks were constructed to store rain water which was not to be allowed to go waste. He purchased cows and gave them free to poverty-stricken families. He got trees planted at suitable places. He spent ten months in this tour, and visited numerous places. Attar Singh, chief of Bhadaur, in his book entitled "The Travels of Guru Tegh Bahadur and Guru Gobind Singh" in 137 pages, mentions some of the important places visited by the Guru.

The local officials were upset at the Guru's activities, and they submitted alarming reports to the Emperor. They accused him of having a large following, exacting money forcibly, and instigating people in revolt. Sayyid Ghulam Husain who compiled his history of India under the title of *Siyar-ul-Mutakhirin* one hundred years later, baselessly charged the Guru with plundering people. George Forster who met Ghulam Husain in Calcutta, and who journeyed in the Punjab, about the same time writes:

> "No document for the elucidation of this passage appearing in any of the memoirs of Hindostan that have reached my knowledge, I am prevented from discovering the quality of the crime which subjected Tegh Bahadur to capital punishment."

The exaggerated reports by Government officials alarmed the Emperor who had already gone through a bitter experience of a revolt on the frontier. He was not prepared to find the border province of Punjab in a disturbed condition, and he decided to punish Guru Tegh Bahadur.

The Guru had hardly settled down again at Anandpur when another catastrophe took place. Some of the Kashmiri Brahmins who were not prepared to embrace Islam under persecution called on Guru Tegh Bahadur to seek his guidance. They had heard about Guru Hargobind's visit to Kashmir in company with the Emperor Jahangir, and had knowledge of his warlike activities. The Guru's heart melted at their tale of woe. He became uneasy and restless at the said plight of innocent people. At this time the child Gobind, not even nine yet, appeared there. He innocently asked about the cause of sadness of the Guru and the visitors. The Guru replied that the nation required a holy man to sacrifice his life. The child remarked that there could be no holier person than the Guru himself. This was enough. The Guru took the child's observation as God's own oracle. His resolve was made. He informed the Brahmins that they should tell the rulers to convert Tegh Bahadur first and then they would follow his example.

The Pandits went back and told this to the Governor, who conveyed it to Aurangzeb at Hasan Abdal, situated close to the borders of Kashmir. The Emperor's mind was already prejudiced against Guru Tegh Bahadur. He hated the word *Sachcha Patishah* used by the Sikhs for the Guru. It implied that the Guru was a true king while the ruler of India was a false king. He also detested the word *Bahadur* in the Guru's name, as this was reserved for the nobility of the Mughal Court only. He ordered his deputies to summon him to the capital and force him to accept Islam or to lose his life.

The Guru realized that his end had come. He composed four stanzas marked as Dohiras Nos. 53, 54, 55, 56. In Nos. 53 and 55 he describes his difficulties and trials, and in Nos. 54 and 56 he expresses hope and faith in God's succour.

Dohira No. 53

Bal Chhutyo bandhan pare
Kachu na hot upae
Kah Nanak ab to Hari
Gaj jiyon hot sahae

(My strength is exhausted, I am in bondage,
I have no resource:
Saith Nanak, God is now my refuge;
May he succour me as He did the Elephant.)

Guru Tegh Bahadur then gave the reply himself:

Dohira No. 54

Bal hoa bandhan chhute
Sab kichh hot upae
Nanak sab kichh tumre hath main
Tum hi hot sahae

(Strength has come, the bondage is broken,
All the resources are there;
Saith Nanak, Lord! everything is in your power,
You are my refuge).

"The Emperor divided his residence between Delhi and Agra, but Delhi was the chief capital, where most of the state ceremonies took place." Tegh Bahadur was accompanied by five Sikhs. His life-long companion Bhai Mati Das, a Mohyal Brahmin of Kariala in Jehlam district, 10 km from Chakwal on the road leading to Katas Raj and his brother Sati Das were among them. Gurditta, a lineal descendant of Bhai Buddha was also there. Dyal Das, the eldest brother of Bhai Mani Singh Shahid, was the fourth. Jaita of the sweeper caste who attended to the menial work of the Guru and his companions, completed the group.

They were first taken to Agra where the Wazir of the Empire was staying; but latter on they were brought to Delhi. The Wazir under orders of "Emperor Aurangzeb," writes Syed Muhammad Latif, "whose efforts were directed to converting the whole world to the Mahomedan faith urged the Sikh Guru to embrace Mahomedanism." Tegh Bahadur turned down the proposal with contempt. He was then asked to show miracles. The Guru rejected the idea by saying that he could not interfere in the work of God.

Guru Tegh Bahadur was thrown into prison and was shut up in an iron cage in chains. He was subjected to severe tortures, both physical and mental. His companions were imprisoned elsewhere and the Guru was falsely told that they had fled away. The darogha of the gaol was Sayyid Hasan Abdullah of Mani Majra near Chandigarh. He treated the Guru with consideration as far as the circumstances permitted. In this situation the Guru composed two more chants:

Dohira No. 55

Sang sakha sab taj gae
Kou na nibhyo sath
Kaho Nanak yeh bipt men
Tek ek Ragh Nath

(My associates and companions have all
abondoned me;
No one has remained with me to the last.
Saith Nanak, in this calamity
God alone is my refuge).

He gives a reply in *Dohira* No. 56:

Nam rahyo sadhu rahyo
Rahyo Gur Gobind
Kauh Nanak eh jagat men
Kin japyo Gur mant.

(The Name remaineth, saints remain,
The Lord remaineth;
Saith Nanak in this world,
Few are God's devotees).

The Guru took five paise and a coconut, prayed and bowed before them. He sent these articles to his son Gobind Rai as a token of his nominátion to Guruship, through Gurditta.

The Martyrdom

The authorities now decided to finish this matter. Of the five companions of the Guru, Jaita remained free, as he had taken to sweeping the road in front of the Kotwali. Guruditta had escaped and gone to Anandpur disguised as a rustic.

Dyal Das, Mati Das and Sati Das were brought into the presence of the Guru. Then the most diabolical drama was staged at the place where now stands the Fountain in front of the Kotwali. Bhai Mati Das was asked to become a Musalman. He refused, saying that his own faith was true and he had no desire to change it. He was tied between two posts, and while standing erect, was sawn across from head to the Joins. He faced the savage operation with such composure, tranquility and fortitude that the Sikh theologians included his feat in the daily prayer (ardas) of the community. Dyal Das was tied up like a bundle and thrown into a huge cauldron of boiling oil. He was roasted alive into a block of charcoal. Sati Das condemned these brutalities. He was hacked to pieces limb by limb. Jaita was also present, disguised as a sweeper with a broom and a basket in his hands. He collected the remains of these martyrs at night and consigned them to the river Jamuna flowing at a stone's throw.

All this happened before the very eyes of Guru Tegh Bahadur. He was all the time repeating "Wah Guru." He knew his turn was coming next. He remained composed, unruffled and undismayed. His energy, thoughts, ideas, feelings and emotions had concentrated on God, and the dazzling divine light was beating upon his face. He realized that such immortal sacrifices could not go in vain. Their name would live forever. In this holocaust he saw a new nation of heroes. It was not the English nation as misinterpreted by some apologists for the British Raj but the Khalsa, the Sikh warriors, whose daring exploits and heroic deeds were to fill the pages of history later on. His followers were done to death on November 10, 1675.

At the end of this devil's dance the Guru was asked either to embrace Islam or show a miracle, or face death. The Guru refused to apostatize himself. About the performance of miracles, he turned down the demand with contempt. In the words of *Bachittar Natak,* an autobiographical fragment composed by Guru Gobind Singh, he is stated to have replied:

> 'The performance of theatrical acts is low,
> At which the devotees of God should feel ashamed.'

The Guru, contemplating the sufferings of the Indian people and the Kashmiri Brahmins who had sought his succour, was determined to offer the supreme sacrifice. The famous words of a poet express his resolve:

> Bahen jinahn di pakariye,
> Sir dije bahen na chhoriye
> Guru Tegh Bahadur boliya
> Dhar paiyai dharam na chhoriye

> (Give up your head, but forsake not those
> whom you have undertaken to protect.
> Says Guru Tegh Bahadur,
> Sacrifice your life, but relinquish not your faith).

On the morning fixed for the martyrdom, the Guru got up early. He bathed and sat in meditation, recited the *Japji* and *Sukhmani*. He reflected upon the supreme sacrifice of his grandfather, Guru Arjan, on the duties of the office of Guruship, and on his own responsibilities at this crisis. His resolve was already made.

The nobles and courtiers had gathered near the Kotwali in the open space. Thousands of spectators had flocked there. At 11 O'clock the Guru was produced before the multitude. "The Guru said before the assembly of the Omerahs that the duty of man was to pray to the Lord, but since he had been commanded by His Majesty to show a miracle, he had resolved upon complying with the King's orders. He wrote on a piece of paper, which he said was charmed, and then, having tied it round his neck declared that the sword would fall harmless on it by the effect of the charm which was written upon it. The executioner was now summoned to test the miraculous charm. The blow was given and the head of the Guru rolled on the floor to the amazement of the court.

A grand Gurudwara, called Sis Ganj (The Holy Head), stands at the place where the Guru was executed. Its adjacent building, the Kotwali Prison where the Guru was kept confined, was acquired by the Sikhs from the Delhi Administration on October 11, 1968.

The people of Delhi were so terror-stricken that none came forward to cremate the body of the Guru for fear of the authorities. Jaita, the sweeper, managed to steal the Guru's head, and carried it to Anandpur, 340 km distant, a prodigious performance, and presented it to Guru Gobind Rai, the nine-year old child. The new Guru bestowed all affection and love on this hero and remarked, "Ranghrete Guru ke bete", meaning "the untouchables are the Guru's own sons." The Gurudwara Sis Ganj at Anandpur Sahib marks the site where the head was reverently received and cremated.

A Labana Sikh, Lakhi Shah, a trader by profession, stole the decapitated body in a cart laden with cotton and cremated it in his village later named Rikab Ganj, 8 km distant from the Kotwali, by setting his own hut with all its belongings on fire to avoid detection. The ashes of the body were collected, placed in a brass vessel (*gagar*) and buried. A magnificent Gurudwara has been erected recently at this site.

This was the great turning point in Sikh history. The execution of the Guru and his companions in the most barbarous manner set ablaze the hearts of Hindus no less than of the Sikhs. They were convinced that any attempt at reconciliation with the Mughal authorities was impossible. It was realized that the people themselves must find their own salvation against a cruel and corrupt government. This task was taken up by Guru Tegh Bahadur's son and successor, Guru Gobind Singh.

As is well-known, Guru Gobind Singh transformed the Sikhs from a quietist sect of God-fearing people into a martial people, a church militant, that urged endless war against Aurangzeb and his successors. After untold sacrifices for nearly three quarters of a century, the Khalsa (militant Sikh Order) of Guru Gobind Singh liberated the Punjab and its neighbouring areas. Guru Tegh Bahadur's sacrifice was only the starting point for a mighty revolution. In the words of *Bachittar Natak*, already referred to:

> The Lord protected the paste-mark and the sacred thread.
> And in Kali-yuga performed a mighty heroic deed.
> This deed he performed for the protection of Dharma,
> Gave up his head, but not his passion.
> For men of God he spared himself no suffering,
> Gave up his head but uttered not a groan.
> Breaking the vessel of his life on the head of the monarch of Delhi,
> He departed for the celestial Realms—
> None has performed a mighty deed like Tegh Bahadur's.
> At Tegh Bahadur's departure the whole world was plunged in grief;
> The world wailed, but the Celestial Realms echoed with his glory.

2

On Human Rights

I

In order to understand the outlook that Guru Tegh Bahadur brought to bear upon the challenging problems of his contemporary social situation, it may be both useful and necessary briefly to refer back to the ideological base of the Sikh society, established by his illustrious predecessors. Guru Nanak, the founder of the Sikh faith, had propounded the fundamental principles which became the basis for subsequent developments under his successors. The ideology thus crystallised had at its rock-bottom the belief that the world, in its essence, is a spiritual and moral order (*dharamsal*—the abode of *dharma*), all-embracing and all-pervading. The Lord of the Universe, the Truth Absolute (*satinam*) permeates His entire creation. The word is "the True One's dwelling place" (Guru Angad Dev); it is "the ocean in which all beings move" (Guru Ram Das), or the thread on which the whole creation is strung" (Guru Arjan Dev). The mythical bull supposed to be supporting the Universe, is made out to be the self-same *dharma,* the Moral Law, born of *daya* (compassion) that holds the world in equilibrium. "God by His will made the world; God at His Will controlleth it; He beholdeth all things set under His Will", said Guru Angad Dev. It is this Divine Will or *hukam* which constitutes the sanction behind the Moral Law or *dharma*.

Mr. D.M. Brown in his book, *Indian Political Thought from Manu to Gandhi,* (p. 15) thus writes with regard to the connotation of *dharma* in ancient India: "The conception of Dharma was a far-reaching one embracing the whole life of man. The writers of Darmshastras in the ancient period meant by Dharma not a creed or religion, but a mode of life or code of conduct which regulated a man's work and activities as a member of the society, and as an individual it was intended to bring about gradual development of a man and to enable him to reach what was deemed to be the goal of human existence." Guru Nanak's conception of *dharma* was even more comprehensive in scope, as he disapproved of the conduct of all such people as renounced worldly life and chose to reside in recesses of mountains and forests. Mr. C.H. Payne has rightly remarked: "In the doctrines of Nanak morality has a higher place than in those of any other Hindu reformer. Few, even of the world's greatest philosophers, have laid down a more exalted moral code than is to be found in the pages of *Granth Sahib.* Purity of life is set forth as the highest object of human endeavour. Loyalty, chastity, honesty, justice, mercy and temperance are among the virtues on which vital stress is laid."

In the moral order of the conception of the Sikh Gurus, the individual (not caste as was the case in the earlier periods) had the pivotal position. He was regarded as one endowed with a unique personality worthy of all respect. The soul within him is a spark of Divine Light—*joyti sarup*. "If thou wouldest seek God, demolish not the heart of anyone, for God lives in every heart." (Guru Arjan, *Adi Granth,* p. 1384). A two-fold objective was set forth before the individual: to realise the best in him and thereby to merge his little self with the Infinite; to uphold the cause of *dharma* in the world. In his efforts to achieve his goals, he is supposed to act in a spirit of full responsibility always realising that all his actions are subject to the supreme Moral Law. "Truth is higher than other things but higher still is the life lived in truth" (Guru Nanak, *Adi Granth,* p. 62). The world being a divine revelation, is to be shunned in no case. On the other hand, the individual must live in it, work in it, participate in its affairs, grapple with its difficulties and challenges and endeavour to make it into an ideal place to live in. The world or society is valuable and must be valued as such, it being at once the theatre of our activities, the testing ground of our faith and principles as well as the measuring yardstick of our personal attainments. Guru Nanak had roundly condemned the *jogi* and *sidh* recluses who had equated religious life with a life of renunciation. He had categorically said that a truly religious man is one who practises religion in his everyday life. "Abide pure amid the impurities of the world; thus shelt thou find the way of religion—true *jog jugat.*" (Guru Nanak, *Suhi Rag, Adi Granth,* p. 730). Such a religion cannot be separated from morality. The person who is not a useful member of the society contributing his mite towards its welfare, is worthless and good for nothing. In fact an individual's very salvation depends upon how sincerely and zealously he tries to serve his fellow human beings. Guru Nanak's clear injunction in this regard was: "Only he finds the true path of life, who earns his bread by the sweat of his brow and shares the fruit thereof with his fellow-beings" (*Var Sarang, Adi Granth,* p. 1245).

Society which is a complex of social relations rather than a mere aggregate of individuals, if properly organised, can facilitate for the individual his task of self-fulfilment. The Gurus had made it clear that all social institutions and associations are intended to help the individual to achieve this main object of his life. Therefore, society must be organised on the healthy basis of justice, tolerance and equality and should be free from oppression of any kind. Subjection had been dubbed a curse, for it was said that under it happiness is not possible even in a dream. Likewise, encroachment upon what rightfully belongs to others was denounced. Exploitation, whatever its brand, was also condemned. All these evils, according to the Gurus, had their roots in the narrow self-interests of the people themselves. The problem could, however, be largely solved by inculcating in the minds of people a consciousness of the underlying unity of mankind. Lack of faith in the brotherhood of man blunts our vision and we easily fall into the habit of lending greater weight to dissimilarities than to similarities. To the Sikh

Gurus the principle of equality was a natural corollary from their faith in the unity of Godhead. If the Creater of all human beings, God, is one, then all his creatures, irrespective of their caste, creed, colour and sex, are equal.

Equality implies tolerance of differences existing in dress, food, faith, custom etc. It is difficult for one to endure for long without the other. Equality, if it does not promote tolerance, is a sham and tolerance if it is not based on a sense of equality, is a mirage. Guru Amar Das made it amply clear when invoking God he said, "Save them, O Lord: through whatever entrance they approach."

The state as the most powerful organ of the organized society has a vital role to play in the creation of an ideal society. Monarchy which was the established form of government then, was accepted by the Sikh Gurus as a legitimate and God-ordained institution. Kingship was regarded as a gift from God, a reward of good deeds done in previous life or lives. Not only that the king was believed to derive all his authority from God. However, this belief in the divine origin of kingly power was different from the Western doctrine of divine right of kings in one important respect. Unlike the West, the Gurus gave no countenance to the idea that kings can act as they like, owing no responsibility to the people placed under their rule. On the contrary, it was stressed that they should always be dispensers of justice and equality and must never wield their authority arbitrarily or despotically. They are responsible to God, "King of Kings", the Supreme Sovereign, for all their actions. They are only His agents commissioned to govern, in the manner of Platos' philosopher-king, with justice, kindness and sympathy and to promote the welfare of their people. They are to conduct their functions, so to say, as a mandate from God. Thus viewed, the monarchy or the state was held by the Gurus to be an inseparable part of the over-all moral order, intended to subserve its primary ends.

It is essential that the ruler must posses a high moral character if he is to carry out his mission successfully. As an individual, he must try to realise the same moral and spiritual aims as are necessary for other individuals. As a ruler, his responsibilities are even greater, for he is required to create, by means of benign-government, such conditions of life as are most needed to enable the individuals to develop their personalities to the full. The state is in fact meant for the betterment of the individual and not vice versa. If a king neglects his duties, oppresses the weak, indulges in activities prejudicial to the general welfare of his subjects and sets the fulfilment of his material pleasures as the primary goal of his life, he incurs the wrath of God and forfeits his mandate. God then, in His displeasure, snatches always the exalted office from him by way of chastisement and bestows it on some body else more suitable. Guru Nanak called Babar for his invasion of India a *Yama* sent by the Almighty as a chastiser of the "dogs" and "butchers" that the Lodi Sultans ruling over North India then were.

To the above views of the origin and functions of the state not wholly unknown here or elsewhere, the Sikh Gurus gave a revolutionary turn by emphasising that kings are not responsible to God alone, but to the people as well, for whose good they are set up by God. The people with the divine spark enshrined in them, are capable of knowing and interpreting the Divine Will. In fact, the people's will is also God's will. Therefore, if a ruler deviates from the path of justice and duty, it is just, the Gurus believed, to offer resistance to his wrong and unjust policies. "Both are fools—he who confers authority on those that deserve not and shameless are those who accept it" Z(*Adi Granth*, p. 1286). Herein lies the sanction for the people's right of resistance in the case of an unjust and tyrannical ruler who is beyond correction by any other means. The exercise of such a right is a sort of religious duty, as injustice and oppression are contrary to the Moral and Spiritual Order of God, as ordained in the world.

Granting the right of resistance inevitably led to sanctioning the use of force (*shakti*). The need for the use of force was realised immediately after the execution of Guru Arjan Dev in Lahore in 1606 A.D. and the martyred Guru's son and successor, Guru Hargobind laid aside *saili* and *topi*, previous symbols of guruship, and put on two swords, respectively standing for the concepts of *miri* (temporality) and *piri* (spirituality). Soon after he started militarising his community so as to be able to meet tyranny with force, if necessary. The implied theory behind this way of thinking, was that force by itself is no evil, that it is its misuse which makes it so, just as we say today that it is not science as such but its misuse which is reprehensible. On the use of arms for a noble cause, Guru Hargobind's statement is unambiguous and authoritative: "*Shaster garib ki rakhya jarvane ki bhakyya*"—arms are protection to the poor and destruction to the tyrant.

As a result of the new policy adopted by Guru Hargobind, the relations between the Sikhs and the Mughals became strained and a number of open armed clashes occurred between them. Guru Tegh Bahadur who was the youngest son of Guru Hargobind, was an eyewitness to most of them and is even said to have personally participated in the battle of Kartarpur and shown rare feats of bravery.

II

Sikhism and Mughal rule came into being almost simultaneously early in the 16th century. The founders of the two organisations, Guru Nanak and Babar, were contemporaries and by a popular but not yet confirmed Sikh tradition, they even had a meeting and exchanged ideas with each other. The remainder of that century passed off practically without any clash or disharmony between them. Rather, the long reign of the Emperor Akbar proved a great boon for the spread of Sikhism and the number of its votaries multiplied at a very fast rate.

Akbar held a high ideal of sovereignty. Unlike his predecessors, he abandoned the idea that he was primarily the king of his own Muslim co-religionists. Like a true liberal he raised himself above communal prejudices of the age and removed all discrimination between Muslims and non-Muslims in matters of public employment, taxation, religion and culture. *Jizya* and pilgrimage taxes which had all along been a great eyesore to the non-Muslims were abolished and in respect of the taxes which were retained, uniform rates for all, irrespective of creed or caste were prescribed. In the sphere of administrative and military service, an open-door policy was adopted and although the predominance of Muslim employees remained as before, opportunities of recruitment for others were greatly augmented and now it even became possible for non-Muslims to rise to the highest rung in the State ladder. Similar liberalism and equality of treatment marked the fields of religious and cultural fields.

Under the next two emperors, Jahangir and Shah Jahan, the liberal policy of Akbar was maintained to a large extent. But already certain forces had been generated by way of reaction of Akbar's policy, whose avowed purpose was to counter the new trends of liberalism in the name of safety of Islam. The leadership of these reactionary elements came from the Naqshbandis of Sirhind headed by Shaikh Ahmed and his successors. Assuming the title of *Mujaddid-Alif-i-Thani* (Reformer of the Second Millennium), Shaikh Ahmed Sirhindi took it upon himself to bring political, social and religious affairs of the Muslims in line with the orthodox *sunni* line. His conclusions were based on his personal prejudices, upon the conditions prevalent in and around Sirhind and in the reports which the distinguished Muslim officials conveyed to him from time to time. He thought that Akbar's policies had succumbed to the unwholesome influence of Shaikh Abul Fazl, Faizi and certain other nobles who had diverted him from the line of orthodox Islam. Akbar's appointment of Hindus to high positions, marriage with Rajput ladies, introduction of *Din-i-Ilhai* and *Sijda* and celebration of Hindu fairs and festivals were all viewed by the *Mujaddid* as posing a serious danger to Islam. He cherished the apprehension that a liberal policy, such as Akbar's, would strengthen and embolden non-Muslims to weaken and ultimately liquidate the Muslim rule. This kind of propaganda by the Naqshbandis had an adverse effect, albeit limited, on the policies of Jahangir and Shah Jahan, so that each one was less liberal than his predecessor. Thus, a departure from Akbar's wide outlook began. Though it was quite slight in the beginning, the rupture grew larger and larger with the passage of time until under Aurangzeb, it assumed the dimensions of a total reversal of Akbar's tolerant policy.

Aurangzeb was the most characteristic product of this Sirhindi School of thought. He held Akbar's eclaticism to be wrong and as ill-conceived, a grave danger to Islam, both as religion and as state organisation. The vast majority of Indians being non-Muslims, the best guarantee for the safety of Islam, he thought, was that they should be kept perennially in a state of abject subjection. Any attempt, in his view, to treat them liberally would in fact be tantamount to endeavouring to undermine the very basis of the Muslim society in India. And to reinforce him in is convictions there were already certain signs of stirrings noticeable among the non-Muslims, the most striking examples of which were provided by the Sikhs in the Punjab and the Marathas in the Deccan. His heart, therefore, from the very beginning, was set on the total reversal of Akbar's policy. "The accession of Aurangzeb to the throne in 1658 heralded the triumph of Muslim theologians. He invited their intercession in the affairs of the state when after the capture of Dara he had him tried and condemned as an apostate." (Sri Ram Sharma, *Religious Policy of Mughals,* 1972, p. 127). This was bound to be so, as the object dearest to his heart was to establish a purely Islamic state on the soil of India. The failure of the liberal-minded Dara Shikoh and later his execution spelt a great disaster to all trends to catholicity in the land just as it also marked the triumph of orthodoxy.

Aurangzeb began with puritanical measures. In the second year of his reign he discontinued the celebration of *Nauroz* (first day of the Solar Year). A few years later, music and dancing were prohibited. *Jharokha Darshan* was discontinued on the ground that it seemed too much like human worship; *tuladan* (weighing of the Emperor's body against gold, silver and various other valuables) was given up; royal astronomers and astrologers were dismissed; drinking was stopped and public censors were appointed to enforce prohibition strictly. Severe punishments were awarded for anything that was construed by the theologians as violating the spirit or even letter of Islam. Permissible length of the beard was fixed at four fingers and offenders against this order were penalized. Garments of golden weave were forbidden. Clay figures of birds, animals, men and women produced for children were disallowed and violations, if any, were punished. Lighting of lamps on the tombs of the saints and other persons was declared an offence. Shia Musalmans were prohibited from celebrating their festival of Muharram. Any talk on anybody's part creating the slightest suspicion of disrespect or want of respect towards Islam, the prophet, and his companions was severely punished, often with death.

But most of those restrictions were of a general nature and covered all communities. Non-muslims were singled out for discriminatory treatment in four specific fields, namely public services, construction and repair of temples, conversions and taxation. The Emperor's deep-rooted suspicion about the Hindus' bonafides seriously affected their position in the services, particularly in the higher echelons. Sri Ram Sharma, (op. cit. pp. 155-56) after careful comparison of relevant figures for Hindu *mansabdars* in the reigns of Shah Jahan and Aurangzeb has this to say on the matter: "This means that towards the end of Aurangzeb's reign there was a smaller number of Hindus occupying the *mansabs* of 1000 and above, than the number of similar *mansabdars* towards the end of Shah Jahan's reign. But the decrease in number becomes still more significant when we take into account the increase in the total number of the *mansabdars* which rose enormously in the reign of Aurangzeb. In 1657 under Shah Jahan there were 8,000 *mansabdars* in all, whereas in 1690 the number of *mansabdars* had risen to 14,556.... The percentage of the Hindus in the higher ranks of the State could not have been more than 50 per cent of what it was towards the end of Shah Jahan's reign."

Even before Aurangzeb, in the reigns of Jahangir and Shah Jahan, there were several instances of destruction of temples, but then these occurrences were generally part of military operations. It was only under Aurangzeb that religious considerations dominated the formulation of state policies and a carefully planned attack was launched forbidding the construction and repair of temples. The provinces of Gujarat and Orissa were among the first targets of Aurangzeb's fanaticism. Both of them witnessed wanton destruction of numerous sacred shrines. In 1666 the stone railing of the famous Keshav Rai Temple of Mathura was removed by imperial orders. Three years later in 1669 a general order was issued for the destruction of all schools and temples of Hindus. "Orders were now sent to the governors of all the provinces that they should destroy the schools and temples of the infidels and put an end to their educational activities as well as the practices of the religion of the Kafirs." (Sri Ram Sharma, op. cit., p. 171).

Soon after the issuance of the order, reports of the destruction of temples began to pour in from all parts of the Empire. A royal messenger was sent to demolish the temple of Malarina in May 1669. In August, 1669 the temple of Vishvanath at Benares was demolished and later a mosque was raised on the site of the demolished building. The temple of Gopinath in Benares too was destroyed at about the same time. An attempt was also made to destroy the Shaiva temple of Jangamwari in Benares, but the idea was somehow given up for the time being. Then came the turn of the temple Keshav Rai at Mathura built at a cost of 33 lacs of rupees by Rai Bir Singh Bundela in the reign of Jahangir. The temple was levelled to the ground and a mosque was ordered to be built on the site.

Similar destruction were ordered in the various Rajput States and Ajmer, Ujjain, Bengal and other provinces of the Empire. The temples of the Deccan, however, escaped the wrath of the Emperor because of his delicate position in the South on account of the Maratha rising. In this hour of crisis, the Sikhs suffered equally with the Hindus for "Aurangzeb ordered the temples of the Sikhs to be destroyed and the Guru's agents (*masands*) for collecting the tithes and presents of the faithful to be expelled from the cities" (Khafi Khan, *Muntkhab-ut-Tawarikh*, p. 652).

In the sphere of taxation discrimination against the non-Muslims was re-introduced. Although *Jizya* was not re-imposed till 1679, the pilgrimage tax was relevied. In 1665 it was ordered that the customs duties on the Muslims be fixed at 2.5 per cent and on the Hindus at 5 per cent. For gardens Hindus were required to pay the rate of 20 per cent, whereas for the Muslims the rate was 16.6 per cent. In 1669-70 it was ordered that in a lunar year the Muslims should pay 2.5% and the Hindus 5% on the price of their cattle.

Equally critical was the position of the non-Muslims in the matter of conversions. This had occurred in earlier periods as well. Islam being a missionary religion and the ruling Muslim community being in minority, great importance had always been attached to conversion work and many ingenious devices had been employed to attain this much-desired goal. However, the tempo was greatly intensified during the reign of Aurangzeb. There is certainly a lot of exaggeration in the Hindu and Sikh traditions that the Emperor made it a habit of collecting a maund and a quarter of sacred Hindu *janeus* (sacred threads) every day, but that he took considerable personal interest in the matter is well borne out. The fact that a deputation of Pandits appeared in the *durbar* of Guru Tegh Bahadur in May, 1675 and complained of the Government conducting a wholesale campaign of conversion is a historical testimony too strong to be ignored.

III

Having seen the Sikh spiritual thought that had been emerging before Guru Tegh Bahadur appeared on the scene, which he also inherited in all its richness, and the grave challenges posed by the triumph of Muslim orthodoxy under Aurangzeb, we now proceed to a brief study of Aurangzeb's attitude towards the Sikhs.

In the very first year of his reign, sometime in July or August 1658, an incident occurred which prejudiced his mind against the Sikhs greatly. Dara who was in flight, posted a large force under Daud Khan on the Beas river to ban the passage of the river by the pursuing troops of Aurangzeb. A similar but much weaker attempt had been made by him a little earlier to block the passage of Aurangzeb's troops across the Sutlej river. On one of these occasions, Guru Hari Rai, at the request of Dara no doubt, sent his small contingent of 2,200 troops for his help. But Dara faltered and the Guru withdrew his men immediately. It is difficult to say whether it was out of any bonds of personal friendship, or in view of the vital issues at stake that the Guru took this step, but perhaps both of these considerations might have been present in his mind.

Getting the necessary handle for interference in Sikh affairs the Emperor sent for the Guru, asking him to present himself at the Court and answer the complaints made to him against the Sikh teachings. The Guru sent his elder son, Ram Rai, for this purpose. Ram Rai answered all the points raised successfully, and apparently satisfied the Emperor. However, Guru Hari Rai was not happy about his manner of replying to the Emperor's inquiries and disowned him. In October, 1661 Guru Hari Rai breathed his last and his younger son, Harkrishan, succeeded him. Aurungzeb took advantage of the change in Sikh Guruship and summoned the child Guru to Delhi. The Guru accepted the invitation and proceeded to Delhi where he had a meeting with the Emperor. While staying in Delhi, Guru Harkrishan was attacked by small-pox and passed away in March, 1664. The Emperor's prejudices, however, continued as before and in 1665 when Guru Tegh Bahadur who had succeeded Guru Harkrishan, was staying at Dhamdhan (Bangar, now Haryana), he was suddenly arrested and brought to Delhi. After a month or so, the Guru was released on the intercession of Raja Ram Singh of Amber, who had developed deep devotion to the Guru. As if this was not enough, when Guru Tegh Bahadur was returning in 1670 from Assam, he was again taken into custody and kept in confinement for about two months and a half. Again he was released and he returned to the Punjab *via* Lakhnaur.

At this time the country, particularly North India, was in the grip of a terrific wave of consternation resulting from the general orders issued by Aurangzeb in 1669 for the demolition of old Hindu temples and schools and the ban on new constructions for their religious and educational institutions. In the course of his homeward journey from East India he had acquired ample personal experience of the feeling of awe and dismay assailing the minds of non-Muslims. As mentioned earlier in Section II, Sikhs too were made targets of official wrath and their local missionaries called *masands* were expelled from several towns and their temples were demolished. Seeing all these dark happenings, the heart of Guru Tegh Bahadur went out in sympathy to the suffering humanity. He toured extensively in the Malwa and Bangar areas and moved among the people to brace up their crestfallen spirits. Thousands of them came to have his holy *darshan* and to receive his message of courage and hope embodied in the dictum, "Fear not, nor give fear to others." After nearly a year and half of travelling about in this region, the Guru finally repaired to his headquarters, Chak Nanaki, presently called Anandpur Sahib.

One month and fourteen days after the visit of the Kashmiri Pandits, on 8th July, Guru Tegh Bahadur nominated his son, Gobind Das, as his successor and two days after departed in the direction of Delhi in company with three of his eminent Sikhs, Diwan Mati Das, Bhai Sati Das and Bhai Dyal Das. The Government was already aware of the Guru's views and sympathies and had even issued orders for his apprehension. Only two days after his departure from Chak Nanaki, on 12 July 1675, he was arrested along with his three Sikhs at a village called Malikpur Ranghran, near Ropar. The arrests were made by Mirza Nur Muhammad Khan, Thanedar of the Ropar Kotwali. From Ropar the prisoners were carried under heavy guard to Sirhind where they were confined till the arrival of definite instructions from the Emperor Aurangzeb, then encamped at Hasan Abdal on the North-West frontier. On the receipt of these instructions the Guru and his followers were removed to Delhi. The Subahdar of Delhi who was deputising for the Emperor made three conditions to Guru Tegh Bahadur, namely: (i) to show a miracle, (ii) to embrace Islam, or (iii) to suffer death.

IV

What was the noble cause for which Guru Tegh Bahadur made the supreme sacrifice? What motivated him to do so? These questions may best be answered in the light of the following factors:

(a) The ideology he had inherited from his distinguished predecessors;
(b) the circumstances which lead to the sacrifice;
(c) the evidence recorded by his son Guru Gobind Singh in *Bachittar Natak*; and
(d) the stage of historical development in which the society was found at the time.

(a) The ideology inherited by Guru Tegh Bahadur from his predecessor Gurus has been noticed earlier in Section I. It will be seen from there that this ideology was based on a clearly recognised sense of social commitment. Spiritual development founded on renunciation of worldly life and social responsibilities which go with it, accordingly, was considered of little merit and life lived away from society was not commended. In this system of thought there was no room for *banbas* (living in jungles) and *sanyas* (hermitage) which was rated so highly prior to the origin of Sikhism. Living in the midst of society and facing all its challenges bravely was a hallmark of this mode of thinking of Guru Nanak and his successors. But the basis of all social life was to be *dharma*, morality. Whatever activities one may indulge in, always the governing principle of one's conduct should be the moral values of truth, social justice, compassion, love, contentment and other such elements which may be categorised under this head. These moral values, the Gurus emphasised, are not meant for any particular segment of life but are to constitute the very bedrock of total social living embracing all aspects of society. Therefore, anything which is in accordance with *dharma* was considered right and anything which is not, was held wrong. Similarly, anybody who helps the cause of *dharma* by regulating his life according to it and by defending it when necessary was rated a good man (*sant, sadh* or *bhagat*) and anybody who acts contrary to it, was reckoned as a wicked man (*dushta* or *sakta*). From this is naturally followed that wickedness or tyranny, whatever its form, is to be resisted, as after the execution of Guru Arjan Dev, his son and successor, Guru Hargobind held the use of arms for the noble fight against tyranny as valid and embarked upon a well-thought-out programme of militarisation of his community. An important implication of the moral basis of social life, as stressed by the Gurus, was respect for other people's modes of living and thinking. All these modes contain a degree of merit, more or less and as such are to be tolerated, if not accepted. The concept of plural society in which different approaches used by people are recognised as legitimate was an essential characteristic of the emerging Sikh ideology and any attempt to impose unity upon the people unmindful of their varying beliefs and practices was considered a violation of *dharma* and an act of tyranny. Such an act of tyranny or breach of morality ought to be resisted as a moral obligation. To sum up, acceptance of social responsibility, recognition of *dharma* as the basis of society, compassion for the suffering humanity, concern for the good of mankind, resistance to evil, if necessary with force, and acceptance of a plural society with respect for other people's modes of living and thinking were the leading highlights of the Sikh ideology which the Ninth Guru inherited from the previous Gurus. Since it is firmly accepted among the Sikhs that all the ten Gurus thought the same way, this ideology was no mere inheritance for the Ninth Guru, but was fully shared by him.

(b) Defeat of Dara and the triumph of Aurangzeb ushered in a new era in India. Dara's defeat marked the end of Akbar's liberalism and Aurangzeb's victory portended the ascendency of Muslim orthodoxy and of the Sirhindi school of thought. True to his convictions, Aurangzeb was determined to convert India into a *Dar-ul-Islam* which meant rejection of tolerance of other people's modes of life and thought, whatever their merit. Along with other non-Muslims, Sikhs too had their share of troubles and difficulties on account of the new regime. Aurangzeb's interference in Sikh affairs started from the time of Guru Hari Rai, and although all his doubts and queries were satisfied authoritatively, he did not refrain from his policy of harassment. Guru Tegh Bahadur himself was arrested and kept in confinement at Delhi first in 1665 and then in 1670. Even more important than these acts of harassment was the all-out campaign of religious intolerance on the part of the Emperor started in 1669. The woes of the suffering humanity had a deep impact upon the sensitive mind of Guru Tegh Bahadur and he, both at his headquarters, Chak Nanaki, and in course of his travels through the country, endeavoured to brace up the disspirited minds of the distress people with his brave message about sheding all fear. The appeal of the Kashmiri Pandits for help, coming towards the end, played a decisive role in so far as it helped the Guru in making his final resolve on the issue. However, from the manner in which the circumstances shaped themselves and finally led to the crucial point, it may be clear that the issues involved were wider and deeper than the compassion for a few woe-striken Brahmins of a distant area.

(c) Guru Gobind Singh's statement in his famous composition, *Bachittar Natak,* on the martyrdom of his father, Guru Tegh Bahadur, is the most authentic of all references to the event.

What Guru Gobind Singh meant by the word *dharma,* comes out very clearly from what the Guru says about his own mission, a few pages later, in the same work:

> (For this purpose was I born into the world;
> For *dharma's* sake I am sent here by the Lord:
> Ordained to promote *dharma* here and there.
> And to demolish the wicked and the evil-minded,
> Let all good people understand that I am born for this purpose:
> To promote *dharma,* to protect the good, to extirpate the evil).

Here the connotation of the term *dharma* is so clear that there can be no mistake about its meaning. It stands for the Moral Law which includes truth, justice, righteousness and other moral values.

Now coming back to Guru Gobind Singh's account of his father's martyrdom, referred to earlier, it would be absolutely erroneous to understand his words *dharma hetu* in any narrow sectarian sense. Such a restricted usage of the term would be not only unfair to the high human ideals of the great Guru, but also foreign to the long-standing valuable Sikh tradition based on the social philosophy of *dharma,* previously noticed in this essay.

(d) Whether we consider the long-standing Sikh ideology preached and practised since the time of Guru Nanak, or we take into account the circumstances that led to the martyrdom of the Ninth Guru, or the evidence of *Bachittar Natak*, it becomes clear that Guru Tegh Bahadur performed the mighty deed under the inspiration of high human ideals and values. Some of these may be mentioned as: (i) Compassion (*karuna*) for suffering humanity, for oppressed and exploited people; (ii) protection of *dharma* (Moral Law) recognised in Sikh tradition as the basis of human society; (iii) resistance to tyranny resulting from a breach of the norms of *dharma;* and (iv) respect and tolerance for modes of living and thinking other than one's own, what is today termed as the ideal of plural society. At the then stage of historical development of Indian society, there was very little consciousness of human rights as such. Only the right of private property, not however in its absolute sense, was definitely known and also to a large extent recognised by the State. The consciousness about the human rights of speech, movement, association, worship etc. is of comparatively recent origin and has appeared everywhere as part of the struggle for democratisation of the springs of political power. So far as our own country is concerned, such a consciousness first made its appearance in the 19th century and ever since then it has been growing in strength. Before our people began to grow conscious of their basic rights under the impact of Western ideas and influences, the fort in India was held by the concept of duty tracing down its roots in the remote past of India. However, duties and rights are closely interlinked and are the two sides of the same coin. What were regarded as duties then, are in the modern period, in the presence of a strong consciousness of human rights, looked upon as corelates of rights. It is in this sense that it may be and is valid to speak of the right of freedom of conscience or worship or some other human right in connection with the motivation with which Guru Tegh Bahadur elected to sacrifice his life.

3

Hukamnamas

The one *Nisan* (emblem or signet) and twenty-one *Hukamnamas* (Epistles) are of the Ninth Sikh Guru, Guru Tegh Bahadur (1621-1675). He was at once a seer, a saint, a poet and a warrior. His writings incorporated in the Sikh scripture, *Guru Granth Sahib,* under the head, *Mohalla 9,* are a spiritual and didactic composition of a very high order and have a unique appeal for the human mind. The feats of chivalry exhibited by him in the battle of Kartarpur in 1635 A.D. are a proof positive of his great skill in the warrior's art. With all these eminent qualities of head and heart. Guru Tegh Bahadur was easily the most respected saint and teacher of his time in North India.

The youngest son of Guru Hargobind, born at Amritsar in 1621 A.D., he spent his early years mostly in loving adoration of God and visiting holy shrines. In 1664 when Guru Harkrishan Dev passed away at Delhi, Guru Tegh Bahadur was called upon to shoulder the responsibilities of *Guruship*. Soon afterwards, he decided to go to the Eastern parts of India where since the time of Guru Nanak, founder of Sikhism, numerous Sikh congregations (*Sangats*) had sprung up. The main purpose of the Guru in visiting these places was to reinvigorate and coordinate the activities of these religious bodies. In the course of his travels he had to visit Assam at the special instance of his Rajput devotee, Raja Ram Singh of Amber.

In the meantime in 1669 had been issued a *Farman* by Emperor Aurangzeb enjoining upon his local authorities to demolish schools and temples of the Hindus. The new imperial orders sent a thrill of horror through the length and breadth of the country. Realizing the gravity of the situation the Guru returned to Punjab poste-haste. His soothing words had good effect on the unsettled minds of the people. About this time, in May 1675, a group of Kashmiri Pandits waited upon the Guru at Chak Nanaki (present Anandpur Sahib) and narrated their tale of woe. Deeply impressed by their appeal, the Guru decided to espóuse the cause of the oppressed and soon after he sacrificed his precious life in defence of his truthful mission at Delhi in November 1675 A.D. Three devoted Sikhs of his, namely Bhai Mati Das, Bhai Sati Das and Bhai Dyal Das, also laid down their lives on this occasion. The Tenth Master, Guru Gobind Singh, has made the following comments upon the martyrdom of Guru Tegh Bahadur:

> The Lord (Guru Tegh Bahadur) protected their paste-mark and sacred thread;

And performed a mighty deed in the *Kali* Age.
To protect the Good he spared no pains;
Gave his head but uttered not a groan.
For the protection of Righteousness he did this noble deed; Gave his head but not his ideal.
To do theatrical acts and such unclean deeds,
Would make devotees of God ashamed.

He broke the pot-sherd of his body on the head of the King of Delhi,
And departed for his Divine Abode.
None ever performed a great deed like Tegh Bahadur.
The world was in mourning;
The whole world wailed but the world of Gods showered acclamations.

(Bachittar Natak)

The *Nisans* and *Hukamnamas* of the Ninth Guru constitute a fresh source of evidence regarding his life and work and it is gratifying indeed that through this publication this new source is being introduced for the first time to the Hindi and English knowing Indian and foreign scholarship. The *Nisan* is primarily a special piece of writing in the Guru's own hand carrying the authority of the Master and on that account is a sort of a seal on epistles. However, sometimes when the same personal mark is affixed on a copy of the Sikh scripture or any portion thereof, it is more in the nature of a sacred memento than a symbol of authority. The *Nisan* thus helps us in authentication of epistles—and this is something most important.

The *Hukamnamas* of the Ninth Guru given here will be found to be useful in many respects. First, they provide the Guru's own evidence regarding his travels in the eastern regions of India. The main problems to be faced in regard to them is that they do not bear dates and as such create hard enigmas for the scholars. However, this is not a problem wholly beyond solution. It is possible now, with the help of other contemporary sources, chiefly *Bhat Vahis,* to unravel, if not completely, the mystery of dates. A kind of attempt in this respect has been made here and the various epistles have been arranged in the chronological order considered most likely. The earliest of these letters cannot be earlier than April or May 1666. Those of them which bear connections with Patna, Banaras, Mirzapur and Monghyr, fall within the period 1667-1668. The five *Hukamnamas* which are addressed to the congregation of Pattan and its chief functionary, Bhai Batha, in all probability belong to the years 1671 to 1675. Usually, it was on the festivals of Diwali and Baisakhi that such letters were despatched to the congregations. Calculating on this assumption, it may be possible to infer that two of the letters addressed to Bhai Batha belong to 1671, two to 1672, and one to 1673, or to 1675. This estimation is based on the fact that from the middle of 1673 to the end of 1674, the Guru was away in the Malwa and Bangar Desh, busy meeting his devoted people and delivering to them his message of courage and hope.

The evidence of the *Hukamnamas* is quite definite on some points: (i) The Guru had a fairly long stay at Monghyr as he addressed letters from here to many of his *Sangats* to come and meet him there. (ii) He was not present at Patna at the time of his son, Gobind Das's birth. (iii) He felt greatly concerned about the accommodation and other arrangements made for the members of his family and addressed a number of communications on that subject. This clearly shows how seriously the Guru took his responsibilities towards his family. (iv) The Guru was a very great organizer and it was mainly due to his genius that the network of relations with and between the divergent Sikh *Sangats* functioned so well and smoothly. These organisations were grouped together areawise with devoted and able coordinators separately earmarked for each one of these groups. The Guru being at the centre of the entire complex maintained his links with them through the coordinators by means of personal correspondence. (v) The financial requirements of the central headquarters of Sikhism were met with voluntary offerings made by Sikh devotees. The Guru's *Golak,* the central treasury of Sikhism, had been created long back in the time of Guru Arjan, may be even earlier, to carry on the missionary work of propagation of the Guru's teachings, to conduct the Guru's kitchen, *Langer,* on a regular basis and to execute other important projects of the young community. How this essential function was performed, becomes amply clear from the 9th Guru's *Hukamnamas* listed here.

A few other things about which these *Hukamnamas* furnish information, though not definite, are these: (i) Somewhere in the vicinity of Monghyr a certain Raja met him, and the Guru accompanied him. The name of this Raja is nowhere mentioned but the expeditious manner in which the Raja is depicted in these letters to be marching and the respectful style in which the Guru has addressed him, are hints significant enough to show that this Raja was none other than Raja Ram Singh of Amber, now Jaipur. (ii) The Guru's visit to Dacca of East Bengal is implied in some of the *Hukamnamas* though there is no direct clue pertaining to this fact.

The *Hukamnamas* have much historical importance in another respect also. They provide specimens of Punjabi prose in the seventeenth century. More significantly, they throw valuable light on the shaping of Gurmukhi letters and as such furnish useful clues in the study of origin and evolution of Gurmukhi script. On the mode of writing, too, they provide significant information. For instance, it becomes clear from them that Punjabi was then written in two principal ways, namely (i) *Kitabti,* i.e., the normal style usually adopted in the writing of books; (ii) *Shikasta, Chaprela, Tirmukhi, Chalant,* or *Chalant Nastalik,* i.e., the running style which is more difficult to read. A comparison of the 9th Guru's *Hukamnamas* with those of the earlier Gurus shows that the latter style was first effectively developed by Guru Tegh Bahadur. Subsequently, it became more popular and Guru Gobind Singh adopted it on an extensive scale. The S.G.P.C. publication on *Nisans* and *Hukamnamas,* brought out in 1967, has given at the end two photostate copies of the *Shikasta* style of Punjabi writing pertaining to the period of Guru Gobind Singh.

Another point, again not entirely unrelated to the domain of history, is the deep reverence in which the Sikhs have held the *Nisans* and *Hukamnamas* of their Gurus. To them they are most sacred documents, the mere sight of which is regarded as a holy blessing or an act of great religious merit. The Sikhs are noted for their passionate devotion to their Divine Masters and any sacred relic, piece of writing, article of clothing, weapon, or any other article, belonging to any of their Gurus evokes the deepest possible sentiments in their hearts.

As remarked earlier, only one *Nisan* and twenty-one *Hukamnamas* have been included in this book. But this in no way means that there are no other. The Sikh Reference Library. Amritsar, already possesses a few more of them and it may be reasonably hoped that a vigorous search conducted on a carefully planned basis may yield encouraging results, though of course it is an established fact of our history that much of our precious historical material was unfortunately destroyed during the upheavals of the turbulent eighteenth century.

1

From the *Pothi* (Sacred Volume) completed on 10 Bhadon, *Samvat* 1728 BK (11 August 1671 A.D.) *Mul Mantar* in Guru Tegh Bahadur's handwriting :

Ek Oankar Gur-Satt

(In the Name of the One Indivisible Supreme Being. Lord Eternal)

Reality Eternal, Creator-Purusha,
Without Fear, without Rancour,
Form Eternal, Unborn,
Self-created,
Realized by Divine Grace

(Preserved in the Sikh Reference Library, Amritsar)

2

Epistle, through Bhai Jawehari to the Congregation of Benaras (Varanasi)

In the Name of the Lord Eternal
Addressed to Bhai Jawehari :
The Lord shall cherish the entire Congregation.
We enjoin upon all to look after Sridhar well.
Let him be well supplied with provisions.
Let Sridhar be conveyed to Patna on its recovery.
Through obedience to the Guru's command the Congregation shall find blessing.

(Preserved in Gurdwara Bari Sangat at Benaras)

3

Guru Tegh Bahadur's Epistle to the Congregation at Benares (Varanasi)

In the Name of the Lord Eternal

Addressed to Bhai Jawehar Mal:

The Lord shall cherish the entire Congregation of Benaras. Bhai Kalyan Das appeared before us, and presented offerings from the Congregation. All should give Bhai Kalyan Das all manner of help. May the Lord's blessing be on you all!

(Preserved in Gurdwara Bari Sangat at Benaras)

4

Epistle to the Congregation of Patna

In the Name of the Lord Eternal

Addressed to:

Bhai Dayal Das, Bhai Ram Rai, Bhai Darbari, Bhai Chain Sukh, Bhai Mehar Chand, Bhai Subha Chand, Bhai Jeth Mal, Bhai Ded Mal, Bhai Nand Kaur, Bhai Din Dayal, Bhai Mehar Chand, -Nath, Bhai Hira Nand, Bhai Ragho Das, Bhai Pehlad Das, Bhai Bansi Dhar, Bhai Murli Dhar, Bhai Mohan Das, Bhai Nain Sukh, Bhai Harkesh, Bhai Chhabil Das, Bhai Bhagwan Das, Bhai-, Bhai Sada Nand, Bhai Ghanishyam, Bhai Kanwal Nain, Bhai Ram Rai, Bhai Murli Dhar, Bhai......, Bhai Singha, Bhai Sangat Das, Bhai Baijnath, Bhai Sukhdeo, Bhai Jhabar Singh, Bhai......, Bhai Jagman, Bhai Chhabil Das, Bhai Roopan, Bhai Lal Man, Bhai Anant Das, Bhai.... Chand, Bhai Nain Sukh, Gulal Chand, Bal Gobind, Bhai Bhagta, Bindra Ban, ...Pala, Pheru, Bansi Dhar, Sukhdeo, Machhi, Sucha Ram, Chain Sukh, Hira Nand Paras Ram, Mittar Sain, Gaj Mal, Jagdeo, Dalpat Das, Bhai Maluk, Dasiya, Chetan...., Lachhua, Raghunath, Fateh Chand, Sister Peri Bai, Dina Nath, Pran Nath.

The Lord shall grant the wishes of the entire Congregation of Patna, that has meditated on God. The Congregation has incurred expense on jubilation at Gobind Das's birth. At this the Guru expresses his pleasure. Each rupee spent has earned the blessing of a *mohur*. The offerings sent previously too have met with the Guru's pleasure. Whoever serves the Guru in future, shall earn merit. The Congregation's prosperity shall increase. Friends! we are sending a robe of honour. Patna is the Guru's own home. The Congregation thereof shall be blessed.

(Preserved in Gurdwara Hari Mandir Sahib at Patna)

5

Epistle to the Congregation of Patna

In the Name of the Lord Eternal

Addressed to:

Bhai Dayal Das, Bhai Ram Rai, Bhai Darbari, Bhai Chain Sukh, Bhai Mehar Chand, Bhai Subha Chand, Bhai Jai Singh, Bhai Chimna, Bhai Lal Man, Bhai Jeth Mal, Bhai Ded Mal, Bhai Pehlad Das, Bhai Bansi Dhar, Bhai Murli, Bhai Ragho Das, Bhai Pritam Das, Bhai Nand Lal, Bhai Pran Nath, Bakhshi Murli Dhar, Bhai Hira Nand, Bhai Sangat Das, Bhai Jhabar, Bhai Gurdas, Paras Ram, Manohar Das, Nain Sukh, Bal Gobind Shankar Das, Sada Nand, Suja Ram, Bhagwan Das, Gujar Mal, Shankar Das, Nand Lal, Chhajju Mal, Nand Kaur, Bhai Jasodha Nandan, Mehar Chand, Pran Nath, Bali Ram, Sobha Chand, Jagdeo, Dalpat Rai, Ani Rai, Ghanishyam, Sukhdeo, Gaj Mal, Gujua, Bhag Mal, Chhabil Das, Suphera, Amaliya, Pheru, Kirpala, Bansi, Sukhdeo, Peri Bai, Ram Chand, Harkesh, Chhabil Das, Shubh Karan, Kewal Ram, Bhag, Ananta, Man Sukh, Basant Rai, Lachhua, Bala, Sada Nand, Sadhu.

The Lord shall succour the entire Congregation of Patna. Meditate ye ever on God. Thus shall your lives be blessed and good befall you. The offerings of clothing sent through Bhai Mehar Chand and Bhai Kalyan Rai have been received in our Presence. The Guru shall bless the Congregation with increase in prosperity. Patna is the Guru's own home. The Congregation therein shall be blessed.

(Preserved in Gurdwara Hari Mandir Sahib at Patna)

6

Epistle to the Congregation of Patna

In the Name of the Lord Eternal

Addressed to:

Bhai Dayal Das, Bhai Ram Rai, Bhai Darbari, Bhai Chain Sukh, Bhai Mehar Chand, Bhai Sobha Chand, Bhai Jeth Mal, Bhai Ded Mal, Bhai Nand Kaur, Bhai Din Dayal, Bhai Mehar Chand, Bhai Pran Nath, Bhai Hira Nand, Bhai Sobha Chand, Bhai Kanwal Nain, Ragho Das, Bhai Pehlad Das, Bhai Murli, Bhai Mohan Das, Bhai Bhagwan Das, Bhai Harji Mal, Bhai Sada Nand, Bhai Kanwal Nain, Bhai Ram Rai, Bhai Nand Lal, Bhai Bal Gobind, Bhai Jag Man, Bhai Sangat Das, Bhai Baij Nath, Bhai Jhabar Singh, Amaliya, Kirpal, Pheru, Bhai Bindraban, Bhai Lal Man, Chhabila, Nain Sukh, Bhai Mula, Bhai Mehar Chand, Bhai Chetan Jado, Sister Peri Bai, Bhara, Maluka, Lachhua, Bhai Pran Nath.

The Lord shall succour the entire Congregation of Patna. Let all meditate on the sacred Name of God. With this their lives shall be blessed and fulfilment shall come to them. All who meditate on God. He shall grant fulfilment of their wishes. Patna is the Guru's own home. God shall succour the Congregation thereof. Service to Gobind Das shall find approval at the Divine Portal, and blessing come to it.

The camp equipment received from Bhai Raja may be sent to us: one fine canopy along with three screens along with equipment for the privy. Send also three screens and one enclosure for the kitchen. Send another tent of five yards measure. Chamber equipment and screens etc. may be sent through Bhai Mula Mehra. The Lord shall succour the Congregation. Patna is the Guru's own home.

(Preserved in the Hari Mandir Sahib at Patna)

7

Epistle to the Congregation of Benaras

By Grace of the One Indivisible Supreme Being. Lord Eternal.

The Lord Eternal

Addressed to :

Bhai Jawehari, Bhai Kirpal Das, Bhai Jat Mal, Bhai Rama, Jado Ghasi, Bhai Kalyan Das, Bhoti Seth, Bhai Babu Rai, Bhikhari Das, Maharaja, Dalpat Das, Hira Man, Durga Das, Ganga Ram Raghunath, Mahanand:

The Lord shall cherish the entire Congregation of Benaras. Let the Congregation entrust to Bhai Jawehari their donations out of their earnings; which Jawehari shall convey to Bhai Dayal Das. These shall then be conveyed to the holy stores. The Congregation shall be blessed. Now is the time to serve the Guru.

(Preserved in the Gurdwara Bari Sangat at Varanasi)

8

Epistle to the Congregation of Benaras (Varanasi)
and the Province thereof

Ek Oankar Sati Guru

(The One Indivisible Supreme Being. Lord Eternal)

In the name of Lord Eternal

Addressed to Bhai Jawehar Mal Masand, Bhai Kirpal Das, Bhai Jat Mal, Bhai Seth, Bhai Kalyan Mal, Bhai Mahanand, Bhai Babu Rai, Bhai Maharaj, Bhai Bhikhari, Dalpat Das, Bhai Ramanand, Bhai Manji, Bhai Man Singh, Phagu Shah, Bhai Bal Kishan, Bhai Chhut Mal, Bhai Mani Ram, and the entire Congregation of Benaras and the province of Benaras.

The Lord shall fulfil the cherished desires of the Congregation.

The donations recently sent through Bhai Dayal Das have duly been received in the holy Durbar.

Let Dayal Das's communication be obeyed by the Congregation as the

Guru's own command. Any Sikh possessing even a *cowrie,* dedicated to the Guru, should make over the same to Bhai Dayal Das. The Lord shall bless the Congregation with prosperity.

(Preserved in Gurdwara Bari Sangat at Varanasi)

9

Epistle to the Congregation at Benaras (Varanasi)

In the Name of the Lord Eternal

Addressed to:

Bhai Jawehar Das, Bhai Kirpal Das, Bhai Kalyan Mal, Bhai Bhoti, Bhai Seth, Babu Rai, Bhai Bhikhari, Maharaj, Rama, Bal Kishan, Man Singh, Chhut Mal, Nand Rup.

The Lord shall succour the Congregation of Benaras and its environs. Ever meditate on God. By this your lives shall be blessed.

Eighty rupees for offerings have been received. May the prosperity of all increase! The Congregation may make over their offerings to Bhai Dayal Das. He will present them to the Guru. May the prosperity of the Congregation increase! The present is the occasion for the Guru's service.

(Preserved in Gurdwara Bari Sangat, Varanasi)

10

Epistle to the Congregation of Benaras (Varanasi)

In the Name of the Lord Eternal

Addressed to:

Bhai Dayal Das, Bhai Ram Rai, Bhai Jawehari, Bhai Kirpal Das, Bhai Bhoti, Kalyan Das, Bhai Sibboo, Seth Dalpat, Bhai Babu Rai, Bhai Bhikhari Das.

The Guru's adjuration to the entire Congregation of Benaras is to meditate on God: Thereby your lives shall be blessed. The Lord shall fulfil the wishes of the Congregation. The offering of one hundred and sixty-six rupees from the Congregation, sent through Bhai Dayal Das, has been received by the Guru. The Congregation has been blessed with the Guru's pleasure. In future all offerings may be sent through Bhai Dayal Das. The Guru shall grant to the Congregation increase in prosperity and fulfilment of wishes.

(Preserved in Gurdwara Bari Sangat, Varanasi)

11

Epistle to the Congregation of Mirzapur

In the Name of the Lord Eternal

Addressed to:

Bhai Bal Chand, Bhai Harikishan, Bhai Chatarbhuj, Bhai Lalu.

The Lord shall succour the entire Congregation of Mirzapur. Send your collected offerings through Bhai Dyal Das, who shall convey these to our Presence. The Lord shall grant increase in prosperity. Offerings previously made have been received.

(Preserved in Gurdwara Bari Sangat, Varanasi)

12

Epistle to the Congregation of Patna, addressed to Bhai Dayal Das

In the Name of the One Indivisible Supreme Being, Lord Eternal.

Addressed to:

Bhai Dayal Das, Bhai Ram Rai, Bhai Darbari, Bhai Chain Sukh, Bhai Mehar Chand, Sobha Chand, Bhai Jaith Mal, Bhai Ded Mal, Bhai Nand Kaur, Bhai Pehlad Das, Bhai Bansi, Bhai Murli, Bhai Pritam Das, Bhai Ragho Das, Bhai Mohan Das, Sister (Bebe) Peri Bai.

The Guru shall fulfil the wishes of the Congregation and his disciples (Sikhs). Friends! We are camped at Monghyr. This is the occasion for the Congregation to serve the Guru. Friends! Inform the Masands of your province in the farther direction to come for a sight of the Guru along with the Congregation of their areas. All Sikhs who come shall be blessed with prosperity. Friend! further we wish to write to you about the tent of our camp of Shahzadpur. We shall send our commandment to the Congregation according as you inform us. Send two score turbans of Bihar, of the value of forty rupees a score. May the Congregation find increasing prosperity!

(Preserved in Gurdwara Hari Mandir Sahib at Patna)

13

Epistle from Guru Tegh Bahadur to the Congregation of Benaras (Varanasi) Province

In the Name of the Lord Eternal

Addressed to:

Bhai Jawehar Mal, Bhai Bhoti Seth, Bhai Kirpal Das, Bhai Jat Mal, Bhai Kalyan

Mal, Bhai Babu, Mani, Bhikhari, Man Singh, Maharaj, Rama Jado, Ghasi, Koka, Mana, Balkishan, Sukhedeo, Phagoo Shah, Chhutman, Rup Narain.

The Lord shall succour the entire Congregation of Benaras Province. May their prosperity increase!

The Congregation is hereby instructed to hand over their offerings to Bhai Dayal Das. He shall convey these to the Guru. The Congregation shall be blessed thereby. We are camping at Monghyr. All Sikhs who come for having the Guru's sight, their wishes shall be fulfilled.

(Preserved in Gurdwara Bari Sangat at Varanasi)

14

Epistle to the Congregation of Patna

In the Name of the Lord Eternal

Addressed to:

Bhai Dayal Das, Bhai Ram Rai, Bhai Darbari, Bhai Chain Sukh, Bhai Mehar Chand, Bhai Subha Chand, Bhai Jeth Mal, Bhai Dev Mal, Bhai Ragho Das, Bhai Pehlad Das, Bhai Mohan Das, Bhai Nand Kaur, Bhai Pritam Das, Bhai Ghanshyam, Jagman, Murlidhar, Bhai Singha, Sada Nand, Kanwal Nain, Ram Rai, Lalman, Chhabil Das, Bal Gobind, Amaliya, Pheru, Kirpal, Sangat Das, Baij Nath, Jhabar Singh, Bhagwan, Gujar Mal, Peri Bai, Ram Chand, Dina Nath, Pran Nath, Jagdeo, Bhoj Raj, Dalpat Das, Bhara, Dariya, Chinta, Bindraban, Pran Nath, Mehar Chand, Hira Nand, Pran Nath.

The Lord shall fulfil the Congregation's wishes. The departure is fixed for the month of Asuj. Articles worth seventy rupees, as per detail, may be sent for our camp immediately on receipt of this epistle. Let there be no delay. The camp is to be made ready. Brother! Come to have the Guru's sight with the entire Congregation. Delay not. The Lord shall bless the Congregation with prosperity. Patna is the Guru's own home.

(Preserved in Gurdwara Hari Mandir Sahib at Patna)

15

Epistle to the Congregation at Patna

In the Name of the Lord Eternal

Addressed to Bhai Dayal Das, Bhai Ram Rai, Bhai Darbari, Bhai Chainsukh, Bhai Mehar Chand, Bhai Sobh Chand, Bhai Jeth Mal, Bhai Ded Mal, Bhai Pehlad Das, Bhai Bansi, Bhai Murlidhar, Bhai Ragho Das, Bhai Dina Nath, Bhai Mohan Das, Bhai Pritam Das, Bhai Nand Kaur, Bhai Mehar Chand, Bhai Pran Nath, Bhai Murlidhar, Bhai Singha, Bhai Sada Nand, Bhai Kanwal Nain, Bhai Ram Rai, Bhai Lalmani, Bhai Chhabil Das, Bhai Bal Gobind, Bhai Amaliya, Bhai Kirpal, Bhai Baij

Nath, Bhai Sangat Das, Bhai Jhabar Singh, Sister (Bebe) Peri Bai, Bhai Ram Chand, Bhai Bhagwan Dass, Gujar Mal, Bhai Jagdeo, Bhai Bhoj Rai, Bhai Dalpat Das, Bhara, Dariya, Chinta, Bindraban, Pran Nath:

The Lord shall cherish the entire Congregation of the province of Patna. Those of the disciples (Sikhs) who have meditated on God (Wahguru), shall have their cherished desires fulfilled. We are travelling out along with the Raja, and have left our family in Patna. Such of the disciples (Sikhs) as have meditated on God (Wahguru), should render service. Their sacrifice of *paisa* shall be rewarded with a *mohur*. Now is the occasion for the Congregation to render service to the Guru. Whichever of the disciples (Sikhs) renders service on this occasion, shall be blessed with prosperity.

Lodge our family in a good, large mansion. The Lord shall bless the Congregation with increase in prosperity. Now is the occasion for serving the Guru.

(Preserved in the Hari Mandir Sahib at Patna City)

16

Epistle addressed to Bhai Dayal Das and Ram Rai

In the name of the One Indivisible Supreme Being.

Lord Eternal.

Addressed to Bhai Dayal Das, Bhai Ram Rai, Bhai Darbari, Bhai Ded Mal:

The Lord shall cherish the entire Congregation. We started four days ago. The Raja set out seven days ago. We have made a halt here in order to meet you. Travel day and night, and reach here at the earliest. Take a fast mount, and reach here within twenty-four hours. Delay not even a quarter *ghari*. We are anxiously waiting for your arrival. Reach here at the earliest. The Lord shall succour the Congregation.

(Preserved in the Hari Mandir Sahib at Patna City)

17

Epistle to the Sikh Congregation of Pattan

(The matter below is in the Guru's own handwriting)

Addressed to Bhai Batha.

The Lord shall be your protector.

The Lord shall succour the entire Congregation of Pattan. The Lord shall cherish the Congregation, and fulfil their wishes. Let the entire Congregation come over on occasion of Diwali to have the Guru's sight. All who come shall be blessed. The Congregation of Pattan is the Guru's own (*khalsa*). All blessings of the Guru shall come to it. Bhai Batha is the Guru's own son. Let the entire Congregation follow him. The Guru shall cherish all.

(Below the above, the same matter is given in the calligraphist's hand. Only in the last sentence, in place of 'The Guru shall cherish all' (bahuri) occur the words *'Khushi hai* (This is the Guru's pleasure).

18

Epistle to Bhai Batha and the entire Congregation

In the Guru's handwriting

The Guru's blessing is on Bhai Batha. The Guru shall succour the Congregation. Bhai Batha, thou art the Guru's own son. Reach along with the Congregation for the Guru's sight. The Congregation is enjoined upon to obey Bhai Batha.

In the calligraphist's handwriting

In the Name of the One Indivisible Supreme Being. Lord Eternal

This is the Guru's commandment to Bhai Batha and the entire Congregation. The Lord shall succour the Congregation. The Lord shall bless the Congregation with prosperity. All their wishes shall be fulfilled. Bhai Batha, thou art our *devoted* disciple. Reach our presence along with the Congregation. Those accompanying Bhai Batha to our presence shall be blessed. The Lord shall confer fulfilment on them. Bhai Batha is the Guru's own son. Let the Congregation obey his injunctions. The Lord shall bless the Congregation with prosperity and happiness.

(Preserved in the Sikh Reference Library at Amritsar)

19

Epistle to the Congregation of Pattan of Sheikh Farid

In the name of the One Indivisible Supreme Being. Lord Eternal

The Guru's blessing on all! Bhai Batha is enjoined upon to come to the Guru's presence along with the Congregation. All who come shall be blessed. Bhai Batha is the Guru's own son. The Congregation should follow his injuction.

(Preserved in the Sikh Reference Library at Amritsar)

20

Epistle to the Congregation of Pattan

In the Guru's own handwriting

The Guru's blessing on all! Bhai Batha, come to our presence along with the

Congregation. All who come shall be blessed. Bhai Batha is the Guru's own son. The Congregation is hereby enjoined upon to follow him. Our blessing on the entire Congregation of Pattan!

In the calligraphist's handwriting

Addressed by the holy Guru's command to Bhai Batha and the entire Congregation. The Lord shall succour the Congregation and confer prosperity on them. All their wishes shall be fulfilled. Bhai Batha, reach our presence. All who accompany Bhai Batha to our presence, the Guru shall bless them with fulfilment. Bhai Batha is the Guru's own son. His word should be obeyed as the Guru's own. The Guru shall confer prosperity on the Congregation. The Congregation shall get all blessings from the Guru. The Guru has blessed the Congregation of Pattan. The Guru's pleasure is on you. The Guru shall bless the Congregation with prosperity. Fail not to reach the Guru's presence.

(Preserved in the Sikh Reference Library at Amritsar)

21

Epistle to the Congregation at Pattan

In the Guru's own handwriting

The Guru shall bless Bhai Batha and the Congregation of Pattan. The Guru shall succour the Congregation, and fulfil their wishes. The Congregation of Pattan is hereby enjoined upon to come to our presence. All who accompany Bhai Batha shall be blessed. Now is the occasion for the Sikhs to render service to the Guru.

In the Calligraphist's handwriting

In the Name of the One Indivisible Supreme Being. Lord Eternal

Herein the holy Guru's command to Bhai Batha and the Congregation of Pattan: The Lord shall succour the Congregation, and confer on them prosperity and fulfilment of their wishes, Bhai Batha, thou art the Guru's own son. Come to our presence along with the Congregation of Pattan. All who accompany Bhai Batha shall be blessed. Now is the occasion for our disciples, *who are our beloved sons,* to render all service. The prosperity of the Congregation shall increase with their faith. The holy Guru's pleasure and blessing is on the Congregation.

(Preserved in the Sikh Reference Library at Amritsar)

22

Epistle to Bhai Malla and Bhai Bagha

In the Guru's own handwriting

The Lord shall succour you. Let not the mule of the Guru's stables be lost. These have to be charged for.

In the Calligraphist's handwriting

In the Name of the One Indivisible Supreme Being, Lord Eternal
Written by command of the holy Guru to Bhai Malla and Bhai Bagha.

The Lord shall succour the entire Congregation. All their wishes shall be fulfilled. Bhai Malla and Bhai Bagha to please note that a mule and two bullocks of the Guru's stables have been lifted from Jamalpur by cattle-lifters of Dhardeo. As is known to you. Dhardeo is in the Bakala area. The bullocks were recovered from the lifters. You are hereby charged to get back the mule. Herein fail not. The Lord shall send prosperity to the Congregation. Now is the occasion for you to make up this loss. Our great pleasure is on you.

(Preserved in Naushehra Pannuan in Amritsar District)

4

Meditation and Religious Tours

I

My father and mother,
Meditated on the Incomprehensible;
They both practised the highest *yoga*
Through diverse spiritual efforts;
Their devout service in the love of God
Pleased the Almighty, and He blessed them.

Guru Gobind Singh *Bachttar Natak: Apni Katha:* Ch 6:3, 4

Bakala is a historic village in the Amritsar district, about two and half miles North of Beas Railway Station. In the seventeenth century it was a flourishing business centre, situated at a short distance from the banks of the river Beas, which has since then changed its course.

Here in Bakala lived Bhai Hari Chand Lamb and Hardevi, father and mother of Holy Mother Nanaki. Here also lived Bhai Mehra, a well-to-do and devout disciple of Guru Hargobind. Just before the birth of Baba Tegh Bahadur, Bhai Mehra had built a beautiful house, and had invited Guru Hargobind and his mother, Mata Ganga, to be the first to step into the house and grace it with their presence. During their stay of about a week, Mata Ganga breathed her last. The day she left for her heavenly abode was also the martyrdom day of her husband, Guru Arjan. According to her last wishes, she was not cremated, but her body was interred in the flowing water of the Beas, in the same way as Guru Arjan's body was disposed in the river Ravi.

After performing the last rites of his mother Guru Hargobind left the place, blessing Mehra, and the house, he had built. Mehra begged the Guru to make the house his permanent abode. Guru Hargobind appreciated his devotion and sentiments, and assured him that one of his successors would come to the place, and stay there for quite a long time.

It is quite possible, that when Guru Hargobind asked his son Baba Tegh Bahadur to go and stay at Bakala, he had this promise to Bhai Mehra in view. But a more obvious reason was that, for the type of meditative life Baba Tegh Bahadur wished to lead for some years, Bakala was an ideal place, where he could live in elected solitude, away from the storm and stress of political upheavals, under the tender care of his maternal grandparents, and Bhai Mehra. Another possible reason for sending him away from Kiratpur was that Guru Hargobind thought it better that two suns did not shine in the same place. His deep spirituality, and glowing personality, backed by his rights of inheritance could attract personal admirers, and tempt them to create an innergroup which could be embarrassing to the seventh and eighth Gurus. As Tegh Bahadur was destined to live longer, he could wait for his turn, lest the seventh and eighth Gurus, who though younger, were equally gifted in perfection of spirit, should not miss their chance of leadership of the Sikh Community.

For nearly twenty subsequent years, Tegh Bahadur lived at Bakala in elected silence. He was amply provided by income from Hargobindpura and the whole of Amritsar district was deemed as his diocese. He had a meditation cell constructed in the house, in which he sat in contemplation and prayer for most of the day and night, giving a few hours to sleep and few to work, study, and spiritual discourses with special visitors. Now and then, he even went out for hunting. In the deep forest, he would spend many hours alone, with nature, and his God. He avoided crowds, because he shunned the blare and bluster of publicity. He lived in silent communion with the all pervading Spirit. He had conquered the senses in the clear light of insight, and now he entered the realm of divine knowledge and truth. All his feelings and emotions were submerged into a vision of reality and experience of truth.

Yet Baba Tegh Bahadur did not practise any self-mortification. He did not torture his body and mind with those cruel austerities, through which Hindu ascetics sought to purchase birth in heaven, and taste divine tranquillities, before they are again launched into the dreary sea of mortal existence. He did not chastise his body, and embrace a life of misery, as the price of eternal happiness. He did not despise life, and show disdain for the decencies of civil society. He did not execute any monastic penance of the ascetic who goes to the forest or desert saying, "Full of hindrance is the house-holder's life."

He lived in the heart of a city with his family. As his son, Guru Gobind Singh, later on testifies, Mata Gujari lived the same life, practised the same meditations, and like him, prayed for the salavation of humanity, and participated in all his silent life of devotion to God and His Will. She too achieved the vision, and received blessings of God, in active spiritual comradeship of her prophet husband. She showed that in the Sikh way of life, home ties are never snapped in the pursuit of spiritual freedom. The ties of true love between man and wife help them to transcend all bonds, and develop a spirituality of mind and soul which inspires them to identify themselves with the well-being of the whole universe. Marriage is an intensely human, and perfectly normal way of attaining self-fulfilment.

Baba Tegh Bahadur's solitude was not a state of isolation which leaves man at the mercy of self-love and all its miseries. His life was not that of a walled-in anchorite of romantic legend. His solitude and quiet meditative life depended not so much on physical isolation, as on the inner apartness, that bears witness, even in the busiest setting of social life, to man's true communion with the divine Spirit.

Through communion with the Perfect Being. Baba Tegh Bahadur acquired a bond with humanity, which far from being broken, tended always towards what is the model of true society: the brotherhood of man in the Spirit of God. Thus his meditation was not only a perpetual communion with the Supreme Being, but through the realisation of His all pervading Spirit; it was communion with all mankind. He and his devoted wife Mata Gujari prayed and meditated not for themselves, but for the whole of humanity. They also sought from God the knowledge and inspiration, for the task they were waiting to be assigned to them. They both prayed for strength and power to fulfil it. They both responded humbly and sincerely to each inner call.

Baba Tegh Bahadur was intimately in touch with the world outside him. He was deeply concerned with the fate and freedom of his country, and watched with keen interest the social and political changes that were taking place, as an artist watches a drama in which he is to play a hero's part. His brother-in-law, Kirpal Chand, who was a soldier in Guru Hari Rai's army, came twice a year, and informed him of all the small and great things that were happening at Kiratpur. Baba Dwarka Das, the descendant of Guru Amar Das, and eminent Sikhs of Amritsar district, like Bhai Garhia, Baba Gurditta, came to pay him homage, and brought with them the news of Lahore.

The people of Punjab were very happy during the Vice-royalty of Dara Shikoh, the eldest son of Shah Jahan. Dara Shikoh developed great personal affection and respect for Guru Hari Rai. Young Guru Hari Rai lived the life of a detached king and prophet, who concerned himself mainly with the moral and spiritual regeneration of the people. He scrupulously avoided getting involved in the internecine aggressive wars of the feudal chiefs of the Himalaya range or the Imperialistic exploits of the Mughal rulers. For his own defence, he maintained a well-equipped army of 2200 horsemen.

Spectacular and eventful changes took place even in the Kahlur State, in which Guru Hari Rai was living. "Kalyan Chand, the Raja of Kah-lur, was killed in 1635 A.D., when he tried to invade the territory of the Raja of Suket, whose daughter he had married. His son Tara Chand tried to avenge his father, but with only partial success."

Raja Tara Chand was a rebellious prince, who did not tolerate interference in his territory even by the Mughal Emperior. He refused to pay tribute to Emperor Shah Jahan, who was so annoyed with his attitude, that in 1645 A.D. He sent Najabat Khan, son of Mirza Sharuk, to attack his territory. Najabat Khan mobilised a large army and took Raja Tara Chand prisoner. Guru Hari Rai was only 14 years old at this time. To keep out of the conflict, he moved his army to Thapal near Sirhind. Raja Tara Chand was released, and his kingdom restored to him when he agreed to pay the tribute.

The ill feeling between Dara Shikoh and Aurangzeb was so bitter even during the lifetime of Shah Jahan, and had continued growing bitter for so many years, that it was the talk of the whole Empire, and peace had been maintained between them only by keeping Aurangzeb far away from the court. Shah Jahan had given clear indications that he wished to leave the crown to Dara, the eldest of the four sons, by the same mother. In order to train him in the administration of the Empire and to smoothen the transfer of the supreme authority to him, the Emperor had kept Dara by his side for many years past, and allowed him to govern his Viceroyalties by deputies. He was given the title of Shah Buland Iqbal "Lord of Exalted Fortune" and invested with a robe of honour, studded with diamonds and pearls, and a splendid ruby for his turban. Most significant of all, a golden couch had been placed for him below the imperial throne, and Dara alone of all the royal family, was allowed to be seated in the presence of the King. No clearer sign was needed to show the court that Shah Jahan intended his eldest son to succeed him. Aurangzeb contrived to give a slow poison to Dara, and the prince became seriously ill. The physicians informed the Emperior that poison could be removed through *chebulic myrobalan (barad)* weighing two ounces and a clove weighing a few grams, which could be acquired only from Guru Hari Rai. These things were very rare. The Emperor wrote a polite letter to Guru Hari Rai expressing his regret at his past attitude towards the House of the Guru, and requested him to send the *chebulic myrobalan* and the clove of the required weight, and save his son's life. To these articles the Guru added a pearl, which was to be grounded and used as subsidiary remedy. Dara Shikoh was perfectly cured, thereafter, both he and his father maintained very friendly relations with the Guru.

During all these years Baba Tegh Bahadur lived in elected solitude amid the busy surroundings of Bakala, like a moon moving among the faint stars. They, who saw him living in the silence of godly love were deeply impressed by the kingliness of his manners. His head was high, and the flame of God was in his eyes. Self-possessed and serene, he looked a little said, but it was the sadness of the prophet, who sought power and love, to show compassion to those in sorrow and suffering, and comradeship to the lonely and despised. When he smiled, in his smile was the knowledge of the universe. It was like the dust of the stars falling on the face of beauty. The pensive smile of Baba Tegh Bahadur was a golden veil over his flaming soul.

Having power, he kept it under grand self-control. Having wisdom, he lived in the silence of innocence. Having light, he carried it with the humility and poise of a sage. The more he discovered the secret resources of his own incommunicable personality, the more determined was his preparation to contribute to the redemption of humanity. Whenever he turned his glance inward, he opened the window of his inner silence on the world. Following the footsteps of her husband on his spiritual ascent, like a shadow, Mata Gujri rose from contemplation to contemplation, till she stood fully enlightened on the Mount of Vision, in the supreme realisation of *Nirvana*. Wisdom rose from within her, like a wind of fire, and burnt away all dross and alloy. She entered the realm of Truth, perceiving the Love, in which all love is one. She held within her heart the treasure of divine wisdom, and the wondrous knowledge that is Light and peace. Holy Mother Nanaki silently watched the enlightened life of her son, and daughter-in-law, who loved and served her with exemplary filial piety.

"Within the country a profound peace reigned. The peasantry were carefully cherished; harsh and exacting governors were in many cases dismissed on complaint of the people. Wealth and prosperity increased on all hands. The wealth of Ind under the great Mughal, Shah Jahan, dazzled the eyes of the foreign visitors. A kind and yet a wise master, Shah Jahan had gathered round himself a band of very able officers and made his court the centre of the wit and wisdom of the land. But, one by one the great ministers and generals, who had contributed to the glory of the reign, were being removed by the pitiless hand of death."

The Punjab was strongly attached to Dara, the province that had long been under his Viceroyalty, and was now held by his faithful deputy, Sayyad Ghairrat Khan. On the way to Lahore he stopped at Goindwal, to pay homage to Guru Hari Rai in the last week of June 1658 A.D., where Guru Hari Rai had come on the invitation of Baba Dwarka Das. Sikh chroniclers have recorded an interesting spiritual discourse between Guru Hari Rai and Dara Shikoh. Guru Hari Rai talked to him of the Kingdom of the Spirit and the transience of the world. He blessed him with the moral and spiritual courage which he needed most. It also appears that Guru Hari Rai also refused to be drawn into his war of succession.

For nearly a month the whole of Punjab was under Dara Shikoh. He stationed an army of 200,000 at Rupar to guard the ferries over Sutlej. A month later Aurangzeb's General, Bahadur Khan attacked Dara's defences and made his army retreat to the ferry at Goindwal. While Dara's army was fighting at Goindwal, he escaped from Lahore to Multan.

After weary wanderings and bitter bereavements, Dara took shelter with an Afghan clansman, whose life he had once saved, when Shah Jahan had ordered him to be trampled to death by an elephant. During this period his wife died of hardships and misery. To crown his misfortune and sufferings, his Afghan host betrayed him to Aurangzeb. On August 29, Dara was seated on an elephant, covered with dust and dirt, along with his fourteen-year-old son. The pity of the citizens swept every other feeling away. At night he was hacked to pieces, and the next day his corpse was placed on an elephant and paraded through the city.

There were significant changes in the Kahlur State also. Twenty-year-old Raja Dip Chand succeeded his father Raja Tara Chand in 1653 A.D. He was a man of religious tendencies, and so evil were the omens of his succession, that he removed his capital from Sunhane to a place on the Sutlej, close to where a shrine of Ranganath Shiva, and a cave of Byasji was situated. Here he founded the present Capital of the state which was first called Byaspur, a name subsequently corrupted as Bilaspur. He assisted the Emperior Aurangzeb in his military campaigns, and received as a reward for his services a *Khilat* of five lakhs, and a *sanad* authorising his suzerainity over no less than 22 hill states, including Kulu, Kangra, Mandi, Suket, Chamba, etc. But on his way home from the Imperial army, he was poisoned at Nadaun by the Raja of Kangra."

In the year 1657 A.D., Bhai Mai Das, son of Bhai Balu Ram came from Alipur near Multan and presented to Guru Hari Rai his three elder sons: Jetha (later Bhai Jetha Singh) 18, Dayal Das 15, and Mani Ram (later Bhai Mani Singh) 13 years old. For two years all the three sons served the Guru with great devotion, and Guru Hari Rai blessed them all. Mani Ram performed the humblest duties of washing utensils in the community kitchen (*langar*). After two years Bhai Mai Das sought the permission of the Guru to go to Alipur to perform the marriage of Mani Ram, who was now fifteen. Mani Ram's marriage was performed with Sito Bai, daughter of an eminent Sikh, Lakhi Rai (also known as Lakhi Shah), a Yadav Kshatriya whose original home was at Khairpur Syadat, in Tehsil Alipur or Muzaffargarh district. He was also a prominent trader and contractor of the Delhi Court who provided provisions to the Mughal army. After the marriage, the three brothers Dayala, Jetha and Mani Ram, remained in the service of the Guru.

During these years Bhai Hira Nand left for his heavenly abode. Before leaving his body, he sought the Guru's blessings for his two sons: Mati Das and Sati Das. Mati Das and Sati Das were Persian scholars. Guru Hari Rai blessed them assuring the great warrior Saint Hira Nand, that his sons would continue to receive the same honour, respect and love, which he had received. The two brothers took a vow to lead their lives in complete dedication to the Guru's cause.

Aurangzeb had now crowned himself Emperior. While in Punjab, he did not see or hear of any active part that Guru Hari Rai might have played against him in his war of succession, but he knew of Guru Hari Rai's personal relations with Dara Shikoh. Some bigoted Muslims and Hindus reported to the Emperor that the Sikh Scriptures and teachings were an attempt to corrupt both Hinduism and Islam. But some of the closest advisers of Aurangzeb, like Mirza Raja Jai Singh, spoke highly of the Gurus and their teachings. These Rajput princes, like the Sikh Gurus, were descendants of the Solar dynasty of Ayudhia, and deemed the Gurus as their kith and kin. Ever since Raja Bhagwan Das' stay at Lahore and his personal association with the Sikh Gurus, these princes maintained great respect for the Sikh Gurus and their teachings. Aurangzeb expressed his desire to meet the Guru.

Guru Hari Rai did not go personally, but sent his son Ram Rai, who was about fourteen, to explain Sikh Philosophy to the Emperior. As heir presumptive to the Guru's throne, he was asked to maintain the integrity and veracity of the faith of Guru Nanak, whom he was to represent. He was strictly advised not to be cowed down, or intimidated, but to give exposition of Sikh Scriptures without fear or guile. He was asked to be loyal to his ideals, firm in his convictions, frank and truthful in his exposition. He was given a recently prepared copy of the *Adi Granth,* in which the proem (*Mulmantra*) had been written by Guru Hari Rai in his own hand. Although Ram Rai was quite young, his intellectual and spiritual training was very nearly complete. His assignment to the Emperor's Court was a test of his ability, his spirituality, and his veracity.

Whenever Aurangzeb wanted to put a non-Muslim Saint to test, he first gave him three days to perform a miracle. If he failed to perform a miracle, he was asked either to accept Islam, or face death. In some rare cases he was spared, if he proved to be politically useful. Ram Rai was an adept in occult powers. He showed nearly seventy-two miracles, which impressed the Emperor very much. The Emperor, himself a great theologian, then discussed Sikh Philosophy and asked innumerable questions to probe whether there was any thing un-Islamic in Sikhism. It goes to the credit of Ram Rai, who was only fourteen years old, that he made a spirited exposition of Sikhism, and almost convinced the Emperor that there was nothing un-Islamic or anti-Muslim in Sikh philosophy. It was a universal faith grounded on the experience of Truth and Absolute God. But a courtier, most probably a Hindu able to read Sikh Scripturers, mischievously pointed out two lines from a composition of Guru Nanak, which was apparently critical of Muslims. The question about this line came as a surprise to Ram Rai, and when Aurangzeb asked him to explain the following verse he quailed, fearing that the literal meaning of the first two lines might annoy the Emperor and he might refuse to hear the symbolic meaning, and the philosophical explanation might not be accepted. Anxious to maintain the excellent impression he had already created on the Emperor, he told a lie: The hymn as read by the courtier was as follows in English translation:

> *miti musalman ki pedai pai ghumiar*
>
> The clay of a Muslim's grave,
> Falls into the hands of the potter;
> Pots and bricks out of it he makes;
> In the fire burns the poor clay.
> As it burns it weeps and wails,
> Shedding tears of cinders at its fate.
> Says Nanak: God the Creator
> Who is the Causer of all the causes,
> Knows where departs and what befalls
> The soul of man hereafter.
>
> Guru Nanak: *Asa-di-Var* 2:6.

The verse only gives Guru Nanak's theory that the soul of man leaves the body and does not remain in the grave, as Semitic faiths believe, till doomsday. The graves of poor men are often dismantled by the potter who makes pots out of the clay, while the fate of the soul is known only to God. Out of cowardice Ram Rai said that the scribe had by mistake written the word "Musalman" in place of *'beiman'* meaning wicked man.

Ram Rai's cowardice proved suicidal for him. Guru Hari Rai was seriously disturbed, when he came to know at what cost of truth and courage, his son had purchased safety. He loved his young son, but he did not let paternal sentiments sway his stern disapproval of his son's cowardice, and disloyalty to Guru Nanak's faith and philosophy. He forthwith disinherited his cowardly son and refused even to see his face. Ram Rai went to Lahore in the hope of persuading the Guru to accept him, through the Sodhis and *Sangat* of Lahore. Guru Hari Rai sent a *Hukamnama* to the *Sangat* of Lahore to disown Ram Rai and not to make him any offerings. He could not forgive a son who out of fear of an earthly Emperior, stooped to such cowardly acts of sacrilege as distorting a composition of Guru Nanak. He was certainly not fit to carry the burden of spiritual sovereignty of Guru Nanak. About a month later he appointed his second son Hari Krishan as his successor and passed away on October 6, 1661 A.D. Hari Krishan, though only a little over five years old, had been tried and tested as a perfect, fearless and fully illumined soul.

During all these years of silent meditation and prayer, Baba Tegh Bahadur's life had become a perennial psalm of God. He was deeply conscious of the political and other changes that had taken place. With his mind's eye, he saw from his retreat his countrymen groaning under oppression and fear, and sinking in cowardice and hypocricy, even as an eagle suspended on unmoving pinions, floating in supernal sunshine, looks down to behold the earth spread like a picture below him.

The cries of suffering humanity reached his ears. The Rajput fighters for freedom, and many Hindu and Muslim divines, had abandoned themselves to greed, court favours and earthly desires, which like sea water enraged the thirst they seemed to quench. The whole country wept uncomforted. Baba Tegh Bahadur was determined to offer his life blood, as unguent to its wound, as soon as he received the call.

He had spent nearly twenty years in prayer and meditation to be as perfect as Guru Nanak, to be as self-effacing as his grandfather, Guru Arjan, to be as bold as his father, Guru Hargobind, and to fight and resist evil till it was conquered. He was now fully prepared to awaken his country from the sleep of ignorance, and abject submission to tyranny. He was waiting for the final call to go out, holding aloft the torch of Guru Nanak, to tame the barbaric spirit of rulers, to bring light to the souls that were plunged in darkness, to transpose indifference into hope, bitterness into love, and to change the most hard-hearted into a hymn of praise.

Baba Tegh Bahadur now lived at the transcendent level of Reality, which we, immersed in the poor life of illusion cannot conceive. He breathed in an atmosphere of abundant life, indicating humanity's claim to the possible and permanent attainment of Reality. His life and achievement testified to the advent of triumphing spiritual power. The deepest and richest levels of his personality had now attained to perfect light and freedom. He was imbued with divine Light and consumed with eternal Love.

It was the midnight of March 30, 1664. Suddenly a great resplented Light blazed within him. His face was radiant with the splendorous beams of illumination. The call had come. He sought, from the Hidden and the Divine, strength to face the problems, his agonising country faced, and to bind the terrors of the time. The perfect and Supreme Spirit of Guru Nanak was ablaze within him. God had crowned him with spiritual sovereignty of the world. He had become, the yet unproclaimed, King of the Kingdom of Spirit. In utter humility, he maintained a veil of silence over it. Why need the sun proclaim the advent of its own light? It will blaze and shine and announce its dawn on humanity through its burning silence.

II

For many months Makhan Shah dominated the stage of eventful Sikh history, as defender of faith, champion of truth, revealer of the ninth Guru, a terror to impostors and a relentless fighter against falsehood in all spheres of life. Penetrating and passionate rather than genial and urbane, and consumed with religious enthusiasm in the literal sense of the word, Makhan Shah was a practical soul, powerful and imposing in action, capable of laborious organisation and always impatiently patient in upholding and revealing the glory and greatness of his beloved Master. His faults and virtues were near allied and mutually indispensable. Impetuous and courageous, Makhan Shah was decisive and uncompromising in his conviction, domineering and energetic in the execution of his plan. He was inspired and creative in his vision, ambitious and proud before man, submissive and humble before his God and Guru.

In his six months of quest for the true Guru and his grace, he had made history. The more he lived in communion and associated with Guru Tegh Bahadur, the more God-intoxicated he became. The charity and humanity radiated by the Master absorbed all his attention. He spent all his time, money and energy in the labour of love, which under the guidance and inspiration of the Guru sought to remove the physical, mental and spiritual hungers of the toiling and suffering humanity. One day, one of his men reminded him that the rainy season was over and it was high time to attend to his trade commitment. With a heavy heart he asked his men to get ready to depart.

He first met holy Mother Nanaki and sought her blessings. "Makhan, my dear child," said the Holy Mother, the services you have rendered will be remembered for all time to come. To me you shall always be as dear as my son and wherever you go and wherever you are, my blessings shall always be with you. Makhan was speechless. He wept like a child, as he touched the Holy Mother's feet in humble adoration. He then bowed in devout reverence to divine Mother Gujari who affectionately said: "Would you leave us so soon Brother Makhan? What will be the Guru's durbar without you?" "There are such great souls in the Guru's durbar, Mataji," said Makhan Shah, "that I am not worth the dust of their shoes. Remember this humble creature and pray for me always. Thy blessings are my salvation divine Mother."

Makhan Shan then went to the Guru's durbar to bid farewell to the Master. He was happy to see Guru Tegh Bahadur in resplendent glory but he was sad at the thought that he might never get an opportunity to see him again. The sight of thousands of disciples coming from far off places to acknowledge him as the Guru gave great joy to Makhan.

With folded hands Makhan Shah stood before Guru Tegh Bahadur, who bestowed on him very costly robes of honour and blessed him with a godly grace. He and his men were given precious gifts which a king only could bestow on a prince and his *entourage*. Overwhelmed by the love and respect shown to him by Guruji, Makhan Shah said: "Forget me never, Gurudeva, forget me never. Ever remember this humble creature with compassion and mercy. Protect me ever, O Redeemer, with thy saving grace. Keep me ever close to thy lotus feet. Separation from thee will be unbearable."

Blessing Makhan Shah with tender affection, Guru Tegh Bahadur said: "You are the most sincere devotee of Guru Nanak. All your bonds of birth and death are broken. You have taken refuge in Truth. Ever contemplate the divine Word which shines like a diamond in your soul and ever live in the peace of your spiritual enlightment. How can you ever be separated from me dear Makhan? You are the noblest example of a Sikh, and like a true Sikh you live in unbroken spiritual communion with the Guru. When you are so deeply and eternally united with me in the life of the spirit, the temporary separation in the physical world is no separation. You have achieved the perfect self-illumination of *Nirvana* in the light and wisdom of which neither joy nor sorrow, neither pleasure nor pain will ever disturb your peace. You are a *jivan mukta,* "the liberated in life."

Mute in the joy of blessings and love, Makhan Shah bowed low and placed his head on the lotus feet of Guru Tegh Bahadur. The Master's hands blessed him with tender affection and urged him not to make the parting so painful. But Makhan Shah would not leave his affectionate hold of the Master's feet, which he adored in complete self-consecration. His heart heaved with the poignant thought of parting from the Guru, and his soul trembled in a thousand reveries. He could not control his tears. His whole life throbbed on the lotus feet of the Guru. Under the persuasion of the Master he got up, but he bowed in utter dedication and love once again. The will of the Guru to him was the Will of God. Without turning his back to the Guru, he came out of the durbar. All the Ministers came to bid him farewell. Again and again he looked back to have a last look at the glorious durbar of the Guru. Then greeting all the Ministers with folded hands, he rode away at full speed.

In the first decade of the sixteenth century, Guru Nanak set out on the mission of sowing the seeds of his new religion of Love (*Gurmat Marag*) in the old places of pilgrimage and centres of faith. By visiting every Hindu sacred place, Buddhist shrine, Muslim centre and other holy places, Guru Nanak not only established a bond between them in the light of his philosophy but his spiritual dialogue with them gave a new outlook and evoked a new vision of unity and cooperation in the religious firmament of Asia. The very spot in these places of pilgrimage where he sat and delivered his message to Sufi pirs, Buddhist Bhikkus, Hindu pundits, yogis and sannyasins, became a place of worship and centre of Guru Nanak's faith known as the *Sangat.* Thus all the places of pilgrimage which were sacred to Muslims, Hindus, Jains, Buddhists also became sacred places of pilgrimage and historical shrines for the Sikhs.

In all these places Guru Amar Das established remarkable missionary centres under the leadership of inspired and thoroughly trained men and women, who kept the light of faith blazing in full splendour upto the time of Guru Hargobind. The Heads of these missionary centres visited the Guru in the Punjab once a year either at *Diwali* or at *Baisakhi.* But for over a century no successor of Guru Nanak was able to visit these places beyond Benaras to illumine them with his Presence and reorganise them according to the changing needs and times.

Guru Nanak had undertaken these missionary journeys after spending many years in elected silence at Rori Sahib and his first journey was to the East. Guru Tegh Bahadur likewise, after many years of *tapasya* (concentrated communion with God), deemed it his first and foremost task to put in new life, new spirit and new activity into these places of pilgrimage. His aim was positive and not negative, as some cynical historians seeking pessimism in everything Guru Tegh Bahadur did, assert by saying without any evidence, that he wanted to avoid conflict with his close rivals at Kiratpur. When he had already established an independent religious capital where was the question of rivalry? Why did he then come back to the place, when conditions were favourable for the rivals and quite unfavourable for him? If his aim was just to escape trouble, why did he not quietly rest in one place, and why did he go to those regions of the country which were a terror even to daring travellers and conquerors? Guru Tegh Bahadur did not run away from the Punjab but he felt that the Sikh mission was for the whole country, for the whole world, and the provincial boundaries should be broken again and again. The country divided by languages, narrow provincial loyalties and political barriers should be united in spirit, in peace and the love of God.

> "Then my father went to the East.
> He visited various places of pilgrimage."
>
> Guru Gobind Singh: *Bachittar Natak: Apni Katha.*

Elaborate plans and arrangements were made as Guru Tegh Bahadur had decided to take his wife and mother with him. His wife had participated in his *tapasya* (Life of Elected Silence) and now she must participate in his prophetic mission. A true prophet is not an unsocial lonely recluse. He is a symbol of a living existential world and not the world of men only. Woman the mother, and woman the partner in life must share the burden and the responsibilities as well as the fruit and glory of creative life. All activities of Guru Tegh Bahadur were unthinkable without his mother, his wife and his enlightened men and women disciples by his side.

Bhai Dayal Das, as the House Hold Minister, was to look after the comforts and requirements of the ladies in the moving camp of Guru Tegh Bahadur. His second brother Bhai Jetha remained at Anandpur to look after the completion of the city under construction. His third brother Bhai Mani Ram (Mani Singh) left for his home town Khairpur (Alipur) near Multan. Diwan Mati Das, the Guru's Prime Minister was in overall command of the moving durbar. His brother Sati Das was the chief scribe and interpreter. Being a great Persian scholar, he transiated the sermons and hymns of Guru Tegh Bahadur for the benefit of those Muslim visitors who could not properly understand Punjabi or Hindi. Kirpal Chand was the treasurer and camp organiser. There were about twenty more excellent administrations assigned different duties. The whole tour was financed by the *Sangat* of Allahabad (Prayag), Benaras, Patna and Dacca. Dacca being the richest centre made the largest contribution. A representative from each major centre was with the Guru's camp.

Guru Tegh Bahadur left Anandpur near about August 1665 A.D. About ten prominent Sikhs were left in charge of Anandpur. Guru Tegh Bahadur and his ministers moved on horseback, the ladies in chariots, the luggage on bullocks and carts. Well equipped tents were a part of the camp equipment and throughout the journey Guruji and his entourage generally rested in their own camps and not in way side inns or rest houses.

The first camp was pitched at a village three miles from Kiratpur. Guru Tegh Bahadur was deeply moved by the pitiable plight of a deserted village near his camp. There was great scarcity of drinking water. Rains had destroyed the crops and mud houses of many people. The poor villagers, though so hard working and virtuous were on the verge of starvation. Guru Tegh Bahadur immediately ordered his treasurer to give all the money he had to relieve the suffering of the people. He asked one of his trusted disciples to undertake the resettlement of the destitute and to reconstruct the whole village. His first and foremost task was to build a well and to give money to the homeless to build their houses. A free kitchen was started, in which people of all castes and creeds could take their meals. He further gave hope and courage to the hardworking people of this village saying: "Whoever causes any trouble to you will perish.

There was a very large gathering of men and women from the neighbouring villages. Sikh chroniclers have recorded the following sermon delivered by the Master when someone asked: "Lord, what shall we do to overcome temptations and walk in the ways of God? What penance should we perform to break through the barriers of desires?" Spoke Guru Tegh Bahadur: "Listen my disciples, human existence is a precious pearl of life. All efforts should be made to preserve its purity and its inherent glory. Never lead a life of purely materialistic pursuits. For the sake of the healthy living and welfare of your family, work honestly and earn your bread by the sweat of your brow. In all your work and professional labour be sinless and pure. Remember God every moment of your life. This is not an age for self-mortifying penances to seek personal occult powers. Service of humanity is the highest austerity and the noblest penance.

Selfless service is the essence of religion. It is the nature of man's mind to wander away like flowing water and be out of control. The mind should be steadily and patiently curbed and controlled. Accept sorrow and joy as the will of God, and never blame God for your suffering. Accept everything with calm forbearance. By accepting everything as the will of God we negate our ego and fix our mind in the divine Ground. Desire nothing but union with God and in this spiritual effort you will find once for all the efflorescence of love. This is the essence of Sikhism. This is the path of truth.

Guru Tegh Bahadur passed through Rupar and camped in a large garden at Saifabad, a city founded by Nawab Saifuddin, said to be holding a mansab of 5000 rank. Both the Nawab and his Begum were known to be religious, devout, liberal and extremely charitable. As soon as they came to know that Guru Hargobind's son Guru Tegh Bahadur had camped in their garden, their joy knew no bounds. The Nawab came to the Guru with gifts, dry fruit and other offerings and bowing reverentially said: "Blessed is my garden Master, blessed is the city and blessed am I that thou hast been gracious enough to come here and sanctify the place with thy presence." "We have come here friend Saifuddin, because your pure and noble soul attracted us. It is joy to rest in the garden of a pure souled man of God. You entertain the love and fear of God in your heart. God's grace shall be on thee and thy descendants." Said Guru Tegh Bahadur.

"Not in the garden, Master not in the garden must thou spend the night," said Saifuddin in utter humility and live, "My house, my mansions are thine; everything in them is thine. Honour me by sojourning in my humble dwelling. The Begum Sahiba would be most happy to entertain divine Mother. Deeply moved by the sincerity and devotion of Saifuddin, the Guru readily agreed. When Guruji mounted his horse, Saifuddin himself held the reins, as a mark of profound respect and reverence for the Guru. While the Guru was riding the horse, he walked on foot, as an act of piety, and conducted the Guru to his palatial mansion which was not far away from the garden. Similar courtesy was shown to Mata Gujari, and Mata Nanaki, who were carried in palinquins (*palkis*). When Guru Tegh Bahadur entered the gate, a peace shedding mansion attracted his attention, and he moved towards it. "That is the House of God (*mosque*) Guruji," said Saifuddin, "Your place is on this side." "This House of God," said Guru Tegh Bahadur, "is as beautiful and enchanting as the Man of God who built it."

Saifuddin conducted Guruji inside his newly built mansion, and after seating him on a special prepared couch, he offered gold coins, and some precious articles, and bowed in reverence. Guru Tegh Bahadur gave him a *siropao* (robe of honour). Saifuddin's wife received Holy Mother Nanaki and Mata Gujari with profound respect and offered them brocade, gold ornaments, and jewels. Guru Tegh Bahadur asked Saifuddin, what made him build his new house in the form of a fortress Saifuddin explained, "I one day saw a wolf attacking a sheep which was trying to protect her young lambs, in this place. The sheep heroically fought the wolf, and compelled it to flee. I had the impression that this place was unconquerable. So I built a house looking like a fortress.

Such was the devotion of Saifuddin that Guru Tegh Bahadur stayed with him for nearly a fortnight. As he had to undertake a long journey, he explained to Saifuddin, that as the rains had ended, he must depart, as many people were expecting him in other large cities of the country. Saifuddin offered to the Guru a fine horse, which he wanted the Guru to ride himself, costly utensils for the *langar* (free kitchen), excellent tents, a chariot for Mata Gujari, and camels for carrying loads of the convoy. Deeply touched by his spirit of dedication Guru Tegh Bahadur embraced him, and blessed him. It was the embrace of Sikhism and Islam at its best, symbolising, that whenever and wherever both these virile faiths shine, in their pristine purity and glory, they will be interlocked in an embrace of love, co-operation, and unity; and they will feel and inspire the essential unity of mankind in the Spirit of one God. With tears in his eyes Saifuddin asked: "Lord of both the worlds, when shall I see thee again? Every day and every moment of my life I shall be waiting for that blessed hour, when I may again feel the presence of a prophet in my home, and within myself?" "In life and death we shall be never separated spiritually. But even on the earthly plane, your sincere love and noble soul will impel me to come again and again," said Guru Tegh Bahadur.

Guru Tegh Bahadur had planned to visit the places of pilgrimage. The first place of pilgrimage he aimed at making was to Kurukshetra, where a large gathering was expected on the day of a solar eclipse. On the way to Kurukshetra he stopped at Kainthal. He camped outside the city, where a poor carpenter who had been anxiously waiting for the Guru met him, and invited him to his humble dwelling. He informed him that there were only three Sikhs in the city; two others besides him were Banyas (shopkeepers). As the high way robbers looted everyone, there was fear of attack by some gangsters. So he begged the Guru to spend the night in his house. Guru Tegh Bahadur calmly said, that he was not afraid of any robbers and decoits. He would spend the night there, and visit the carpenter's house the next day. The carpenter then asked Guru Tegh Bahadur: "What are the most auspicious days which the Sikhs should specially celebrate?" Guru Tegh Bahadur replied: "The days of worshipping and paying homage to the eternal Guru are as follows: *firstly Baisakhi,* the New Year day; *secondly Diwali,* (the festival of illumination); *thirdly* the *Sankranti* of the month *Magh*. There are two auspicious days connected with the life of Guru Nanak: his birth-day which falls on *Kartik Puranmashi* (October-November), and his ascension day, which falls on *Asu Vadi* 10. But remember whenever and wherever the *Sadh Sangat* meets and prays together, it is an auspicious day. The Guru and the *Sangat* are one in spirit."

The carpenter then informed the Guru that the next day was the ascension day of Guru Nanak, and he desired the Guru and the *Sangat* to celebrate it at his residence in Kainthal. Guru Tegh Bahadur readily accepted the invitation. Mata Gujari was received by the carpenter's wife. The carpenter spent all his fortune in entertaining the *Sangat*. Bhai Gurditta, the High Priest performed the congregational prayers. The carpenter then offered the little money he had to the Guru. Guru Tegh Bahadur blessed the carpenter saying. "Your devotion reflects the true spirit of Sikhism. Your home will be the temple of God in future. The seekers of God will chant His praise here." The carpenter's house became a temple of God, and it still is.

From Kainthal the Guru's camp moved on to Pehowa, Barna and Karan Kheda by stages till it reached Thanesar (Kurukshetra). At Pehowa he visited the shrines built by the Sikhs, to commemorate the visits of Guru Nanak, Guru Hargobind the Guru Hari Rai. At Barna, a Sikh peasant serving the Guru said, "Sir, the Revenue Officer has come to measure land and fix the taxes? May I please be permitted to go and get some concession in taxes." Guru Tegh Bahadur assured him that God will help him and because he was selflessly serving the people, the assessment of the taxes on his land would be quite adequate."

When later the Revenue Officer reached Barna he asked the Sikh peasant how much land he had. The peasant frankly stated he had 125 *bighas* of land. "But every time I measured the land, said the Revenue Officer, "I found it to be, only 25 *bighas*. My assessment is on 25 *bighas* only." What is this strange thing that has happened?" The Sikh peasant then told him that the Guru had assured him that the assessment would be adequate. The Revenue Officer met the Guru and asked him the explanation of this mysterious happening. Guru Tegh Bahadur said: "The letters on the seal are inverted, but when you fix the seal with the help of ink, the letters appear straight. Similarly, a Sikh who bows and dedicates himself to the Guru, finds himself protected by the unseen Hand of God from exploitation error, and harm."

"Give me instruction, my Lord," said the Officer, so that I am my family may live in peace and prosperity. "Give up smoking and the use of tobacco" said the Guru. Lead an honest and charitable life. Share whatever you have with those who are in need. Serve the saints and learn humility and imbibe the devotion to God from them. For some generations this man's descendants led a pious life but towards the end of the eighteenth century they fell into evil ways, and started smoking and drinking. Kavi Santokh Singh, the eminent historian, guided them to the right path and under his moral and spiritual influence the whole family was baptised into the Khalsa Holy Order.

Guru Tegh Bahadur's camp then moved on to Kurukshetra, where there were already three Sikh shrines commemorating the visits to the historic city of Guru Nanak, Guru Amar Das and Guru Har Gobind. The city was full of monks, yogis, Brahmins, hermits, and anchorites. Devotees from all parts of India had come to seek solace and enlightenment. The Hindu conception of a prophet had now come down to be a man who had no family ties with the world and who begged his food. But into the historic city of Kurukshetra stepped a strange prophet, who was riding a white horse, wearing a sword, carrying bow and arrows, and had been hunting wild animals even on his journey to Kurukshetra.

He was married, and moved about with his family and disciples. The Brahmins were upset, but his sermons of illuminating wisdom silenced them, and awakened them to the light of truth. The *yogis* were fidgety, but his discourses on the *Sahajya yoga* of Sikhism, and the philosophy of the divine. Word opened a new vista for their spiritual vision. For three days a free kitchen remained open for all. Whatever was offered to the Guru by the devotees was distributed among the needy. Guru Tegh Bahadur then paid homage to the shrines of Guru Nanak, Guru Amar Das, and Guru Hargobind. Food and clothes were distributed in all these three places. The Brahmins, says a chronicler, asked for a special gift. Guru Tegh Bahadur gave them a *Hukamnama* (a letter of blessing) engraved on a copper plate.

After leaving Kurukshetra Guru Tegh Bahadur camped at a place now known as Banibadarpur. There was a cluster of trees under which the Guru's entourage pitched their camp. A peasant from this place complained that there was great scarcity of water, and he had very little land. Finding him very hardworking and pious, Guru Tegh Bahadur gave him a bag full of money (known in old Punjabi as *badar*) with which the farmer bought land and constructed a well, and built a temple to commemorate the visit of the Guru. The place was known as Banipur. After the Guru's gift of a bag full of money to develop that area, it came to be known as Banibadarpur.

From here Guru Tegh Bahadur went to a place named Sudhail, on the banks of the Jamuna. From here he moved on to Kadamanakpur. In this place lived a very pious Vaishnava, named Maluk Das. At first, Maluk Das was very anxious to meet the successor of Guru Nanak, but when he came to know that Guru Tegh Bahadur wore arms, and indulged in such sports as hunting, and allowed his disciples to take meat, his vegetarian tendencies, and strong Vaishnava sentiments created some doubt about the holiness and spirituality of the Guru. In his subconscious mind he felt impelled to go. But the thought of a prophet with a sword, bow and arrow, and holy men eating meat was too repulsive to his Vaishnava sentiments. Against the temptation of being impelled to go, he closed the doors, and started repeating the name of Lord Krishna, in front of the idol of his god. As he concentrated on the image of Lord Krishna, he reflected on the historical Krishna also. The image of Krishna, the Flute player, at once changed into Krishna, the warrior prophet, standing with a bow and arrows, and a sword in his hand. So the thought came to him that Guru Tegh Bahadur could also be a Saviour with the sword. He had concentrated too much on the romantic image of Krishna. After his prayers he made a formal offering of food to his god. It was pure vegetarian food, the only food fit for gods and saints. He kept it covered with a piece of cloth before the idol, a ceremonial way of offering food. When he uncovered the food, he saw to his dismay and shocking surprise a dish of meat among other dishes. Was it a vision or a dream? He could not understand it. Do the gods accept meat also? Is it a food suitable for holy men? The thought of Guru Tegh Bahadur came to him again and he reflected "If he is as great as Krishna let him divine my inner desire to see him. Krishna is said to have gone to his devotees wherever he was remembered. Cannot Guru Tegh Bahadur come to me, when he is already in the city?" Such were the confused thoughts of Maluk Das when there was a knock at the door. When he opened the door he saw Guru Tegh Bahadur standing there. "Forgive me Master, how greatly I have sinned in my vanity of vegetarianism. And yet, O Saviour thou hast forgiven me, and come all the way to save me from getting lost in darkness. Inscrutable are thy ways, Lord. Forgive me all the sinful thoughts I have been having in my troubled soul. How could a petty creature like me understand thee?" According to one historical record Maluk Das was over a hundred years old and Guru Tegh Bahadur sent a palanquin (*palki*) for him to be brought to his Camp-durbar with respect and due reverence. Maluk Das begged the Guru to leave his wooden slippers with him as a gift which could remind him every moment of his lotus feet. Guru Tegh Bahadur gave him a Book of Hymns and wooden slippers which have been preserved in the historical temple.

Camping after every twelve to fifteen miles journey, Guru Tegh Bahadur reached Delhi. He was received with great enthusiasm by the Sikhs of Delhi, the leading among whom was Lakhi Rai, a Yadav *Kshatriya* of the Badhtiya clan. With him were his eight brave sons: Naghayia, Hema, Hadi, Situ, Pundara, Bakhshi, Bala and Jawahar. Lakhi Rai's wife, Paran Devi, received Holy Mother Nanaki and Mata Gujari. The wives of Raja Ram Singh and Raja Jai Singh came to pay homage to the Guru and Mataji. Here Guru Tegh Bahadur received the news that the brave Shivaji had surrendered to Raja Jai Singh, who was persuading him to go to Agra and make peace with Aurangzeb. No freedom loving person was happy at the turn of events. Aurangzeb was at this time at Agra.

After a very brief stay, Guru Tegh Bahadur left Delhi for Mathura, where during two day's sojourn he paid a visit to Vrindaban also. As he did not stop at Vrindaban, there is no historical place commemorating his visit. From Mathura Guruji went to Agra, where there was already a very important Sikh centre built in memory of Guru Nanak's visit to the place. Guru Ram Das and Bhai Gurdas had stayed in Agra when they were assigned important missions to represent Sikhism in Akbar's court. A devout lady invited Guru Tegh Bahadur to her house where the Guru spent a day or two. Tradition gives the name of this lady as Mai Jassi. Her, house became a shrine and is now known as Mai Than Gurdwara.

From there the Guru and his *entourage* moved on to Etawah, Kanpur, Fatehpur, and reached Allahabad early in January 1666 A.D. Neither history, nor tradition has preserved any anecdote relating to these places, but the places where Guru Tegh Bahadur camped are still preserved as shrines. The historical temples in these large cities, where there are thousands of Sikhs now a days, being located in old localities, are in a very miserable condition. While Sikhs have built imposing new Gurdwaras, and even some saints have erected large Gurdwaras of their own in these cities, not a penny is being spent to maintain these historical shrines. A large section of the public does not even know about their existence.

Allahabad (Paryag) is the place where the Ganges, the Jamuna, and the fabled subterranean Saraswati unite, thereby giving it the name Triveni, 'the triple braid.' It has always been a celebrated place of pilgrimage. There was a suicide tree here, to jump from which and die, was considered an act of piety. Many ignorant people gave their belongings to the Pandas and Brahmins and committed suicide in the hope of jumping down to heaven. Jahangir had this tree unprooted and wisely put a stop to this folly. Guru Tegh Bahadur camped in a place now called Ahiyapur.

Guru Tegh Bahadur was known for his benevolence and charity. The poor, the needy, and the destitute gathered around him for food, clothing, and other gifts, which he freely gave. In the building, which the disciples had prepared for his residence, there was a room set apart for his meditations also, and its sanctity is preserved to this day. Here a great and joyful thing happened which created a stir and thrill in the knowledgeable spheres. Here the Spirit and Light of Guru Gobind Singh descended, and manifested itself by the Will of God, in his mother's womb. The divine Mother Gujari conceived the Son of God, an event which Guru Gobind Singh himself describes thus in his Work "*Apni Katha*: (Autobiography), which forms the first Book of his great historical work: *the Bachittar Natak.*" Says Guru Gobind Singh: "God brought me into the world as I was doing austerities on the *Sapat-sring* mountain which is near Hemkunt, where I performed such penance hat my soul blended with the Supreme Spirit. My father and mother meditated on the Incomprehensible. They both practised the highest Yoga through diverse spiritual efforts. Their devout service in the love of God pleased the Almighty. Then God commanded me to take human form in this world. I was then born into this dark age. My mind was fixed on the lotus feet of God. I did not like to come; God sent me into the world with a mandate saying, I cherished thee as my Son, and send thee to establish the path of Truth. Go into the world, establish virtue and keep the people from evil. When my father came to Triveni (Allahabad) he daily devoted himself to boundless charity, and humanitarian acts of piety. There, at Allahabad, my Light first manifested in human form. (i.e. my Spirit descended into my mother's womb).

The conception of the Son of God was a great event which thrilled everyone. Guru Tegh Bahadur was forty-five, while Mata Gujari was about forty-three years old. They were going to have their first son, a prophet of God, born for saving humanity in answer to decades of prayer, service and meditation, on the Supreme Being. After a stay of one month at Allahabad, Guru Tegh Bahadur moved on the old Grand Trunk road along the Southern bank of of the Ganges. The place where Guru Tegh Bahadur stayed is known as Gurdwara Pukka Sangat.

The next important place where Guru Tegh Bahadur camped was Mirzapur, where there was a small temple commemorating the visit of Guru Nanak. Four prominent Sikhs, Bhai Bal Chand, Bhai Hari Krishen, Bhai Chatar Bhoj, and Bhai Lalu were the missionaries stationed here, who worked under the *masand* of

Benares. Guru Tegh Bahadur rested in a garden belonging to a local zamindar, who later on dedicated the whole garden, and all the land attached to it, to the cause of the Guru. Unfortunately, the shrines of Guru Nanak, and Guru Tegh Bahadur have disappeared. Either they were desecrated during some political upheaval, or the buildings collapsed, and were never rebuilt. The place where Guru Tegh Bahadur sat is till clearly marked. The descendant of the *masands* of this place have become the owners of the garden worth two lacks. The man who claims to be the direct descendends of the *masands* possesses a copy of *Adi Granth* which is quite old. The people of all the neighbouring villages come to pay homage to the place, where Guru Tegh Bahadur pitched his camp. Married couples, and the newly born children are brought here for blessings and grace. After three days stay here, Guru Tegh Bahadur moved on to Benares.

There was already a large religious centre under the *masand* Jawehri Mal commemorating the memory of Guru Nanak's visit to the holy city. A new one had now been built for Guru Tegh Bahadur in the heart of the city. In the labyrinth of streets which link temple to temple, and which in themselves are strewn with shrines, and altars, with different gods, and goddesses in every temple, the Sikh shrines known as the *Sangats* were the only ones where there were no idols and no images. As a matter of fact, Guru Nanaks disciples were vigorous preachers against idolatry, without of course offending any god or goddess. Bhai Gurdas had spent nearly two years in Benares, during which he had written about six hundred poems in high Hindi on Sikh mysticism containing about a hundred poems strongly criticising idolatry. In every verse he presents the worship of gods and goddesses in the light of the true worship of one God. While he deems the life of a worshipper of the One God as ethically pure, as that of a loyal wife loving only her husband, he considers the life of worshippers of many gods and goddesses as immoral, hopeless, and miserable, like that of prostitutes.

Into this city Guru Tegh Bahadur entered into his white horse named Sri Dhar, a gift of his friend Saiffudin. He was wearing a dark brown dress of Rajput style, still preserved in the holy shrine at Benares. A numbers of letters of Guru Tegh Bahadur written in his own artistic hand from Patna, Monghyr and Dacca reveal the names of the following prominent Sikhs of Benares, which unfortunately no other available historical document has recorded: Bhai Jawehri Mal (the Head of the Centre), Bhai Kalyan Mal, Bhai Kirpal Das, Bhai Babu Rai, Bhai Bhikhari, Bhai Maharaj, Bhai Ram Mal, Bhai Bhati Seth, Bhai Jati Mal, Bhai Babu Muni, Bhai Man Singh, Maharaj Rama Joydyosi, Bhai Koka Mana, Bhai Bal Krishan, Bhai Sukhdev, Bhai Phagu Shah, Bhai Chatak Mal, Bhai Durga Das, Bhai Ganga Ram, Bhai Raghunath, Bhai Mohan Das, Bhai Dalpat Das, Bhai Sadanand, Bhai Jai Ram Das, and Bhai Ramanand.

With the coming of Guru Tegh Bahadur into the holy city of Benares the whole atmosphere seemed to have been divinely inspired. The devotees from all parts of the country flocked to have a glimpse of the Guru. The pundits and scholars came to know the depth of the Guru's Knowledge and spirituality.

Benares, as it is even now, was overflowing with the diseased and the infirm. No wonder, a great number of the pilgrims came here to die on the banks of the Ganges. "I have indeed," says Count Hermann Keyserling, "seen more of that which induced Prince Siddhartha once upon a time to leave this world, than ever before." Guru Tegh Bahadur told the pundits that wasteful logic chopping, and intellectual legerdemain, concerned with the conundrums of narrow metaphysical ideas, quite unrelated to life and the spirit of truth, amounts to ignorance of truth and of God. They should not make religion and philosophy a recondite idiosyncracy, but bringing into it the much needed human interest. To the sick and infirm, who came to die, he explained, that human life was precious to the last day. The only death a man must die, is the death in life which gives spiritual rebirth. A free kitchen (langar) was opened for all. Clothes were distributed to the naked. Early in the morning one day Jawehri Mal got up and informed the Guru that he was going to bathe in the Ganges, which was about half a mile from there. With a smile on his beaming radiant face, Guru Tegh Bahadur said: "Why should my disciple go to the Ganges, the Ganges should come to this place. Dig any where in this room, and you will find the clear water of the Ganges." For the Sikh, the word of the Guru was the law of God. There lingered one fear in the disciple's mind, that he might have to dig very deep as the wells in the neighbouring buildings were quite deep. But to his surprise he had hardly dug one foot when the crystal clear water of the Ganges emerged out of the square hole. The Ganges came to this disciple. To this day this strange phenomenon can be witnessed. Guru Tegh Bahadur also perhaps wished to symbolically teach his disciples, that the water in any place where the praise of God is sung is as holy as that of the Ganges.

Guru Tegh Bahadur camped at Benares for about a fortnight. His horse Sri Dhar fell ill. He had to leave it under the care of his disciples. The first letter he wrote from Patna was about his concern about the health of Sri Dhar and the medicine that was to be given to it." "Send Sri Dhar to Patna," he wrote, "as soon as he recovers."

From Benares Guru Tegh Bahadur moved on to Saśaram where there was an important missionary centre under a romantic *masand,* who was addressed by everyone as Uncle Phagu Shah. Uncle Phagu Shah had built a very beautiful mansion, with a stately portico, and a large entrance hall. People wondered why he had built such a large building and such a large entrance chamber. He said that he was expecting the Guru to come on horseback, with a large *Sangat* (congregation), and when he came, he should not have the trouble of alighting from his horse, but could enter the mansion on horseback. He had been saying this for many years, and yet the Guru did not come. Now when the news of Guru Tegh Bahadur's arrival at Benares reached Sasaram, everyone felt that the prophetic expectations of Uncle Phagu Shah had come true. Guru Tegh Bahadur stayed with Phagu Shah for a fortnight, and blessed him for his devotion and service.

From Sasaram Guru Tegh Bahadur went to Buddha-Gaya, the holy site of

Buddhism which had by then been everpowered by sharp witted intolerant Brahmanism. Yet, in the shadow of the 'Tree of Revelation' reflected the peace and nobility of the great Buddha. There was some affinity between the spirit of the Buddha and that of Guru Tegh Bahadur. They were not what people call born prophets. They became gods among men by their strenuous spiritual effort. They were both born in similar atmosphere; both brooded on the suffering of humanity; and both of them spread the gospel of truth by travelling far and wide. Both had a devoted wife and son. Both taught the people of India the unity of humanity, compassion and charity. But for Buddha, and the Sikh Gurus, Indian culture might not have made such a leap forward during the two critical periods of its history, a fact, which narrow-minded Brahmanism refuses to recognise to this day. Guru Tegh Bahadur paid homage to the shrine built in memory of Guru Nanak in the place where along with his Muslim rebeck player Mardana he sang for a week or more the songs of the eternal path to Truth, the songs of *Nirvana*. The place where Guru Tegh Bahadur spent a week and silenced the Brahmins, who, in pride of their wisdom, thought that their high birth, external piety, knowledge of the Vedas, could everawe this strange visitor, whom the people called the new prophet has also, become a historical shrine. These actors of wisdom soon realised, that they were face to face with another living Buddha, with a difference. Lord Buddha had moved from kingliness to renunciation, while Guru Tegh Bahadur had moved from renunciation to kingliness. The superhuman creative energy, and inspiration emanating from both manifestations of the most exalted condition of the spirit of man was the same. India falls into the pit of darkness, corrupt life, and mental slavery, when its masses and political leaders fail to recognise this central fact of our history and culture.

From Buddha-Gaya Guru Tegh Bahadur followed the age old route of Buddhist pilgrims to Patna, camping for a day near the ruins of Nalanda, and for three days at Rajgriha. At Rajgriha we have, till this day, two *Sangats* (shrines), one commemorating the visit of Guru Nanak, and the other that of Guru Tegh Bahadur. Towards the end of May 1666 A.D. Guru Tegh Bahadur reached Patna.

III

King Ajatasutra's capital was Rajgriha, which did not serve as an efficient base of operation against his enemy, the Lachchavi Republic. He had to construct a new base, a fort at a convenient site on the river, and thus was laid the foundation of the new capital, which was first named Kusumpura, or Kusumvaya, and then named Pataliputra. The Greeks called it Palibothra. It is now known as Patna.

The city was first contructed under the supervision of Ajatasutra's Chief Ministers named, Sunidha, and Vassakara. When the construction of this city, built mainly for war and aggressive designs on neighbours was complete, the two ministers invited the prophet of peace and non-violence, Lord Buddha, for dinner so that the great Master might be the first to step into it. They named the gate, through which the Buddha went out of the city, as the *Gotama-gate*, and the *ghat* (landing), from which he was ferried across the Ganges, was commemorated as the *Gotama-ghat.* It was on this unique occasion that the Buddha is said to have made his pregnant prophecy that Patliputra would one day grow to be the chief city of Aryan descent, and the centre of trade and economic prosperity.

Patliputra (Patna) was also the capital of Chandragupta's vast empire. Megasthenes, the Greek ambassador in Chandragupta's court, reports that the city was built at the confluence of the two rivers, the Ganges, and the Son. It was nine-and-half miles long and a mile-and-a-half broad, protected by a moat, and further protected by a massive timber palisade. It had 64 gates, 570 towers, and as protection against floods, the whole city was built of wood. From the ancient times to the seventeenth century, Patna was famous for art treasures, courtesans, goldsmiths, terra cotta and artistic pottery.

The city to this day has the unique distinction of being honoured by the holy presence and foot-prints of the Buddha, Guru Nanak, and Guru Tegh Bahadur, and of being the birthplace of Guru Gobind Singh. When Guru Tegh Bahadur arrived, the East and West had already started mingling in Patna, and other large cities. The Holland company had a house, by reason of their trade in Saltpetre. Tavernier, the famous European traveller, had just passed through Patna on his way to Dacca. English factories had also been already established at Lahore, Hoshiarpur, Patna and Dacca.

It was at Patna that Guru Tegh Bahadur received the news of some of the major political happenings in the country. Shah Jahan was dead. A treaty of peace had been signed at Purandar in June 1665 A.D., according to which Shivaji agreed to handover twenty-three of his forts, and to write a letter to the Emperor, pleading for his favour. By the same postal messenger Jai Singh had sent a secret letter to Aurangzeb, suggesting a cordial reply to Shivaji's letter. Such chivalry was not however, native to Aurangzeb. Frigidly he replied to Shivaji "Your letter couched in humble strain has been received by us. It is agreeable to note that you crave for pardon for your conduct, and that you repent for your past deeds. Our reply is that your behaviour has been so base that it deserves no forgiveness. Nevertheless, at Raja Jai Singh's intercession, we extend to you a general pardon." It was hardly a tone to turn a defeated opponent into an enthusiastic supporter. However Shivaji carried out the terms of the treaty with Jai Singh. Most probably at the suggestion of Raja Jai Singh again, Aurangzeb wrote, another letter, phrased in a very different language,"you are at present serving in our Imperial Camp. In recognition of your services a handsome dress, and a pretty jewelled sword are sent to you herewith. We have a high opinion of you. Therefore we desire you to come here quickly and without loss of time. When we grant you audience we shall receive you with great hospitality and soon grant you leave to return."

In this letter the shrewd Shivaji scented a tiger's caress. Shivaji diffidently suggested that perhaps the invitation was a trap. Jai Singh at once offered his own son, Ram Singh, who had shyly admired the Maratha ever since his arrival in the Imperial Camp; he supported his father's offer, delighted at the prospect of close companionship with Shivaji. Shivaji began his journey to North India on March 5, 1666 A.D., and had reached the outskirts of Agra on 9th May, where the Emperor was holding Court.

The visit was not a success. Aurangzeb clearly did not understand the man he was to deal with, and showed a curious lack of political sagacity in his reception of the Maratha. No prince or General in all India could render the Emperor such aid in his designs against the Deccan kingdom as the rude highlander who had at last come to his feet. A good many points might well be stretched to secure so valuable an ally. But Aurangzeb was a bigot inclined to be fastidous in somethings. He could not forget that Shivaji was according to him, a fanatical Hindu, and a vulgar brigand to boot. He set himself the task of showing the Maratha his real place, and far from recognising him as a Viceroy of the Deccan, let him stand unnoticed among third rank officers in the splendid assembly, that daily gathered before the throne in the great Audience Hall. Deeply affronted, pale and sick, with shame and fury, Shivaji quitted the presence without taking ceremonial leave. According to another account Shivaji fell down in a swoon. There was a stir among the courtiers. The Emperor asked what he matter was. Ram Singh diplomatically replied: "The tiger is a wild beast of the forest. He feels oppressed by the heat in a place like this, and has been taken ill." He also apologised for the Raja's rude conduct saying that he was a Deccani unfamiliar with courts, and polished manners. Raja Ram Singh was ordered to lodge him in the Jaipur House, outside the city walls, and be responsible for his custody. Jai Singh was placed in a dilemma by this unexpected result of Shivaji's visit to the court. He continued to write to Ram Singh, to see to it that Shivaji's life was safe, and the solemn assurances of the Rajput father and son remained inviolate.

On August 19, 1666 A.D. Shivaji escaped. Two months Guru Tegh Bahadur left Patna he was at Rajgriha. It was Ram Singh who broke the news to Aurangazeb. The Emperor suspected that Shivaji had fled with the connivance of Ram Singh. The Rajput prince was punished, first by being forbidden entry into the court, and then by being deprived of his rank and pay.

The news of Shivaji's escape delighted everyone. The news of Raja Ram Singh's disgrace and arrest was deeply felt in the Guru's household. The kindness and support of Raja Jai Singh and Raja Ram Singh to the cause of Guru Hari Krishen had not been forgotten. Many ministers of Guru Tegh Bahadur like Bhai Mati Das, Bhai Sati Das, and Bhai Gurditta, the High Priest, knew the Rajput Rajas personally.

Ever since Guru Nanak's visit to Patna and about four months stay there, the light of the Sikh faith had been kept burning by a successive band of missionaries. The heads of the diocese which was also the capital of the *Suba* (State), were *masand* Ram Rai and Bhai Durbari. They made an excellent arrangement for the stay of Guru Tegh Bahadur and his family. A devout lady, who is addressed as Bebe Paidi Bai in Guru Tegh Bahadur's letters looked after Holy Mother Nanaki, Mata Gujari who was expecting a child. The names of other prominent disciples who wholeheartedly served the Guru are: Raja Fateh Chand Maini, Bhai Chain Sukh, Bhai Mehar Chand, Bhai Subha Chand, Bhai Jeth Mal, Bhai Dedh Mal, Bhai Nand Kumar, Bhai Din Dayal, Bhai Mehar Chand, Bhai Pran Nath, Bhai Hira Nand, Bhai Gayo Das, Bhai Prehlad Das, Bhai Bansidhar, Bhai Murlidhar, Bhai Mohan Das, Bhai Nain Sukh, Bhai Harikes, Bhai Chabil Das, Bhai Bhagwan Das, Bhai Gujar Mal, Bhai Sadanad, Bhai Ghanishyam, Bhai Kawal Nain, Bhai Ram Rai, Bhai Murli Dhar, Bhai Kishen Das, Bhai Singha, Bhai Sangat Das, Bhai Baij Nath, Bhai Sukh Deo, Bhai Jhabar Singh, Bhai Jagman, Bhai Rupa, Bhai Lal Man, Bhai Anant Das, Bhai Amlia Keskar, Bhai Sufer Chand, Bhai Nain Sukh, Bhai Gulal Chand, Bhai Bal Gobind, Bhai Bhagta, Bhai Bindraban, Bhai Pala Govardan Das, Pala Pheru, Bhai Bansidhar, Fisherman Sukhdeo, Bhai Suja Ram, Bhai Hira Nand, Bhai Paras Ram, Bhai Bhag Mal, Bhai Hirdai Ram, Bhai Mitter Sain, Bhai Gaj Mal, Bhai Jagdeo, Bhai Dalpat, Bhai Mul Dasi, Bhai Achetan, Bhai Bala Mula, Bhai Lachua, Bhai Raghunath, Bhai Dina Nath, Bhai Pran Nath, Bhai Subha Chand, Bhai Nand Lal, Bhai Pritam Das, Bhai Bhoj Rai and others.

Guru Tegh Bahadur had now decided to spend the early months of the rainy season (known as the *Chumasa*) at Patna. During this period the whole missionary work in this region was reorganised. As the Dacca *Sangat* also known as *Hazuri Sangat,* was anxiously waiting for Guruji, it was decided that his family should stay at Patna while he went to Bengal and Kamarup to meet and bless those brave Sikhs who had been keeping the torch of Sikh faith burning in those far-flung areas for over a century.

Bhai Dayal Das was appointed the Suba (lit: Governor meaning Archbishop) over all the missionary centres in East Bengal, Bihar, Uttar Pradesh, and other neighbouring areas Guru Tegh Bahadur gave him complete authority over the *Sangats* of these regions. Every letter written by Guruji from Bengal to the *Sangats* of these areas bears witness to the Master's profound confidence in this noble soul. Again and again Guruji instructs the *Sangats* to consider Bhai Dayal Das an embodiment of his own Spirit, and respect him as his own living image. His command was to be accepted as Guruji' command. His exalted character, dedicated soul organisational ability, tireless spirit of service, and unstinted devotion to the cause of his faith, made him the most outstanding Sikh, deserving such a high and responsible post. Out of personal love and affection for this scion of Bhai Mai Das' family, everyone of whose ten sons fell a martyr to the cause of Sikhism, Guru Tegh Bahadur addressed him as *Bheiya ji* (Respected Brother). As long as Bhai Dayal Das was there at Patna he was no longer worried about the welfare of his family. He new that there would be looked after, with as much care and affection as he could personally bestow on them.

Some Sikhs complained to the Guru that Bhai Jaith Mal (whose name is often given incorrectly as Bhai Jaita), was very dirty in his habit because he never took a bath, never wore clean clothes, never said his prayers regularly and did not visit the temple as frequently as a Sikh should. Guru Tegh Bahadur smiled and asked two of his disciples to find out the truth. To the Guru, Bhai Jaith Mal appeared to be as devout a Sikh as anyone else. These two disciples disguised themselves as travellers and sought Bhai Jaith Mal's hospitality, which was freely granted. At night they keenly watched Bhai Jaith Mal. To their surprise he quietly got up at 2 A.M. took his bath and after putting on very clean clothes sat in his meditations and prayers for nearly four hours. At daybreak he wore the same dirty clothes which he generally wore while working outside, and attended to his guests. Guru Tegh Bahadur was happy to learn about the silent devotion of Bhai Jaith Mal for God, and blessed him.

Elaborate preparations were made for the journey to Dacca and Kamarup. Bhai Bulaki Das from Dacca and Raja Ram Rai of some state in Kamarup, personally came with gifts, money, and plans for the journey. Raja Fateh Chand Maini, and *masand* Ram Rai, the Head of the Patna diocese, took responsibility for arranging a still better accommodation for Guruji's family. Holy Mother Nanaki wanted Guru Tegh Bahadur to say on for a few moths more at Patna and wait for the birth of his child some time in December. But to the detached spirit of Guru Tegh Bahadur, his responsibility to fulfil the wishes of his disciples thirsting for his illuminating presence was dearer than any family affair. He left Patna sometime in August 1666 A.D. along with his prominent disciples Diwan Mati Das, Bhai Sati Das, Bhai Gurditta and others. Covering about thirty miles a day Guru Tegh Bahadur reached Monghyr, a flourishing town on the banks of the Ganges. Here Guruji stopped for nearly a month and wrote letters to the *Sangats* of Allahabad, Benares, Mirzapur, and Patna. To Patna *Sangat* and Bhai Dayal Das, he wrote: "The wishes of the disciples and the whole *Sangat* shall be fulfilled by the Guru. We have camped at Monghyr. It is the time now for the *Sangat* to serve. Bhaiji, bring all the *masands* working under you and also the *Sangat* to Monghyr for *darshan* (personal blessings of the Guru). Whoever comes shall abide in prosperity. This is the opportunity to serve the cause of the Sikhism. Whatever Bhai Dayal Das says should be accepted by the *Sangat* as the command of the Guru. The Guru will fulfil the desires of such disciples. There is one more thing, respected Brother. We are thinking of acquiring some tents for our *dera* (convoy) from Shahzadpur. I leave it to you. You can send any order to the *Sangat* and make them comply with your commands. Please send forty Bihari turbans; also send twenty turbans worth forty rupees. The *Sangat* shall flourish in prosperity."

To the Benares *Sangat* he wrote: "All the tithes and offerings should be given to Bhai Dayal Das. It will reach the Guru's presence. The *Sangat* shall be blessed. We have camped at Monghyr. Whoever comes here to receive the Guru's blessings shall receive his divine favour. His desires shall be fulfilled." Similar letters were written to all the dioceses.

Most of the letters of Guru Tegh Bahadur indicate that some Raja was with him in his itinerary and he accompanied him back to Anandpur. Neither Raja Ram Singh nor any other General of the Mughal Army was with him during his journey from Patna to Dacca. No Mughal General sent with an army on a military expedition, according to the rules, could stop at Monghyr for more than two days. But Guru Tegh Bahadur camped here for nearly a month, and invited his disciples of Allahabad, Mirzapur, Benares to come and meet him. He would certainly not have written to these *Sangats* to send such small amounts of money as eighty to hundred rupees, and such articles as turbans, and tents, if Raja Ram Singh who went to Dacca much later with a huge army had been with him. Some of the costly turbans he was acquiring were to be given as robes of honours to visitors and dignitaries, who met him on the way to Dacca, such as *pirs,* saintly scholars, devout chiefs and *masands*. During his stay at Monghyr and other places where he camped, Kirtan was performed by his bards and musicians, sermons were delivered, and elevating and sweet Songs of *Nirvana* (the *Padavli*) were composed by Guru Tegh Bahadur and recorded by Bhai Sati Das. Says an Assamese chronicler about Guru Tegh Bahadur: "He became the Guru of a large number of Brahmins and Kshatriyas. He would not take the name of Rama and Krishna, nor of any god or goddess. On meeting a disciple of his own faith he would simply say: *"Vah-Guru, Vah-Guru"* and nothingelse. People came from great distances to have a glimpse of the Guru. He was the second Guru of the Sikh faith to come so far, and revive the seeds of faith sown by Guru Nanak.

From Monghyr Guru Tegh Bahadur went to Bhagalpur, and from there to Colgong, Sahibganj and Kantnagar. This village, Kantnagar, was subsequently wiped out by the floods, and the inhabitants moved to a new site towards the North, now known as Lachmipur. A number of villages in these areas of Bihar are still predominantly Sikh villages. Although their dress is Bihari, and the language is Maithili, they retain Sikh traditions and practices in much purer form than we find them in the Punjab. When Patna Sahib was raised to the status of a *Takhat* after the abolition of the *masands,* an army was stationed there. This Khalsa army was such a powerful force that the Mughals and Assamese continued to seek their support in their military campaigns up to the time of the British invasion. The memory of the Guru's visit is still fresh in the minds of the people, and the presence of Guru Tegh Bahadur is still felt in the wonderful legends told and retold by the devout Bihari and Bengali Sikhs of these areas. From Kantnagar Guru Tegh Bahadur went to Raj Mahal, where he stopped for three days. From here he moved on to the great Sufi centre Malda, known for its *Pirs* and *Fakirs*. Here the Sufi *Pirs* gathered around him and discussed many religious problems. They were deeply impressed by the magnetic personality of the Guru and the active associations of the Sikh faith with the major Sufi Schools of thought, like the *Chistis* and the *Qaidriyas*.

From Malda he went to Godagari, Gopalpur and, passing through Pabna, he reached Dacca by the middle or the end of October 1664 A.D. Here he met a reception befitting kings and emperors. The *masands,* the disciples, and innumerable Rajas who were Ministers and Army Generals under the Viceroy of Dacca came to pay homage to Guru Tegh Bahadur.

IV

The origin of the city of Dacca is shrouded in mystery. Various theories have been propounded to explain the derivation of the name Dacca. According to the most popular opinion, the word "Dhaka or Dacca" is derived from *Dhak,* the name of a tree, *Butea Frondos* which bears red blossoms and is plentiful here. Sayid Aulad Hasan gives a tradition according to which Dhaka is derived from the Bengali word *Dhak* meaning drum. Vikramaditya is said to have visited this region and his capital Bikrampur still survives.

European travellers identified Dacca with Bangalla. Dacca consisted of 52 bazars and 53 streets, and from the circumstances it obtained the name of *"Bauna Bazar and Tippan Galli."* One of these the, Bangalla bazar, still exists. Bangalla is one of the older names of Dacca referred to by Rennel. It is not improbable that *"Baunoo bazar and Tippan Galli"* was the city here alluded to, and the name of Bangalla by which one of its many bazars was known was applied by Europeans to the whole town, from the circumstance perhaps of this bazar being the place in which trade was chiefly carried on with foreigners. Want tends to confirm this opinion of the identity of Dacca and Bangalla is the circumstance that only one of them is ever mentioned by the same traveller.

Bengal was known as a country of hellish paradise. Bernier, the French traveller and physician, who visited Bengal in 1665 A.D. very aptly observed that Bangalla has a hundred gates open for entrance but not one for departure. Its wealth and goods attracted all travellers while its climate was killing. The Chinese travellers call it *Pang Kola* (Bangala). Abdul Fazal mentions that Kamarup originally extended to Dacca and a considerable part of the present East Bengal.

Guru Nanak visited this place on his way from Dhubri in Assam to Jagannath Puri in the beginning of 16th century. The place was famous for the Dhakeswari temple, a place of pilgrimage. This part of the country was then divided into a number of petty states which were dignified with the title of kingdoms. There appeared to be considerable scarcity of drinking water. During his short stay Guru Nanak had a well constructed here and a temple and tank were built by some local Raja to commemorate the Guru's visit. In the month of March (*Chaitra*) people of all faiths used to gather in worship and prayer to keep the memory of Guru Nanak's visit alive. The water of the well was believed to possess miraculous powers. Hindus, Muslims, and Sikhs came to drink the wish-fulfilling waters of this historic well until recent times.

A greater miracle was performed by Guru Nanak by leaving the light of his faith burning intensely in the soul of the Bengalis of Dacca and other places visited by him. Guru Amar Das was the first to send missionaries to this region who organised the *Sangat* here and informed the Bengali Sikhs that Baisakhi (New Year Day) had been fixed as the national gathering day, when Sikhs of distant places were expected to come and meet the living Guru. History has preserved the name of Bhai Mohan of Dacca, who visited Punjab during the time of Guru Hargobind.

Shortly after Bhai Mohan's visit to Punjab Baba Gurditta eldest brother of Guru Tegh Bahadur reorganised the Udasi Missionaries of Guru Nanak's son, Sri Chand, and appointed Almast the chief missionary over all the centres in Bengal, Bihar and Orissa. Almast visited all these areas with a band of inspired Sikhs and appointed them *masands* (bishops) at Patna, Rajmahal, Dacca, Calcutta and Jagannath Puri.

Almast appointed Bhai Natha as the Head of the Bengal Missionary centre, while Bulaki Das was the *masand* who assisted him in the work. As the city grew, it was felt that a temple should be built in the centre of the city. Bhai Natha, though of a very caustic temper and flaming tongue was very much respected for his piety and philanthrophy. With the help of donations freely given by Bengali Sikhs, Bhai Natha built a beautiful temple on the right side of the road which now goes from Ramana race course towards Nilket. It is just behind the newly built Public Library. Bhai Natha also built a well, which was repaired later and a stone inscription was fixed which reads: "In the name of the True God, the Creator, and of Guru Nanak (attached to) the Guru *gaddi* at Nanakmata of Almastraj. Baba Natha Sahib's *Sangat* at Shujatpur. Mahant Premdas. Well repaired in 1890 B.S., 1833 A.D. Another Bengali inscription is fixed on the top of the well.

"The Sikh organisation is located in a big compound, which can be entered through an arched gateway from the Northern by-lane. The interior falls into two parts, the temple-cum-residential complex on the East, and the Western half containing a masonry tank, a well, and other *samadhis* (death memorials). The Eastern half consists of a rectangular court, on the Northern and Southern sides of which range residential rooms, while its Western side is occupied by the temple. In the court is a *vedi* (raised seat) on which is set a black stone containing footprints (probably of some Guru). The temple consists of multiple rooms arranged around a central square room,—four rooms on its four sides and other four at the corners, in all nine. All these are interconnected by arched doorways. The roof is a flat vault resting on coping arches at the sides. In the central room is a small platform on which is still kept the *Guru Granth*. The ground plan of this temple exactly follows the arrangement of rooms in Bibi Pari's tomb. (Bibi Pari, or Lady Fairy, better named Iran Dukht was daughter of Nawab Shaista Khan who died in 1684 A.D.).

Nawab Islam Khan (1606-1613 A.D.) named Dacca, Jahangirnagar, and shifted the capital to this city from Rajmahal, which then lost its strategic importance. Shah Jahan visited it in 1624 A.D. Sultan Mohammed Shuja temporarily transferred the capital to Rajmahal for his self-defence, but six years before Guru

Tegh Bahadur arrived Mir Jumla again transferred it to Dacca. In 1664 A.D. Shaista Khan nephew of the beautiful Empress Nurjahan and brother of the Lady who sleeps in Taj Mahal was appointed Viceroy of Bengal.

Shaista Khan was the noblest ruler that India was fortunate to have, after Akbar. He ruled Bengal with great compassion, and noble concern for all communities. While Aurangzeb had started eliminating Hindu and non-Muslim officials, the key posts in his administration were held by the Hindus. Even his Prime Minister (Diwan) was a Hindu. Rankin in his Dacca Diaries (1668 A.D.) states that the following were the principal non-Muslim Officials: *Diwans:* Raja Bhagwant Das, Rai Nand Lall. *Peshdast of Diwan:* Keshi Das; *House Diwan*: Murlidhar: *Munshi:* Parbal Das, *Chief Mutsady:* Manohar Das; *Mutsady*: Shib Ram; *Superintendent of Finances and Ships:* Kishor Das. *Commander* of 15,000: Raja Subal Singh Sisodia. Out of these, Raja Bhagwant Das who was the Diwan at the time of Guru Tegh Bahadur's arrival, is said to be a Nanak Panthi.

From Rajmahal to Dacca Guru Tegh Bahadur and his *entourage* covered the journey in about nine days. A royal reception was awaiting them at Dacca. The Dacca *Sangat* had built a house specially for Guru Tegh Bahadur's stay, which is now known as Guru Tegh Bahadur's *Sangat* and is situated in the Sangat Tola lane. The mohalla is also called Sangat Tola. The rich and the poor, the high and the low, men, women, and children flocked to see the prophet from the Punjab, the eighth successor of Guru Nanak. Dacca was the most prosperous place in India. Wealth and gold were in abundance. The Portuguese Missionary Sebastian Manrique writes in 1640 A.D., "Money is so plentiful in Dacca that it is seldom counted but always weighed. The vastness of wealth in the city is stupefying."

Daily *Kirtan* was held, sermons were delivered, visitors were received, and the number of those who received the light of Guru's faith, and became his ordained disciples also swelled. He won the admiration of Shaista Khan and his nobles. The locality in which Guru Tegh Bahadur was lodged was mainly reserved for foreigners. Close by, was the Christian Mission under Father Bernard de Jesus. Vicar General of Bengal. In the Feringi bazar lived the Portuguese and Englishmen who had already established a colony.

At Patna Guru Gobind Singh was born on December 22, 1666 A.D. (Posh Sudi 7, 1723 B.S.). There was illumination and great rejoicing at the birth of the Guru's son who was named Gobind Das. Later Guru Gobind was frequently addressed as Gobind Rai. When he ordained the Holy Order of the Khalsa and added the suffix "Singh: Lion", to the name of all his disciples, he added it to his own name also. He is therefore known in history as Gobind Singh.

Bhai Dayal Das immediately dispatched a letter to Dacca giving the happy news which was carried post haste to Dacca by Bhai Mehar Chand and Bhai Kalyan Chand. There was great rejoicing at Dacca. Recitation of the Scriptures, *Kirtan* (hymn singing), and illumination were held. Food and clothes were distributed to the poor. Guru Tegh Bahadur immediately wrote the following reply to Bhai Dayal Das and the Patna *Sangat*: "My blessings on the *Sangat* of

Patna and all the *Sangat* who contemplate the Divine Name; *Vah-Guru"*; God will fulfil their desires. The *Sangat* of Patna has spent money to celebrate the birth of Gobind Das. All the offerings made on the occasion shall be accepted and shall receive divine favour in the *Dargah* (Heavenly Court) of God. A rupee (silver coin) shall be accepted in His Presence as a *mohar* (gold coin). All other services rendered on the occasion shall be accepted, and blessed by God. He who renders service to Gobind Das in future shall be blessed, and shall receive the favour of God. Everyone of you will flourish in prosperity and receive the bounties of God. I am sending a robe of honour to you respected brother (Dayal Das). Patna is the Home of the Guru. May the *Sangat* of Patna live in prosperity.

Guru Tegh Bahadur now wished to visit other areas in Bengal. The sensitive soul of the Bengali people had responded so enthusiastically to his call for spiritual life that invitations from all regions of Bengal were pouring in. Guru Tegh Bahadur was anxious to establish religious centres of his faith in all major towns. Raja Ram Rai, who accompanied him on this itinerary, probably belonged to one of these regions. Between Chittagong and Sylhet there were many small independent kingdoms which accepted the suzerainty of the Mughals. Raja Ram Rai was the ruler of one of these states, most probably some state of the Jaintia Hills near Sylhet, known for its white elephants, and other rare products, and included in the boundaries of old Kamarup.

The journey through these regions was hazardous and required special camp equipage and preparations. Raja Ram Rai had sought one favour from the Guru. Now that a son had been born to the Guru he begged the Guru to pray for him so that he might also be blessed with a noble son who would serve Gobind Das with the same pride and devotion with which he was serving him. Guru Tegh Bahadur granted his request. Preparations were now underway to go first to the Jaintia Hills, Sylhet, and from there go South to Chittagong, and Sondip, and then come back to Dacca within a year or so. In connection with this journey Guru Tegh Bahadur wrote another letter to Patna *Sangat* saying: "The Guru's grace will redeem the *Sangat* of Patna; repeat the divine Name and ever remember the Guru. Sikhs who contemplate the divine Name, *Vah-Guru*, shall be blessed by the Guru and their wishes shall be fulfilled. Patna is the Home of the Guru. The *Sangat* of Patna is devoutly serving Gobind Das. The service of Gobind Das and of the Guru shall be accepted in the *dargah* of God. May the *Sangat* ever live in prosperity. If Bhai Raja has sent the tents from the other side, (some city West of Patna), then please send them. Our requirements are as follows: One special tent (*subela*), three awnings, (*qanats*), one *peshkhana* (duplicate tent) and one kitchen tent, a five yard *ravti*. Send some enclosure tents, and the awnings necessary for that also. All these things may be sent with Bhai Mallu Mehra. The Guru will bless the *Sangat*. Patna is the Home of the Guru."

Accompanied by his disciple Raja Ram Rai, Guru Tegh Bahadur left for Jaintia Hills and Sylhet. He felt that the house in which his family was lodged was not spacious enough for the upbringing of his son, who would soon require a playground a garden, rooms for his governesses, and other attendants to look after him, and train him in the best possible manner. So he wrote the following letter to Bhai Dayal Das and the Patna *Sangat*: "The Sikhs who contemplate the divine Name, *Vah-Guru*, shall be redeemed by the Guru. We are now going beyond (Dacca) with Rajaji. I have left the family at Patna; devout Sikhs who remember God are expected to look after them and serve them. A penny in service will bear the merit of gold coin in the presence of God. This is the opportunity for the *Sangat* of Patna to render service. Whoever renders any service shall be blessed, and his offerings in the name of the Guru shall bear fruit. Now is the golden opportunity to render service to the cause of the Guru. Find a first class, large, and spacious house (*aval haveli hovai, badi havai*) and lodge my family in it."

It was probably in response to this request that Raja Fateh Chand Maini of Patna built a large house which was completed and dedicated to the Guru's family on Guru Nanak's ascension day, Assu Vadi 10 in the year 1725 B.S., 1668 A.D. The Child, Gobind Das, developed a deep personal affection for the wives of Raja Fateh Chand, named Kishori Devi and Visambhara Devi.

Sylhet at this period was divided into three principal states Laur, Gaur, and Jaintia, and it is highly probable that Raja Ram Rai was the ruler of one of these states. These three states covered Sunamganj, Khasia Hills, Habiganj, Amirganj, Nabiganj, Sankarpasah, Jaintia Hills and the present town of Sylhet. The place became famous for Sufis and eunuchs. The first Sufi Khanqah was established by Shah Jalal who came to this place with three hundred disciples and settled here. Shah Jalal was a contemporary of Shaikh Farid and Nizamudin Auliya. His spiritual and cultural influence on Bengal was tremendous. Guru Tegh Bahadur visited early in the year 1667 A.D. Here he also established a missionary centre known as the Sylhet *Sangat*, under which there were minor *Sangats* of the neighbouring area. The Sufis of Sylhet, though far more bigoted than the Sufis of the Punjab, Patna, Delhi and Malda, were impressed by the mystic light which the Guru and his disciples radiated. To Guru Tegh Bahadur's son Gobind Singh later on Sylhet provided war elephants.

After spending the rainy season at Sylhet Guru Tegh Bahadur moved South towards Chittagong, and Sondip. He passed through Shaistaganj, and stopped at Agartala, the Capital of independent Tripura State. From Agartala he moved on to Commilla, Laksam, Daulatganj, Sitakund, and Hathazari. From here he went to Chittagong where he stayed towards the end of the year 1667 A.D. During his stay at Chittagong he established a large religious centre of his faith, and even went to Sondip Island, and established a *Sangat* there. We have the letters of Guru Gobind Singh addressed to the chittagong and Sondip *Sangats*, which show that these dioceses, founded by Guru Tegh Bahadur, must have made tremendous progress because less than thirty years after the death of Guru Tegh Bahadur the Sondip Island *Sangat* and the chittagong *Sangat* were prosperous enough to provide weapons, and war material for the freedom fight of Guru Gobind Singh.

Guru Tegh Bahadur stayed for a few weeks at Dohazari also. Here it is believed a dog belonging to the Guru was seized by a crocodile. The local Mohammadan Zamindar had an autograph of Guru Tegh Bahadur which was preserved till the other day, with a reverence due to a valued family heirloom, and holy relic. The paper may yet be found in the court of wards." The priest at Banskhali informs the visit of Guru Tegh Bahadur, and the places where he camped, and delivered his melodious sermons, *Sangats,* (dioceses) were also established at Agartala, Jorarganj, Feni, Mirsarai Sitakund, Kursira, Bhatian, Comilla, Kulgaon, Hathazari, Rangunia and Kanchannagar. It is this chain of religious centres which clearly indicate that Guru Tegh Bahadur came from Sylhet to Chittagong. Kumira and Kanchannagar had two *Sangats*. The *Sangat* at Banskhali survives to this day. A *jaghir* of Rs.1,000 is still attached to it. The Sikhs in a subsequent period acquired so much importance in Bengal and Assam that their help was always acquired by the authorities to repel Portuguese and Arakanese attacks, and also for the freedom battles of the Assamese. The *Takhat* Patna maintained a standing army under the Jathedars of Patna Sahib. Because of such help rendered by the Khalsa Army of Patna, a learned Sikh, Sardar Mohan Singh was appointed Governor of Chittagong.

Passing through Noakhali, Chandpur and Narayanganj Guru Tegh Bahadur reached Dacca early in the year 1668 A.D. As soon as he arrived, he received happy news about his son Gobind Das and his family. Though Patna *Sangat* and his family was eagerly waiting for him, he had put his heart and soul into the great work of the moral and spiritual regeneration of his country. He was also determined to revive all the old religious centres established by Guru Nanak in Assam. Had he waited for another three months at Patna he would have seen and blessed his new born son, Gobind Das. Had he spared just one month, he could have easily gone to Patna, met his family and come back. But to the detached spirit of Guru Tegh Bahadur nothing was dearer and more important than the awakening of his country to the grim realities of the impending cloudy future. Unfortunately history has not preserved his beautiful sermons delivered to the people of Bengal for whom he developed a deep and tender affection.

Raja Ram singh then met Guru Tegh Bahadur with great reverence. The Guru had already completed his tour of Bengal, and now he wished to revive the religious centres built by Sikh Missionaries to commemorate the visit of Guru Nanak at Dhubri and Kamakhya. By a happy coincidence he was now able to accept Raja Ram Singh's request to accompany him, though the Raja knew that the Guru could not afford to say for more than six to nine months in Assam.

The personal ties of Raja Ram Singh with Shaista Khan brought the Sikh *Sangats* in greater respectful favour of the peace and harmony loving Governor than ever before. It was at this period that an extensive portion of the modern Dacca was given as *jaghir* to the Nanak Panthi *Akhara* and *Sangat Tola* Gurdwara. Some years ago land for the Dacca University, the Dacca Medical College and Hospital, and the Public Library was all acquired from the Mahants of these Gurdwaras. All this land and much more comprising nearly one-third of present Dacca was sanctioned as *jaghir* by Shaista Khan.

It was at about this time that a son was born to Raja Ram Rai, whom he named Rattan Rai. According to a local tradition his name is also said to be Anup Rai. But the historical records are almost unanimous about his name being Rattan Rai. Guru Tegh Bahadur and his ministers were very happy that God had fulfilled the wishes of his devout disciple, who had accompanied him on his Bengal tour and was now ready to accompanied him on his Assam tour also.

Guru Tegh Bahadur and his ministers left Dacca along with Raja Ram Singh. Both Raja Ram Singh and Guru Tegh Bahadur marched a little ahead of the army with a few chosen attendants. Raja Ram Singh and the Guru left Dacca some time in the middle of December 1668 A.D. and reached Assam in February 1669 A.D. The total distance of about two hundred miles was covered in about forty days. Ram Singh's army consisted of 21 Rajput Chiefs, 4000 troopers in his own pay, 1,500 gentlemen troopers, and 500 artillerymen, and with his reinforcements from Bengal his total army swelled up to 30,000 infantry, 18,000 Turkish cavalry, and 15,000 Koch archers. While Guru Tegh Bahadur camped at Guru Nanak's shrine at Dhubri, Raja Ram Singh camped at Rangamati about fifteen miles from Dhubri.

5

Hymns

1

Adore and Love God

gun gobind gayio nahi janam akarath kin

You have never sung the praise of God,
You have lived your life in vain;
Says Nanak: Worship and adore the Lord,
As a fish loves deep sea waters.

Life devoid of the wisdom and love of God is wasteful and purposeless. Life has meaning and significance only if man comes out of his lust for transient pleasures and is devoted to the divine Presence within himself, and in humanity. To love and adore this eternal Spirit is to love and truly served humanity. To sing the glory of God is to harmonize our self with the essence of the Supreme Being. We must participate in the existence of the Immanent Spirit through love and dedication as the fish participates in the deep and boundless waters of the sea. The mind and soul of man must live like a fish in the eternal waters of life. A man cut off from the living Spirit of God is a self-centred being cut off from Reality. He is dead in mind and spirit like a fish out of water. The love and adoration of a devotee for the Beloved should have the intense thirst of the fish for the waters of the sea. It is through such longing and zeal that an inseparable union with the Beloved is attained.

2

Reality Behind the Unreal

sadho racna ram banai

O seers, how strange is God's creation:
Some take earthly life to be transient,
Others consider it to be permanent.
Strange is this human world. Refrain
Man is a slave of lust, wrath and delusion
He has forgotten the living Presence of God.
He foolishly believes,

That this fleeting body,
Will last for ever.
But it will vanish like a dream overnight. 1
All that you see will disappear,
Like the shadow of moving clouds.
Know this world, says Nanak,
To be transient and unreal,
And take refuge in the Presence of God. 2

There is a world which only our physical senses grasp. This world and its delights cater to the animality of man. Everything in this material world would appear to be a means to excite and satisfy our lower passions, and feed our lust and desires. But pervading and sustaining this material world is the living Spirit of the Eternal. The root principle of this Reality behind the unreal world is the wisdom and light of God. When the consciousness of a seeker of Truth awakens from the heedless life of lust and ambitions, he finds courage to renounce and overpower his animality. He realizes that the essence of an enlightened human life is to move mentality and spiritually away from all that is false, transient and disgusting, to that which is real, eternal, inspiring and blissful.

Enjoyment of transitory pleasures without concentrating on higher values and wisdom is a never ending wild-goose chase, which brings in turn stimulation and grief. Desire produces the terrible entanglement and mad ambition keeps it on. Unless one does not free his mind from this blind race for dizzy pleasures, he cannot realize the meaning and purpose of life and existence.

"The strangest thing in this creation of God which is difficult to comprehend," says Guru Tegh Bahadur "is that there are some people who consider the world to be the only one to be enjoyed, and they abandon themselves with intense zeal to its pleasures. They are completely blind to the living Presence and Image of God *(Hari-murat)* which can be felt by sensitive minds and souls everywhere. For such people, the body and this satisfaction of the senses is the sole aim of their life. For them divine wisdom, higher values, art, music, meditations are useless pursuits. But Guru Tegh Bahadur points out that this animal life of existing and living only for the sake of physical pleasures will vanish like a passing cloud. Man should take refuge at the Feet of God. Concentration on his divine presence will unveil the mystery of human life in this world.

3

The Worldly Man

prani ko har jas man nahi avai

Man contemplates not the glory of God,
Day and night in mammon he is absorbed;

O how can be glorify the Lord? Refrain
He is deeply engrossed,
In his sons and friends;
He is enslaved of his own accord,
In the delusion of wealth.
He is bewitched and hankers after
The world, which is like a mirage; 1
The ignorant fool disregards God:
The source of sustenance and salvation of all.
Few out of millions, says Nanak,
Attain the love and contemplation of God. 2

The endless night of ignorance clouds the light within a man engrossed in the world. He realizes sometimes too late that he has been running after a mirage. His human relations with his friends, sons and brothers are based on selfishness, egoism and greed. His very love and affection for them is motivated by material interest. Neither his love nor his kith and kin, nor his friendship is ever fruitful. He considers his sons and friends worthy of his affection only if they can satisfy his agreed and selfish interests. He foolishly forgets that all he possesses comes from God, and He can take it away when He likes.

Guru Tegh Bahadur brings home the truth that God is the source of sustenance *(bhukta)* and of liberation from bondage *(Mukti)*. It is disastrous both for the mind and soul of man to be so absorbed in worldly pursuits as to completely disregard moral and spiritual enlightenment. Although the majority of the people in this dark age of spiritual ignorance are busy crazily hunting for material wealth and pleasures, there always are a few sensitive minds who dedicate themselves to the search of truth.

All earthly happiness ends in sorrow and misery. But there is a type of sorrow and suffering which ends in joy, and that is the suffering, seekers of truth readily undergo for the sake of freedom, justice and love of God. By making himself a slave of purely worldly affairs man lives in the delusion of false achievements. The millions that he has accumulated ultimately prove to be a mirage leading the soul to a burning desert and not to an oasis of peace.

4

Misguided Mind

sadho eh man gehio na jai

O Seers, the uncurbed mind strides,
Wavering from all self-control;
Stormy passions within it resides,
Lost is the governance of the soul. *Refrain*

Wreckless wrath in the heart abides,
And shakes all the mind's repose.
Sense passions steal the jewel of the soul;
Every goodness and virtue they oppose. 1
In vain the yogis struggle and strive,
The singers have sung their carol.
When the Lord bestows His grace, says Nanak:
All mysteries and misgivings unfold. 2

We live in a world which is full of trials, tribulations and temptations. Lust, anger, greed and egoism prowl around our mind ready to cause it mortal injury. Those who abandon themselves to temptations become reprobates. Hermits, ascetics, *yogis, sufis* have devised many ways to control the mind and become immune to temptation. But even after performing penance and yogic practices of self-mortification, the mind is a pray to the senses and bodily passions. They find it difficult to be completely free from earthly desires.

Within the depth of man's heart God has placed the spark of His Light. It is clouded from our vision by ignorance and dark passions. We can discover the pearl of life within us not through any self-asserting practices but through the grace and love of God. Any acts of self-centred self-mortification, or *hatha-yogic* feats may discipline the body but they cannot control the mind. Before striving and struggling to control the mind we must give up egoism and practices which inflame our vanity. Grace comes from trusting, striving and patient suffering for the love of God. Life is full of darkness, temptations and incomprehensibility. The balance of our soul is disturbed by stormy passions and the persistent feeling of the absurdity and cruelty of human existence. Our mind guided by evil instincts continually comes into conflict with our conscience. Only the Light of His grace can strengthen our soul.

5

Let Your Heart for God Aspire

sadho gobind ke gun gavo

Sing O seers the praise of the Lord,
You have been given a precious life,
Why art thou wasting it in vain? *Refrain*
God is the Saviour of sinners,
He is the Redeemer of the meek;
Seek sanctuary at His Feet.
Even the drowning elephant,
So the story goes,
Lost the fear of death,
Through prayer sincere and earnest.

Why have you forgotten Him? 1
Discard all pride and worldly desires;
Let your heart for God aspire.
Sayeth Nanak: this is the path of Liberation.
Be God-conscious and achieve illumination. 2

Cynics and anchorites generally preach contempt for human life, but says Guru Tegh Bahadur, "Human life is precious and a rare opportunity to break the bound of birth and death. Unlike animals man is gifted with a mind which thinks about the meaning and significance of human existence.

Pride and purely material interests are the greatest hindrance in man's moral and spiritual development. These things drive man to the pit of mental darkness, where he ceases to believe in his own moral and spiritual destiny. He finds it difficult to believe that man can rise even above the viscious circle of his earthly desires.

Guru Tegh Bahadur strikes a very optimistic note for those who feel that thy carry such a heavy load of sin on their head that they cannot be redeemed. He also inspires those people with hope and vision of moral and spiritual exaltation who believe that they are doomed in this life to perpetual suffering for the evils they did in the past life by the law of *karma*.

The Guru assures us that God responds to the prayers and appeals of people who are sincere, unselfish, meek and genuine seekers of truth. He gives as a proof of the legendary story of the elephant which has taken strong roots in the Indian tradition. The incident is said to have taken place on the banks of Brahmaputra river opposite Patna in a grove called Rtuman. It is quite possible that the hymns having reference to this elephant were addressed to the people of this region. Reference to this legendary story is found in the composition of other mediaeval saints also. An annual fair is held in the place on the day this incident is said to have taken place. According to this legend an alligator once caught hold of an elephant and tried to drown it by taking it into deeper water. In this dire difficulty the elephant remembered God. Here Guru Tegh Bahadur suggests that even this animal who concentrated his mind on His Creator and sought His help was blessed with the state of fearlessness, and through this fearlessness, the elephant was able to free itself from the clutches of the alligator. If human beings remember God sincerely and inwardly, His Light descends on them as grace and illumination, and under this inspired state of soul they can work wonders. The thought and remembrance of God inspired the elephant with the state of fearlessness and he freed himself from the alligator and was saved from drowning. Guru Tegh Bahadur identifies liberation *(Mukti)* with the state of fearlessness and this state is achieved by sincere soul through the love and grace of God.

6

The Uncurbed Mind

kou mai bhulio man samjhavai

Ah mother, if only some one
Could instruct the misguided mind;
Man listens to the scriptures,
He hears the sermons of the saints,
Yet he signs not for a moment, the glory of God. *Refrain*
Having acquired so precious a human vesture,
Man wastes and dissipates life.
The illusive world is wilderness of affliction,
To it he is attached and allured. 1
God is within us and outside us.
He ever remains close to us.
To Him man does not devote himself.
Says Nanak: Know that man to be a liberated soul,
Whose heart is illumined by God's love. 2

Many people read and listen to scriptures to impress others with their piety. Many others read and recite scriptures to perform formal rituals and rites, to invoke divine powers, to fulfil their material desires. Darkened by sin, agitated by remorse and obsessed by evil passions and low desires, such people visit the temple regularly, recite their prayers and listen to scriptures, yet they live in darkness of ignorance, and wilderness of affliction. The reading of the scriptures and reciting of prayers, without understanding and imbibing their spirit and meaning neither changes a man's character, nor elevates him spiritually. That is why Dionysius says, "Let us therefore read and learn, not for the purpose of killing time or loading our memory, but for refreshing our spirit and kindling our heart to divine love."

Guru Tegh Bahadur also emphasises the point that "the gate of the open heaven is the human heart, the heart that is pure, annointed and hall-marked with truly divine feelings." When the love of God dawns on man he is transformed. When God looks into his eyes and sheds His resplendent Light on his heart, he is transfigured. He is the liberated one. He is a god in flesh. Such an attunement of human to divine life is the real, moral and spiritual aim of Sikhism.

7

The Enlightened Philosopher: Gyani

sadho ram saran bisrama

O seers, real peace is at the feet of God,

The virtue of studying scriptures,
Lies in contemplating His Name. *Refrain*
he who discards greed and desire,
He who gives up lust for wealth,
He who serves not evil passions,
And is undisturbed by happiness and grief,
Know him to be embodiment of the Divine. 1
Heaven and hell, nectar and poison,
To him are alike as gold and copper.
Praise and calumny are to him alike,
Who is free from greed and attachment, 2
Know him to be enlightened philosopher (gyani):
Who remains unperturbed by joy and sorrow.
O Nanak, a man who lives such a life sublime,
Consider him to be liberated and divine. 3

Guru Tegh Bahadur defines a philosopher, a man of divine wisdom *(Gyani; Sanskrit; Jnani)* in this hymn in terms of Sikh philosophy. He is compassionate and free from arrogance and self-love. He is patient and contented and gives up greed and lust for wealth. He is serene, well balanced, unperplexed and detached. He scorns none, he dotes on none. He neither grieves in sorrow nor displays childish jubilation in joy. He bears shame and glory with quiet dignity. Evil thoughts and passions do not disturb him. He is steadfast in the contemplation of His Presence. He cares not for fame or, gain. With senses controlled, he is tranquil in spirit, free from fear, devout and absorbed in the vision of Reality. He has subdued his passions for ambitions and pleasures. He would rather accept the tribulations and adversities of this earthly life than submit to lust for power and riches. He is convinced that to live absorbed in worldly things, pre-occupied solely with one's stay on earth, in to insult both reason and the truth of human existence.

"He is a *mukta* (a liberated soul) who lives in sublime detachment.' Sorrows and earthly pleasures do not bind him to a purely mundane life. So profoundly is he absorbed in higher values of life that worldly praise or calumny pass away touching him like hot or cold wind. His attitude towards heaven and hell is that of the well-known woman Sufi Saint Rabiya who said: "O God, if I worship Thee for fear of Hell burn me in hell and if I worship Thee in the hose of Paradise, exclude me from Paradise; but if I worship Thee for Thy own sake, grudge me not Thy everlasting Beauty." In Sikhism the problem of Hell and Heaven is ontological, and is not connected only with justice and retribution, but also with freedom and personality. God gives man the moral right to prefer hell to heaven, and to prefer divine love to both hell and heaven. Hell is pictured symbolically as an intense and agonising experience which proves ultimately the indestructible nature of personality. Sikh theology and mysticism rise to the heights of disinterestedness and are free from the fear of hell or a craze for joys of paradise.

8
Why do You Behave Like a Maniac

man re kahan bheo tain baura

O Man, why do you behave like a maniac?
Day and night your life is curtailed,
with greed you have ruined yourself; *Refrain*
The body which you call your own,
And the beautiful wife who adorns your home;
None of them is yours, none will last;
Think and reflect over it seriously. 1
This jewel-like life you have frittered away,
You have given no thought to the path of God.
For a moment you have not contemplated His Feet.
Precious years are wasting away. 2
Sayeth Nanak: that man is truly happy,
Who glorifies the Name of God.
People infatuated with material pleasures,
Attain not the fearless state of a Saint. 3

The fundamental purpose of life is quest for Truth. When man sets aside this purpose and seeks fulfilment of life in marriage, family, property power, fame, wealth, he is disillusioned. His life ends where it began. It ends in moral sickness and spiritual emptiness. In the silence of loneliness, his soul cries for deeper joy and profound peace.

After all our earthly achievements, we live in fear and uncertainty. We are crazily running after some prop in life which are swept away by time and change. Every path of glory and power which we pursue ends up in a blind alley. We rush madly after high standards of life, well paid positions and wealthy associations. But all these neither bring real joy nor give lasting satisfaction. People feel emphtiness inside their heart in spite of the power and wealth they possess.

Guru Tegh Bahadur stirs the conscience of those who madly pursue wealth and power to reflect seriously over their moral and spiritual future. They are working up their own ruin. Life is far more precious than what the average man thinks it to be. The object of life is to attain the fearless state of an enlightened philosopher, a condition of mind in which he enjoys the bliss and grace of God's love and has shed all fear of earthly authority and even death. The essence of life is not gain, success and affection. It is not the work one accomplishes outside himself but that which one shapes within himself.

9

Take Refuge in the Lord

nar acet pap te dar re

O ignorant man,
Fear all sins and wicked deeds,
Take refuge at the feet of the gracious Lord,
Who is compassionate to the humble and meek,
And is the destroyer of all fear. *Refrain*
Remember the Lord in your heart,
Whose glory is sung by scriptures and lore,
The Lord's Name is the most sacred thing;
Ever contemplate the holy Word,
And purge yourself of evil and sin. 1
This human body you may not get again,
Make some effort to attain liberation.
Sayeth Nanak, sing the praise of the Merciful,
And cross the fearsome ocean of life,
To meet the Eternal on the other side. 2

Without inward peace and without outward security man lives in a pitiable state. Fear has replaced faith, confusion and bewilderment has overtaken their lust for pleasures. The moral destitution and spiritual infirmity of man is revealed in all his ambitions and desires. Out of ignorance of higher ideals and life man becomes unconscious of the evils and crimes he commits against truth, justice and humanity. But he who repents and turns from darkness to light is saved from the doom of divine justice. He who abandons self-sense breaking the moorings of his proud, avaricious and sensual egoism and fully trusts God, is not only guided by divine Power but is literally carried to perfection.

"How very, very few people," says a Savant, "there are who as talented artists, philisophers, writers strive after their ideals, and how very, very many idlers are wasters, there are who know nothing of ideals and spiritual life." The scriptures of all higher religions point out to the one royal road to Truth, but how many are there who read and recite the scriptures fruitfully.

Within an inspired soul, meditations begin to unfold from within. The moment we start purging our hearts of evil and sin, the light of God starts dawning on us. Let us go forward with head held high and eyes open. No temptation should distract us, neither sweet not bitter. Man must make a concentrated effort to turn his back on darkness and take refuge in His grace and love, which is the Light of life.

10

The Snare of Worldly Pleasures

birtha kahon kaun sion man ki

Ah, to whom shall I express
This sorrow of my heart,
Ensnared in greed, it drifts and shifts,
Craving more, ever more, for wealth. *Refrain*
In seeking worldly pleasures,
My mind comes to acute grief,
As it slaves before everyone.
Going like a dog from door to door,
Blind to the devotion of God.
Man wastes a precious human life. 1
He is shamelessly heedless,
Even when people chide and ask:
"Why singest thou not the glory of God
Says Nanak: all evil from your heart will depart. 2

Sensitive souls realize that there are too many ignoble and evil propensities in us which have become too powerful for shattered minds. We cannot have a glimpse of the Eternal if we carry darkness and death in our hearts. Anger selfishness and other perverse feelings oppress faint hearted souls. The words of Buffon are true: "Men do not die, they kill themselves by senseless way of life."

Guru Tegh Bahadur condemns that feverish. Egoistical life of mad cravings which pushes on to one's ultimate ruin and puts others into peril. He condemns that senseless desire for riches which wants more and more. Those who heedlessly knock from door to door, degrading themselves before others and slaving before the wealthy, the autocrat and the despot, for more riches, are compared by the Guru to a dog who is indifferent to the humiliation and disgrace which he suffers knocking from door to door. Even if he is driven away from the door of the people having wealth and weilding great power, his inner craving again compels him to run after them. This is the condition of men with low ambitions, ignoble desires and sensuous passions.

By seeking the love and Presence of God man can get release from all his instinctive, sensual and distorted existence. So we must break all evil inclinations and mould the instinctive animal element into the shape of virtue and discipline. Just as an artist breaks shapelessness into shape and conquers material beauty, so the divine hand of the Lord breaks the instinctive man by the art of moral and spiritual recreation and fills him with holiness, beauty and divine power.

11

The Crazy Mind

yeh man naik na kehio karai

Alas, the mind listens not to what I say;
I counselled it as best as I could;
It refrains not from evil ways, *Refrain*
Mad with craze for wealth,
It utters not a word of His praise.
To satisfy base hunger and desire,
The mind cheats and exploits the world
With its deceptive and hypocritical ways; 1
As a dog cannot keep its tail straight;
The crazy mind disregards what I say.
Sayeth Nanak ; Ever contemplate the Lord's Name,
Your work will be fulfilled by His grace. 2

Impurity of people's soul poisons the very life of nations. It is the fire which consumes life in its blossom. Our zeal for formal religious life is usually a painted mask with which we pretend to be holy and pious. Morally and spiritually we pretend to be what we are not. The husk of good actions exist but their seeds have fallen out. Our heart is an empty vessel and our soul is a shadow. Our conscience utters a suppressed cry against our hypocrisy and sins concealed under piety, but our mind, ever so crooked as the tail of a dog, goes on cheating, betraying and exploiting others to amass wealth and gratify low passions.

"As rains breaks through an ill-thatched house," says the *Dhammapada*, "passions will break through an unreflecting mind. As rain does not break through a well thatched house passion will not break through a well reflecting mind. The evil-doers mourn in this world, mourn in the next, he mourns in both. He mourns and suffer when he sees the evil results of both." Earnestness is the path of immortality, thoughtlessness is the path of death. Those who are in earnest do not die, those who are headless err as if dead already." Follow not after vanity, nor after enjoyment of love and lust. He who is earnest and meditative obtains ample joy. Earnest among the thoughtless, awake among the sleepers, the wise man advances like a racer, leaving behind the hack."

Guru Tegh Bahadur urges man to contemplate the divine Presence within and outside us, and ever live in the sublime wisdom and power of God. A heart filled with the grandeur and light of God will be free from evil and sin. The love and grace of God will dawn on his soul. All noble aspirations, all sublime wishes of such a seeker of truth are fulfilled.

12
Worldly Ties
sabh kich jivat ko bivhar

All worldly ties,
Are only for earthly life;
Be it father, mother, sons or kinsmen,
Or be it even a devoted wife. *Refrain*
As soon as the soul leaves the body,
"Take away this phantom" they cry,
Even for an hour they would not keep it.
Out of the house it is hastily carried away. 1
Man, reflect in your heart, on its fate.
Consider the earthly creation of mirage.
Sayeth Nanak: Contemplate the Name of God.
Thy soul will be saved by the Lord. 2

"If any man came to me and hate not his father and mother and children and his own life also," said the divine Christ, "he cannot be my disciple." (Luke xiv, 26). The Guru likewise does not teach hatred or contempt against father, mother or children. Least of all could Guru Tegh Bahadur do it, whose father was Guru Hargobind, mother the divine Nanaki and son the great Guru Gobind Singh on whom he bestowed all his powers and authority when he was hardly nine. These human relations are to be cherished and developed if they help us in our aspirations for Truth, Justice and Goodness; but we have to inwardly break away from them if they induce and tempt us to abandon the path of righteousness and virtue. Human relations and worldly ties are put to test by poverty, adversity and death.

When honour has faded, wealth is lost, those who sue for favours have departed in disappointment, friends have dwindled, kith and kin look down upon him, man still has hope in the love and grace of God. If one is overtaken by harrowing difficulties, and no one renders any help; enemies chase him and kith and kin flee away; all hope of any support is lost, all succour and possibility or relief fade away; if he remembers God no harm will come to him. If a man is extremely femished, naked and on the verge of starvation; he has no money, nor anyone to console and help him; no one shows compassionate charity towards him, and he succeeds not consequently in any work; If he sincerely remembers God he shall attain the sovereignty of the Spirit." (Guru Aryan: *Ashtpadi Sri Rag,* p. 70). The path of righteousness demands that man must be prepared to sacrifice his all for the sake of the Eternal. He must renounce all that he has for the sake of self-sacrifice, so that the salt of his life does not lose its savour.

The seeker of Truth must renounce everything that would prevent his dependence on God alone. We cling to the body of our kith and kin when he is alive and use his life as an instrument of our wishes and desires. Be he father, mother, friend, wife, when he dies, he is nothing more to us than a heep of dust. We never care to establish moral and spiritual relations with our kith and kin and with our friends and companion. Moral and spiritual relations are everlasting. They do not end in death. They bloom and flower in life. They bear fruit in death.

13
Strange are the Ways of the World

jagat mai jhuthi dekhi prit

All earthly love in this world,
Have I found to be false;
Everyone seeks his own happiness,
Be it wife or friend, however fast. *Refrain*
Everyone proclaims, "he is mine, he is mine."
In life everyone is deeply attached;
Friends and dear ones forsake you in death.
Strange are the ways of the world. 1
O unwise and indiscreet mind,
How oft have I tutored thee,
Says Nanak: Life's perilous ocean you can cross.
If you sing the praise of the Lord. 2

Passion" says La Rochefoucould, "often turns cleverest men into idiots and makes the greatest blockheads clever." "Love as it is practiced in society," says Chamfort, "is merely the exchange of two momentary desires and the contact of two skins." Guru Tegh Bahadur clearly distinguishes between the true love and the false skin deep love. *saci prit na tutai, jug jug rahi samae;* True love never breaks even after death. It matures age after age" says Guru Nanak.

False is the love and attachment of purely worldly relations. It is based on selfish interest and greed. Such a love fades away and becomes extinct during troubles and trials. When a man's wife and children love him only for the comforts and material blessings he bestows on them, he loses their affection and respect as soon as he becomes poor and destitute. But true love is based on the love of truth and God. It inspires and ennobles all those who come into contact with a man disciplined in true love. True love orientates human passions, corrects and rejuvinates the sensual and slothful minds. Human relations based on false love are strained and even come to the point of breaking during adversity. But human ties based on true friendship and love last in life and death.

If love is pure, simple and well ordered one cannot be in bondage of any earthly ties. A true lover seeks wisdom and enlightenment. False love is narrow, selfish, lustful and avaricious. True love is divine, peace-shedding, ennobling and eternal. False love ends in delusion and grief while true love yields the golden harvest of grace.

14
God's Inscrutable Ways

hari ki gat nahi kou janai

No one knows the Lord's inscrutable ways:
Monks, yogis, hermits and many men of wisdom,
Have tried to fathom His mystery in vain. *Refrain*
In a moment, God makes the pauper a prince,
And brings on kings penury and shame.
The penniless are made wealthy and rich,
The rich are turned beggars,
Such are His inscrutable ways: 1
He Himself has created the panorama,
He Himself is the Spectator of it all.
Innumerable are the forms of the Universal Spirit.
Yet from all forms He remains apart. 2
Beyond expression and Infinite is He,
Inconceivable and Transcendent is He,
He has kept the world in dark ignorance.
Discard all doubts and delusion, says Nanak.
Let His lotus feet rest in your heart. 3

The mystery of God's infinite power and ineffable depth is unfathomable. Yogis, *sannyasis,* hermits doing penance, and intellectuals, poets and seers have tried to probe His mystery through concentration, penance, meditations. They acquire some occult powers, but they neither receive the true light of God nor are they able to unveil the mystery of God.

Many *yogis* and ascetics who acquire some powers forget the omnipotent Will of God. God manifested His omnipotence by calling the world into existence. He is the Creator, the Moulder, the Maker and Destroyer of life and civilizations on earth. "He does things great and incomprehensible, deeds wonderful and without number." God created man and even though he has given considerable autonomy and free will to man within the limit of birth and death, time and space, man is ultimately wholly dependent upon God. The might of man is nothing in the eyes of God. He can annihilate decandent nations and civilizations and create new ones. God has shown His omnipotence through centuries of history. He shows it in daily life. "He pulls down the mighty from their seats and raises the humble to sovereign power." We find slaves raised to the position of kings, and emperors reduced to penury and utter grief. During his own time Guru Tegh Bahadur saw the fall of Dara Shikoh, the imprisonment of Shah Jahan, the imprisonment and escape of Shivaji.

Yogis and ascetics probe the depths of mind and human existence, but they hardly touch the fringe of the mystery of God. "They who travel in pursuit of wisdom" says Goldsmith "walk only in a circle and after all their labour at last return to their prestine ignorance."

> *The traveller has to knock at every alein door to come to his own, and one has to wander through all the outer worlds to reach the innermost shrine at the end.*
>
> *My eyes strayed far and wide before I shut them and said, 'Here art thou."*
>
> —*Rabindranath Tagore*

It is from this intuitive awareness of the ineffable which comes alike to the poet, philosopher and the scientist, that our search actually begins. The mystery of God, or even the mind and soul of man cannot be known if a man takes either a fatalistic or a positivist attitude towards knowing Him. It is revealed to the man who seeks communion of the Spirit with God, through humility and love. God has created the world and kept the human creation ignorant about His existence, He grace and power. He unveils Himself to the true seeker. Man searches God in the depth of his heart and soul and God reveals Himself in the creation in His Immanent form and beyond creation in his Transcendent form.

15

Contemplate God Ere Death

re man ram sion kar prit

Man, devote yourself to the Lord,
Turn your ears to the praise of God,
And let your tongue sing His hymns. *Refrain*
In the company of holymen, contemplate Him.
You will be pure and free from sin.
Death is at large, O friend,
Like a blood-thirsty beast,
Ready to devour any prey. 1
Bear it in mind and never forget;
It will pounce on you some day.
Contemplate the Lord, sayeth Nanak,
Life's precious years are passing away. 2

"Blessed is he that has always the hour of death before his eyes and everyday disposes to die." People are generally so absorbed in the present charms of life that they never care to think of death. Those who live in the confidence of dying happily or fearlessly live a full and fruitful life. But there are people who are so indifferent and careless to the vicissitudes of life that they remain completely ignorant of death. Death pounces on them like a hawk sweeping unaware on a bird of prey. To such people Guru Tegh Bahadur gives the call: "Death is at large O friend, like a blood-thirsty beast, ready to devour any prey. It will pounce on you unaware."

No one stops to think that the silence and darkness of death broods over all. It is death which gives meaning and purpose to life. It is death which makes man think whether he will end up in the grave or conquer death and be immortal. For those who are transfigured by the love of God and are initiated into the comprehension of immortality, death is a transition from Time to the Timeless, from earth to the realm of the Spirit.

We deceive ourselves through the inordinate love we bear for our physical desires and sensuous ambitions. We dissipate the best gifts of life in utter forgetfulness of death. Says a Yiddish proverb, "Everyone knows he must die, but no one believes it." Man lives in conscious ignorance of death. He can conquer death by unveiling the mystery of life. If in life man contemplates the Eternal, he will one day embrace the spirit of immortality. "Love alone maketh light all that is burdensome and bears equally all that is unequal. Let every seeker of Truth sing the canticle of love and lose himself in the glory and wisdom of God."

16

The Sorrows of a Repentant Soul

man ki man hi mahi rahi

everything to which my mind aspired,
In my mind remains unfulfilled;
Neither have I contemplated God,
Nor worshipped at holy shrines.
Death has caught me by the forelock. *Refrain*
Friend, wife, son chariots and wealth,
Even the treasures, of the whole earth,
Know them all to be transitory.
The love of God is alone enduring. 1
After suffering a frustrating cycle of births in many lower lives
You have attained a human life.
This is your opportunity to meet the Lord;
Says Nanak: Why do you not contemplate God. 2

"Vanity of vanity and all is vanity. It is vanity therefore to seek riches which must perish. It is vanity to be ambitious of honours and to raise oneself to high station. It is vanity to follow the lusts of the flesh and to desire that for which thou must afterwards be grievously punished" (Thomas Kempis). This awakening comes to man when he finds that his passions for material pursuits has ended in sorrow and despair.

He who avidly seeks earthly riches, looks for happiness only in physical pleasures, becomes a slave of wealth, women and worldly attachments. To live totally absorbed in material pursuits, solely to enjoy earthly pleasures, is to insult both reason and faith. When death holds man by the forelock, then comes rude awakening that he has neither done any good deeds, nor ever remembered God. Then comes the feeling and knowledge that even though he was given special gifts of a human being, he had led the life of an animal. Human life had a meaning and purpose. But he has wasted it in transient pleasures and material pursuits and the spectre of moral and physical death coming one after the other looms large before him.

Guru Tegh Bahadur reminds Man of his past which he has forgotten. There was never a time when he did not exist and there will never be time when he will not exist. He has acquired human birth after a cycle of births and deaths in lower animal, and perhaps animal-like human existence. Human life is a golden opportunity for man to rise to god-hood, and break the bonds of the cycle of births and deaths. The Persian mystic Rumi puts it beautifully:

First he appeared in the realm of inanimate,
Thence came into the world of plants and lived
The plant life many a year, nor called to mind
what he had been; then took the onward way,
To animal existence, and once more
Remembers naught of that life vegitive.
Again the wise Creator whom thou knowest,
Uplifted him from animality
To man's estate; and so from realm to realm,
Advancing, he became intelligent,
Cunning and keen of wit, as he is now.
No memory of his past abides with him,
And from his present soul he shall be changed.

Jalalu'l Din Rumi (Tr: Nicholson) 188.

This belief is deeply rooted in Sikh theology and eschatology. Man either sinks to the animal existence of births and death in lower lives, which is the real hell, or rises to more blessed states of human and divine existence. In this context of the grim reality of our past and future, Guru Tegh Bahadur reminds us that human life is golden opportunity for exalting oneself to spiritual communion, and mystic union with God.

17
Wasteful Live

man re kaun kumat tain lini

Man, why do you lead a sinful life,
You indulge in calumny and adultery,
And contemplate not the love of God. *Refrain*
The path of liberation you have ignored,
And to hoard wealth you hanker ever more,
In vain are you forging chains for yourself. 1
Nothing will abide with thee in the end.
You have neither contemplated God,
Nor ever served the saints;
Devoid of divine wisdom you have remained,
Within you resides the Immaculate Lord,
But in vain you search Him in forests. 2
Wearily you have wandered from birth to birth,
Still you have not acquired wisdom and peace.
Nanak tells thee an important fact,
Having attained this precious human birth,
Contemplate, His lotus feet. 3

It is futile and vain to seek riches, accumulate goods of luxury aspire after earthly honours and devote all our energy to narrow, selfish ends. Man wastes his life indulging in calumny, adultery and sinful deeds, but he never thinks of the path of liberation. His low ambitions are always striving after the wind.

In his pre-occupation with material interests man neither remembers God, nor serves enlightened saints. He remains steeped in ignorance of moral and spiritual values of life. He lives in bondage of his material gains which give him no peace but only multiply his sorrows. There are two or three types of ignorance which keep people in the dark about life and existence of God.

Firstly, there is the ignorance of the slothful and idle people who remain indifferent and blind to virtue and truth. To such people the sensuous life and keeping themselves busy in the accumulation of wealth is the only life worth leading.

The second is the ignorance based on wrong belief and misleading practices. Out of such ignorance, some people performing formal acts of piety imagine themselves to be living in heaven, and they are quite indifferent to the welfare of their human beings. There are still others who leave society and go to the forests and mountain caves in search of God. While God resides within them, they wander for the peace of Yoga in wilderness.

Guru Tegh Bahadur says that our body is the temple of God, where we can find the Light of His Living Presence. The Light of God is within us. It supports and sustains our mind and soul. Without this right faith and right knowledge no one can achieve divine Wisdom and enlightenment.

18

Reflect on the Presence of God

man re prabh ki saran bicaro

Man, think of the Presence of God,
Enshrine Him in you heart
Remembering whom the adultress was saved, *Refrain*
By contemplating Him,
Dhruva attained the fearless state.
Why hast thou forgotten, O Man, the Lord,
Who is dispeller of agony and sorrow. 1
As soon as the elephant remembered the Treasure of Mercy,
He was saved from being drowned by the alligator.
O to what extent can I enumerate.
The greatness of His Name.
By meditative rememberance of divine Name.
Man is released from all bondage. 2
Even Ajamal, the great sinner was liberated
When he called on the Name of God
Nanak: Meditate on His Name, the precious pearl,
You will also cross the perilous ocean. 3

The theme that is closest to Guru Tegh Bahadur's heart is the Divine concern of God for even the greatest sinner who repents and remembers God sincerely. This Divine concern is extended even to animals. "A man entirely unconcerned with his self is dead" says Heschel, "and a man exclusively concerned with his own self is a beast." Truly human is he who is concerned with his own self and with others as well.

God who is immanent in us and Transcendent everywhere is seriously concerned with our character and destiny. Guru Gobind Singh says, "God hears the feeble cry of an ant long before the trumpeting of an elephant reaches Him." "It is within my power" said Tolstoy, "either to serve God or not to serve Him. Serving I add to my own good and the good of the whole world. Not serving Him, I forfeit my own good, and drive the world of that good which was in my power to create." "God did not deprive thee of the operation of his love but thou didst deprive Him of His co-operation," says Francis de Sales. "God would never have rejected thee, if thou hast not rejected love."

The remembrance and devotion to God is rewarded with infinite grace. Bhakta Dhruva became immortal in Indian history and tradition. Sinners like Ajmal and Ganika the adultress were liberated from the pit of hell even though they remembered God too late. The drowning elephant remembered God and was saved from the clutches of the alligator." The greatest sinner can through off the load of sins and shatter the laws of *karma,* if he seeks the love and grace of God through moral rebirth and discipline of spiritual contemplation. Man does not see God who constantly watches him with motherly love and fatherly concern. The pearl of Wisdom within us is His veiled Presence. By contemplating the Named one through His Name, His Presence within us is visibly revealed. The perilous world-existence of delusion and ignorance is crossed.

19

What Should Man Do

prani kaun upao karai

O what should man do,
To attain the love of God
And dispel the fear of death. *Refrain*
What knowledge he must acquire?
What virtue must be practise?
What divine Name should he contemplate
To cross the perilous ocean of life. 1
In this dark age of ignorance.
There is but one divine Name.
The Name of the merciful Lord.
Contemplating which liberation can be gained.
This is the highest Religion.
So do the scriptures proclaim. 2
The Lord who is above joy and sorrow.
Even reside within us.
Like the image in the mirror. 3

"Religious life" according to Guru Tegh Bahadur has twofold purpose to dispel the fear of death and attain the love of God. These are two fundamental aims of all higher religious. "Fear and love" says Guru Nanak, go side by side. The fear of God is reverence and awe and not the fear that strikes terror. It is a fear *(bhau)* which changes into love *(bhao).* This love is the descent of the illumined Spirit into the body and the soul. There is one practical path, a spiritual exercise, recognized by all higher religions: that is to attain the revelation of God within us through intense devotion and dedication. With this devotion is connected the spiritual discipline of the contemplation of His Name.

This spiritual discipline is the *Nama-sidhannta,* or *Nama Japa* called *Zikar* in Sufi tradition. It is the meditative contemplation of the mystic Word, the Name of God, imparted by the Guru, the divine Preceptor. It is considered by the Gurus to be the easiest and most efficacious path for liberation. It has a great bearing on the art and music of North and South India. The Name is at first the symbol, the collective attribute of God. When the music of the Name sinks into our consciousness, it becomes the essence of the One whose Name is sung. The Name becomes the Spirit and Being of God.

The well-known Sufi mystic Shebli used to inscribe the Name of God in every place he could find. Suddenly a voice addressed him, "How long will you go about the Name? If you are truly a seeker, stride forth on the quest of the Named." These words affected him so deeply, that peace and composure altogether deserted him. So, powerful was the love possessing him so completely was he overwhelmed by mystical tumult that he went and flung himself into Tigris. The river surged and cast him up on the bank. Then he hurled himself into the fire, but the flames affected him not. "Woe to him" said Shebli, "whom neither water nor fire will accept, neither wild beasts not mountains." "He who is accepted of God," came a voice "is accepted of no other." Arberry: *Muslim Saints and Mystics.*

Thus the Name becomes the Light and Being of the Named One: God. The Name or *Shabad Brahma* is considered the supreme gateway to God-realization. The Name of the Lord is the instrument of invoking Him and unveiling His Presence in the mind.

20

How Can I Express my Lowliness

mai main keh bidh lakhon gusain

Mother, how can I have a glimpse of God,
My mind is enmeshed in dark ignorance,
And the infatuating spell of the world. *Refrain*
I have wasted my life in bewildering delusion,
I have not acquired tranquility and poise.
Day and night I have lived a sinful life,
Viscious ways I have failed to discard. 1
Company of the saints I have never sought,
Nor have I sung the glory of the Lord,
Sayeth Nanak, there are no virtues in me,

Keep me, Lord, at Thy Feet. 2

"When the heart weeps for what it has lost," says a Sufi aphorism, "the spirit laughs for what it has found." A soul in search of peace and light wakes up from the stupor of delusion. The darkness that oppressed his soul before wisdom dawned reminds him of his sorrow and affliction caused by the sinful life he led.

What a pitiable life it was with which the awakened soul wishes to break away. He avoided the company of the saints and virtuous men. He indulged in viscious ways of life to enjoy sensational pleasures. He was steeped in ignorance and completely disregarded the moral and spiritual values. The temptations and tribulations of life have kept him cut off from love, charity and knowledge of truth. But the sorrows of these very temptations and afflictions have humbled him and made him conscious of the real purpose of life. He has learnt patience and humility. He now shuns vice and seeks the company of the holy and the virtuous.

It is said fire tries iron, temptations try the just man. But even the man who is devoid of any virtue has the right to seek the solace of His Wisdom, when he feels impelled to move from sin to virtue, from darkness to light and from ignorance to Truth His search and prayer begins with a prayer: "Give me the dust of Thy lotus feet," and ends with the exaltation of Spirit and perpetual communion with God.

21
The Headless Mind

mai man mero bas nahi

Mother, over my mind,
I have lost all control,
Day and night it hankers,
For viscious ways of life,
O how shall I curb it or control? *Refrain*
After listening to scriptures:
Vedas, Puranas and Simritis,
Man imbibes not the teachings,
Even for a moment in his heart.
It craves for the wealth of other people;
It covets the wives of other people;
In utter waste my life whiles away. 1
Mad in the intoxication of worldly wealth,
Man understands not the wisdom of life.
The blesmishless Lord resides within him,
Whose mystery he fails to unveil. 2

When man takes refuge at the feet of a Sage.
All evil thoughts are dispelled.
Says Nanak: he who contemplates, the divine Word,
Which is life's most precious pearl,
He cuts off the noose of death. 3

"Great is human frailty which is always prone to vice. Today a man repents over the sin he has committed, tomorrow he would be again tempted to commit the same sin. No man is so perfect as not to have any temptation. Sometimes when we seek arbitrary escapes from temptations, we fall even more grievously into them. By flight alone we cannot overcome them. When the *yogis* in mountain retreat proudly told Guru Nanak that they keep away from towns and cities to escape temptations, Guru Nanak remarked, Quite so, but your mind wanders back to the cities and towns and broods over the charms of the housewives to whom you go periodically for begging your food."

"He who lies, culminates, hates, offends, he who is greedy touchy, impatient and selfish, he who takes his duties too lightly, is like an unwashed unkempt ugly visage, and not at all the child of God." The world riches and power are good, but only if they serve great aims. We should not allow our souls to shrivel either from riches or from poverty. We should not allow our hearts to dry up from mere earthly cares and sensuous dissipation.

For Guru Tegh Bahadur life was not a noisy huckstrong affair where sharp dealing is the order of the day, nor a circus display of sham strength. He firmly believed that in every type of life there can be but one aim for all knowledge, learning and moral struggle and that is the fashioning of the mind, the heart and the *soul, so that man may become lofty, pure, free, truthful* and conscious of his own dignity. He shows us that our greatest task is the overcoming of all that is base, material and evil. Those who neglect this duty will lose their free and spiritual nature and will be failures as human beings in the truest and highest sense of the world.

Man's fundamental error in understanding life is to be ignorant of the mystery that God resides within us. The dust that clouds the mind will be removed in association with enlightened saints and sages. They will dispel all evil thoughts by the light of their wisdom and personal inspiration. Then will the misguided, man conquer death and bask in the sunshine of eternal life.

22

Cherish this Truth in your Heart

re nai eh saci jia dhar

O Man, cherish this truth in your heart;
The material world is but a dream,

In no time will it vanish and pass. *Refrain*
Mansions of sand which you have built,
Will last not for more than a few days,
So are the pleasures of wealth.
Why are you engrossed in them, silly lout. 1
Hearken even now, not much is lost.
Contemplate the Name of the Lord.
Such is the eternal wisdom of the saints,
Which Nanak loudly proclaims. 2

Guru Tegh Bahadur looks at the world from a transcendent plane of Reality. He clearly distinguishes the world of blind animal existence from the world of enlightened living. Both exist side by side on earth. The Guru brings to light the dangers of discursiveness of a fickle and irresolute mind, and unfettered pursuit of vagrant desires. He is against a forced isolation from the world. He also does not advocate the destruction of sense life, but lays stress on inward withdrawal, and poignantly comments on this purely material worldly life, unconcerned with anything except personal aggrandisement and pleasures, as an empty dream.

The reflections of Guru Tegh Bahadur are aptly summed up in the words of *Dhammapada:* "Look upon the world as you would on a bubble, look upon it as you would on a mirage; the king of death does not see him who looks down upon the world. Come, look at this world, glittering like a royal chariot; the foolish are immersed in it, but the wise do not touch it. He who was formerly reckless, and afterwards became sober brightens up this world, like the moon freed from clouds. This world is dark, few only can see here, a few only go to heaven, like birds escaped from the net. If a man has transgressed the one law, and speaks lies and scoffs at another world, there is no evil he will not do." This is the fundamental truth of human existence in this world which we should cherish in our heart. "It is never too late." Says Guru Tegh Bahadur, "to give up life of sin and vices and turn to wisdom and Truth." This is the perennial wisdom of the sages and prophets of God which the Guru proclaims.

23
None Stands by Thee in Sorrow

eh jag mit nà dekhio koi

True friends one finds not in this world,
All people are engrossed,
In the fulfilment of their pleasures,
None stands by you in sorrow. *Refrain*
Wife, sons, friends, kith an kin,
All are with you if you have wealth.

They run away from you in disgust,
As soon as they find you penniless. 1
How shall I explain to you, O insane mind,
The futility of all such cupidity,
God is the protector of the destitute,
He is the Dispeller of fear,
Whom you have utterly forgotten. 2
Like the tail of the dog,
The mind straightens not.
I have made strenuous efforts and failed.
Sayeth Nanak: Protect me, Lord, from my shame,
Because I have taken refuge in Thy Name. 3

Friendship in this world is as rare as love. Both friendship and love are proved false or true when they are put to test. Life is so full of trails and tribulations that we see, almost everyday, children abandoning their parents when they needs their help most; wife running away from her husband when he is in dire misfortune. Seneca closed the vast circle of his knowledge by learning that a friend in power was a friend lost.

"Friendship" is like money "easier made then kept," said Samuel Butler. "The worst disease is gradual decay of friendship and dislike hourly increased by causes too slender for complaint and too numerous for removal," said Dr. Johnson. Nietzsche remarks, "Shared joys make a friend, not shared suffering." Guru Angad comments:

Friendship with a shallow mind,
Devotion to a man of wealth,
Is like a line drawn on water,
Such friendship is fleeting and purposeless.

Friends and relatives whose attachment for us is based only on greed, selfish interest, should awaken us to a conscientious search for true friends. "True friends," says Guru Nanak, "are those on meeting whom one has a vision of the Beloved. The sage, the divine Teacher, the philosopher, the mystic who opens the portal of our soul to divine knowledge is the best and most abiding friend."

But human minds is so twisted by oppressive thoughts, desires and passions that like the tail of the dog it never becomes straight. One must seek refuge in the love and friendship of God, who will purify our mind of all impurities and dispel all fears. He is the only Friend of the lonely, the only saviour of the destitute.

24

I Invoke Thy Forgiving Grace

man re gehio na gur updesa

The teachings of the true Enlightener,
You have grasped not, O Recluse;
What matters if you are a clean-shaven monk,
And ochre dyed is your garb. *Refrain*
From truth you live apart,
And waste your life in falsehood.
You indulge in hypocricy and fraud,
Only to feel to the full,
And sleep like a bull. 1
The path of devotion to God,
You have never sought;
You have sold your soul to mammon.
Engrossed in venemous pleasures, madman,
You have forgotten His Name: the Wisdom-pearl. 2
Unconscious of divine life,
You have wasted your life in vain.
Says Nanak: Man ever sins and errs,
Lord, I invoke Thy forgiving grace. 3

"Hypocrisy is the homage that vice offers to virtue," says La Rochefoucauld. The ochre robe, the clean shaven head are symbols of holiness, but they do not make a man virtuous and holy. There are monks and priests who put on the grab of holiness but eat and sleep like animals and indulge in depraved activities. The holy robe is only a veil to cover their hypocrisy, greed, and lust for wealth. It is a means to deceive and exploit innocent people. They turn their back on truth and waste their life, living sinfully under cover of external piety. "What makes the Sufi?" Rumi was asked. He answered, "Purity of heart, not the patched mantle and the perverse lust of those earth-bound men who steal his name." This is the very idea of a holy man which the Guru desires to convey through this hymn.

It is not the knowledge of scriptures, acts of formal piety and the sack cloth, or the ochre robe of the monk which makes a man holy, but noble and virtuous deeds which make him dear to God. There are holymen who display their piety only through their sermons, their garb and other pretentions. Though outwardly they are ascetics they are at heart as worldly as any other man living indulgently. They sat lustily and sleep lustily like men living in luxury and ease. In their hearts there is not a trace to true love of God.

Such hypocrites who grow like mushrooms in every faith have brought religion into disrepute. They do not have an iota of sincere love of God in their hearts. Outwardly they pretend to have renounced the world, secretly they crave for wealth and women and other venemous pleasures which turn a man's mind away from higher values of life.

All who commit evil and sin in the name of religion have but one hope. They should give up hypocrisy, take life seriously and seek the forgiving grace of God. God can ennoble all repentent souls.

25

The Enlightened Sage

jo nar dukh mai dukh nahi manai

He who grieves not in grief,
From avarice, pleasures, and fear is free,
And considers gold as good as dust. *Refrain*
Who indulges not in slander or flattery,
And is immune to greed, attachment and vanity,
Who in happiness and sorrow, self-poised remains.
And in immune to greed, attachment and vanity,
Who discards all hopes and desires,
Who lives detached from the world,
And is not affected by lust and wrath.
In such a one shines the Light of God. 2
The man who receives the Guru's grace,
Discovers the secret of spiritual life,
Sayeth Nanak, the soul of such a man blends,
With God, as water mingles with water. 3

The Sikh Gurus aimed at not only giving doctrines and hymns of divine wisdom but at establishing the kingdom of righteousness and enlightened men. The Enlightened Man created by the Sikh Guru's Way of Life was what Marcus Aurelius called a god in flesh' who made full use of that indwelling power which can keep a man unsullied by pleasures, proof against pain, untouched by insult and impervious to evil. He is a competitor in the greatest of all contests, the struggle against passion's mastery; he is imbued through and through with uprightness, welcoming whole heartedly whatever falls to his lot and rarely asking himself what others may be saying or doing or thinking except when the public interest requires it. He confines his operations to his own concerns, having his attention fixed on his own particular thread of universal web seeing to it that what befalls him must be for the best—for his own directing fate is itself under higher direction. He does not forget the brotherhood of all rational beings nor that a concern for everyman is proper to humanity.

"The Sage *(Gurmukh)* is distinguished for self-control, fixity of purpose, and cheerfulness under ill-health or other misfortunes. His character is an admirable combination of dignity and charm, and all duties of his station are performed quietly and without fuss. He gives everyone the conviction that he speaks as he believes and acts as he judges right. He is never hasty any never dilatory. He indulges neither in despondency nor forced geity, nor has anger and jealousy and power over him. His kindliness, sympathy and sincerity all contribute to give the impression of rectitude that is innate and not calculated."

The darkness of error is dispelled by the light of truth and strengthens him in life and death. He loves Truth, he loves God intensely and the love of God descends on him as abiding grace and light which shines in his heart. He attains an inseparable union with God.

26

Commune with the Beloved

pritam jan leh man mahi

Commune with the Beloved in your heart,
The world is ensnared,
In personal pleasures;
No one for others really cares. *Refrain*
In prosperity friends gather around thee
In adversity they turn back and fee.
In misfortune no one will come near thee. 1
Even your own dear wife,
Whom you love so deeply,
And endears herself to you day and night,
Will shun you as a phantom and ghost.
When the soul leaves the body; 2
Such is the way of the world,
Which you love so passionately.
At the last moment O Nanak,
Nothing will be of use to thee,
Except the love and grace of God. 3

Guru Tegh Bahadur urges human beings to reflect on there inner loneliness in a world in which everyone is engrossed in the pursuit of his own personal pleasures. During his times Guru Tegh Bahadur saw around him, as we see even now around us, "that the rich live like reprobates in the dens of wealth. The hypocrite exploit the innocence of the faithful to wear the golden crown of piety, the politician fattens on gossip and misfortunes of the people."

Friendship with the ignorant, and the selfish is like living with drunkards and gamblers. In prosperity they will follow you like a shadow, but in adversity they will turn them against you. In sorrow and misery the closest relatives shun you. During moments of trial and utter misery even the wife and children desert a person.

The wise man is he who lives an communes with God. Guru Tegh Bahadur urges man to let the lamp of Divine grace burn with resplendent flame in one's heart.

It is with this torch of divine wisdom, man can light his path and come out of the dark valley of despair.

It is the love and grace of God that illumines a man's life even in death. The light of love and the fragrance of His grace strengthens the soul, deepens our conviction and illumins our vision.

27
Wherefore Search God in the Forests

kahe re ban khojan jai

Wherefore go to the forest in search of God?
He is all-pervading and ever detached.
He is the Indwelling Spirit in thee. *Refrain*
Just as fragrance resides in the flower
Just as the image is reflected in the mirror,
So the Light of God dwells within thee;
Seek Him O brother in thy own soul. 1
This supreme Truth the Guru has revealed;
Know the One Eternal outside and within thee.
Says Nanak, without realizing your true self.
The mind's delusion shall never be dispelled. 2

Ascetics, anchorites, *yogis* and *sannyasins* run to the deserts and forests to escape the temptations of society and to seek solitude, peace and God. Reflecting on typical ascetic contempt for life in society, the great Yogi. Bhartrihari writes in his *Viragya Shaktam:* "In our servile attendance on the wealthy wicked, their shabby manners and talk we have somehow put up with: suppressing tears that welled up from our hearts, we have smiled out of vacant minds; obeisance we have made to dullards stultified by too much wealth; in what more fooleries wouldst thou have me dance, Oh Desire, thou of ungratified yearning." (4) Then he adds, "Blessed are those who live in mountain caves meditating on Brahman, the Supreme Light, while birds devoid of fear perch on their laps and drink the tar-drops of bliss that they shed in meditation; while our life is fast ebbing away in the excitement of revelry in palatial mansions or on the banks of refreshing pools or in pleasure-gardens, all created (and brooded over) merely by imagination. (14) For food, now I have what begging brings and that too tasteless and once a day; for bed, the earth, and for attendant, the body itself; for dress I have a worn out blanket made up of hundred patches. And still alas! the desires do not leave me." Eminent Yogis left society to run away from temptations, but temptations and desires chased them to remote mountain caves and hermitages. It is this cynical types of ascetic life which the Gurus strongly criticised and discouraged A good many such Yogis, particularly of the *Nathpanthi* and *Saiva-Siddhanta schools,* aiming to be *siddhas,* who went to extremes in their cynical contempt for social life which the Gurus strongly criticised and discouraged. Although the Gurus never doubted the sincerity, the normal greatness, and the *yogic* achievements of great *Siddha Yogis* known to history. But most of them later on, betrayed a repulsive egoism and lack of good taste.

"Why go to the forest," says Guru Tegh Bahadur, in search of God? The Spirit of God pervades not only in Nature, in the forests, but also in the human world of a civilized society. It dwells in the heart of humanity like fragrance in flowers and can be perceived by sensitive minds and aesthetic insight of noble souls. The heart and soul of human being is the mirror in which the Eternal spirit is reflected. You can see His Light in others if you search Him in solitude of your heart. The divine Teacher unveils His Light to the initiate and sincere seekers of Truth. The clouds of doubt and delusion begin to disappear when one realizes his own self. God walks invisibly amongst us. From Him, existence continually rises, souls are in contact with Him with their deepest roots. He reaches and flows into our life.

28

The World Lives in Delusion

sadho eh jag bharam bhulana

The world O seers,
Lives in delusion;
Discarding contemplation
Of the Name of God;
To material pursuits,
People sell their souls. *Refrain*
Son, father and mother,
Wife and brothers:
To these man is passionately endeared.
Intoxicated with glory and pride,
Of youth, wealth and power,
A mad life man leads day and night,
He concentrates not his mind on God. 1

The Protector of the lowly,
The Dispeller of pain and grief.
Sayeth Nanak: One in a million,
By leading divine life of a Sage
Has realized the Perfect One. 2

For those who do not know, feel or understand the Eternal Spirit that sustains the world, the earth is full of incomprehensibility, suffering and darkness. The essence of life is not gain, success and material achievement, not the work one accomplishes outside oneself, but that which one shapes in oneself. The impurity of our desires and the selfishness of our attachments to our friends and kith and kin profane the soul and drag it down to shame of blind passion.

For small pleasures in this mortal life we incur eternal death in our souls. We live in the joys and sorrows, ambitions and desires of our false and private selves. We try to exist outside the radius of God's Will and outside the grace of God's love. We live in the illusion of wild passions and we chase the enchanting mirage of our pleasures.

"Three things" says Guru Tegh Bahadur "corrupt a man most: the blind passion of youth, the intoxication of wealth and the madmen of Power. We consider them to be blessings of life but they end up as fetters to our feet." As prisoners of our own pleasures and captives of our own desires, we live a wild life in the intoxication of youth, wealth and power. In his vanity man forgets the Protector of the lowly and the Dispeller of sorrows.

The true wisdom of life on earth is to escape from the prison of our self-hood and enter through love into communion with the Eternal Spirit who dwells within the essence of every creature and in the core of every heart. So long as we live in self-hypnotism we walk in darkness.

29

An Enlightened Yogi

teh jogi ko jugat na jano

That yogi knows not the art of living
Whose inner-self abounds with low carvings,
And is deluded with avid leanings. *Refrain*
Know such a one to be a true yogi,
Who dwells apart in self-control,
From false praise or blame,
To whom cheap iron and gliterring gold
Appear all as one and the same.
In joy and sorrow, in happiness and misery

Tranquil and detached he remains. 1
The shilly shally mind is drifting and shifting.
Aimlessly in all directions;
One must hold the mind in self-restraint.
Know such a one, says Nanak,
To be a liberated and enlightened yogi. 2

The word *yoga* means 'to bind together,' 'to hold fast,' 'to yoke" and has for centuries inspired detachment from matter and emancipation with respect to the world.

From Patanjali's cryptic *Sutras* it developed into an ascetic discipline and technique of meditation. No other system of practical mysticism has been so abused and misused and even corrupted as this system. The *Hatha Yoga* has concentrated on developing physical techniques and training the body. The practices and said to make dynamic a latent force in the body called *Kundalini*.

With all such control of breath and physical system this brand of *yogis* have not been able to control their egoism, their craving for many other low desires. After years of *Yoga* practice, they rarely achieve a healthy mind, capable of adjusting itself in society, still less a healthy and enlightened soul.

True *Yoga* (union with the Divine) is attained by the spiritual discipline of contemplation of the divine Name and the love of God. The Sikh Gurus called it *Sahajya Yoga*. It should not be confused with the *Sahajya Yoga* of Tantric Leftists *(Vamacharis)*. Guru Tegh Bahadur here described the divine state and moral achievements of a true *Yogi* and spiritual discipline of a *Sahajya Yogi*. Such a yoga acquires a sublime self-control without any practice of penance and self-mortification. He achieves the spiritual state reflecting the highest moral and mystic achievement. During our time Vivekananda reintrepreted *Yoga* and made it relevant to modern conditions. But Sri Aurobindo has given almost the same meaning and significance to *Yoga* through his own meditations, philosophic and mystic reflections and after achieving the highest State as the Gurus did in their *Sahajya Yoga*. He sums up his achievements and spiritual discipline in the following poem:

Then, falling silent in himself to know
He meets the deeper listening of his soul.
The Word repeats itself in rhythmic strains:
Thought, vision, feeling, sense, the body's self
Are seized unalterably and he endures
An ecstasy and an immortal change;
He feels a wildness and becomes a Power,
All knowledge rushes on him like a sea:
Transmuted by the white spiritual ray

He walks in naked heavens of joy and, clam,
Sees the God-face and hears transcendent speech.

—*Sri Aurobindo*

Praise does not make such a man feel flattered. Blame and calumny do not disturb his mind. To him all that glitters is not gold. He does not judge men by the material wealth they possess. In joy he does not lose his mental balance. In sorrow and grief he remains calm and composed. About such a man it is said, "The good give up attachment for everything; the saintly prattle not with sensual cravings. Whether affected by happiness or pain, the wise show neither elation nor depression."

30

Lord Save a Sinner Like Me

ab mai kaun upao karaun

Now, what shall I strive to do,
To dispel the dark delusion of my mind,
And cross the perilous ocean of life? *Refrain*
After acquiring human birth,
No good deeds have I done on earth.
That is what frightens me.
I have chanted not the glory of God,
With the sincerity of mind, speech and deed;
Over this I brood and grieve. 1
Even on hearing the teachings of the Guru,
No wisdom has dawned on me;
Like an animal I eat and sleep.
Sayeth Nanak, I invoke Thy gracious mercy,
Lord, save a sinner like me. 2

This *padavali* rings forth the sorrow and agony of a repentent mind oppressed by the remorse of his sins. This mind has been suddenly awakened to the grim reality of inner life. The fetters of lust and cravings bind man to darkness and delusion. While the mind aspires for illumination, the flood of cravings throw him off his feet and keep him in bondage.

The awakened soul broods over his life of his past sins and transgressions. The thought that virtue and goodness give peace and joy while the wages of sin is death, awakens him to turn his back on the life of evil and sin. Pride and sensuality keep the mind in darkness. Agitated by remorse, the mind strives for peace and tranquility. The repentent soul feels that he has wasted the most precious part of his youth in eating and sleeping like an animal. There a suppressed realization in such minds "that no one can be enlightened unless he be first cleansed and purified. Purgation has the negative aspect of determined detachment from all that leads the mind away from God and Truth and the positive aspect of achieving the highest state. The Sikh Gurus repeatedly stress the point that both detachment and illumination should be achieved without the physical gymnastic of self-mortification. Eckhart emphasises the point which is given the highest importance in Sikh scriptures and philosophy." God is Good in Himself and therefore will He dwell nowhere but in a pure soul." It is for such purgation and purity the soul cries aloud to *Niranjan* (Blemishlessly Pure God): "I invoke Thy grace Lord, save a sinner like me."

31
God Resides Within

bhulio man maya urjhayo

Out of ignorance the mind,
Is in material pursuits entwined,
All its actions done in greed,
Have made it a prisoner self-deceived. *Refrain*
Never has it realized,
That, absorbed in venomous delights,
Devotion to God it has despised.
The misguided man knows not,
That God resides within;
To the forests he runs to search Him. 1
The precious pearl; the Word divine,
Within you is ever enshrined.
Knowledge of the world you have never sought,
Says Nanak, without the Love of God,
Life is wasted and comes to naught. 2

"It is not love but lust, the very food of self-hood, which poisons the relations between the Self and the external world, and immediately fatigues the soul," says Evlyn Underhill. Divide the world into "mine" and "not mine" and the unreal standards are set up, claims and carvings begin to fret the mind. The self-regarding instincts and desires of man keep his vision clouded, and his thoughts absorbed in self-interest.

When man learns of higher life and the Eternal Spirit he reaches for them outside himself. He imagines God to be residing in the starry heavens and expects Him to visit him if he prays to Him in some lonely place. To suppress his desires he submits himself to self-mortification. The thraldom and painful travail of mortifications generally produce an ascetic whose heart is empty and the soul is still dark without the love and grace of God. Just to lull the desires to sleep by mortification of sensuality is no great moral or spiritual achievement.

At first man abandons himself to greed and avarice and becomes prisoner of his own low cravings. When he wishes to escape from the temptations, he runs to the forests and monasteries for solitude and peace. He does not know that God resides within him. He is ignorant of the fact that the pearl of divine Wisdom also resides within his heart. Whoever finds this pearl of wisdom throws everything in the joy of its possession. "The kingdom of Heaven is like merchant in search of fine pearls; when he finds a single pearl of great price he goes and sells all that he has and buys it." (Mathew XII 45-46).

This precious pearl is the strength and divine power within us for disciplining and shaping our life here and now in the crucible of truth. For this precious pearl we have to give up everything and we willingly give up all, after we have found it. The treasure is buried within us but layers of dust, stone, rubble of sensual and beastly existence cover it. It has to be dug out. The pearl swims in the hardships of life's ocean. It has to be fished out. The storms of disappointments, ship-wrecks and sufferings divert our attention. Economic strife, work, worries about our daily bread, change the earth to an arena of combat. No one believes the treasure is there. But Guru Tegh Bahadur emphatically proclaims that "the pearl of Wisdom is in your heart. The Light of God dwells within you. The Divine Teacher will unveil it."

32

Bless me with Gift of Fearlessness

hari ju rakh leh pat meri

Beloved Lord, save me from dishonour,
The fear of death torments my soul;
O Treasure of Mercy
I have taken refuge at Thy feet. *Refrain*
I am disgracefully fallen, foolish and greedy,
Sinning ever, I am fed up of sinning,
The fear of death constantly weighs on my mind
And keeps me burning in agony. 1
Hard I have tried to attain liberation.
Restlessly I have wandered in all directions,
within resides the Lord, pure and sublime.
The mystery of His indwelling Presence I have not known. 2
Alas, virtues I have none,
I have not practised meditation nor performed penance,
What deeds should I do to win His love.
Says Nanak, I have taken refuge at Thy feet.

Bless me with the gift of fearlessness, Lord. 3

The first underlying theme of the hymn is that all strivings of spiritual or moral discipline outside ourselves are fruitless. The mystery of God is not unveiled by religious practices which do not lead the mind to divine Presence within us. He who is illumined within the heart attains the state of fearlessness. The second theme of the hymn is that the purpose of all meditations, prayers and divine worship is to seek the state of fearlessness *(nirbhai pad).* Guru Tegh Bahadur identifies fearlessness with godliness and the Kingdom of Heaven.

"The first duty of man is that of subduing fear" says Thomas Carlyle: "we must get rid of fear, we cannot act at all till then. A man's acts are slavish, not true but specious; his very thoughts are false, he thinks too as a slave and coward, till he has got fear under his feet." Emerson pointed out at another aspect of fear. He says, "Fear is the instructor of great sagacity and the herald of revolutions. One thing he teaches, that there is rottenness where he appears. He is a carrion crow, and though you see not well what hovers for, there is death somewhere. Our property is timid, our laws are timid our cultivated classes are timid. Fear for ages has boded and mowed and gobbered over government and property. That obscure bird is not there for nothing. He indicates great wrongs which must be reversed." That is why Neitzsche calls fear, the mother of morality.

India's great Yogi-King Bhartrihari says, "In enjoyment, there is the fear of disease; in social position, the fear of falling off; in wealth, the fear of hostile kings; in honour, the fear of humilitation; in power, the fear of foemen; in beauty, the fear of old age; in scriptual erudition, the fear of opponents; in virtue, the fear of traducers; in body, the fear of death. All things of this world pertaining to man are attended with fear." The fear of death is the greatest fear. Whoever acquires calm fearlessness in the face of death attains godliness. The eminent Sufi mystic Dho-L-Nun Al Mesri writes:

Fear wasted me,
Yearning consumed me,
Love beguiled me,
God revived me.

Dho-L-Nun Al Mesri

Guru Tegh Bahadur describes the highest spiritual state of *Nirvana* as the state of fearlessness *(nirbhai pad).* The fear which man has is first changed into awe and reverence and then into love. The fear which demoralizes and degrades a man is a curse and sin. Greed, selfishness and sin torment a man with agonising fear. Such a fear says Virgil, "is proof of a degenerate minds." The only escape is by taking refuge at the feet of God who inspires man with fearlessness when the Light of His Presence shines within the soul, man becomes fearless, and attains the supreme state of *Nirvana.*

33

Seek The True One

man re saca gaho bicara

O mind, reflect and seek the True One;
Besides His Name, the sacred Word,
Transient is the whole world. *Refrain*
He whom the yogis tire of searching,
And have known not His limit and mystery,
Know the same Lord to be ever near thee.
He is distinct and unique,
As He is without form, and features. 1
His Name is pure and eternal in the world.
On His Name I have never meditated.
O Thou whom the world adores and worships;
Nanak takes refuge at Thy Feet.
Lord, through Thy abiding grace, save me. 2

"It always strikes, and it is very peculiar," says the French artist Van Gosch, "that whenever we see the image of indescribable and unutterable disolation—of loneliness, poverty and misery, the end and extreme of things—the thought of God comes into one's mind." The hymn centres around four themes; Firstly, the unicity of God; secondly, the nearness of God to man; and thirdly, God is achieved through the meditative discipline of His Name, and fourthly, the Name is identified with eternal Verity behind the unreal world.

God is one and exists from eternity to all eternity. He is the only reality. One God created the universe and governs it. God is eternal and unique. He is without beginning and without end. He is changeless, formless, infinite and supreme. "In whichever direction I look" says Guru Gobind Singh, I see Him manifest as Love (Jap: 80). "God is nearer to man than his neck vein" says the Koran. It is this profound truth of the Koran on which the whole experience and mystic achievements of the Sufis were built, and it is this fundamental belief of the Sufis which brought them very close to the Sikh Gurus both in their ethical and spiritual outlook. God is close to us as a Living Spirit. Not our physical eyes, but our inner vision can see Him vividly. Man lives his earthly life as such a low moral and spiritual level that a Yiddish proverb says, "If God lived on earth, people would break His windows."

But God ever lives close to our minds and soul. He is revealed to us in our hearts through the mystic power of the Word, His Name, or the inspired songs of His Presence. Our inner eyes clouded by darkness see Him only when we approach Him with humility and pure mind. "Some there are" says Plotinus "that for all their effort have not attained the vision. They have received the authentic

Light, all their soul has gleaned as they have drawn near; but they come with a load on their shoulders which holds them back from the place of vision. They have not ascended in the pure integrity of their being, but are burdened with that which keeps them apart. They are not yet made one within." (Ennead VI, 9). The love and grace of God changes even a sinner into a saint.

34

How Can I Express my Lowliness

kahau kahan apni adhimai

Alas, how can I express my utter lowliness,
Ensnared in the lust for gold and women;
I have never sung the glory of God.
Considering the transient world to be rèal,
My mind in it is deeply engrossed. *Refrain*
Alas, I have contemplated not the Lord,
The Protector of the poor and the oppressed,
Who would abide by me in distress.1
Day and night, night and day,
Absorbed in worldly ways,
From cockle and weeds my mind is free.
Says Nanak, there is no other way,
Except taking refuge in Thee. 2

The most important trait of a great character and sincere seeker of Truth is that he has the courage and humility to look straight into his failings and frankly express his shortcomings. Such a humility gives him strength to fight them and conquer.

Such a humility endears us to our fellow men. "Comes pride, comes disgrace, but with the prudent there is wisdom. "Do not exalt yourself lest you fall and cover yourself with shame." "The humble man's greatest glory is God's good pleasure." "To the scorners God will be scoirners, to the humble he gives grace." Yet the Sikh Gurus time and again warn us against false humility which is sheed hypocrisy and urge us to sincerely repent over our past deeds and reflect seriously on our deeds. "Repentence is change of minds," says Aldous Huxley, "and without it there cannot be even a beginning of the spiritual life—for the life of the Spirit is incompatible with the life of the "Old man" whose acts, whose thoughts, whose very existence are the obstructing evils which have to be repented." This necessary change of mind is normally accompanied by sorrow and self-loathing. Self-reproach is painful but the very pain is reassuring proof that the Self is still intact. It is in this mood of repentence the human mind is depicted in this hymn as emerging out of darkness into light. "Joy shall be in heaven over one sinner that repenteth more than over ninetynine just persons which need no repentence." (St Luke) The repentent soul not only becomes conscious of his sins and transgressions, but his faith in the mercy of God is awakened, and with an inner determination he seeks refuge in God, the Eternal Spirit that sheds light and love.

35

Still All is Not Lost

cetna hai to cet lai nis din mai prani

Man, if you want to think of God,
Remember Him day and night;
Every moment life fleeteth fast.
As an earthen pitcher of water breaks,
Thy vesture will one day collapse, *Refrain*
Why chantest thou not, O ignorant fool,
The praise and glory of the Lord.
So absorbed are you in vain ambition,
You have never thought of death. 1
Still all is not lost;
Ye, chant the glory of God.
Says Nanak: by devotional worship of the Lord,
You shall be blessed,
With the supreme state of fearlessness. 2

Guru Tegh Bahadur is the prophet of hope and profound optimism. He repeatedly stresses that the fallen man can still make an effort and through the grace and love of God reach the highest spiritual state. As long as there is life, there is hope for every sinner. While the wise and virtuous trust Him for His justice and power and love, the sinner too must trust Him for His mercy and compassion. Highlighting God's mercy in utter humility, Bhai Gurdas, father of Sikh philosophy, writes: "From my own deeds I do not expect a place even in hell, but your infinite mercy and compassion gives me hope that You will forgive me and be the cover of my shame." Without such hope and trust in the grace of God, life of meditation and prayer is impossible People sin more for lack of trust in God than in complete ignorance of God's existence. We rely too much on the body and our biological instincts which are paralysed with one stroke of mental or physical illness. We are too absorbed in our physical existence of superficial relations with other human beings. We completely forget our moral and spiritual relations with the society in which we live and with humanity at large. The mad passion for wealth, power, domination over our fellow beings has obsessed our mind so much that we fail to realize how frail is human life.

Mortal beings are but grass that wither and flowers that fade. We live as if we are never going to die, and there will be no reckoning of our deeds. Few ever realize that life may cut off while the web was still in the making. Our passions reflect the things of the world in false light but death will unmask them. With all our wealth and power, a grave, a coffin and ashes are our lot.

"It is never too late," says Guru Tegh Bahadur, "to turn from sin to virtue, from falsehood to righteousness, and from evil to good. Even if a person turns to Truth for too late in life, the Merciful God will reward all sincere worship, prayers and meditations, contemplating His true love. Even such a one can attain the highest spiritual state of *Nirvana,* the state of fearlessness."

36

Awake ! Arise !

jag leh re man jag leh kahan gafal soya

Awake O man! awake and arise!
Why sleepest thou in reckless indifference,
The body which was born with thee,
Will not accompany thee after death. *Refrain*
Father, mother, sons and friends,
For whom you have deep attachment,
Will throw you in the flames,
As soon as your soul departs. 1
People pretend to love thee,
They feign to be ever thine,
Only as long as you live in the world,
Awake! Arise! says Nanak; sing His praise;
Like a dream the earthly life will pass away. 2

Long is the night of life which is spent in egoistic indifference to truth, in reckless ignorance of righteousness,, justice and wisdom. Short is the day in which man toil and suffers for Trust, Beauty and Love. The Guru reminds us of the perennial call of the Spirit: "Awake! Arise! live in the love and glory of God." "The face of Truth," says Isa Upanishad, "is hid as it were by a golden lid, O Pushan, uncover that Truth, so that I who love Truth, may visualise it." (15)

For a majority of people ignorance is bliss, and the comforts of sensuous pleasures are the joys of paradise. "Thus, the Orient lies upon its soft bed," says Khalil Gibran. "The sleeper wakes up for an instant when stung by a flea, and then resumes his narcotic slumber." Whoever tries to awaken him is berated as rude person who neither sleeps himself nor lets others sleep. Shutting their eyes again they whisper into the ears of their soul: "He is an infidel poisoning the minds of the youth and undermining the foundation of ages. If awakening were a virtue, modesty would prevent me from claiming it. But it is not a virtue, but a reality that appears suddenly to those who have the strength to rise. To be modest in speaking the truth, is hypocrisy."

The call of the spirit awakens sensitive minds to a new firmament and lights a fire within the soul which never afterwards subsides. We become conscious of a life which is quite different from the false life which we lead. We see human relations not in terms of wealth and riches or in response to lower passions, but quite differently.

"Man" says the Sufi mystic Rumi consists of two parts: "that which feeds on animality in this world on these lusts of desire. But as for that which is his true essence its food is knowledge and wisdom and the sight of God. The animality is man flees away from God whilst his humanity flees away from the world." (Discourse)

The truest test of human relations comes in suffering and death. All that absorbs our attention is transient and phenomenal existence and impels and induces sensitive minds to seek wisdom and Light.

37
Sing the Glory of God

hari jas re mana gae lai jo sangi hai tara

Sing my mind, the glory of God,
In life and death it will abide by thee,
The years pass by, ye listen to me. *Refrain*
To wealth, riches, elephants and chariots
You are attached so deeply;
When the noose of death falls around your neck,
All you deem yours will cease to be thine. 1
Knowingly you have brought your doom, O fool;
From sin and vice you desist not,
Nor pride and vanity you give up. 2
Listen to the teachings of the Guru.
Nanak giveth the call;
Take refuge at the feet of the Lord. 3

The divine Songs of Guru Tegh Bahadur are strung to music because music according to the Gurus, when used with enlightened spirit inspires the soul with beauty and exalts the mind. All the Sikh Gurus were poet-musicians. Music has the greatest power to lift a depressed spirit to the heights of poetic vision. That is why all the hymns of the Gurus are captioned with *ragas, talas,* and *gribas (ghar).* Music wedded to lust and degrading club revelry excites only lower passions. But music by itself or wedded to inspiring divine poetry liberates the soul from bondage.

The 59 *padavalis* of Guru Tegh Bahadur are strung to fourteen *Ragas*. Each *Raga* has a different atmosphere, a different tonal mood and depth of feeling and sublimity. The very word *Raga* means something that colours and tinges the mind. When the hymn is read it stirs the mind, but when it is sung in the *Raga* indicated, which is done by very few musicians only, it stirs the soul. To sing the glory of God is to dive deep into the Spirit of God.

Guru Tegh Bahadur continues to write on the theme, the various aspects of which have been discussed in the foregoing hymns. He gives the call to human beings wandering in wilderness to desist from working up their own doom and take refuge at the feet of God. This can be done by discarding vanity and lust for low ambition of power and wealth by seeking the love and grace of God and by humble submission to truth, charity and service of humanity.

38

The Word of God

dukh harta hari nam pachano

Know the Word of God,
To be dispeller of sorrow
Ajamal the sinner,
Ganika the adultress,
Were all liberated and saved,
By contemplating His Name. *Refrain*
The drowning elephant,
Lost all fear of death,
As soon as he remembered,
The Name of God.
Taught by the Sage Narada,
Child Dhruva contemplated the Lord. 1
Immortal and Ineffable became his Spirit,
And attained the fearless state.
The world wondered at his great feat.
Sayeth Nanak, God is the saviour of saints:
Know Him to be ever near thee. 2

God, the Almighty Power remains hidden behind his own creation, only to reveal Himself to Man within his own heart. From age to age He reveals His Light to humanity through gifted prophets and mystic sages. These prophets express His immensity and glory through attributive and symbolic Name, which is truly expressive of God's Light and Being. The Mystic Word, and the utterances of these Masters have rightly been termed the divine Name or the Word *(shabad)*. The Word, thus becomes what the Greeks called the Mind and the Spirit of God (Logos).

The mystic Word *(shabad)* uttered by the Prophet in transcendental communion with God is truly the Mind and Spirit of God, not distinct from His Light. Eternally latent in Him the Word appeared as His Activity in creating, energising and illuminating the universe. But as God alone exists in Reality His creative Word is divine in nature. It was this Word about which the Gospel of John declared." In the beginning was the Word and the Word was with God; and the Word was God." (John. 1) Bhai Gurdas, the father of Sikh philosophy says, "In God is the Word, and in the Word is the Light of God." He calls the Word, *(shabad)* the Unseen Presence *(agocar),* supremely Wonderful *(parmadabhut),* and Ineffable Testament *(akatha-katha)."* "From Him who is Light, Music and Truth, comes everything except sin, because sin is nothing but defect, a lack of righteousness." God alone is real, but apart from His immortal Transcendent Existence. He lives in all creation as the poet in his poems. When the Guru baptizes us and imparts His Light and Spirit, the Word of God becomes fresh and tabercled in us."

"The deep and meditative rememberance of God *(Simran* as it is often called in Sikh scriptures) is the planetary march of our life round the higher life of Heaven." Says Poet Puran Singh. "The heart beats, the breath, the tongue, the pores of the skim, the mind, the footfalls all must repeat `Hail Master,' with a rosary made of the beads of love, of tear-drops for all. In all tempests, with our tiny arms twined round His Mother Neck, our tresses flung free in breeze of time, we sleep like babes in His firm Embrace. No fire can burn, no waters can drown, no sword can cut, no kings destroy the children of the Masters. We are the sons of Guru Nanak—Guru Gobind Singh."

Sinners who take refuge in the Light of divine Name have been liberated. Adultresses who remembered Him became saints and singers of the Divine. Sinners have been exalted to moral heights of great poets and mystics. The distinterested boy prince Dhruva, when initiated by the sage Narada into the mystery of divine Name became immortal and from times immemorial shines in Indian history and religious traditions like the pole-star. Indeed, the discerning sages named the pole-star after him, to symbolize his stead-fastness, and unshakable devotion to God. Thus the rememberance of His Name inspires the seeker with the divine Presence of God, who is very close to us.

39

Without True Devotion to Him

hari ke nam bina dukh pavai

Without contemplating His Name,
Man suffers sorrow and pain,
The Guru reveals this mystery;
That without true devotion to Him,
Man cannot be free from delusion. *Refrain*

What use is going to pilgrimage,
What use are all fasts,
If you take not refuge in the Lord?
Know such yoga and worship to be useless,
Which neglects praise and love of God. 1
He who discards all attachment and pride,
And sings the glory of the Lord of Light,
Deem such a man, says Nanak,
To be, jivan mukta: liberated in this life. 2

The mystic Name of God is the divine stream of life which flows from the eternal Guru to the sincere and deserving disciple. It is life that begets life. It is not achieved through penance, yogic practices and ascetic habits, but through devotion, love and grace. Yet the contemplation of His Name has nothing to do with ritualistic empty repetition of any Name of God without inner communion and devotion. It is not mere lip-service. It begins with the Guru lighting the lamp in our heart. After this baptism of the spirit, the contemplation of the Name becomes a constant pouring of the oil in the lamp, till the lamp (our heart and soul) becomes ablaze with the flame of Light.

A true Sikh, a true seeker of truth is never free from striving. He wanders restlessly and ceaselessly about the Light and majestic splendour of God.

Bhai Gurdas compares the love of a true Sikh with that of Majnu for Leila. Why so, may ask? Leila was not a spiritual being, but corporeal and of the fresh, fashioned of clay. Yet Rumi tells us, "Majnu's passion for Leila produced such absorption and so utterly seized and overwhelmed Majnu that he had no need to see Leila with the eye, no need to hear her words by the voice, for he never saw Leila apart from himself, so that he cried:

Your name is on my tongue,
Your image is in my sight,
Your memory is in my heart,
Whither then shall I write?

Thus the Name of the Beloved whose attributes are true and eternal can bring a man into a state in which he never sees himself apart from the Beloved. He sees nothing around him which does not proclaim His praise.

40

Fasts and Pilgrimages

ja mai bhajan ram ko nahi

Bear this in mind,
Wasted is the life of the man,

Who is devoid of devotion to God. *Refrain*
He who keeps fasts and goes on pilgrimage,
And performs acts of piety,
Without purity of mind and self-control,
Useless are all his pious acts:
Believe me, I speak the truth. 1
Place a stone in water,
It remains hard and insensible,
Such is the lot of a man,
Who is devoid of the love of God. 2
The true Guru has revealed to me:
In this dark age of Kaliyuga
Enlightenment can be attained,
Sayeth Nanak: that man is truly great,
Who sings the glory of God. 3

In orthodox Hinduism and Islam facts and going to places of pilgrimages are accepted as means of salvation though many eminent Sufi Saints and medieval Bhaktas rejected these views as positive articles of their faith, after attaining the highest mystic experiences. In Islam, the month of Ramzan, the ninth month of the lunar year is observed as a period of fasting, with complete abstinence from food and drink during the hours of daylight. Those sick and on journey are exempted. Pilgrimage to Mecca constitutes a religious obligation. The Hindus keep fast mostly on *ekadashi* and a number of other auspicious days and do so to attain salvation. In Sikhism, visiting holy places of historical interest is done out of reverence and to perpetuate the memory of the Gurus and the events connected with their lives but is not obligatory as a means to salvation. Fasting is rejected as part of religious discipline, and is even considered hypocrisy when it is done merely as superstitious ritual. But at the same time gluttony is strongly condemned. "Those who eat little or sleep little and lead of life of contemplation succeed in breaking the bondage of life." says Guru Nanak. "Eat little and sleep little and entertain compassion and forgiveness in your heart" says Guru Gobind Singh *(Shabad)*. Fasting under medical advice, or for reasons of health, or for any other cause, not connected with personal salvation is a different thing. In religious life, anything that promotes health must be accepted "But those who undertake fast for self-mortification and bring undesirable suffering to the mind and body achieve nothing," says Guru Nanak.

Pilgrimage to holy places, or places of historical interest connected with lives and deeds of the prophets or to any culture institutions built by the founders of a religion, when done only to pay homage to holymen residing there or for any religious and cultural gatherings of community worship is appreciated by the Gurus and they themselves built such shrines as ideal centres of the Sikh Church. But the Gurus made it clear again and again that merevisit to such holy places, or bathing in holy tanks without imbibing any ennobling influence from congregational hymn singing, or association with devout souls residing there, is meaningless and will not save anyone from his sins. "What use is bathing in such places if the mind is not made clean by accepting truth."

Eminent Sufis took the same views about pilgrimage as the Gurus did. The Sufi saints of the Chisti order were great and devoted friends of the Gurus. They discreetly avoided going to Mecca for pilgrimage, because for them the place where one sincerely worshipped God was in-itself pilgrimage to Mecca. Other eminent Sufis and mystics also gave it a secondary place in devotional life. "A Muslim youth missed the pilgrimage and he sighed. The eminent Sufi Sofyan al-Thauri said to the youngman," "I have performed forty pilgrimages, I bestow them all on you. Will you bestow this sigh on me?" "I do" said the youth. That night Sofyan was told by a voice from the Unknown, "You have made such a profit on the transaction that if it were divided up among all the pilgrims at Arfat. They would be rich indeed." *(Tazkirat al-Auliya)* A man devoid of love is like a stone in water, incapable of feeling and finer perceptions of life. No pilgrimage or bath in holy water can help him. Communion with the love and wisdom of God alone can breath life into dead souls, exalt them and lead them to the realization of highest truth.

41

The Miracle of Grace

re man ot leh hari nama

My mind, seek refuge in the Lord's Name,
Contemplating which all evil is dispelled,
And the divine state of Nirvana is attained. *Refrain*
Blessed are those who sing His praise,
Erased are the sings of their past lives;
Their souls are exalted to celestial abode. 1
Ajamal, the sinner, gained consciousness of God.
Just before death when all was lost,
By remembering the Saviour, God:
Within a moment he attained the divine state,
For which great sages aspire and crave. 2
The elephant that was saved,
From drowning by the Lord,
Had neither any virtue or learning,
Nor spiritual consciousness and thought.
No pious act the elephant had performed.
Such O Nanak, is the ennobling grace of God,
That even when the elephant remembered Him

He was blessed with the fearless State. 3

The Name of God is the essence of His Spirit. It is the symbol of His unseen Presence. He who contemplates His Name seeks the fragrance of His Presence. Through this spiritual discipline the highest mystic state of *Nirvana* is attained. The sins of the past life are destroyed. The mind comes out of the clouds of mental darkness and basks in the sunshine of enlightenment.

Not only human beings but even animals, and more so human beings with animal and brutish nature have a spark of divine flame deep down in their heart. The story is told of an elephant who was rescued from death when he was dragged into deeper waters, by remembering God, His creator. Guru Tegh Bahadur says that if God responds to the speechless agony and the call of an elephant who was devoid of knowledge, wisdom, forethought, he would certainly answer the prayer of human beings who have better understanding and spiritual perception than animals. God would certainly respond to the sincere prayer of the most depraved human beings, living like animals, even if they turn to him in extreme distress with the determination to completely give up their dark past and seek the Light of God. "Blessed are those who remember Him," says the Guru "Even the greatest sinner can acquire liberation through His grace, if he remembers God with single-minded devotion."

42
Divine Discipline

sadho kaun jugat ab kijai

O seers, what discipline should I adopt,
To destroy all evil thoughts,
And contemplate the love of God, *Refrain*
My mind is absorbed in material persuits,
It has acquired not divine wisdom.
What is that divine Name,
Contemplating which Nirvana is attained? 1
The apostle of God blessed me graciously,
And unveiled this mystery to me.
Know that: he who sings the praise of God,
Thereby practices all religious duties. 2
He who within a day or night,
Contemplates God even for a moment,
Loses, O Nanak, all fear of death,
And illumines his life and self. 3

Every serious tinker searches for a way of life, and discipline which can change him mentally, morally and spiritually. A mind engrossed in material desires remains ignorant of spiritual knowledge. The mystery of His Presence, the essence of His Name and Power is never revealed to such a man.

Awakening comes on meeting a divine Master. The ever living Spirit of the Guru unfolds the mystery through the World, the Name of God. To contemplate His Name is the most illuminating meditation and practical spiritual discipline. But the contemplation of His Name should not be merely a formal repetition of the *mantram* (Mystic Word). There should be inward faith and singleminded devotion. He who sincerely contemplates His Name attains peace and immortality. Guru Tegh Bahadur once more stresses that the noblest aim of religion is to attain *Nirvana,* the highest spiritual state.

43

You Still Realize not Your Error

prani narayan sudh leh

Man, reflect and think of God,
Day and night life lessens every moment,
The body is wearing away.. *Refrain*
Childhood passed in ignorance,
Youth was spent in venemous pleasures,
Old age has now overtaken thee,
You still realize not your error.
In what false belief you are engrossed. 1
Why have you forgotten the Lord,
Who gave you a precious human life?
You have never sung His praise for a moment,
Contemplating whom man attains liberation. 2
Why are you intoxicated in the vanity of wealth.
With thee will not abide thy pelf,
Or help thee in life and death.
Says Nanak: Contemplate His Name, the precious pearl,
Which will help thee even in death. 3

Man should reflect on all the stages of his mental and spiritual development. Childhood passes in blissful ignorance. Youth is wasted in thoughtless pleasures. Even when old age overtakes him he realizes not that he has wasted his whole life in petty and vain ambitions. False doctrines and beliefs misdirected his life and thoughts. By forgetting God man remains blind to his own real self and to the purpose of his life.

Guru Tegh Bahadur urges us to turn our mind away from the phenomenal world, not to escape from the realities of the world but to participate here and now in eternal life and face the challenges of the demonic forces within his own heart and outside him in society. He must not be swept away by the stormy waves of the world, but he must acquire power to sail against the current.

44

Eternal Spring of Peace

hari ko nam sada sukhdai

The Name of God is the eternal spring of peace and joy,
Contemplating Him, Ajamal, the sinner, acquired liberation;
And Ganika, the adultress, experienced spiritual exaltation. *Refrain*
When Draupadi was being stripped naked in royal assembly,
She remembered the Merciful Lord,
Who compassionately covered her shame,
And thus enhanced God's glory as Saviour. 1
The Lord bestows His grace and protection,
On one who glorifies the Treasure of Mercy.
Says Nanak, with this confidence and belief,
I too have taken refuge in Thee. 2

Every sinner has hope of coming out of the mental and moral darkness if he makes a sincere effort to strive towards God and His Light. The grace of God descends on all repentent sinners as much as on sincere devotees. From ancient Indian religious lore are given two examples. Ajamal the adulterer remembered God on death bed and cried for protection in the terror of agonizing darkness. God mercifully showed him the path of Light. Ganika, a prostitute met a saint who awakened in her a repulsion for the life of sin and asked her to contemplate God. She was saved. The Guru suggests that the law of love conquers the law of karma. The flame of pure love burns all, base passions and desires. The sins of a whole life can be erased by genuine repentence and love of truth. The grace of God is ever there awaiting repentent souls. This is one aspect of the grace and love of God.

The second aspect of God's protective grace and mercy is depicted through the well-known story of Draupadi, daughter of the King of Panchala and wife of the Pandu princes. Draupadi was a damsel of dark complexion, but of great beauty. In the great gambling match which Yudhistra, the eldest of the Pandus played against his cousins, the Kauravas lost their kingdom and even Draupadi, a lady of rare virtues.

Duryodhana tried to treat Draupadi as a slave girl and ordered her to sweep the rooms. She refused and then Dussasna dragged her by the hair into the pavilion before all the Chieftains, and tauntingly told her that as slave girl she had no right to complain of being touched by men. He also abused her and tore off her veil and dress to strip her naked, while Duryodhana invited her to sit on his thigh. She cried for help in her sorrow. Lord Krishna miraculously restored her garments as fast as they were torn. This classical story is given as a historical example of God's power and compassion to protect the destitute and helpless who seek His protection.

45
Remorse

ab mai kahan karon ri mai

What shall I do now O Mother,
The whole life I have wasted in sensuous pursuits,
And have contemplated not the Beloved. *Refrain*
When the noose of death falls around the neck,
All sensuous pleasures the mind will forget.
Nothing will help man in the hour of death,
Except the Name of God. 1
The wealth which as his own he considers,
In a moment becomes the possession of others;
Says Nanak: Only one thought disturbs me now,
Why have I not sung the praise of the Lord. 2

"The grief of the dead is not on account of death," said the Persian poet-mystic Rumi, "it is because they dwelt on the phenomenal form of existence and never perceived that all this foam is moved and fed by the eternal sea." This *padavali* is the lament of a soul plunged in the gloom and unrelieved sense of misery for which he is himself responsible. Vividly portraying the remorse of a pent up soul, Guru Tegh Bahadur, presents the two sides of a repentent mind seeking light. On the one hand comes the feeling that a precious portion of life has been wasted in dissipating pleasures, and on the other hand there is a strong urge to save the soul from the doom of darkness and death. The man who has wasted all his life in sensuous pleasures, thus suddenly wakes up to the grim realization that the sap of his life has rotted and his consciousness is filled with an inexpressible agony. With his joyless life he totters towards the grave. Low dark ideas, unclean imagination, flaming passions have sucked all his spiritual strength like a tape worm. He is spiritually dead and lives in the grave of dark ideas. Even for such a moral leper of society there is hope and brighter future. The compassion of God is boundless. He is always ready to forgive a sinner who sincerely repent over his past and seriously and looks for the path of light and wisdom. The Merciful God is ever ready to bestow grace on one who turns to Him. But one must have courage enough to turn away from transient charms of wealth and material acquisitions. One must learn to seek peace and strength in the glory and power of God.

46

When His Love Dawned on Me

mai mai mam ko man na tyagio

O Mother, I have abandoned not the pride of my mind
I have wasted my life in the intoxication of wealth,
I have never devoted myself to the worship of God. *Refrain*
When over the head hangs the mace of death,
Out of slumberous stupor you will wake up, my soul.
Of what avail repentence and regret,
I cannot escape the doom of death. 1
When on my heart dawned the love of His feet.
Over my plight I began to grieve.
Nanak: when I abandoned myself to the Songs of the Lord,
My life found spiritual consummation. 2

Guru Tegh Bahadur continues to reflect on the same theme of the stifled cry of penitent soul. It is the expression of a heart overwhelmed by shame, humbled and broken by guilt and yet saved from despair through penetential faith in the mercy and grace of God. There is no evasion of responsibility here on the grounds of chance circumstance or an instinctive urge; no blaming of ignorance, necessity or evil agency. There is an unreserved confession of guilt. In this penetential state he thinks of death. The understanding of death awakens his moral and spiritual consciousness. There is a healing of inward distress and anguish when the Light of God's love shines on the disillusioned soul. Penitence in Sikhism implies the dispossession of sinful desires.

The hymn begins in the depth of distress and ends in the heights of confident hope. Faith has triumphed over despondency. The fear of death brings of magic awakening from the deep sleep of apathy and ignorance. The thought of being suddenly torn from earthly ties hurts us. It is terrible to slide down the unknown roaring depths.

47

God Within

sadho eh tan mithiya jano

Know the body to be transient O seers,
The Spirit of God that resides within,
Know it to be true and real. *Refrain*
Why are you engrossed in glamorous illusion
of the world: a transient dream.
Beyond death nothing will accompany thee,

Why are you attached to your possessions. 1
Discard all thought of praise or blame,
Entertain in your heart the glory of God.
In every heart dwells the Perfect One,
Sayeth Nanak: the One Supreme Being is the Lord. 2

Many people believe in a God dwelling in a remote heaven, a God whom they would meet only after death or on the Day of Judgement. The body is the temple of God, eternal in time and place. The presence and power of God dwelleth within us. The Light of God is not to be found on mountain tops or forest dwellings but within the individual beings.

God is not an abstract idea, a myth. He is a visible Reality, a resplendent Light. Compared to the eternal existence of God the world is a dream. The Light of God shining in our hearts reflects the true and real existence behind the phenomenal world. Our ignorance, self-will and pride have veiled this Light from our eyes. Says Goldsmith, "God is within our own consciousness, closer than breathing and nearer than hands and feet. If we are ever in a place of discord, let us never forget that salvation is closer than breathing, because I and the Father are one. Man must turn away from the materialistic interest. Nothing will last with him beyond death. For false pride and transient honours man turns away from wisdom and truth. He should maintain a stoic attitude towards praise and blame and live in the love of God. Turning away from the phenomenal world he must concentrate his contemplative attention to the Supreme Light within the Self.

48

Victims of Lust

papi hiai mai kam basae

O sinners, lust is aflame in your soul,
The unsteady mind has lost all self-control. *Refrain*
Yogis and Jains, ascetics of all creeds,
Are victims of passion's storms. 1
Those who contemplate the Name of God,
The Ocean of Fear they easily cross. 2
Humble Nanak takes refuge in Thee,
Bless me with Thy Name, Lord.
So that I may live singing Thy glory. 3

Guru Nanak says in his *Omkar* "Lust and wrath waste the body as borax melts the gold." Lust is the most powerful animal instinct in man. Pointing to the power it wields over the heart and soul of man, Guru Arjun says, "Lust, thou native of hell, that goadest man into the cycle of births and death, thou art enchanter of hearts, wielding vast power on earth. Thou destroyeth meditation, austerity and virtue offering petty passing delight." *(Shloka Sehaskriti)*.

Not only the common man but even Yogis, Jains, and ascetics who live under the vow of chastity and continence lead outwardly a pious and holy life, but are inwardly victims of lust for women. No ascetic discipline can suppress this passion by merely keeping away from society. Those who seek the Presence of God through contemplation of His Name are able to sublimate and rationalize lust by leading a normal family life. To sing His glory is to imbibe His Name.

The divine Buddha said, "The truth is not for the hermit alone, it concerns every human being, priest and layman alike. There is no distinction between the monk who has taken the vows and the man of the world living with his family. There are hermits who fall into perdition, and there are humble householders who mount to the rank of *rishis.*" "Hankering after pleasure is danger common to all; it carries away the world. He who is involved in its eddies finds no escape. But wisdom is the handy boat, reflection is the ladder."

49
Delusion Dispelled

mai mai dhan payio hari nama

Mother, I have acquired the wealth of His Name,
My restless mind wanders no more,
It has acquired peace and self-control. *Refrain*
All attachment for material wealth,
Has parted from my body;
The light of pure Wisdom has dawned on me,
From greed and low cravings the mind is free.
The love of God it has espoused. 1
When I was blessed with the pearl of His Name.
The delusion That prevailed from past lives has disappeared.
All desires have been calmed;
The mind has found peace in the bliss of soul. 2
He who is blessed by the merciful God.
Sings the songs of the glorious Lord.
Says Nanak, some rare and Enlightened men,
Get so precious a spiritual wealth. 3

The Name or the Word of God, is the spiritual wealth of divine Wisdom. Whoever is blessed with the treasure acquires peace and self-control. The mind finds rest and illumination. All material attachments fade away. Such purity and sinlessness prevails that the love of God overpowers all petty passions like greed. Pure and perfect Wisdom is revealed *(upjai nirmal gyan)*. All confusion and fear of birth and death departs when the precious pearl of divine Name is achieved. When the springs of inner happiness and bliss *(nij sukh)* are revealed, all desires disappear. Only through His mercy and grace one feel inspired to sing the glory of God. Few enlightened Sages acquire this inner treasure. The Word of the Guru, the Name of God calms the storm of passions and dispress the winds of temptations. The divine Name orientates the whole person with a new impetus. The Name of Gold cannot be understood and imbibed as a spiritual discipline without the illuminating grace of God.

50

Death Will Knock at Your Door

man kahan bisario ram naam

Why O Mind have you forgotten the Name of God,
Death will knock at your door,
And thy body will be no more, *Refrain*
This world is a mountain of smoke,
What made you think it is true and lasting. 1
Know that wealth, wife, mansions and riches,
None will accompany thee beyond death. 2
The love of the Lord alone will abide with thee.
Says Nanak: Adore God with singleminded devotion. 3

Everyone knows that he will die but no one believes it. Everyone knows that death comes unawares, yet no one is conscious of the fact that life may end suddenly and his connections with all his kith and kin snapped and he will be suddenly deprived of all his worldly possessions.

For an ordinary human being death is the valley of darkness, about which he need not be worried as long as he is alive. A saint looks at death quite differently. When the Sufi mystic Al-Shebli was dying, people thronged around him to pray for his soul. Shebli exclaimed, "How marvellous, a throng of dead men are come to pray over one living."

After enjoying the wealth and glory of a kingdom, Bhartrihari cried in despair, "Alas! youth has passed away from the body, the virtues have proved barren for want of appreciative admirers. The powerful, all-destroying, unrelenting Death is fast hastening in. What is to be done? Earthly possessions are as transient as thought; the whole series of our enjoyments are like occasional flashes of autumnal lightning, the embrace round the neck given by our beloved ones linger only for a while. To cross the ocean of fear of the world attach your mind to God." Says Guru Tegh Bahadur on the same theme; "Remember death so that you may contemplate life. Love Truth and God so that you may live in eternity."

51

The Lord Abides Within Thee

kahan bhulio re jhuthe lobh lag

Why are you deceived by lust for greed,
Awake, arise, all is not lost, be free. *Refrain*
Consider the world to be a dream.
It will vanish in no time; know this truth. 1
The gracious Lord ever abides within thee,
Contemplate Him day and night O Friend. 2
His remembrance will help even in death.
Says Nanak: Sing His praise and glory. 3

Man is dazzled by his immediate surroundings and prevented by custom, habit, misleading diversions from looking into his own heart and soul, where lies dormant the seed of infinite life. He is bewitched by his lovely body and beautiful earth. His greed and desires cloud his inner life. The instinctive man who lives for the outward spectacle of life is unconscious of his real self. He is unconscious of his spiritual destiny. He attends to the exterior and he has made no effort to emancipate his consciousness.

He does not see inwardly, but has craze for things outside himself. Guru Tegh Bahadur urges these moral dwarfs, these crippled souls to wake up and see the reality. Instead of following instinctive nature they must discipline themselves. In everyone of us the Lord is present; He hides Himself in the foliage of our ideas and feelings, which when sublimated become the shades of Paradise. Bhai Gurdas says, "If we go one step towards him in this inward pilgrimage He takes a thousand steps to meet us to bestow His grace on us. We must love Him truly. We must contemplate Him day and night."

52

No one will Save Thee Ultimately

hari bin tero ko na sahai

No one will save thee ultimately.
Besides the Merciful Lord,
Father, mother, son and spouse,
None, none will be of help of thee, *Refrain*
All earthly riches, wealth and wife,
Which you say are thine,
None after death will accompany thee;
Why cling to them, ignorant man. 1
God is the Saviour of the destitute,

God is the dispeller of sorrow.
Even such a one you have not adored.
O Nanak, transient is worldly life.
Like a dream you see at night. 2

A Sikh lives in the world, but he is not of the world. He lives in the family and society and yet he is free and illumined spirit and not slavishly attached to the cravings and clamour of the family and society. Riches, wealth and a beautiful wife give every physical satisfaction to a man, but if he thinks not of God whose gifts he enjoys, these material objects of achievement may make him utterly blind to the refined life of the mind and the soul. Unhampered by earthly pre-occupation, a true Sikh serves the Lord fervently by word, dead, and labour. Work and labour without contemplation of God is like fire without heat, destined to die. To work, to earn, to spend only for amusement and distractions, to follow sensuous instinct unaided by enlightened reason is to march deliberately on the road to ruin. Man should not cling to transient pleasures. He should devote all his energies to the love and power of God.

53

Why Cling to Your Body and Wealth

kahan man bikhya sion laptai

Why my mind, crave for poisonous pleasures;
Nothing in the world ever lasts.
Through birth some come into the world,
Through death some depart. *Refrain*
Wherefore cling to your body and wealth,
Why crave for earthly treasures?
Whatever you see will fade away like clouds. 1
Discard your pride, my mind,
And take refuge at the feet of the saint,
You will be liberated in no time.
Says Nanak: without devotion to God,
One knows no peace even in a dream. 2

Devotion to God, the ultimate Truth, is the road to peace. Without contemplative love of God, one knows no happiness and joy. But he who avidly seeks earthly riches becomes their slave and a restless beggar at the door of men with power and wealth. But he who lives detached from all material pleasures is completely free and constantly serene. To the devotee of God the senses are servants. In the life of a man leading materialistic life, the senses become serpents. The fire of concupiscene is not extinguished by formal prayers and observation of religious rites. "It is the fire" says Don Giovanni Rossi "of which the fuel is gluttony, the flame is vanity, the smoke is dishonour, the ashes are shame and the end is hell." When one wants to put out a fire observes Saint Jerome, "he first removes the wood." If one wishes to extinguish the flame of sensuality, he must begin denying himself many legitimate pleasures. Each pleasure sought, each craving gratified, each idleness consented, each lower passion satisfied leads man to the pit of darkness. One must discard pride and take refuge at the feet of the Enlightened One.

54

The Transitory World

kahan nar apno janam gavavai

Why O man, have you frittered away your life,
Mad in the intoxication of wealth;
You indulge in sensuous pleasures.
You seek not the sanctuary of the Lord. *Refrain*
This world is transitory like a dream;
Why are you charmed by its spell?
Whoever is born will one day depart;
Nothing in the world will last. 1
Considering the transitory body to be real,
Man chains himself in bondage.
Says Nanak, he is a liberated soul in the world
Who praises Him with singleminded devotion. 2

Guru Tegh Bahadur urges man to direct all his attention and energy to a single-minded devotion to the Eternal Spirit. Only such a devotion leads men to the path of liberation and illumination of Reality. The Guru deplores the lot of those who turn away from the path of Truth and devotion to God and waste all their life in acquisition of wealth and indulgence in low sensuous pleasures.

Man gives himself only to physical pleasures because he wrongly believes that his body and wealth will last long enough. He forgets death. He forgets God. He is ignorant of the indwelling spirit within Him which can awaken him to the lasting values of life. He can be saved if he seeks refuge in God.

"It is bondage" says the author of *Ashtavakra,* "when the mind desires or grieves at anything, rejects or accepts anything, feels happy or angry at anything. Liberation is attained when the mind does not desire or grieve or reject or accept or feel happy or is angry. Rare is the man who knows the Self as one without a second as well as the Lord of the Universe. He does what he knows; he has no fear from any quarter. Only those who have sincere yearning for truth can be exalted into God-experience:

55

Self-Willed Deeds

man kar kabhu na hari gun gayio

Never have I sung the Lord's praise,
With devotion sincere and true,
Victim of vices night and day,
Self-willed deeds I do. *Refrain*
To the Guru's Word I have never given ear;
I have sinned by coveting another's wife;
I have a craze for slandering others,
Restraining not when advised self-control. 1
Lord, how shall I describe my sinful deeds,
In evil ways I have wasted my life.
I am a sinner full of vices and iniquities,
Merciful Lord, Keep me in Thy sanctuary. 2

Man sins wilfully, but there is always one door open to him, the door leading to the refuge of the Lord. In this hymn is the poignant cry of the repentent sinner who admits, that he has been saying formal prayers, but never has he prayed inwardly and sincerely. He has outwardly been pious, but has wilfully drifted into sinful acts of calumny and adultery. He has neither listened to the divine Word and peace-giving message of the Guru nor exercised any control over his passions. But the repentent soul sincerely prays for divine guidance. It is pathetically crying for grace and forgiveness. It is smothered and suffocated by the misty darkness of sinful life. It gropes for peace and light.

It is neither good to indulge in pleasures of the body, nor it is good to neglect bodily needs and to heap filth upon impurities." The lamp that is not cleansed and not filled with oil will be extinguished, and the body that is unkempt, unwashed, and weakened by penance will not be fit receptacle for the light and truth. One who takes refuge in His Presence is liberated from the bondage of temptations.

56

Unreal is All This Panorama

ram simar ram simar ehai terai kaj hai

Contemplate the Lord, meditate on God,
In life this is thy real task.
Discard all attachment to wealth.
Take refuge at the feet of the Lord.
Know earthly pleasures to be false,

Unreal is all this panorama. *Refrain*
Ephemeral like a dream is your power of wealth;
Wherefore art thou priggish and vainglorious,
Like a heap of sand is the kingdom of the earth. 1
Nanak, the servant of God proclaimeth the truth.
When you die your body will perish;
The 'yesterday' of earthly existence has vanished,
So will face away 'today.' 2

The pleasures of physical life are unreal; its paradisian labyrinth is the road to misery, and its fading beauty kindles the flames of desires that never can be satisfied. Human frailty is great, for man is a vessel of clay; furious are the winds of passion; strong are the winds of allurements of the world; terrible are the temptation of lust and greed. Every passion of pride is a gust of wind which blows open the door of the soul to all other evil passions. The bliss of divine life is attainable by everyone who contemplates the Presence of God.

It is not wealth and power that enslave men but craze for wealth and power which destroys the mind and soul of man. We cleave to earthly pleasures which keep on slipping through our hands. Man must free himself from the illusion of false pleasures, and the delusion of earthly gains. The Guru does not at all suggest that the world should be renounced. We are to live in the world like lotus in the pond, which growing in dirty water, remains untouched by any filth or the disturbance of water. We are to live not a life of self but a life of truth.

57

Precious Life is Melting Away

ram bhaj ram bhaj janam sirat hai

On the Lord meditate,
On Him alone contemplate,
Thy precious life is melting away.
I have cautioned thee time and again.
Why O ungracious fool,
You still realize it not,
Your body is like a pellet of hail,
That will in no time melt away. *Refrain*
Dispel all doubts from your heart,
And contemplate the Name of God
This alone will light thy path,
In thy journey beyond death. 1
Discard all poisonous pleasures.
Let His glory be your heart's treasure.

Nanak in humility proclaims: Listen Man,
Your life is dissipating away. 2

The fundamental theme of this and similar hymns is to orientate human passions with compassionate concern and rejuvenate the sensual and the slothful. With one hand he points to the sorrow and misery of the lowest depth of human degradation, with the other he lifts man from his disgusting depths and elevates him to divine heights of perfection. The Guru says that the human body is precious, but to ignore the indwelling spirit and turn our mind to the body alone is a folly. The body is like a pellet of hail which will melt away at the approach of death. Sensuous pleasures do not give any lasting joy and happiness. Man must conceive his journey to be going beyond death. It is one continuous journey to the realm of Truth. One may achieve it during life time and conquer death. Death for such a one becomes the most important and beautiful event of life. He lives in eternity, and, death is the only victory gate to heaven.

58

Reflect What May be Your Fate

re man kaun gat hai teri

Man, reflect what may be your fate,
The Name of God is the light of the world,
To it you have never given thought.
You are deeply attached to venemous pleasures
And turn not your mind away from them. *Refrain*
You are born as a human being,
And still remember not God for a moment.
Engrossed in the attachment to wife and family
Thy feet are bound in chains. 1
Know ye, Nanak proclaims:
The world-spectacle is like a dream.
Why rememberest thou not the Lord.
Maya, the material power is the slave of God. 2

Maya, the earthly power manifests itself in many forms in the creation. Guru Tegh Bahadur wonders why man should forget God the Creator of *maya* and run after such transitory ambitions like wealth and power. The very purpose of human life is to rise above animality and be conscious of one's destiny as a human being.

Man can break the mental trappings of the flesh and rise to communion with the Eternal within his soul. Family and friends can be helpers and, inspires, when one seeks their participation in the divine quest. But when he abandons himself to their earthly cravings, they are menacles chaining his feet to low type of life *(pagoh pari beri)*. Guru Tegh Bahadur strongly proclaims *(kahai pukar)* the truth that this aspect of the world to which man is deeply attached is transitory. The world is transitory but life is immortal. Life may move from suffering to wisdom and peace or it may fall from the pinnacle of sensuous pleasures into the pit of sorrow and death, *Maya,* the material power behind human existence is the slave of the Enlightened man, because he use it for noble ends, but it is the Master of the man who abandons himself to the senses, and ultimately destroys him.

GURU GOBIND SINGH

1

Guru Gobind and Creation of the Khalsa

Immediately after the demise of Guru Tegh Bahadur, his son Gobind Rai was installed on the *gaddi* of Guru Nanak. It is said that the way of self-sacrifice chosen by Guru Tegh Bahadur had full consent of the young Gobind Rai. He started the mission entrusted on him with a more vigour and strength under the able guidance of his maternal uncle Kirpal Chand and with the help of sincere, honest and pious devotees of the Sikh faith. Moreover, the young successor of Guru Tegh Bahadur himself paid a proper attention towards the atrocities done by the Mughal authority and therefore, the Guru launched a vigorous programme of militarisation of his devotees.

It is said that the martyrdom of Guru Arjun, had already led to the taking of the two swords of Miri and Piri by Guru Hargobind. The martyrdom of Guru Tegh Bahadur produced the militant brotherhood of Khalsa in the time of his immediate successor, Guru Gobind Rai. The seeds sown by Guru Tegh Bahadur with his blood soon grew into a crop, with the birth of the Khalsa. A well-entrenched Sikh tradition also connects the origin of five K's with the tragic event of 1675. After that Guru Gobind Singh determined to below on his followers such distinctive marks as would render impossible for future repetition of what had earlier happened at Delhi in 1675.

As a matter of fact, the Sikhs were convinced that for their meaningful existence they would have to take up arms. Guru Gobind, though nine years old at the time of his father's martyrdom, was a foresighted person with great intellect. Instead of losing time in weeping and mourning, he utilized it in the strict military training of his Sikhs. He asked his devotees to solemnly declare that from the day he created the Khalsa, they had changed their occupation, their previous family ties and their earlier creed. In the view of Gordon, "The execution of Guru Tegh Bahadur sowed seed in Delhi, which soon brought its harvest."

The Sikh Movement took a new turn after the martyrdom of Guru Tegh Bahadur. Guru Gobind was convinced that the Mughal rulers were not moved by the supreme sacrifice of Guru Arjan and Guru Tegh Bahadur. The Hindus for whom the Guru laid down his life, continued to be persecuted ruthlessly. Gobind Rai wanted to prepare his followers to fight against the tyrannical rulers. He took up arms and made up his mind to meet force by force. He proved that the sword when taken up for a right cause has a different strength and splendour and cuts through the forces of tyranny and injustice.

Guru Gobind instilled into his devotees a strong determination to fight aggression and tyranny and to root out evils, both political and social, wherever they existed. The Guru's fight for the cause of 'Dharma' or righteousness is also stated in the *Bachitar Natak:*

> The divine Guru sent me for religious sake; I come into the world charged with the duty to uphold the right in every place and to destroy the wicked and the evil, that the good may live and tyranny be torn out by their roots.

Some of the historians believe that the main cause of the creation of the Khalsa by Guru Gobind was 'the avenging policy to Islám.' For instance, Cunningham writes, "The violent end and the last injuction of the martyr Guru made a deep impression on the mind of Gobind,... he became the irreconcilable foe of the Muhammadan name, and conceived the noble idea of moulding the vanquished Hindus into a new and aspiring people. G.C. Narang too has recorded the similar opinion when he writes, "Gobind himself, in fact, as well as his work, was the natural product of the process of evolution that had been going on even since the inception of Sikh brotherhood. The seed blossomed in the time of Guru Gobind Sing had been sown by Guru Nanak and watered by his successors. The sword which carved the Khalsa's way to glory was, undoubtedly, forged by Gobind, but the steel had been provided by Nanak." Thus, the creation of Khalsa was the need of the time. Guru Gobind Singh created Khalsa for the protection of Dharma i.e. righteousness. He realised that for this pious task he must prepare with the strong determination.

The Guru had also determined to abolish the caste system and untouchability so that these evils should not be made a arm of disunion amongst his 'Khalsa brotherhood' and thus he stressed on the disciplined life for his followers. The Guru went further than that. He taught by practical examples. When a low caste, known as Bhai Jaita, brought the head of Guru Tegh Bahadur from Delhi, he embraced him affectionately and said, "Ranghreta Guru Ka beta" i.e., Rangretas are the Guru's own sons.

The tenth Guru ordered that all Khalsas must drink Amrit out of the same vessel at the time of their baptism. The destruction of caste in the matter of inter-dining was a hallmark for the unity and integration of the devotees. In this way caste-pride was totally eradicated.

The Hindu masses were bitter against the galling yoke of Mughal tyranny. But the Hindus of position and rank, were most efficiously loyal to the government. They were feared that any activity which show sympathy with these movements would displease their Muslim masters and deprive them of their office, land and power. G.C. Narang writes that the Hindus at this time were too mild by nature, too contented in their desires, modest in their aspirations, too aversed to physical exertion and terror-stricken and demoralised, even though strongly attached to their religion. He further says that the Hindus had religion, but not national feelings, whereas Guru Gobind Singh sought to make nationalism their religion.

Both Rajputs and Kashatrias alone as a class followed the function of arms. This distinction had made the Hindus very weak because only some selected people could turn out as affective in the time of need. The Guru now ordered that every Khalsa must be trained in arms. He thus, made all the four Varnas and even the untouchables to share in the pride of the defence of their Dharma and Country and thus increased the number of effectives in the small community that had gathered around him.

In fact, Guru Gobind was determined to fight tyranny with arms and with the cooperation of Hill Chiefs. However, the Hill Chiefs betrayed. It is already stated that a severe and bloody battle was fought between the Hill Rajas and the Guru at Bhangani in October 1698. It was the first decisive battle and a battle for self-defence. It set the ball rolling towards a major clash. Not only this, the battle gave the Guru and opportunity to understand the real character of his people. It is said that "it was Gobind's first baptism of steel." After that the Guru utilised the period of peace for making preparations for the ensuing struggle. The relations between the Guru and the Hill Chiefs again become cordial for a moment. Since Aurangzeb was busy in the south, therefore, the Hill Rajas (Hill Chiefs) did not want to pay the tribute of Mughal Government and sought the help of Guru Gobind. Both the Hill Rajas and the Guru were jointly fought against the Mughals in the battle of Nadaun, but the selfish Rajas deserted the Guru after the battle of Nadaun. They made an agreement with the Mughals against the Guru. In other words, again, the relations were strained between the Hill Rajas and the Guru.

The differences between the Guru and the Hill Rajas remained unsolved and the Hill Rajas were compelled to think for the assistance of the Mughals. Now, the Guru found himself completely isolated. The forbearance of the Shahzada, no doubt, gave him a temporary respite but the storm might burst at any moment and the guru had now none to depend on but himself and his followers. In the words of I.B. Banerjee He, therefore, immediately busised himself in putting his house in order and in bringing about a transformation in the ideology of his followers. They were to be fitted to meet the situation with their own unaided strength and the steps that the Guru took to achieve this end brought the Khalsa into existence.

Harbans Singh writes, "A preparatory measure he undertook was the reformation of the Sikh ecclesiastical organisation." The Masands, who at one time were the representative agents of the Guru with something of his delegated authority, were an important link between the Guru and a large number of the Sikhs. The Masands formed the pivot of the organisation that Guru Arjan had created. The institution flourished rapidly under Guru Arjan, who patronized them for the sake of spreading the true religion. However, during the days of Guru Hargobind some problems were created by the Masands. But Guru by his force strength, and imagination put a curb on their activities and they could not act according to their own wish. Though the Masands system had been developing on wrong lines and difficulties had been felt even by Guru Hargobind, but the worst feature of the system appeared after Guru Har Rai's death. The Masands appear to have lost Guru Gobind's confidence. Guru Gobind's condemnation of the Masands is well known. Now the Guru had determined to free the Sikhs from their clutches. The Masands had become neglectful of their religious affairs and were corrupt and oppressive.

Thus, the Guru had no alternative but to finish this evil's root and branch. This is evident also from two of Guru Gobind's thirty three Sawwaiyas:

> If any one serve the Masads, they will say,
> 'Fetch and give us all thine offering.
>
> Go at once and make a present to us of
> whatever property is in thy house.
>
> Think on us night and day, and mention not others
> even by mistake.
>
> If they hear of any one giving, they run to
> him even at night, they are not at all
> pleased at not receiving.

The Sikh traditions have confirmed that the removal of the Masands was one of the primary objectives of Guru Gobind. The Guru summoned the Masands to come to Anandpur and divested them of their positions. Some of them who had serious charges of misconduct and had no answer to give were punished and a few who were good and honest were honoured by him. In this way the Guru abolished the Masand system and saved his sikhs from their oppression. He ordered that all the Sikhs thenceforth should bring their offerings direct to the Guru, wherever possible.

The Guru decided to put his predetermined plan into operation in 1699 and that too in a systematic manner. For this mission he selected the Baisakhi day on which many Sikhs as well as the Masands used to visit the Guru; and this year they were specially asked to come. "Guru Gobind Singh had ordered special preparations to be made for the festival of Baisakhi in 1699, messages were issued to the Sikhs throughout the country to come to Anandpur in large number, wearing arms and maintaining their beards and hair inviolate. Elaborate arrangements were made at Anandpur for the reception of the pilgrims.

Panj Piyare

As Baisakhi approached, the people began to arrive at Anandpur from every part of the country. The Sikh chroniclers have recorded that twenty thousand person gathered for the occasion. On the first day of Baisakh, Sambat 1756 (30 March, 1699) Guru Gobind, as usual, awoke early and sat in meditation. A large number of devotees had already assembled at Anandpur. A large and beautiful tent was set up. After the daily religious formalities were over the Guru went inside the tent for a while and remained inside for sometime. Suddenly he came out and with his glittering eyes, his naked sword shinking in his uplifted arm, and his whole body transformed like that of warrior and in a voice as that of thunder, said, "My sword wants today a head. Let any one of my true Sikhs come forward. Isn't there a Sikh of mine who would sacrifice his life for his Guru?" When the Guru found no response to his first call, he called forth second time but again there was no response. And for the third time he asked for any one who would lay down his life at a call by him. At last Daya Ram, a Khatri of Lahore, stood up and said with humility, "My head is at thy disposal, my True lord. There could be no greater gain than dying under thy sword." He walked behind the Guru to a tent nearby. The Guru came out of the tent with his sword dripping blood and demanded another head. Now the confusion turned into fear. People started leaving the place. But Dharm Das, a Jat of Delhi, now arose and offered his head, on the second call. Guru Gobind made three more calls. Mohkam Chand, a washerman of Dwarka, Himmat Rai, a weaver of Jagannath, and a Sahib Chand a barber of Bidar cheerfully responded one after another and advanced to offer their heads.

After a while, when the Guru came out of the tent, his sword was sheathed, his face was seaming with joy and satisfaction. "In that tent, erected on a hillock and confidentially guarded, he had kept dresses especially made for the occasion. Decked in saffron rainment topped over with neatly tied turbans of the same colour, the glorious five walked deferentially behind their master, overwhelmed with thankfulness. The Master was himself attired in the same manner as his chosen disciples." It was a great surprise for all present there, the five Sikhs, who were taken inside the tent, were brought out. The assembly was further puzzled to see those whom they had thought to have been sacrificed to the Guru's whim return in flesh and blood. To these five now the Guru bestowed the name of Panj Piyare or "Five beloved" — as they came to becalled.

After a while, the Guru proceed to hold the ceremony of baptism. The method of initiation in the past has been for the disciple to drink the water which the Guru had touched with his toe. It was believed that this method of initiation developed humility and politeness in the Sikhs. He, thus introduced absolutely a new method of initiation. "So far Charanpahul, I shall substitute Kahande Ka Amrit, the system of baptism by water which has been stirred with the two-edged sword." According to Harbans Singh, "Filling an iron bowl with clean water, he kept churning it with a two-edged sword while reciting over it the sacred verses. Mata Jitoji came with sugar crystals which were put into the vessel at the Guru's bidding. Sweetness was thus mingled with the alchemy of iron. The Amrit, or nector Immorality, was now ready."

The five beloved, fully deressed and accounted, stood up before the Guru. They were asked to repeat 'Wahguru' and the preamble of the Japji. The Guru then gave them five palmfuls of the Amrit (Nectar) to drink. He sprinkled it five times on their hair and their eyes, and caused them to all to repeat 'Wahguru ji ka khalsa, Wahaguru ji ki Fateh' (hail to the Khalsa who belongs to the Lord: Hail to the Lord to whom belongs the victory::). On this were given the surname of 'Singh,' meaning lion and were to wear the following five embles whose name began with 'K,' namely—Kesh, long hair and beard; Kangha, a comb; Kara, a steel bracelet; Kachha, short drawer; Kirpan, a sword. "They were enjoined to practise arms, and not show their backs to the foe in battle. They were ever to help the poor and protect those who shought their protection. They must not look with lust on another's wife or commit fornication, but adhere to their wedded spouses. They were to consider their previous castes erased, and deem themselves all brothers of one family."

The Guru addressed to them: "you are the sons of Guru Nanak, the Creator's own, the chosen ones, I name ye the Khalsa, Ye are the disciples of the word and ye shall be the saviours of man. Ye shall own no property and ye shall love man as man, making no distinction of caste or creed, ye shall keep forever this flame of life lit in you, unflickering, in deep meditation on the one Timeless Being. Ye shall bow your heads to your Master only. Ye shall never workeship stock, stone, idol or tomb. Remember always in times of danger of difficulty the holy names of the masters, Nanak, Angad, Amar Das, Ram Das, Arjan Dev, Hargobind Sahib, Har Rai Sahib, Har Krishan, Tegh Bahadur. I make ye a rosary of these names; and ye shall not pray each for himself, but all for the whole Khalsa. In each of you the whole brotherhood shall be incarnated. Ye are my sons, both in fless and spirit.

The Guru asked his five faithful Sikhs to prepare the Amrit as he had done. When it was ready, he stood before them with clasped hands, and besought them to baptise him into their brotherhood. The Khalsa is the Guru and the Guru is the Khalsa. You and I are one forever. He created the Khalsa in his own image. Then the Guru received Amrit from the five Beloved in the same manner as they had received it from him. Like the names of his five Beloved, too, was made to end in Singh or Lion. It was changed from Gobind Rai to Gobind Singh. The Guru invited others to receive baptism. Upon this many others prepared to receive baptism. In a very little time many thousands were baptised. Through his chastening baptism at Anandpur on the Baisakhi of 1699, the nucleus of Guru Gobind Singh's Khalsa had come into existence.

The word 'Khalsa' has been taken from Arabic 'Khalish' which means pious, sacred, pure and noble. But Guru has used it especially in a symbolic and technical sense. The creation of the Khalsa was aimed at making a union (group) of such persons who follow a life of stoice (saints) according to Sikh ideals, who are selfless servants of this wordly life, who are the saviours of the innocent people, helpful and encouraging to people. With the help of it they may be able to release people from sorrows and woes, to set right the guilty so that people may lead a life of peace and comfort. "Ideologically, the creation of the Khalsa aimed at a well-balanced combination of the ideals of Bhakti and Sakti, of moral and spiritual excellence and militant valour or heroism of the highest order." McLeod also writes, "The Khalsa is best described as an order, as a society possessing a religious foundation and military discipline."

By creating Khalsa, the Guru struck at the root of all sorts of prejudices which had crept into the society. The creation of the Khalsa brought a remarkable transformation of Sikh society. All men, according to him, were equal. He said that all men are alike, it is the One God who creates them all. Only good actions elevate human beings and distinguish them from one another. The Guru said, "let all embrace one creed and obliterate differences of religion. Let the four Hindu castes who have different rules for their guidance abandon them all, adopt the one form of adoration and become brothers. Let no one deem himself superior to another. Let men of four castes receive my baptism, eat out one one's dish, and feel no disgust or contempt for one another.

Guru Gobind Singh, through his baptism, poured his life into his Sikhs, and invested them with his own personality. It is said that the Guru imported a stern olympain air to his followers. His mission was not only to elevate and alter the constitution of the devotees' minds contrary to the experience of ethological experts, but also operated materially and gave amplitude to their physical frames. They came to be regarded as models of physical beauty and statelines of manners. A tremendous change was effected in the whole tone of national character. Even those people who had been considered as dregs of humanity were changed, as if by magic into something rich and strange. The sweepers, barbers and confectioners, who had never touched the sword and whose whole generations had lived as gravelling slaves of the so called higher classes, became under the stimulating leadership of Guru Gobind Singh, doughty warriors, who never shrank from fear and who were ready to rush into the jaws of death at the bidding of their Guru.

2

Guru Gobind Singh As A Great Warrior

I

Guru Gobind Singh has been described by Bhai Nand Lal, a poet and the devout votary of the Guru in these memorable words:

> "The victor and the vanquished Guru Gobind Singh;
> Beloved of the Almighty Guru Gobind Singh;
> Righteous in thought Guru Gobind Singh;
> King and Saint Guru Gobind Singh;
> Inspirer of action Guru Gobind Singh;
> Friend of the oppressed Guru Gobind Singh."

This is the most befitting tribute paid to the Guru—the lord of the white hawk who sacrificed his everything to free India from the stranglehold of centuries old slavery and to restore human dignity to those who had lost all moral and ethical values associated with free people. He was the heroic champion of the oppressed and the down-trodden and the valiant defender of the rights and dignity of man.

The Guru was not only a spiritual luminary but also a great leader of men. A dauntless warrior, he wielded the pen with equal ease as the sword. He combined in his person daring qualities and rare administrative ability. A great organiser. He brought new awakening to a society demoralised and crushed under a tyrannic rule.

Guru Gobind Singh infused a new life, a new vigour, a new energy, a new zeal, a new resolve into the hearts of the people who had been humiliated and degraded and had lost all hope of freeing themselves from the perpetual slavery. The Mughal rulers had not only crushed them physically but had also suppressed their souls. The country was in a state of deep frustration and the people saw no ray of hope. Guru Gobind Singh provided them with a silver lining and opened a new era in the annals of Indian history. He created a new nation and a new order. He was the pioneer of a marvellous political force in the country and made history by organising hitherto meek people into a militant group. A warrior class was created in order that the people may be able to stand up and fight vigorously the oppressiveness of the then rulers of the country. Prior to this, the Saints and other religious leaders had not come into conflict with the authorities. They simply operated on the social and religious plane. Guru Gobind Singh realised that without resort to sword at that critical juncture in the history of India, the country could not be saved from utter humiliation. He took to sword out of sheer necessity at a time when all other means had failed for saving the honour of the nation. It will not be for us to forget that, whatever else he might have been, Guru Gobind Singh was first and foremost a great religious leader. None but a person of saintly disposition, highly spiritual and with complete resignation to the will of God, could have behaved as he did during the most acute crisis of his life. Leaving his home and everything in the hands of the enemy he bids farewell to Anandpur, and with his ranks depleted and his family dispersed, his wife going in one direction and his mother with his two younger sons he knew not where, he arrives at Chamkaur and is at once surrounded by the Mughals and the Hill chiefs.

After a super human fight against the heaviest of odds, in which he saw his two dearest sons and his chosen companions fall one after another before his very eyes. He reluctantly left the battle scene. He was haunted and had very narrow escapes. But he kept up his courage. Even when he received the news of the barbarous and brutal murder of his two younger sons and the tragic death of his mother, he remained cheerful and calm. He faced all this with the most supreme composure and went on with his work as if nothing had happened. He compiled a new recension of *Sri Guru Granth Sahib*, added to it Guru Tegh Bahadur's compositions and his own *sloka* and laid strong foundations of Sikhism. Certainly, no mere politician or soldier could have done it.

Guru Gobind Singh's whole life and work are one marathon denial of the promise that ill-will always follows all conflicts. For, in his killing, there was never an element of malevolenie. To him, war was a surgical operation to rid humanity of cancerous growths in its body politic. Only destiny had cast on him the mantle of a fighter. He had to kill his enemies without wanting to kill them. Even on the battlefield he was never the aggressor. It was only after he was attacked that he defended himself and ultimately silenced the enemy everytime.

He was brave and fearless as a lion. He undertook to make sparrows pluck the Imperial falcons; and he succeeded in that ardous task. No odds, however heavy, damped his valour and resolve. No personal danger made him shirk his duty. Wounds only stirred him to greater exertion. He was an able general and an efficient organiser. People, the very dregs of society, who had never handled a weapon for ages, were transmuted by him into the sturdiest soldiers that the world has ever seen under his influence. Men, who had never touched a sword or shouldered a gun became heroes. Confectioners and washermen and barbers became leaders of armies before whom the Rajas quailed and the Nawabs trembled with terror.

From his very childhood, the Guru started procuring all sorts of arms and weapons and practised their use. He exhorted his followers also to perfect themselves in the use of arms. The news of Guru's liking for the arms spread like wild fire to even far off places and people with martial leanings and whose forefathers had fought in the army of Guru Hargobind flocked around him. Guru's *darbar* at Anandpur looked like a war camp. People in beautiful uniforms chaired the Guru on their shoulders. The Guru issued orders to his people to present him with arms and ammunition. He was delighted whenever someone presented him with a special type of a gun or sword. His army gradually grew in size and strength and in course of time it became a fully trained and well equipped force, ready to fight aggression from whatever quarters it came and to face any eventuality. A new spirit was infused in the hearts of the people to fight for truth and justice. Guru's orders were fully obeyed and the people who were in possession of good type of arms presented them to the Guru willingly. However, from the course of events that followed, it was proved that these were not the preparations to attack anybody or to snatch away any one's rights but for defence and protection of the honour of the oppressed people who had suffered a great humiliation in the execution of Guru Tegh Bahadur. People with patriotic fervour and earnest zeal flocked around him and were ready to sacrifice their all at the call of their master.

While still young, the Guru got designed a new war drum called *Ranjit Nagara*. It was a kind of a big drum usually carried by the soldiers while attacking the enemy. It surprised many. The Guru felt that no war equipment could be complete without the big drum. Diwan Nand Chand, the Guru's Minister, got it made taking special care that Guru's directions were carried out. It was the time when only Kings and Rajas had the right to have the big drum rolled in their territories. It was a sign of independence and sovereignty and amounted to a challenge or revolt. Although it was apprehended that the beating of the drum would be objected to by the Hill Rajas, the Guru did not care at all.

Thus, visualising the entire situation, the Guru effectively aroused the dormant energies of a vanquished people and inspired them with lofty ideals for social freedom and national ascendancy. He created an autonomous state at Anandpur and exhorted his followers to lead an independent life in a free atmosphere. His people did not recognise the authority of the Mughal rulers. Authority of the Muslim administration was openly flouted. Justifying the use of force by Guru Gobind Singh, the late Dr. Radhakrishnan, our Philosopher-President once said: "Our country has taken pride in spiritual values but if by spiritual tradition we are unable to resist evil, we have to use military might. In using military might we are not doing anything which is unscrupulous and untraditional. It is something which has been enjoined on us by our own scriptures. Nothing in this world was achieved without suffering and sacrifices."

Guru Gobind Singh pronounced this political theory by creating military might and using armed force against the prevailing tyranny. Prior to the time of the Sikh Gurus, no General ever conceived the idea of raising an army from men who were believed to be unclean and polluted from their birth. The stimulating precept of the Tenth Guru altered what had hitherto been deemed the dregs of humanity into warriors whose promise and loyalty never failed their leaders.

We, as students of history know fully well that right from the invasion of Alexander the Great, we were never able to put up any national resistance worth the name to foreign invasion and exploits of Ghaznavis and Ghori and other Muslim invaders. Aryavarta was subject to a series of invasions and foreign rule for a thousand years. And India produced no hero to resist them, much less to beat back their invasions. For full 700 years, waves after waves of Muslim invaders swept this land and inflicted untold misery, humiliation and even death. It was Guru Gobind Singh who stemmed this course. It was he who was instrumental in ending the mighty Mughal rule in India. He applied a sharp axe on the foundations of this rule and demolished it.

Bravery, heroism and valour of Guru Gobind Singh was unparalleled in the history of the world. Even at a very early age, his duals with roaring lions are unsurpassed. It is said that one day he came to know that a white lion was causing havoc among the hill people of the surrounding areas of Paonta where he was camping. The Guru desired to shoot the lion and in the company of the Raja of Nahan, he proceeded to his lair. A fierce animal, the King of the Jungle, roared at the sight of the Guru. No one else dared advance even an inch. The roars of the lion struck terror in everybody present. But the Guru, undaunted, got down from his horse, took his long sword and shield, and proceeded towards the mighty beast and challenged him to come out of its den. The lion became furious, sprang forward and attacked the Guru. The Guru put forth his shield and checked the attack. While the Guru held the lion by his left hand, he cut him into pieces with his sword in his right hand.

The lion's roars died down and everybody heaved a sigh of relief. The entire episode was over just in the twinkling of an eye. All those present were amazed at the extraordinary prowess of the great Guru. To kill a terrible beast was not an ordinary affair.

The Guru had given a practical proof of what he preached. "Only then I will call myself Guru Gobind Singh, if my one soldier fights against a lakh and quarter soldiers in the battle. When the Guru was compelled by circumstances to leave Anandpur, there was not a sign of grief or sorrow on his face. He remained composed, serene, undaunted and unshaken. On reaching the banks of the Sarsa river, the Guru and his band of few devoted Sikhs proceeded towards Chamkaur. Mata Gujari and his two younger sons lost their way and went towards Morinda side with the Gangu *Brahmin*, the family cook. Only his elder sons, Prince Ajit Singh and Juzhar Singh, were with the Guru. Guru's wives, Sundari and Sahib Kaur, had to go to Delhi under the escort of Bhai Mani Singh.

On reaching Chamkaur, the Guru and his party took possession of a mud house and converted it into a miniature fort. It was just an ordinary building with an upper storey in the form of an attic. The Guru fortified it with the help of his Sikhs, using the outer walls of the house as the main defence line. The Guru had only a few weapons of war with him and the stock of food supplies was also nominal. What was the Guru to fight with? Only his dauntless courage and devotion to a cause, sustained him. It is a unique saga of heroism in the annals of the world. The Guru's example of unmatched endurance will serve as a guiding torch for generations to come. Heroic deeds of many renowned world heroes pale into insignificance before the bravery and valour of the great Guru. It is a lesson for posterity to follow; it will serve for ever as an inspiration to the people fighting for independence.

The Mughal troops hot in pursuit of the Guru reached Chamkaur in no time. The Imperial forces came like swarms of locusts. They were bent upon liquidating the Guru. The Guru, however, did not lose any time. He posted eight of his saint-soldiers to guard each side of the house. The Guru, with his sons, covered the top storey. The historic battle began. For the whole night the Sikhs stood vigilant, as if guarding their destiny. Early next morning even before the sun had beamed its shining rays on the universe, the Imperial forces went into action. The house was stormed from all sides. Stiff resistance was offered by the brave Sikhs. It was a unique scene. Each saint-soldier fought heroically and played his part extremely well under the generalship of the Guru. It was a fight against unprecedentedly heavy odds: a few Sikhs fighting against a mighty army well-equipped and trained. The Guru tells us thus in *Zafarnama*, "What could forty hungry people do against one million who pounced on them by surprise." The Guru's gold-tipped arrows pierced the bodies of the Mughal soldiers. It was a dreadful scene. The situation deteriorated minute by minute, second by second. But the Guru was not perturbed. He stood like a rock; determined, unbent, with full faith in the will of Almighty. The Sikhs at the moment were playing a multiple role—proving their faith in their Guru; in defence of their religion and against tyranny. In due course both elder sons of the Guru, Prince Ajit Singh and Juzhar Singh, laid down their lives for preserving the honour of their country before the very eyes of their father. The Guru, notwithstanding that he had lost two sons, many of his faithful and loyal soldiers, was filled with even greater vigour and zest. His arrows were still piercing the bodies of the enemy soldiers. The bullets from the ramparts of the fortress were still raining death. This continued for some time. Enemy reinforcements in thousands arrived on the spot. The fortress was surrounded from all sides. However, the moral victory was the Guru's.

Guru Gobind Singh's feats of valour and bravery in the battle of Chamkaur were unparalleled in the history of the world. He remained in high spirits throughout and in spite of agony and distress, his patriotic fervour and resolve for serving the nation did not flicker for a moment. His mind did not waver at all.

Then again in the battle of Mukatsar also, the Guru's courage and determination was unique. The Guru from the top of the mound showered arrows on the enemy. Muslim soldiers made bitter attacks and tried their best to dislodge the Sikhs from their vantage position, but all in vain. The Sikhs engaged the Mughal hordes so recklessly that everyone of them, including the courageous heroine, Mai Bhago, fell fighting for a noble cause. A fierce battle followed. It was the bloodiest of the battles ever fought.

However, in spite of several acts of bravery to his credit, the Guru should not be compared with any of the army generals of the world, for this comparison is not correct. The Guru never wanted wars, but they were thrust upon him everytime. He fought battles but did not occupy an inch of anybody's territory. After the battles he forgave people and behaved as if nothing had happened. Kings and generals of the world fought to enlarge their territories, collect booty and to plunder others' property. Attacks were made on the weaker nations simply to grab wealth and annex their territories. People were killed on the battlefields like ants and yet their hearts did not move. They bothered very little for the suffering humanity. Before their very eyes, women in thousands were widowed; property worth lakhs was burnt, innocent children were orphaned. But, on the other hand, Guru Gobind Singh was a warrior with a difference. He fought battles in a different way. After the battle of Muktsar, he went straight into the battle-field and moved about lifting the heads of the dead and putting them into his lap, wiping their faces with a piece of cloth, one by one. It was a heart-rending sight. The Guru's Sikh Bhai Kanahiya, served water to the wounded Hindus and Muslims in the battle of Anandpur. He did not observe any distinction between a friend and a foe.

The Guru was not a political aspirant but toiled throughout only for uplifting the down-trodden. No comparison can be made between him and Napoleon or Charles XII of Sweden. They plundered the world at large but the Guru saved humanity from being looted. Nepoleon was a great soldier, a great military general but the Guru was a warrior-saint. Napoleon dashed across the deserts, flung his armies at the enemy and infused millions with the electric fore of revolution, became the master of Europe at the tender age of 32. But what was the cost. He plundered wealth and crushed under his feet several peace loving nations of Europe. He played with the peace of the world. He became so dreadful that Princess Mary of Austria refused to marry him and prepared for death. She never loved him. People called Napoleon 'The Great Unloved.' He was simply drunk with power. The Guru was 'The Great Beloved.' He had all the humility and mercy in him.

Guru Gobind Singh desired to serve his people and prepare them to fight against tyranny. He was such an adept soldier and a strategic general that his arrows caused havoc in the enemy ranks. He produced an admirable army which faced the relentless war of extermination from its inception and carried the torch of resistance and revolution. Mankind owes him a debt of gratitude which cannot be expressed in words but only in sentiments. He brought into being a new people and released new dynamic forces into the arena of Indian history. He transformed the depressed and the downtrodden into mighty leaders of men. He was far ahead and much in advance of his times. And for the confidence he inspired, the zeal that he infused, and the impulses that he gave, his name shines like aluminous star in the history of mankind.

It was, indeed, a great miracle which Guru Gobind Singh had wrought in turning a mass of heterogeneous, weak and divided people into a single united community of saint-soldiers, brave, fearless and devout, always ready to go to the end of any helpless victim of tyranny and ruthless oppression.

Guru Gobind Singh, in the words of Indubhushan Banerjee, was a "great soldier and a great general." This would perhaps be denied by none who is even cursorily acquainted with the story of his military adventures. In the *Bachitar Natak* the Guru is rather modest with regard to his own performance and instead attributes his successes to the will of the Almighty; but from what little he says it is not difficult to see what an accomplished archer he was and how unperturbed and dauntless he could be even in the midst of raining death. In forming an estimate of the military abilities of Guru Gobind Singh it must not be forgotten for a moment that there was a tremendous disparity in numbers and resources between himself and his enemies and the amazing thing is not that he lost but he could fight so long. The defence that he extemporised at Chamkaur, where, as tradition affirms, the Guru with only forty chosen companions, kept at bay for several hours a whole host of the opposing troops has hardly a parallel, and the keen and discerning eye with which he chose the spot where the battle of Khidrana was fought and the army of Wazir Khan was compelled to retire, leaves us in no doubt as to his tactical genius. As Cunningham says "Success is not always the measure of greatness" and this dictum should be kept in view in judging the achievements of Guru Gobind Singh.

In short, we can say that the Guru fought battles for the sake of saving *Dharma*. He prayed to Almighty:

"O, the Great Lord, grant me this boon only;
That from noble deeds I may never turn away.
I may fear not him, whom I face in fight;
Certain be my victory.

And this be the instruction to my mind
My greed be to sing Thy praises,
When the period of my life draws to a close,
I may fight my foes valiantly,
And die a heroic death."

—Epilogue to *Chandi Charitar I.*

Thus, Guru Gobind Singh being a spiritual leader and without possessing a regular army, war equipment, sufficient funds, defended himself like a skilful general against the mighty Mughal army. Under his inspiration, men who were even afraid of the very name of the sword or hwo had never fired a gun became warriors and inflicted crushing defeats on the enemy. The Guru in his life-time never killed his adversaries by any surprise attack, nor did he ever shoot at those on the battle-field who were taking rest and were not actually engaged in fighting. In the battle-field he maintained a code of conduct for himself and his soldiers. He roused in the people a feeling of nationalism, and infused in them a spirit which would not let them bow before aggression and persecution and he taught them how to die for the sake of their Motherland. He had a great faith in his people—his disciples whom he loved the most. He said:

"All the battles I have won against tyranny,
I have fought with the devoted backing of these people,
Through them only have I been able to bestow gifts
Through their help I have escaped harm,
The love and generosity of the Sikhs
Have enriched my heart and home.
Through their grace I have attained all learning;
Though their help in battle, I have slain my enemies.
I was born to serve them, through them I reached eminence.
What would I have been without their kind and ready help?
There are millions of insignificant people like me.
True service is the service of these people;
I am not inclined to serve others of higher castes
Charity will bear fruit in this and the next world,
If given to such worthy people as those.
All other sacrifices and charity is profitless.
From head to foot, whatever I call my own
All I possess or carry, dedicate to these people."

It was Guru's true democratic spirit which sustained him through all his trials and tribulations. He gave to the world democratic traditions and nationalistic fervour, three hundred years back when these concepts were unknown to mankind.

II

Guru Gobind Singh occupies the pride of place in the galaxy of the great revolutionaries of the world. He performed several revolutionary acts in a short span of 42 years of his life. The greatest of them was the creation of *Khalsa* in order to check the onslaught of the religious fanaticism perpetrated by the Mughal rulers. He infused the spirit of patriotism and fearlessness in the people. The Guru had firm faith that all mankind was created by the Almighty and he preached the ideals of equality, service and sacrifice for the uplift of suffering and down-trodden humanity. It was nothing short of a miracle which the guru performed by turning a mass of heterogeneous, weak and divided people into a single united community of saint-soldiers, who became fearless, brave, ever eager to render all possible assistance to the helpless victims of tyranny and oppression. The soldier-saints of Guru Gobind Singh were devoted, sincere and virtuous, deeply steeped in religious fervour and earnest desire to pursue the teachings of their Master. They coveted nothing and were always prepared to lay down their lives for the honour of the Motherland.

Guru Gobind Singh has carved for himself a unique place, in many respects, in the history of the world. History has no parallel where any child of nine might have advised his father to sacrifice his life to save the religion and honour of the country. It was deep-rooted patriotism which made him make this novel suggestion. Again, who else would have directed his two minor sons to proceed to the battle-field against heavy insurmountable odds, when death was absolutely certain. It was only Guru Gobind Singh who remained composed and unbent when the news of his two younger sons having been entombed alive was conveyed to him. Who else could sacrifice his mother, wife, sons, every other relation, including his maternal uncles, at the altar of the Motherland. History would have been quite different had Guru Gobind Singh not appeared on the scene at the time he did. He changed the course of history and added glorious chapters with his blood and sweat. 'It is yet to be thought, offered and explained as to what would have been the history of India if the *Khalsa* had not given a death blow to the Mughal ruler.' But Guru Gobind Singh accomplished a great miracle and a rare wonder.

The Guru, by his personal example of service and sacrifice raised the spirit of his people and infused a new life in them. He inspired them to fight for their rights to preserve the freedom of conscience and religious worship. He founded the *Khalsa* on the principles of equality, fraternity, justice, fairplay, self-sacrifice, and service of the oppressed and downtrodden people of this land.

The revolutionary step taken by the Guru was unique. But, in fact, the whole Sikh movement was revolutionary in character. Guru Nanak, the founder of Sikhism, revolutionised the whole Bhakti movement and took bold steps to root out the degradation into which the entire society had sunk. Before Guru Nanak, some other Hindu reformers had also tried to improve the manner of worshipping. Thus, "in the beginning of the sixteenth century, the Hind mind was no longer stagnant or retrogressive, it had been leavened with Mohammedanism and changed and quickened for a new development. Ramanand and Gorakh had preached religious equality, and Chaitan had repeated that faith levelled caste. Kabir had denounced images and appealed to the people in their own tongue and Vallabh had taught that effectual devotion was compatible with the ordinary duties of the world. But these good and able men appear to have been so impressed with the nothingness of this life, that they deemed the amelioration of man's social condition unworthy of thought. They aimed chiefly at emancipation from priestcraft, or from the grossness of idolatory and polytheism. They formed pious associations of contented quietists, or they gave themselves upto the contemplation of futurity in the hope of approaching bliss, rather than called upon their fellow creatures to throw aside every social as well as religious trammel, and to arise a new people freed from the debasing corruption of ages. They perfected forms of dissent rather than planted the germs of nations and their sects remain to this day as they left them."

It is beyond any doubt that these reform movements which appeared on the scene before Guru Nanak, were sectarian in character and in many cases only served to make confusion worse confounded.

When Guru Nanak was born in 1469, conditions in the country were awful. People were so mercilessly trampled during the frequent raids of Muslim invaders that they had become completely demoralised and utterly helpless. "The springs of true religion had been choked up by weeds of unmeaning ceremonial, debasing superstitions, the selfishness of the priests and the indifference of the people. Form had supplanted the reality and the highly spiritual character of Hinduism had been buried under the ostentatious paraphernalia of sects. The centuries of invasion, foreign misrule and persecution had produced the greatest depression and spiritual subjection and stagnation had aggravated the demoralisation to an enormous degree."

The Hindu society had been degraded so much that women and children were driven like cattle to Ghazni, before the very eyes of their people, who stood silent spectators. Indian women were sold in the bazars of Gazni like cattle but nobody ever dared raise a finger to save them from humiliation. People had hopelessly succumbed to disgrace and degradation.

This was the pitiable condition of Indian society when Guru Nanak was born. Even when he was quite young, his indignation was aroused at what he beheld and he made up his mind to devote his life to the service of the nation. His heart bled when he was with his own eyes, how thousands of men, women and children were massacred in one of the Mughal raids. His heart was filled with auguish which reflected itself in a verse, Nanak composed. It showed the deep effect the spectacle had made on his mind. He said:

O, God: when there was so much slaughter and groaning,
didst Thou not feel any pain ?
O, Creator, Thou belongest to one and all.
If strong person harms an equally strong man,
there is no cause for grief;
But when a ravenous lion attacks a herd of cows,
the master of the herd must become courageous."

Guru Nanak preached the oneness of God. He declared "that God alone was to be worshipped and that he was not to be degraded by making any images of Him and worshipping those images. He was to be worshipped in the spirit, by constantly meditating over His name, and feeling and realizing His presence in every place and at every time."

The Guru made a significant utterance that 'there is no Hindu, no Musalman.' He laid emphasis on treating all men as equal since God's light is contained in the heart of each. He said:

'Castes are folly, names are folly;
All creatures have one shelter, that of God.'

He preached the gospel of universal brotherhood. He gave a message of truth and peace. It was reserved for Nanak to perceive the true principles of reform and to lay those broad foundations which enabled his successor Gobind to fire the minds of his countrymen with a new nationality and to give practical effect to the doctrine that the lowest is equal with the highest in race and in creed in political rights as in religious hopes.

Guru Nanak preached not only the oneness of man but also equal status for Women. women were not only inferior to men but they had equal responsibility for their action before God.

"He made a powerful attack on the sacerdotal classes of both communities and declared that all people were equal in the eyes of God, who, he said was the common Father of all. Men are brothers, he said, and must live as brothers, guiding their actions by justice and love."

To raise a voice against the caste system was great revolutionary step. The Guru in spite of the opposition from the high class people preached the oneness of man. Nobody was born high or low, it was only through good or bad deeds that man was recognised, was his dictum.

The successors of Guru Nanak implemented his mission both in letter and spirit as best as they could. Sikhism had become a sect of peace-loving disciples, and it retained its original character until the mantle fell on the shoulders of Guru Gobind Singh. He transformed this sect of peaceful devotees into a band of warriors. It is said that Guru Nanak was so much affected by the sight of suffering that he fell down in anguish and went into a trance. What would he not have done, this master of herd, had he been in the position of Guru Gobind Singh? He could then only utter a cry and wish that the cows should become lions, but what would he not have down, if he had a nation at his back? Alas, he had no nation at his back. He and his successors had yet to create it. Still he did not sit down in rage and utter idle Jeremiads. He did as much as was possible to do in the circumstances.

Guru Gobind Singh realised that his followers should shake off the dreamy ways of Saints and turn into active soldiers to put down evil forces which were playing havoc with the lives and the sentiments of the people. To face the prevailing situation, they must all be transformed into a class of brave, fearless and selfless people who would feel the sorrows and miseries of the downtrodden people as if they were their own and would immediately throb to action, and be prepared to lay down their lives bravely for the sake of a sacred cause, so dear to them. "The sad plight in which he found his followers as well as the Hindus in general, religious strifes brought about by the persecuting policy of Aurangzeb, the prevailing corruption, ignorance and superstition, and his own personal resentment at his father's execution must have generated in his mind the earnest conviction that this was undoubtedly the time for the rise of a saviour and his strong impulses and the force of circumstances in which he was placed soon led him to work himself into a belief that he himself was the man the times needed."

The Guru, thus decided to evolve a new order with the sole object of making the people realise the necessity of sacrificing their lives for the cause of *Dharma*. The people should fight against the tyranny of the rulers. They should refuse to be the slaves of anybody. He advocated the use of arms for the extrication of the oppressor. He ordained that the sword was to be used as a weapon against the people who usurp rights of others. He stood for the basic human rights of others, without any interference from the State. He relied on the will of God and the strength of his sword. He fully realised that the previous method of prayers, humility and submission were outdated and resort to arms was the only course left to him.

It was under these circumstances that the Guru decided to create the *Khalsa*. It was a revolutionary decision taken by him. On the Baisakhi festival day, *Samvat* 1756 (1699 A.D.) the *Khalsa* was born. A new creed came into being "which professed complete devotion, unflinching faith and undivided allegiance to prejudices, equality of privileges with one another and with the Guru, common worship, common place of pilgrimage, common baptism of all classes and lastly, common external appearance—these were the means, besides common leadership and the community of aspirations, which, Gobind employed to bring about unity among his followers, and by which he bound them together into a compact mass before they were hurled against the legions of the great Mughals."

The entire outlook of the community was not transformed inasmuch as it no longer represented an humble attempt to live what it considered to be the true life and propagate by peaceful means what it regarded as the true faith but henceforward it took upon its shoulders the responsibility of combating all sorts of tyranny and oppression with means adequate for the purpose. The Guru had declared that in the circumstances of the time a mere negative policy of passive resistance was on the prowess of arms. With love and devotion he grasped the sword, 'the subduer of countries and the destroyer of the armies of the wicked.' The Guru's conception of the *Khalsa*, therefore, was a fully democratic compact community, armed to the teeth, struggling to maintain what it conceived to be the right path and fighting incessantly and without compunction tyranny and injustice in all their forms.

We may conclude that although the Guru introduced a new ideology, it was not a departure from the old ideals preached by Guru Nanak and his successors. His Sikhism in essence remained the same as was ordained by Guru Nanak. It was Guru Nanak's mission that was preached by Guru Gobind Singh. Nanak's objectives were made the basis of Guru Gobind Singh's programme. Guru Nanak had given the inspiration and placed some ideals before his disciples, Guru Gobind Singh showed the practical way to achieve them.

III

Guru Gobind Singh as A Scholar

Guru Gobind Singh was a man of action. He did wonders in his life. He was humane and a brave Soldier, Saint, Philosopher and a Seer. Yet in his turbulent life spent mostly in fighting and nation building, he studied Persian, Sanskrit and Punjabi. He was well-versed in all these languages and wrote supurb poetry, with equal ease. He patronised the men of learning and his *darbar* was attended by fifty-two poets. These poets wrote poetry under his guidance and supervision. Guru Gobind Singh's writings are preserved in the *Dasam Granth*, which was compiled by his contemporary scholar, Bhai Mani Singh. The writings included in the *Dasam Granth* were composed at different times by the Guru himself and his band of 52 poets. There is some confusion about the authorship and authenticity of the writings included in the *Granth*. It was in 1734, some 26 years after the death of Guru Gobind Singh, that a devotee of the Guru, Bhai Mani Singh, collected the compositions of the Guru and his band of poets and compiled the *Dasam Granth*. When Bhai Mani Singh was martyred in 1738, doubts were expressed about the compositions contained in the *Granth*; some scholars thought that all the compositions passed in the name of Guru

Gobind Singh were not written by the Guru himself. They met at Damdama Sahib and debated the spiritual value of the compositions included in the *Granth*. In the words of Macauliffe, the scholars opined: "Many of them are of Hindu origin, others not fit for perusal, and none comparable with the hymns contained in the *Adi Granth*. The Sikhs therefore maintained that the *Hikayats* or Persian tales and the whole of the *Tria Charitar* stories illustrating the deceit of women should be omitted, and included in a volume which might be read, not for religious purposes, but for the entertainment and delectation of the public."

The main purpose of Guru Gobind Singh's heroic hymns was that by reading them, the Sikhs should learn the art of ruling, use of weapons and bows and arrows and other skills like horse-riding to make them fit for warfare.

In *Krishna Avtar*, the Guru himself explained his purpose of writing hymns. He said: "I have rendered in the vernacular the tenth chapter of the Bhagavat with no purpose other than to arouse desire for a holy war—a righteous war of the Lord."

Macauliffe has given three reasons for the translation from Hindu mythology and Hindu epics; first, to dispel cowardice and incite bravery by filling the minds of the Sikhs with heroic examples; second, by showing what a brave woman (goddess Chandi) could achieve in battle, to spur men on to surpass her achievements; and third, to enable the Sikhs to see the inferiority of the Hindu sacred writings so that they can appreciate the writings of their Gurus more.

The arousing of people to fight against tyranny and injustice was the main object of the Guru's writings.

The Guru had fought all the battles for defence. He never had any intention to occupy territory, nor was he a revengeful militarist. All his hymns have only one theme—that of peace and harmonious brotherhood.

Although *Dasam Granth* is a holy scripture of the Sikhs, it is not installed in shrines, nor does it occupy the same position as the *Adi Granth* in which is manifested the Guru himself. Guru Gobind Singh had made *Adi Granth* the Guru of the Sikhs before leaving his mortal coil and gave it an exalted position.

The *Dasam Granth* includes the following hymns:

1.	Jap	—	199 verses
2.	Akal ustat	—	271.5 verses
3.	Bachitar Natak	—	271 verses
4.	Chandi Charitar:		
	(a) First version	—	233 verses

	(b) Second version	—	262 verses
5.	Avtars of Vishnu	—	4,370 verses
6.	Mir Mehdi	—	10 verses
7.	Up Avtar	—	1,201 verses
8.	Shabads	—	9 verses
9.	Sawayyas	—	33 verses
10.	Shaster Nama Mala	—	1,318 verses
11.	Var Sri Bhagwati Ji Ki	—	55 verses
12.	Gian Prabodh	—	336 verses
13.	Zafarnama	—	111 verses
14.	Hikayats	—	756 verses
15.	Charit Pakhian	—	7,569 verses
16.	Miscellaneous	—	59 verse
	Total		17,263½ verses

Bachitar Natak—It is an autobiography of guru Gobind Singh. It is one of the best sources of the Guru's life before the creation of the *Khalsa*. It also gives an idea as to why he came to this world and what was his mission in life. It has a unique position in Hindi literature.

Bachitar Natak begins with an invocation to God.

"I bow before the holy sword with love and devotion. Help me to complete this composition." About himself the Guru wrote that he belonged to the Sodhi clan and also to that of the Bedis. Guru Nanak, the Bedi, established true *Dharma* in this world in *Kalyuga* just as Lord Rama had done in the earlier *Yuga*. God blessed all those who followed the teachings of Guru Nanak. Their sufferings were removed and they attained salvation. The truth preached by Guru Nanak was cherished by his successors who all must be regarded as one with Guru Nanak.

Thus, Guru Gobind Singh himself was the true and real successor of Guru Nanak. He was ordained by the Almighty to spread true religion in the world. He bore no enmity against any human being to whatever caste or creed he belonged. He considered himself a human being like any other, not God. He specifically declared:

"All those who call me the Lord
shall fall into hell's pit.
Call me the servant of God
Have no doubt about this
I am the slave of the Lord."

Guru Gobind Singh was sent by the Lord to defend *dharma* spread righteousness and destroy evil and sin. His mission was to root out the wicked and to create saint-soldiers who could fight evil.

The Guru has given in *Bachitar Natak* description of some of the battles he had fought. Everywhere he attributes his success to God and says that he and his disciples were under the protection of the Lord.

The date of composition of *Bachitar Natak* is given by Macauliffe as 1692, when Guru Gobind Singh was 26 years of age. The book was written at Anandpur. It is divided into 14 chapters and is written in archaic Hindi with a large mixture of Sanskrit. The script is Gurmukhi. Praise of the All Powerful and Immortal God, satire on the religious beliefs and practices of the Hindus and other ascetics, and descriptions of the Guru's ancestors and of his own life form the main themes of *Bachitar Natak*.

The description of the battle of Bhangani is excellent. Something of the ardour aroused by the Guru is evident in an incident in this battle. Kirpal, the *udasi mahant*, sought permission of the Guru to fight Haiyat Khan. The Guru told him that a holy saint like him could not kill Haiyat Khan with words, he better pray for victory. On hearing this conversation the Guru's uncle requested him to permit to fight Haiyat Khan. The Guru asked him as to what weapon he would like to use against the enemy. "With the club," replied the *mahant*. The Guru smiled and allowed Kirpal to fight the adversary. It was a great spectacle to see: the *mahant* with his hair twisted around the head, his body covered with only a thin plaster of ashes and his belly protruding in front of the saddle proceeding to engage a practised warrior armed with the latest weapons of destruction.

When the *mahant* approached and challenged Haiyat Khan, finding that he was not armed with the latest weapons, the latter decided to retreat, scorning to attack a defenceless man. The spectators were also amused and wondered, 'How can that *fakir* contend with a Pathan?" The *mahant*, however continued to challenge Haiyat Khan. As a snake escaping into its hole comes forth and attacks the aggressor when its tail is trodden on, so did Haiyat Khan who had till then been retiring before the *mahant*. He advanced against him goaded by his taunts and aimed a blow of his sword at the *mahant*, which the latter received on his club, and behold, Haiyat Khan's sword had fallen to pieces. The *mahant* then addressed him thus: "Now hold your ground and defend yourself against me." The *mahant* rose in his stirrups and, wielding his club with both hands, struck Haiyat Khan with such force on the head that his skull broke and his brains issued forth and stained the battlefield.

33 *Sawayyas*—There are 33 *Sawayyas* in the *Dasam Granth*. These *Sawayyas* give the gist of Guru Gobind Singh's teachings. In the first *Sawayya*, he defines a pure Khalsa. He who fixes his thought on the Supreme Reality day and night and does not turn his mind to anything else, is full of love and faith and does not put his trust in fasts nor worships

tombs, hermitages or crematoriums, whose place of pilgrimage, charity, compassion, austerity and self-control are all guided by devotion to the Lord, and whose mind is resplendent with the ever shining light is to be called a pure Khalsa. In the next 10 *Sawayyas* the Guru describes the attributes of God-head. Then the fatility of worshipping various gods and goddesses and the so-called incarnations of God is set forth. In *Sawayyas* 18th and 19th the Guru enjoins sincerity and in the next *Sawayyas* discards idol-worship and goes on to explain that the gods whose images men worship were themselves subject to death.

Then he subjects to scathing criticism formal and ceremonial worship and exposes the tactics of sectarian leaders, who care more for self-aggrandisement than for spreading true religious spirit.

In the end, Guru Gobind Singh reminds man that he is morally responsible for all his deeds and that he will have to bear the consequences of his doings. His dear friends and near relations for whose sake he commits inequities will not accompany him when the soul departs from the body.

Jap : This is an introductory invocation of the *Dasam Granth.* It begins with *Sri Mukhwakh Patshahi Das,* 'By the holy mouth of the Tenth King.' The date of its composition is uncertain. According to Sir John Archer, it was written during the Guru's stay at Damdama Sahib which means the year of its composition was 1705, but Macauliffee is of the opinion that the *Jap* was read in the preparation of the *amrit* when the *Khalsa* was founded, which indicates that it was composed before 1699—before the creation of the *Khalsa.*

The *Jap* is the morning prayer of the Sikhs. It is about half that of *Japji* of Guru Nanak and takes about 25 minutes to recite.

Akal Ustat—It was not composed at one time. The different parts were composed at different times and were later compiled together.

In the opening verse, God is addressed as *Akal Purkh,* Immortal, *Sarab Loh,* All steel; Sarab Kal, All death; and later as Maha Loh, Great Steel; Maha Kal, Great death: *Asidhuj, Asiketu, Kharagketu* (having a sword on His banner); and *Asipani* (having a sword in his hand).

The Guru commences the composition with an invocation to the God of War—the All steel. He ends with the hope of tolerance of all religions and even among people living in all parts of the world, seeking the same God and being blessed by him.

Zafarnama—Guru Gobind Singh wrote a historic letter to Aurangzeb called *Zafarnama*—the Epistle of Viceroy. It consists of 111 couplets in Persian verse and is one of the most forceful epistles ever written in any language. It is written in the style and metre of Firdausi's *Shahnama* and begins with an invocation to the Lord.

The Guru tells the Emperor that he had proved to be a liar. He does not have any faith in religion and does not see the truth. He does not fear God nor follows the teachings of the prophet. His ministers and courtiers had been telling lies. The Hill Rajputs who worshipped the idols were also not loyal to them as they swore by the cow and broke their vows.

After forcing him to leave the Fort of Anandpur by taking false oaths and deceiving him, the forces of the Emperor and the hill Rajas had attacked him again near Sarsa which was extremely mean on their part.

In verses 21, 22, and 23, the Guru expresses regret for his having been forced to take arms and to be a spectator of bloodshed.

The Guru then describes the battles of Chamkaur Sahib by saying that his forty companions fought with valour and bravery against the Emperor's forces who fell upon them like a swarm of locusts. There was huge loss of life and the battle-field turned red with the blood of the wounded and the dead.

Mentioning about the martyrdom of his sons, the Guru wrote to the Emperor that it did not affect him at all as the spirit of the *Khalsa* was immortal and the sacrifice made by the innocent young boys had drawn thousands more under his command to root out tyranny and injustice from the land. It was of no avail putting out a few flames while a fire blazed to reduce to ashes the Royal edifice built upon cunning and oppression.

The Guru advised the Emperor to leave his throne as he had performed so many sinful acts that his cup of sins was now full to the brim.

If the Emperor was keen to meet him and bring the long-drawn suffering to an end, he should come forward with a clean heart and issue orders to his Governors to cease all hostilities against the Sikhs. Only after that a meeting could be arranged.

The letter was delivered to the Emperor at Ahmadnagar by Bhai Daya Singh and Bhai Dharam Singh after a long and tiresome journey.

Thus, *Zafarnama* reflects the Guru's erudite learning, dauntless valour, truthful spirit and sympathy for all human beings without any distinction of cast, creed or colour.

Chandi Charitar—Three versions of the story of Chandi or Durga, the goddess of war, are presented. The first is from the *Markandeya Purana*, and the second is from the *Bhagavata Purana*. The third is also based on the *Markandeya Purana*. The Guru's designation *Patshahi* 10 does not appear in the first two versions but appear in the third—the Epic of Chandi.

The time and place of this composition are not certain. The first two parts are written in Braj Bhasha while the Epic is written in Punjabi. All the three run with the lore of the battles between Durga and the demons which indicates that the fight was between good and evil.

It is said that the entire story is imbued with the spirit of battle. At that time in India there was a great need for the inculcation of this spirit. The Guru wanted to show how pure women of this country, fighting in bloody battles, saved their own faith. Now too, the blood of these heroines was present in the veins of the people of India. The guru wanted to arouse enthusiasm for war to protect the *dharma.*

Var Sri Bhagvati ki or Chandi-di-Var—It is the first *Var* of its kind in Punjabi and can be said to be of the finest poems in this language.

Shabbad Patshabi Das—These *Shabads* are in the several *ragas.* The verses exhort men to worship only one God and not His manifestations or His creations.

Hikayats—The concluding sections of the *Dasam Granth* are in Persian and follow *Zafarnama.* The *bikayats* are 11 in number. None of them bears the Guru's signature although all of them contain the words *Wahi-Guru Ji Ki Fateb.* The language is extremely powerful and all the *bikayats* are rhymed. They contain moral instruction given to Emperor Aurangzeb.

Thus in one part of the *Dasam Granth*, Guru Gobind Singh attempted to give an account of Hindu mythology whose knowledge was very essential to understand Sikhism which flourished on the Indian soil with mythology as its background. However, this does not mean that the Guru accepted these mythological tales.

III

Guru Gobind Singh as a Man

Guru Gobind Singh occupies a very high place in the history of mankind on account of his versatility. He was a rare combination of multiple qualities and his activities were also varied. The guru was a Saint, Soldier and Man of letters, confined into one.

Behind every specific idea and institution there is a man; behind every man there is an age; and behind every age there is a past. The man preaches his ideas through his personal example and qualities of the great order. Guru Gobind Singh had a manifold personality, both idealistic and practical. He was a handsome, tall, robust youngman with very active habits. His face ever shined with a benign grace. Even in the grim days of fighting, his face did not show any sign of sorrow or distress. He had attractive black eyes and a body full of vigour and strength. His courage had no parallel. Full of youth he performed miracles in the battle-field.

Guru Gobind singh loved humanity. His love embraced one and all without any discrimination. He received with open arms whosoever came to him. Even his enemies were welcomed and honoured in his darbar. He did not bear any illwill against anybody and always kept in view, his father's dictum "fear no one and strike fear in no one." It is a well-known fact that when Raja Fateh Shah of Srinagar (U.P.), who had a long standing enmity with Raja Medni Prakash of Nahan expressed his desire to remain on good terms with the Guru who had come quite near to his territory and was now strong enough, the Guru not only showed his willingness to meet him but also received him with full honours at Paonta Sahib. The Guru made magnificent arrangements for the reception of the Raja. A huge Pandal was constructed to receive him. Precious carpets were spread on the ground and special ministrels were engaged for the entertainment of the Raja. On his visit, the Guru expressed the desire to come to an amicable settlement with the Raja of Nahan, who showed a gesture of goodwill. The Guru was pleased and appreciated the attitude of the Raja and calling Raja Medni Prakash in the open *darbar*, asked him to embrace Raja Fateh Shah and forget their old enmity. It was a unique scene, two enemies became fast friends, by the goodwill inspired by the Guru.

The Guru was humane in his approach to men and matters, he could even forgive those committing the worst offence. Whenever any of his erring follower apologised and promised good behaviour in the future, the Guru gladly pardoned him. His heart mettled at the very sight of the sufferer. He could even pardon his enemies and persons who had betrayed him earlier. It is a well-known fact that at Anandpur, some of his Sikhs deserted him for fear of death. But when the battle of Muketsar, the last battle fought by the Guru, was over he went to look after those who had been slain or wounded in the battle. The Guru felt that all those who had died were his sons. They were all his Beloved Ones who were fighting with him shoulder to shoulder against tyranny and aggression. The Guru moved about lifting the heads of the dead and putting them into his lap, wiped their faces with a piece of cloth, one by one. When the Guru reached near the body of Bhai Mahan Singh, one of the Sikhs who had earlier deserted him, he was still breathing. The Guru affectionately lifted his head and putting it in his lap asked him if he was not Mahan Singh, one of his sons. Mahan Singh nodded meakly. The Guru told him that he was dying as a martyr and could ask for whatever he desired. Mahan Singh was delighted and opened his eyes, wet with tears. Mumbling in a choked voice he said to the Guru that he was a sinner and had no right to be made immortal. He had deserted the Guru when he needed him. The doors of heaven were closed for him. He requested the Master to forgive him. That was the only prayer he had to make. He requested that the document of denunciation; *Bedava* should be destroyed and he be pardoned along with other deserters, and accepted back into the *Khalsa* fold. The Guru smiled and took out the document, which he had carried with him all the time. It was like an ulcer in his body. The Guru tore it off and forgave all the deserters and blessed them. Mahan Singh heaved a sigh of relief and breathed his last peacefully-nay he was immortalised. Who else could be large-hearted than the Guru! He forgave them with an open mind, the people who had been instrumental in compelling him to leave Anandpur. On yet another occasion, when the Guru was on his way to Anandpur from Patna, he went for game shooting. He was then camping at Lakhnaur in Ambala district. Suddenly he met one man, Ghogha by name who was afraid of the Guru and tried to hide himself as he had earlier committed the crime of abducting the maid-servant of Guru Tegh Bahadur. The Guru did not possess any revengeful spirit and pardoned, Ghogha, when he asked for it. Such stories could be multiplied manifold.

The Guru had a strict routine of life in his personal affairs. He was strictly punctual and observed prevalent customs of the family. He used to get up in the dead of night and perform his prayers. He was particularly delighted to listen *Asa-di-var.* After daybreak, he gave his Sikhs divine instructions and then practised martial exercises. In the afternoon he received his Sikhs, went shooting, or raced horses; and ended the evening by performing the service of the *Rahiras.*"

"The Guru was a great riddle. Not many understood him aright. At times for sixteen hours together he was in trance ecstatically singing Tui,' Tui,' Tui' when the bullets were flying about, he would sit down to chant Guru Nanak's morning service of *Asa-di-var.* For eleven months, he was alone in a solitary cave at Bhabour, on the rocky side of a chiff overlashing the Sutlej. And yet this great saint was a great scholar and a warrior."

The Guru had a strong moral character. He was as perfect in his moral behaviour as he was high in his spiritual life. "Throughout his life, not even once did he stoop to unfair means, falsehood, deceit, or lies. In war, as in peace, his policy was the same; truth above everything else. He taught his sikhs to be content as far as possible, in any case never to go near the bed of another's wife even in a dream." The Guru practised whatever he preached. *Rehatnama*, which he gave to the Sikhs in short says that the Sikhs should not borrow at all and if they are forced by the circumstances to borrow out of dire necessity, they should return the money without any delay. They should not speak a lie nor should they associate themselves with falsehood of any kind. They should associate with holymen and live by honest labour. They should recite *Japji* before eating. They should not look at a naked woman nor cohabit with another's wife. They should deem other's property as filth and keep their bodies clean, obstain from using tobacco in any form and remember the one Immortal God. Guru Gobind Singh, like Guru Nanak, gave great importance to purity and simplicity of life. But he placed brave deeds and devotion to the Sikh's cause at the same level as a pure life. There was no higher duty for a Sikh than to die fighting in defence of his faith.

The Guru desired his Sikhs to be of spotless character as he himself was. Once when the Guru went to Rawalsar in the hills, some ladies, including the wives of the hill chiefs, came to see him. Padma, Princess of Chamba, who accompanied them was very much impressed by the Guru's creative qualities and his poetic ability of the highest standard.

On her saluting the Guru in reverence, he patted her back with his own bow. She was rather surprised. When asked by his Sikhs the reason for his doing so, the Guru explained that he did not want to touch any other woman with his hand except his wives. By his single act the Guru proved himself a real practitioner of restraint and combinance both in word and deed and this is expected of every true Sikh.

On another occasion, some Sikhs captured a Muslim Amir's young bride. But the Guru said that she was to be treated like a sister and did not allow his Sikhs to molest her. Later she was conducted with proper escort to a safe place honourably. The Guru himself once fell into the secret snare of a vile, rich woman. She threatened to raise an alarm unless he agreed to her proposal. He decided to risk his reputation if necessary and protect the purity of his character at any cost, and he finally escaped unseathed, preserving both character and honour!

The Guru attached highest importance to the dignity of labour and working with one's own hands. He preached throughout his life Guru Nanak's message of '*Kirt Karo*,—work honestly, 'one day when the Guru felt thirsty, he asked a Sikh to fetch him some fresh water. Before the Sikh had time to do so, a young boy, who had come to see the Guru, volunteered to perform the service. The Guru, noticing that the boys's hands were soft and clean, asked him if he had any occupation. He replied in the negative. That was the first time he had ever offered to fetch water for any one. When he brought it the Guru refused to drink, saying it was impure. The boy protested and insisted on its being quite pure. The Guru replied, 'Hear me, O Sikh, it is an important article of the Guru's faith that performing service for Saints contributed to man's salvation. The hands are purified by serving them. The feet are purified by going to behold the Guru. Without serving holy men a man's body is as unclear as the limbs of a corpse; which all fear to touch.

The Guru was very keen that every visitor to his *darbar* should be served well and should neither remain hungry nor thirsty. All his devotees should eat in the common kitchen. One day thinking that his kitchen was not well-served, he paid a surprise visit to it in disguise, and asked for something to eat. The cooks gave various excuses. One of them said that prayer must first be offered. Another observed, we must first give the Guru his desire.' When the Guru had received several similar excuses but nothing to eat, though he had urged that he was very hungry, he went to Nand Lal to beg for his dinner. Nand Lal atonce brought forth flour, vegetables, salt and clarified butter, and handed them to the supposed mendicant, who took them with delight. Next day the Guru told in the open court how he had paid a visit in disguise to his kitchen and how he had been treated. The cooks were very much ashamed and craved forgiveness. He then gave orders that every wandering Sikh, who came to his door should atonce receive food, whether raw or cooked, without any excuse or delay. The Guru continued: There is nothing equal to the bestowal of food. "Blessed is the man who giveth to the hungry. Let no one fix a time for exercise of this virtue. It is not necessary to consider whether it is night or day, evening or morning, whether the moon is dark or full, or if there is a particular anniversary. Nor it is necessary to consider what the social position of the supplicant may be. Avoid all delay in such a matter. In such a matter, charity is of all gifts, the greatest for it seventh life."

The Guru had great power of tolerance and forbearance. He lost his all, his father, mother, hearth and home. In fact, he did not keep anything for himself but sacrificed his all at the altar of the Motherland. Which father can hear the woeful tale of the death of his sons and yet be not moved! While he was at Dina a devotee, Mahi by name, narrated the sad tale of the bricking alive of the two younger sons of the Guru. Everybody present wept bitterly. The painful story was heard by the congregation of Sikhs with rapt attention. Not a voice was heard and everybody overcame with grief. But the Guru sat unmoved and unnerved, digging at a shrub. He simply declared that his sons were not dead rather they had been immortalised. Inspite of the unprecedented happenings the Guru remained composed, undaunted and in high spirits. Agony and distress did not unbalance him. His patriotic fervour and resolve for serving the Motherland did not flicker for a moment. Both in weal and woe his will remained unshaken. He moved about in the forests of Machhiwara; a king became pauper. He was all alone and later on he got the news of the execution of his two younger sons and the death of his mother as well. Yet with such complete resignation did he accept all this, and made the event to look in only significant. After all this happened and after he had suffered such a great loss, he sat down with a composed mind to compile a new recension of the *Adi Granth*, in which the mental exercise of the highest order was required, and then he undertook the religious preachings in the Malwa, as if fresh in mind. Such habits only super-human, and Saints of the highest order could posses.

The Guru was altogether immune from the evils of '*Kam, Krodh, Lobh, Moh* and *Ahankar*'—meaning sexual indulgence with a woman other than ones own wife, short temperament, greed, craving wordly things and pride. These wordly evils did not fit in with the very nature of the Guru who though living in this world as a man, enjoying the pleasures of this life and suffering the sorrows and miseries was above all these evils. The Guru not only himself remained aloof from them that when the Guru at the young age of nine had completed all his worldly education, he was called one day by his father, Guru Tegh Bahadur. The young Guru sat in his lap affectionately and received a kiss from his dear father. The Guru (Tegh Bahadur) told him the necessity of leading a pure and simple life and asked him to make a promise with him to this effect. The young Guru atonce bowed his head before the Guru (Tegh Bahadur) and promised to fulfil the undertaking throughout his life. Writing about this incident Guru Gobind Singh says:

> "When I was young The God told me to fulfil this promise that in my youth I would not have company with any women other than my wife and I would not sleep with her even in my dream."

Further events in the life of Guru Gobind Singh have clearly showed as to how he obeyed the order of his father.

The Guru was never haughty or arrogant, although he had reasons to be such in view of his achievements. He was the image of Guru Nanak who had preached the virtues of humility and simplicity. Guru Nanak, had declared himself as the servant of God, a humble creature and Guru Gobind Singh said he was the servant of the Almighty, who had come to see the spectacle of the world. He never preached his 'self' but always preached the message of God. The word 'self' had no meaning for him. He won victories in the battlefield against heavy odds but even then called himself an insect. He was one of the greatest poets and creative writers of the world, who enriched the world's literature with his superb genius, yet he himself praised the Lord's glory. He declared again and again that whatever he had composed was God's creation and not his.

In temperament he was always invariably cool and composed. He was serene like the sea and had limitless tolerance. He never uttered any harsh words, nor allowed his passions to get the better of him. Once when the Guru was attacked by a young Pathan at Nanded and was seriously injured, the Guru did not lose his balance of mind. He remained absolutely calm and composed and unsheathing his sword he attacked the Pathan with his might. The Pathan tried to escape from the Guru's tent, but in vain. As he lay dying, the Pathan cried 'mother, mother,' but the Guru raising his voice said, "Don't cry mother, it is time to remember God, the Almighty who created you."

The Guru, even in the battle-field never lost his temper. He showered arrows after arrows on his enemies but never lost his calmness and poise. Love for worldly goods had no place in Guru's mind. He loved his God and his creatures, and not the worldly possessions. When he was a child of five years he once threw away his gold bangle into the river. When his mother enquired about the lost bangle, the Guru threw the second one also into the river and said: 'there.' On another occasion when Emperor Bahadur Shah presented him with a diamond, he threw it into the river in the presence of the Emperor. The Emperor was very much surprised at this action of the Guru. The Guru, in fact, had no love for gold, for he thought that these diamonds, silver and other precious things, made the people forget God.

One day, while at Nanded, a Sikh devotee presented him a diamond ring. The Guru was meditating and without seeing it threw it into the river. The Sikh was surprised at the action of the Guru. He did not relish the idea of the Guru throwing such a precious thing into the river without even looking at it and seeing its beauty and splendour. He requested the Guru to let him know the place where he had thrown the ring so that he might jump into the river to fetch it out. The Guru smiled in his usual benign way and threw the other equally valuable ring which he was wearing, into the river. All the people gathered were simply amazed. But the Guru desired to impress upon his followers that one should not have any attachment for the worldly belongings however valuable and lovely they might be. The Guru always taught his followers the futility of the love for worldly goods. He says:

> "No sooner you are dead, then your wife will desert you calling you a ghost; young sons, wife, relatives and all dear friends will cry with one voice 'make haste to take him out.' The palatial mansions, the valuable treasures; the land, the wealth, all will pass into other's hands as soon as you give up your soul.
>
> Always bear this in mind, O, unthinking brute! In the end you will be going alone.
>
> —*Sawayyas*-(33)

The Guru did not have any love in the worldly sense, even for his near and dear ones. Although they were part of his household, he thought them to be the creatures of God who had come into the world to perform certain duties and then return to their true homes in the heaven. And it was only a matter of time.

It could only be Guru Gobind Singh who sacrificed his father, mother and sons, nay, in fact, all which he possessed, without ever uttering a single word of sorrow or distress. While at Damdama Sahib the Guru's two wives Sundari and Sahib Kaur, who had been separated from the Guru while crossing Sarsa after the besiege of Anandpur, now joined him. Sundariji most humbly and respectfully asked the Guru as to where were his four beloved sons. Where had he left them? With tears in her eyes, she bowed before the Guru and wanted to know the fate of their dear ones. Thousands in the huge congregation listened to the mother's tearful cries of agony. It was a heart-breaking scene. No eye was dry. But the Guru sat composed and emotionless. His beaming face shone as before. The Guru closed his eyes for a while and opening them shortly afterwards told Sundariji that her sons were not dead, they had become immortal and were playing in the lap of their Eternal Father. He consoled her by saying that she should not lament for the four who had gone. They had courted martyrdom for the sake of true religion and have performed their duty. What a father!

The Guru was a perfect *yogi*—a true *yogi.* He lived and died for others. He sacrificed his all for the cause of the honour of his Motherland. "His whole life, from cradle to the grave, was one long vigorous and persistent struggle for the uplift and liberation of his vanquished race. He held back nothing, he gave all and everything."

No sacrifice was to him too dear if it led to a furtherance of his lofty and selfless ideals. He could have, if he had the liking, spent a life of peace, comfort and honour, among his disciples, or carved out a kingdom for himself. But his heart was set the other way.

Guru Gobind Singh was a perfect man. He was an obedient son, a considerate father, a kind master and a loving husband. Although man of a detached nature, he did look after his family-members well and never thought of neglecting them for a moment. He nourished his sons, giving them full parental love and affection and even gave them worldly education as was possible under the circumstances. He gave them guidance, not only when sought for, but even in the daily life. He always emphasised on worshipping one God and held that no sacrifice should be thought too great for achieving a certain cause.

They were told to be firm and determined inspite of the provocation by the enemy. As Guru Nanak, his Master, the Guru did not desire to leave his house and worship the God in jungles. Remember Him as a part and parcel of his worldly life, the Guru remembered the Name of Almighty and living in this world tried to fulfil the mission of his life.

"I have come into this world,
To spread righteousness everywhere,
To destroy the evil-doers and sinners,
Understand ye holy men,
I was born in this world,
To help good to flourish and to save Saints,
And to uproot all tyrants from this world.

— *Bachitar Natak*

He did not feel it necessary to renounce the world though he knew it was full of evils, miseries and agony. But instead he preferred to live in this world and preach against evil customs and rituals. He was an ideal householder; words of his father and mother were orders of God for him. He never disobeyed them, never hurt their feelings and never went against their wishes. When the Guru was surrounded in the fort of Anandpur, he was called by his mother and told to consider the offer of Mughals to evacuate the fort. The Guru's mother tried to convince him the utility of the offer but the Guru told her time and again that Mughals and Hill Rajas were liars. Their promises were false. They could not be relied upon. But Mata

Gujari insisted that the Guru give a chance to the enemy in the interest of saving the starving Sikhs. The Guru was put in an awkward position; to obey his mother or act according to his own judgement. The Guru took the historic decision—to leave Anandpur—never to return there again. It was the desire of his mother, the Guru carried out against his own wishes. What an obedient son?

The Guru also possessed great wit and humour. These are qualities to be found in a spiritual leader. The Guru's life was one long string of strains and stresses, yet his sense of wit and humour did not abandon him. Whenever an occasion arose, the Guru made the people laugh. But through his wit also the Guru preached his ideals and made his followers learn lessons from small incidents of life.

Once a devoted Sikh, Udhey Singh by name, came to his *darbar* without any offering. The Guru asked him the reason for the same. He replied that he had one beast killed but was unable to carry it on his shoulders. It was a heavy gift. He had killed a tiger in the nearby jungle but he could not lift it. The Guru sent his men to bring the tiger. When it was brought, it was skinned. A donkey was brought covered with the tiger's skin, and then let loose. The donkey with the tiger skin on frightened all the other animals as he wondered around. The Guru rejoiced and enjoyed the feats of the disguised donkey. Requests were made to the Guru to kill the animals as it was a menace to others. The Guru, alongwith his few Sikhs went out to shoot the animal, which on hearing the noise, was afraid and ran to his old master for protection. The potter, noticed that his behaviour and movements were those of donkey and not of a tiger, and leaving him, took off his tiger's skin, gave him a sound drubbing, and took him away for his usual labour. The Guru told his Sikhs to learn a lesson from the incident that as long as they were bound by caste, they were like disguised donkeys to be used by low persons. They had been now freed by him from these entanglements and given all worldly blessings. They have been clothed in the garb of a tiger and made superior to all men. They would enjoy happiness in this world and were assured of glory in the next. When the donkey wore a tiger's skin he was formidable, but when he fell into the hands of the potter, and discovered of his real nature, he was severally beaten and was loaded with heavy burden. Similarly when they preserved the tiger's outlook, their enemies would fear them and victory would be theirs, but if they parted with it and observed caste distinctions, they would be subjugated. They had been made real tigers. These words of the Guru heartened his followers and they were convinced of the futility of the caste system.

We could also find several instances of wit and humour from the Guru's writings. While describing the Bhangani war, the Guru writes in *Bachitar Natak*: Mahant Kirpal took up his club and hanged it on the head of Hayat Khan, the brave, and crushed his brains out. The grey matter spilt on the ground as if Kahana (Lord Krishna) had broken the pot of a milk-maid and made the streaks of butter spread all round."

In short, the Guru was the embodiment of great human virtues. He possessed a rare character, high morality and goodwill for one and all. Even his enemies praised his rare qualities of head and heart.

3

War-I Against Hill Chiefs

According to a Muslim historian, Ghulam Mohyiuddin, the emperor was duly informed by the news-writer of the address given by Guru Govind Singh to his followers on the birth of the Khalsa. "He has abolished caste and custom, old rituals, beliefs and superstitions of the Hindus and banded them in one single brotherhood. No one will be superior, or inferior, to another. Men of all castes have been made to eat out of the same bowl. Though orthodox men have opposed him, about twenty thousand men and women have taken baptism of steel at his hands on the first day. The Guru has also told the gathering: 'I'll call myself Govind Singh only if I can make the meek sparrows pounce upon the hawks and tear them; only if one combatant of my force equals a lakh and a quarter of the enemy.' "

The Hill chiefs were also greatly scared. While the Guru one day went out hunting in the Doon Valley, two of them, Balia Chand and Alim Chand, challenged him with a large detachment. Though the Sikhs were few in number, they gave an excellent account of themselves. The Guru's arrows brought havoc in the enemy's camp. Balia Chand was shot dead; Alim Chand lost one of his arms and fled. With many dead left on the battle-field, the hill armies beat a retreat, humbled and in disarray.

When the other Rajput Hill chiefs heard of this encounter, they were gravely alarmed. Finding themselves weak, if not helpless against the Guru, they decided to approach the emperor at Delhi through a petition. The emperor was in the Deccan, engaged in grim battles. So, in his absence, the Subedar of Sirhind heard their representatives. The memorandum said, "The present Guru is tenth in succession to Nanak, the Guru who preached the gospel of peace and human brotherhood. That's how we raised no objection to his finding residence in our midst. But, his ideas and intentions are different from Nanak's. When we tried to curb his rising power with which he aims to challenge even the emperor himself, he repaired to the Nahan state, made friends with the raja there, and then came into conflict with him and Raja Fateh Shah of Srinagar. A battle was fought between us and him at Bhangani where human blood flowed in abundance. Then, he returned to Anandpur, and established a new order, called the Khalsa, which is contrary to all our cherished beliefs and customs. He says his religion is distinct as much from the Muslim, as from the Hindu faith. And, yet, he wanted us to join hands with him to fight our emperor against whom he harbours profound grudge. This we have refused to do, much to his annoyance and discomfiture. He is now gathering men and arms from all over the country to challenge the Moghal empire. We cannot restrain him, but as loyal subjects of your Majesty, we crave your assistance to drive him out of Anandpur and not to allow grass to grow under your feet. Otherwise, he would become a formidable challenge to the whole empire, as his intentions are to march soon on Delhi itself." This representation was duly forwarded by the Viceroy of Sirhind to the emperor.

After some time, the imperial Government replied to this representation saying that the Hill chiefs could be assisted by imperial troops if their expenses were paid for. To this the Hill rajas readily agreed. Accordingly, two Moghal generals, Painde Khan and Din Beg, were despatched to help the Rajput princes with a force of ten thousand troops under both. At Rupar, they were joined by the Hill forces under the direct commands of their rulers. The purposes of this assault, as advertised, was to drive the Guru out of Anandpur, but if he promised to live as a loyal subject, then, he would be allowed to abide there on payment of a tribute.

When information reached the Guru that a strong force was advancing against him, he organised his men also in battle array. He appointed the five Beloved ones as five generals of his army, and himself also decided to fight along with his troops. The fire-power of the Sikhs inflicted heavy losses on the enemy. Though the Moghal forces on the one hand and the Rajputs on the other were haranguing their troops separately that it was a religious war, nothing availed them. At last General Painde Khan decided to engage the Guru in a single combat and thus determine the result of the battle. He challenged the Guru to come out and face him personally. Hearing this, the Guru galloped his steed towards him and roared, "I'm Govind Singh come to settle accounts with thee." Painde Khan taunted the Guru, "Why don't you settle with me then? Strike first so that you have no regrets." The Guru smiled and said, "It's not the custom of my house to fire the first shot. You have aggressed against me. So, I give you the privilege!"

Painde Khan moved his horse around the Guru in many positions to strike him with the sword, but the Guru was so swift with the movements of his horse that the Pathan general felt helpless. He, then, discharged an arrow which whizzed past the ear of the Guru. The Guru taunted him, "Thy archery is perfect!" Painde Khan discharged another arrow which also missed its mark. Upon this, he hastened to retreat, but was challenged by the Guru: "You dirty coward, why don't you let me have my chance also?" Saying this, the Guru aimed an arrow at the ear of Painde Khan which was the only part uncovered by armour. The aim was so sure that Painde Khan fell off the horse-back and died. The other general, Din Beg, now took the command. The Moghal troops fought desparately, while the Hill troops fled in disarray, seeing the battle going in favour of the Sikhs. Din Beg was himself badly wounded and seeing no chance of victory beat a retreat. He was pursued by the Sikh forces upto Rupar, but the Guru advised them not to harass them any further. The Sikhs captured a large booty from the battle-field and having wrought much destruction to the enemy troops, were greatly enthused over this decisive victory.

The Guru now sent instructions to his Sikhs that whosoever came to see him must bring either an arm or a horse. When the news of the Guru's victory reached far and near, many people came to join the ranks of the Khalsa. The Guru employed armourers to make muskets, swords and arrows and collected a large quantity of gunpowder and lead.

Some of the Hill chiefs felt panicky and decided once again to approach the emperor for assistance, and make valuable presents to him. One of their number advised them not to do so, and to muster their own forces, surround Anandpur from all sides and starve its occupants to death or submission. This advice was later accepted. Each Hill chief, among them, the rajas of Jammu, Nurpur, Mandi, Bhutan, Kulu, Kainthal, Guler, Chamba and Srinagar, contributed his contingent. Raja Ajmer Chand, son of Bhim Chand of Bilaspur, was to be in overall charge of the invading force and everyone agreed to submit to his decisions. Ajmer Chand first sent an emissary to the Guru asking him either to abandon Anandpur or pay them the arrears of yearly rent on the land on which the city stood. Failing this, the town was to be blockaded from all sides.

The Guru spurned this demand with the contempt it deserved adding, that as the site of the Anandpur town was bought by his father for cash, no one could claim from him a rent on it. And if it was the desire of the Hill chiefs to deprive him and his followers of their lawful habitation, through force, then the Guru had no choice but to fight back in self-defence. The Guru said he meant no harm to them whatever, if only they would let him in peace and not join forces with the Moghals against whose tyranny he was preparing to fight. Indeed, he sought their help and assistance in this holy war.

The rajas were furious at this reply. They were convinced that the Guru would not buy peace at the cost of honour, and would much rather fight than surrender or sue for peace. Thereupon, they collected a large army contributed by every chief of the Hill states. There were not many Sikhs residing in Anandpur at this time. But, they were joined soon by the devout from many corners of the Punjab. The Guru's eldest son, Ajit Singh, in his teens, also was permitted to command a company of one hundred. The two forts at Anandpur, Lohgarh and Fatehgarh, were put incharge of two separate commanders with a force of one thousand to guard each fort. The Guru advised his forces not to move beyond the town, but to remain on the defensive.

The Sikh chroniclers say the Hill forces swarmed in like the locusts. But, though outnumbered and outweaponed, the Sikhs fought with such bravery and self-assuredness that the enemy was thrown in confusion and the

Ranghars and Gujars sought to flee. These two castes were known for their fighting qualities, and bearing a grudge against the Guru over an earlier fight in which they had lost and their towns of Nuh and Bajpur had been sacked, had mustered a strong force under their leader, Jagatullah. But nothing availed them against the accurate marksmanship and death-daring chivalry of the Sikhs. Jagatullah was shot dead and the Sikhs would not even allow the enemy to remove his dead body. The Guru himself, seated on a mound, aimed his deadly arrows at the enemy accounting for innumerable heads.

At this, the rajas decided to make one final assault from three directions. But, even this did not yield any result. Jagatullah's body lay on the cold dust, but inspite of determined attacks of the enemy, the Sikhs made it a point of prestige not to let it fall into his hands. After bloody skirmishes, the enemy retired to his camp. Here, they were counselled by some, like the Raja of Mandi, to sue for peace with the house of Nanak, there being no dishonour involved in approaching a high spiritual personage with a petition for peace. But some of the rajas thought this would further embolden the Guru, that he was not as strong as he was feared and that if they did not lose heart, they would soon gain an upper hand. So, they made a desparate try again. This time they concentrated all their forces on a single point. The Guru's son, Ajit, showed exemplary courage. His horse was wounded, so he fought on foot. This electrified the atmosphere. The Sikhs fought with their backs to the wall and wrought havoc in the enemy's forces. In the end, the Hill chiefs thought it was useless to continue the fight any longer and after a siege of two months, they withdrew. But, before they did so, they tried another method of breaking through the defences of the fort. They sent an intoxicated elephant to make a breach in the walled defences. Seeing this, a Sikh, Duni Chand, who had brought a detachment of five hundred from the Central Punjab to aid the Guru, fled in terror, secretly. The Guru on hearing of this remarked, "He who flies from death in the face of danger to his nation finds death awaiting him in another garb." It is said when Duni Chand reached Amritsar and his foul deed was known to the community, he was ostracised from society and died a lonely man soon thereafter, stung by a cobra.

The elephant, except for his trunk, was covered with a steel coat-of-mail. He had to make an assault to the front door of the Lohgarh fort with a spear stuck in his forehead. The Hill forces were to march in his rear so that when the front gate was breached, they would storm the troops within and a great massacre would follow. The fort would thus fall into their hands. The Guru appointed one of his valiant soldiers, Vachitter Singh, to pierce the elephant's trunk with a lance. Another Sikh, Ude Singh was appointed to chop the head of Raja Kesri Chand who was leading this assault.

Vachitter Singh was successful at the very first go, in driving his lance into the mad head of the elephant advancing menacingly towards the fort. The animal got furious in his rage, turned back and trampled many of his own troops to death. Ude Singh challenged Kesri Chand in a single combat and cut off his head. After much massacre of their men, and abandoning much war-booty, the Hill chiefs took to their heels in the dead of night losing the most prominent of their ranks, Raja Ghummand Chand, also on the battle-field.

However, they decided to give no peace to the Guru and made frantic appeals to the emperor to assist them in their designs. On hearing of it, the Guru this time decided to meet the enemy on open ground, some distance ahead of Anandpur. Seeing the Guru thus exposing himself to attack, the hill chiefs advanced upon him. The Guru's forces took positions on an elevated ground, and soon beat them back. Then, a Muslim gunner was employed for high reward to get the Guru. But in this also they failed. With one shot, the gunner killed a servant of the Guru, but the Guru employed his skill in archery to devastating effect and killed both the gunner and, also, his brother who had the same mission on hand.

Meantime, the imperial army under the Subedar of Sirhind, Wazir Khan, reached the spot. Though the Guru was advised to hasten back into the fort of Anandpur, he refused to budge from his ground and advanced with about five thousand men, in three detachments, the Guru commanding the rear and his son, Ajit, with another four, the vanguard. There was desperate fighting right upto the bank of the Satluj which the Guru crossed along with his troops to take positions on the other side. But, the losses of the imperial and the Hill armies were so colossal that they decided to retreat, and, offering presents to the Moghal Viceroy, entreated him to go back and not to pursue the battle any more. The Hill chiefs were happy that the Guru had left Anandpur, but their satisfaction was short-lived as after a brief while the Guru returned with the beat of drum. Now Raja Ajmer Chand who was his prime enemy, sued the Guru for peace and sent him costly presents and a very conciliatory communication. The Guru replied in the same friendly tone. The other Hill chiefs also followed suit, and peace reigned for some time in this battle-scarred region.

War II - Against Hill Chiefs

During the Brief period of peace that followed, the Guru instructed his following in the finer, spiritual or social aspects of Sikh life. Men and women trekked long weary distances to have his sight, and, as was the Guru's behest, made offerings of arms or horses to him. Congregations would assemble, morning and evening, in which besides the chanting of the Guru's Word by the musicians, the Guru would minister instructions on dedicating one's life and all one had to the Supreme Being, to keep Him ever in one's remembrance and to do everything in His name and for His pleasure. The Guru also enjoined upon his followers to serve each other, irrespective of any distinctions, and to look upon the whole humanity as one.

One day, the Guru feeling thirsty asked some water to be brought to him. A young boy obeyed the command, but when the Guru looked at his soft, feminine hands, he said to him: "Your hands are so tender that I wonder if you have ever used them!" The boy said this was true. He was born to rich parents who wouldn't permit him any manual work. The Guru threw away the water he had brought, saying, "I wouldn't accept any offering from a hand that has not served another."

Every Sikh was expected to make an offering of the tithe, each year, to the Guru. This the Sikhs did with utmost devotion, taking this to be a favour of the Guru. They came from all over the country, not only from the Punjab, but from as far away as Kabul and Kandhar. One day, a Sikh came to him in quest of peace. "I've earned enough", he said, "now I want to be at your feet to listen to your instructions and redeem myself." The Guru put him under a tutor and asked the tutor teach him reading and writing so that he could read the Guru's Word himself and write it for others. But, when the tutor uttered to him the first stanza of Guru Amar Das's *Anand,* beginning, "Wonder, O wonder, my mother, I've attained unto the Guru", he refused to learn any more! The tutor complained to the Guru of the apathy of the learner. On being questioned by the Guru, the Sikh replied, "What more is there for him to teach and me to learn when I've found the Guru and feel blessed. This is what I came here for!" The Guru embraced him saying, "Blessed art thou who hast found the Guru that soon, and so well."

A Sikh, Kahan Singh by name, was greatly devoted to the Guru. He was once plastering a wall when a drop of mud fell on the Guru's dress as he was passing by. The Guru humorously remarked: "Such a one should get a slap in the face." Many Sikhs rushed forward and gave the poor man a hearty drubbing. The Guru who was witnessing the scene felt distressed and asked, "You have carried out my instruction very thoroughly indeed! Now I ask, is there one who would marry his daughter to him? He is so devoted to my work and ought to be rewarded with a suitable match." Most Sikhs became utterly mute, but a man from Kandhar immediately offered his daughter to the poor man whom the Guru blest with the boon of five powerful sons.

One day, finding the rations in the Guru's kitchen dwindling, his mother stopped the Sikhs from serving food to others. The Guru was greatly distressed on hearing this and pronounced a curse: "Those who have given this evil advice to my mother, may the Turks destroy them!" The mother tearfully begged of her son to pardon her and those that had given her false reports of the dwindling rations.

The Guru said, "O mother, the Guru's kitchen will never be empty, nor my Khalsa's, so long as it is meant to serve others." And, he forgave those who were responsible for this misdemeanour.

In the meantime, Raja Amjer Chand sent a Brahmin to the court of the Guru in the garb of a devotee but indeed to keep a watch over his activities, and the size of his treasury. By giving secret information, he was responsible for two of the finest horses being stolen from the Guru's stable. One day, he suggested to the Guru to grace the fair at Rawalsar, near Mandi, where the Hill chiefs also gathered each year. He said this would be an ideal opportunity for a rapproachment between the two sides.

The Guru agreed on the entreaties of his mother and a large number of the devout. The Guru received the rajas in his camp with great warmth and they and their queens were literally charmed by his manners and sweet speech. They implored the past to be forgiven to which the Guru said: "In my house, we do not store the past, only the present and the future." The Guru arranged a big feast in honour of his visit and invited high and low to partake of it. But the high-caste Brahmins refused the invitation, saying, "He has corrupted the religion of our forefathers. How can we interdine with men of low castes or give up our age-old beliefs in our gods and rituals by following his way of life."

Knowing that the Hill folk were very superstitious and believed in astrology, the Guru said, "My Sikhs will never be a prey to superstitions. For them, one moment is as good as another. He who has faith in God will not like to divine His Secrets through astrology or such like superstitions."

It is said a Vaishnava, Har Gopal by name, being influenced by his father's newly-awakened faith in the Guru, came to visit him wish a handsome offering, but he felt disgust in his mind on seeing the Guru taking a meat diet. Though he pretended to the Guru that he had utter faith in him, and was blest by the Guru who also offered him a steel bracelet, on way back home he confided to a Sikh that he had wasted his money on the Guru who was a meat-eater. The Sikh asked him to transfer to him the Guru's blessings and the steel bracelet in return for the money he had offered to his Saviour. The Vaishnava was much pleased with the deal and received his money back from the Guru's devotee with great joy. But after sometime, he incurred such heavy losses in his trade that he had neither the money, nor the peace of mind. So, he went back to the Guru to ask forgiveness. The Guru pardoned him and said, "The Guru eateth whatever cometh to him from God. He eateth not for the taste of the palate, but to keep him a fit and a worthy instrument of God's mission. Men quarrel over diet, dress and ritual and over caste, community and creed, and have thus torn man from man. My mission is to restore mankind to a single brotherhood. So, how can I love one kind of man and hate another? They whose lives and deeds are dedicated to God find everything that cometh from Him sacred and good. My Sikhs shall never live on charity or religious offerings, but through honest means earn to live and live to share, and will ever keep God in their hearts in whatever they do. All else is secondary and of little consequence."

A Brahmin complained to the Guru that some Pathans had abducted his bride. The Guru sent an expeditionary force of one hundred cavalry under his young son, Ajit Singh, to restore the Brahmin's bride. Ajit Singh fell on the Pathans in the night like lightning and produced the culprits along with their booty before the Guru. The woman was restored to her husband and the Pathans punished for their misdeed.

The Guru's fame was spreading far and wide, thus giving alarm to the Hill chiefs. In these days, two Muslim generals, Sayyad Beg and Alif Khan, were marching from Delhi to Lahore. Raja Ajmer Chand thought this an excellent opportunity to ask for their assistance which was agreed to on payment of one thousand rupees a day. Sayyad Beg, on hearing of the Guru's holy character, refused to fight and indeed joined the Sikh ranks. Together, they gave a hot chase to Alif Khan and his forces and made them retreat with heavy losses. Sayyad Beg transferred all his wealth to the Guru and decided to cast his lot with him in future.

After a brief period of peace, the Hill chiefs with a force of ten thousand attacked Anandpur again. The Guru had only eight hundred men with him, but he asked them to meet the enemy in the open this time, and not from behind the battlements. A great carnage followed. The Guru instructed the Khalsa army to aim their arrows and guns from positions of vantage and not pursue the enemy nor charge him with swords hand to hand. But when the Sikh troops saw the enemy retreating, they pursued him. The Guru was much displeased at this for, as he had visualised, the enemy finding them hopelessly outnumbered fell upon them and inflicted heavy losses. The Guru now himself took the field and this enthused the Khalsa so much that they routed the enemy.

However, the respite after this victory also turned out to be all-too-brief. For, on insistent entreaties from the Hill chiefs, the imperial troops soon advanced against the Guru's house under a Moghal general, Sayyad Khan. The Guru had only five hundred men at his disposal at this time. He put them in battle array under Generals Sayyad Beg and Maimun Khan, another devotee of his. At first they were disheartened to hear of a large army advancing towards Anandpur, but the Guru gave them heart and said, "In the final analysis it is man's heart that leads one to victory, not numbers or arms. And he who has a moral cause to fight for always has God on his side." Sayyad Beg engaged himself thereupon in a single combat with a Hill chief and killed him. Seeing this, a Moghal general, Din Beg, filled with hatred against Sayyad Beg for having deserted the Moghal army, struck him from behind and killed him. Maimun Khan fought with great bravery, as did other Sikhs and took a huge toll of life of the enemy's hosts.

Seeing such fantastic deeds of valour, General Sayyad Khan himself advanced towards the Guru on horseback. But, on beholding his serene and holy face said to him, "You strike first. I do not have the heart to take the initiative." The Guru replied, "In my house, we never fire the first shot. If you wouldn't strike me, I wouldn't strike you either." The General was so much overcome by emotion on hearing these words that he dismounted and fell at the Guru's feet. The Guru blessed him with the name of God and said, "Thou art saved in both the worlds." Sayyad Khan, however, could not restrain his troops who continued to war with the Sikhs. But, he retired to a distance, when another commander, Ramzan Khan, took the field against the Guru. The Guru aimed his arrow and killed his horse. But his forces were far too few to be able to romp victory home this time. The Guru, therefore, decided to leave Anandpur which was captured and looted by the Moghal army. The Sikhs were so much exercised over this defeat that they wanted the Guru to permit them to pursue the enemy and to die fighting rather than suffer the humiliation of a defeat. The Guru permitted them to do so. They gave a hot chase to the enemy and not only killed a large number of them but also relieved them of much of their booty. Many lost their lives but those that remained brought the Guru great joy and he came back to Anandpur with them much relieved.

The emperor was greatly exercised over this debacle of his huge army. The Qazi advised that the Guru be brought to the presence of the emperor. Aurangzeb agreed with this and sent a message to the Guru saying, "Your religion and mine believe in the unity of God. Why should there be any misunderstanding between us? There is no choice for you nor for any one else but to acknowledge my sovereignty which I have obtained from Allah, the Almighty. If you have any grievance, come and see me and I shall treat you as a holy man, but do not challenge my authority, else I shall have to march personally against you."

To this the Guru replied, "There's only one Sovereign, God the All-powerful to whose Will both your Majesty and I are subject. But you recognise this not and discriminate and pursue the Hindus, and instead of doing justice practise discrimination and bring harm to their person and religion. God has sent me with a mission—to restore righteousness on the earth. How can I be at peace with you so long as our ways are different?" The Guru however treated the emperor's envoy with great courtesy, and bestowed a robe of honour on him.

War-III Against Mughals

The Sikhs from various parts of the country, notably the central Punjab, came to visit the Guru in large number. They brought offerings of horses or arms as was the Guru's bidding. They learnt the lessons of warfare at Anandpur. The Guru, however, felt that even though calm prevailed around him, it was a lull before the storm. So, he must not be caught unprepared if the challenge came from any source, at any time.

The Hill chiefs were also secretly planning to have a show-down with the Sikhs in one final, decisive bid in collaboration with the imperial forces. They, therefore, sent another emissary, this time in the person of Raja Ajmer Chand to the Deccan where the emperor was waging war against the Deccan sultanates. The raja met the emperor, personally, and presented a petition on behalf of his fraternity detailing the anti-state activities of the Guru's house for the last over one century which resulted in the martyrdom of his father and great grandfather. The emperor was told that the Guru who had founded a new religion wanted all Hindus to embrace it and to wage war on the Moghal empire. The emperor, alarmed at these reports, ordered the dispatch of all available troops at Delhi, Sirhind and Lahore to march on Anandpur, under the supreme command of Wazir Khan, Subedar of Sirhind. These were joined by the Hill troops. The Guru got information from his devout followers from Delhi and elsewhere of the approaching storm. Though troops from the imperial capital could not be spared, those from Sirhind and Lahore made a formidable combination for the far fewer men the Guru had under arms with him.

When the enemy's hosts reached the outskirts of Anandpur, the Sikhs discharged their artillery fire with such venom and accuracy that it took a great toll of the enemy's life and horse. The Guru's army was shelling from within the forts, while the enemy was without any such cover and was on a lower ground. Two of the Guru's generals, Ude Singh and Daya Singh, were ordered at the close of the day's battle to charge the enemy in single combat. They with their storm troopers rushed into the enemy's ranks and inflicted heavy losses on the enemy. After a reorganisation of forces, the enemy was compelled, as we shall see, to pursue a different strategem. The fear lurking in everybody's mind that the Guru was a performer of miracles was coming true. Macauliffe records nine hundred dead on the enemy's side on the first day of the battle.

Next day, the Guru himself took the field on a charger. He showed magnificent skill in archery and his men fired with deadly precision. All attempts to capture the Guru alive or to kill him failed. So, it was decided to change the tactics and to cut off outside supplies from the fort so that the Guru and his men be starved into submission. The Guru asked his followers not to venture forth, but to hold the forts put under the charge of different commanders, including his son, Ajit Singh. The enemy cut off all supplies. The Sikhs in the dark of night pounced upon the enemy and created much havoc and looted much booty. On the day-break, another assault from the enemy followed, but to no avail against the Sikh guns.

These days, a Sikh, called Bhai Kanihya, was reported to the Guru as administering water to the fallen in battle, irrespective of friend or foe. The Guru called him to his presence and asked him why he was offering water to the enemy's wounded. Kanihya replied: "Since you've taught me to make no distinction between man and man, I do not see amongst the wounded any but *you.*" The Guru was so much pleased with this reply that he blessed him with salvation. His followers, the *Sewapanthis,* whose one aim in life is Service *(Sewa)*, are an honoured part of the community to this day.

The hardships of the beleaguered troops increased with each day. Inspite of the night sorties of the Sikhs, it was becoming near impossible to subsist on the meagre rations left within the fort. Even water supplies were running out. Starvation stared everyone in the face. Some of them complained to the Guru's mother that their hardships were being unnecessarily prolonged, for the Guru would not let them venture out, except occasionally and at night, but the booty they got was not enough to sustain them for long and their losses in such assaults were also heavy. For sometime, they lived on the leaves of trees and bark ground into flour. Hundreds of Sikhs sought the permission of the Guru to leave him. The Guru was much distressed, but said he would permit them to do so only if they denied him, in writing. Even this some of them did, saying, "Neither Thou art our Guru, nor we Thy Sikhs." But when they returned home, they were so shamed by their women-folk that they returned to battle at Mukatsar and each one of them died fighting for the Guru.

Seeing the Sikhs not surrendering even though by all estimates their resources were totally exhausted, the Hill chiefs hit upon another plan. They sent an emissary, a Brahmin, who said both the Hindus and the Muslims promised on oath that if the Guru would only leave the fort of Anandpur, the enemy's forces would retire and the Guru might return to his fort, later, at his pleasure. The sikhs could even take all their moveables with them. The Guru saw in this proposal a trick to drive him out of his entrenchments, and so did not agree. But the entreaties of his mother and devout followers left no choice for him. However, to put the bonafides of the enemy to the test, he asked for pack bullocks to convey his property first. This was immediately complied with. The Guru, however, sent out only the useless and waste material, covering it with brocade. This caravan was to move out at the dead of night with the help of torch lights. When this procession reached the enemy's camp, they pounced upon it with great ferocity, throwing all their oaths and solemn commitments to the winds. But, when, on daybreak, they found to their shame the contents of their booty, they knew that they could not trick the Guru into being caught in their trap.

The Guru now reminded his followers of what he had told them beforehand. But, meantime, the Moghals sensing the Guru's reaction at their foul deed, sent in another emissary, this time with a message, suggested to be in the emperor's own hands, expressing regret at the misbehaviour of the imperial troops and promising safe conduct, should the Guru condescend to quit Anandpur. The Sikhs were in dire straits. The Guru's mother also joined hands with them in making entreaties to accept the emperor's offer and not to let his innocent followers die of starvation. Even if the imperial troops were to betray their trust, it would be better, it was argued, to die fighting than through hunger. The Guru accepted the latter alternative, and so set fire to his possessions: those that could not be disposed of thus, were buried in the ground. The Guru's mother, with the two youngest sons of the Guru, aged 5 and 7, and his wives, were to go first, while the Guru with five hundred of his following was to move out along with his two elder sons, at the dead of night. It was the bitingly cold month of December of the year 1704 A.D.

On reaching Sirsa, the Guru met his mother and his two younger sons and entrusted a devout Sikh to take them to Delhi, to where his wives had already left. But, he took them instead to Rupar to a relation of his. Here, the Guru's mother met a Brahmin, Gangu, who was once their cook, who later took them to their village, Kheri, near Sirhind, and betrayed them to the Nawab of Sirhind. The Nawab offered them the choice between Islam and death. "We are the sons of Govind Singh who knoweth not defeat, nor surrender," the older one is reported to have said, "our grandfather laid down his life, but gave up not his faith. So shall we." When asked to bow before the Nawab, the little heroes kept their backs straight, and refused to pay obeisance to the Vicar of tyranny who was after the blood of their father and his peace-loving followers. When told that their father was dead and so there was no more any earthly hope for them, they are said to have replied: "Our father is deathless. He can never die." Realising that even though tender of age, they were resolute of will and firm in faith, they were ordered to be bricked up alive.

Historians have gone lyrical over the manly and fearless ways of the innocent ones, but what else could one expect from the offspring of Guru Govind? However, for the aged mother of the Guru, the shock was too overwhelming and, on hearing of the heart-rending news, she collapsed.

The Moghal authorities conducted a search in the Brahmin's house, suspecting that he had kept to himself the jewellery and other valuables of the Guru's mother. On his refusal to divulge where he had buried the treasure, they tortured him to death. The only one to protest against this heinous crime against the Guru's sons was the Nawab of Malerkotla who said, "The sins of the father should not be visited upon the tender sons. If we could not defeat the Guru, why wreak vengeance on these poor little things!" But, his pleas went unheard. The Sikhs under Banda Singh Bahadur kept this act of grace on the part of Malerkotla's house so much in their memory that whereas they destroyed Sirhind utterly, and butchered Wazir Khan and his entire family, they spared the state of Malerkotla altogether.

The Guru was in the meantime being pursued by the Moghal army. He took shelter in an improvised mud fortress at Chamkaur, where a bloody battle ensued, resulting in the loss of all but five of the forty Sikhs who were now with the Guru, the rest having been left at Sirsa to withstand the Moghal assault, till the Guru had crossed to safety. The Guru's two elder sons, Ajit and Jujhar, also died fighting valiantly at Chamkaur in single combats. The Guru had insisted, much to the anguish of his followers, that if not the first, they must not be the last to die. Seeing them fall before his very eyes, he offered prayers of thanks giving to God: *"O God, I've surrendered to Thee what belonged to Thee."*

Now, the Guru's own life was also in danger. But, he refused to leave the five who were still with him. They did their best to prevail upon him saying if he were to keep alive, the faith would grow once again into a formidable force. But, the Guru said, "My life is not more sacred than a devoted follower's. I'm going to die in battle along with you, if there's no other choice." On this, the Sikhs were much distressed. So, they hit upon a plan. The five gathered together and passed a *Gurmatta* (resolution) and presented it to the Guru thus: "Thou hast always said wherever there are five of you, dedicated to me, there I shall also be, and whatever ye ask, that shall be granted unto ye. Now, we command thee, as thy Guru, to leave the fort post-haste, and let's deal with the enemy later as best as we can." The Guru felt so helpless. His own injuctions were being quoted against him! He decided to obey, and after hugging each one of them to his bosom and saying, "God be with you, ye are redeemed both in this world and the next," he left. Two of them remained behind to lay down their lives next day, one of them being Sant Singh who wore the Guru's crest to masquerade for him. The Moghals were greatly disappointed to find, on inquiry, that the man of mistaken identity was not Guru Govind, but one of his followers. But before the Guru left, he discharged two arrows which struck the torches in the hands of the Moghal bodyguards, and then pierced through their bodies. Under cover of darkness he walked, barefooted, through the forest and lay down tired at Machhiwara, between Rupar and Ludhiana, where the other three Sikhs also joined him as directed.

On being informed that a detachment of Moghal army was still pursuing him, it became incumbent on him to escape to safety soon. But his feet were blistered, and he could hardly walk. At a Sikh's house where he was putting up now for a day, he met two Pathans, Nabi Khan and Ghani Khan, who had visited his court earlier also, and who now offered their services to the Guru. It was decided that the Guru would be carried on a cot by the two Pathans and two Sikhs while the fifth one would serve as an attendant. The Guru was to disguise as a Muslim *Pir,* recently returned from *hajj,* and fasting. This scheme saw them safely through the Moghal troops who were camping on the way.

It is said the Moghals would offer them safe conduct only if the "pir" would eat with them along with his followers. The Guru, however, execused himself saying he was on fast, and would touch nothing but raw barley. His three Sikhs were, however, advised to eat whatever was served with God's name uttered over it.

On the way, he met Mahant Kirpal who had fought on his side so valiantly in the battle of Bhangani, but Kirpal would not keep him for fear of the Moghals. The Guru went thence to Jagraon and Raikot and met the Chowdhry of these towns, Rai Kalha by name, who offered him great courtsies at his village, called Jatpura. From here, he proceeded to the Lakhi forest where he encamped for sometime in the midst of great natural scenery. Whoever heard of the Guru's coming, came to him overcome with emotion. The Guru himself writes: "When they heard of their Shepherd, they were full of gratitude to God. The flocks would touch not grass nor water, and no one waiting for the other ran to have a sight of the Master and be blest by him." It is here that the Guru received the heart-rending message from Sirhind about the martyrdom of his two young sons and mother. The Guru, composed as ever, bent upon his knees and lifting his hands to God in prayer uttered: "These two, Thy trust, I have also rendered unto Thee," and digging up a shrub with this knife he made this prophecy: "Just as I've torn this shrub from its roots, so shall this tyrannous empire be destroyed, root and branch, and much too soon."

II

From Jatpura, the Guru proceeded to Dina. A Sikh had presented his horse to him on the way and this facilitated his march away from the Moghal forces sooner than was possible otherwise. The Guru halted at Dina for some time. It is here that he wrote his Persian composition, *Zafarnama* (or, the Letter of Victory) in the name of Aurangzeb. This letter breathes defiance and contempt for earthly power which is yoked to tyranny and sin, and lays down the eternal rule that he alone wins in the end whose cause is just. That he alone doeth good who's right.

The Guru says in this epistle, *inter alia*: "O King, I have no faith in thy oaths. Thou vowest to go one way and followest another. I would not have withdrawn my forces from Anandpur if I hadn't put my faith in what thou pledged to me. And what could my forty men at Chamkaur do, when a hundred thousand men of thine fell upon them?

"When there's no other course open to man, it is but righteous to unsheathe the sword. When thy forces advanced against me, I gave them a taste of my arrows. Some of thy men fled, others were sent to the other world. And, I escaped, unhurt, by God's Grace. Not a hair of my head could all thy forces touch.

"I protest thou believest neither in God, nor thy prophet. Thou keepest not thy word, and liest, putting faith in worldly weal and power, and not thy God. Thou knowest not the value of an oath on the *Quran*. If the prophet Mohammad were here, I would present to him this foul deed of thy treachery. Thy envoy and thy Qazi vowed before me on thy behalf, and thou betrayed my trust! If even now thou repentest and comest to see me here in this territory of *Bairars*, who are all my followers, they shall give thee safe conduct and thou shalt not be harmed. I wish I could speak to thee face to face.

"I owe allegiance to only one God, my King. If He so desires, I might come to thee. Did thy God ask thee to tyrannise over others? Fie on thy sovereignty and on thy regard for God and religion! But, hear me: do not employ thy sword to murder the innocent, for the God on high would for sure punish thee. Fear God, therefore, who's the Master of the earth and the heaven, and whose vengeance is terrible, who fears no one and is the protector forever of the poor.

"What if thou hast killed my four sons? Remember, the coiled snake is still alive. By putting out a few sparks thou quenchest not the fire thereby. Thy troops plundered the goods I had sent out (of the Anandpur fort) believing their oath to be true. But just as thou hast forgotten God, God will now forget thee and thou wilt be punished for thy evil deeds. But I wonder if thou knowest God. Thou hast an empire, wealth and pomp, a generous disposition, warlike qualities, but far from thee is religion.

"My protection is God than whom there's no one better, nor higher. He who acteth honestly, him the God saveth to perform His service. How can an enemy touch his person of whom God on high is the friend and refuge? Life is but for a brief few moments. Change is the law of life. Whoever cometh here, also quitteth the scene. So, whatever one's strength, one must annoy not the weak and thus destroy one's roots."

This unusual letter the Guru sent to the emperor through two of his trusted Sikhs, Daya Singh and Dharam Singh. The letter was duly delivered to the emperor, personally, in the south at Ahmadnagar and the emperor expressed a wish that the Guru might come and see him, but before the two could meet, news was received that the emperor was dead.

In the period that intervened, the Guru travelled through the Malva country. Some easy-going Sikhs of the central Punjab (Majha) hearing of the Guru's nearness waited upon him and implored him to return to the peaceful path of Nanak.

They promised to intercede on his behalf with the emperor so that further animosities between the two houses might cease. But, the Guru refused to listen to them saying, "I'm fighting for a cause, not for myself. I have sacrificed my sons, my father and my mother for this cause. And, now you come to ask me to withdraw from the fight to save my person? This will never be. Whosoever wants to live in ignoble peace, may compromise with tyranny. I wouldn't till I have breath in me, nor will those who will choose to follow me." These men then left for their homes, disappointed, but when they reached their destinations and told the people of the Guru's determination to continue the fight, hundreds of them resolved to fight on the Guru's side, led by a woman, Mai Bhago, who, donning a man's dress shamed and censured them back to the path of suffering and sacrifice. Some of them were those who had earlier denied the Guru at Anandpur and escaped from the battle.

The Guru now got news that he was being pursued by the imperial troops, at least ten thousand strong, under Wazir Khan, Subedar of Sirhind. He, therefore, proceeded towards *Khidrana,* in the district of Ferozepur. In the meantime, the large contingent of Sikhs from Majha (whose strength some historians like Latif have put at 12,000, though the Sikh Chroniclers say they were far fewer, some say as few as forty) saw a huge force advancing towards the Guru who was only a short distance away. They engaged the Moghal hots so recklessly that everyone of them including the brave heroine, Mai Bhago, fell on the battlefield. It is said they attracted the Moghal forces towards themselves by spreading their white cotton sheets on the trees and shrubs all around. The Moghals seeing a huge Sikh camp pounced upon it and after a fierce battle, killed everyone of their number. The Moghal forces thinking that the Guru also must be one of the slain, retired from the field quite some distance behind, as they could not find water for their troops. When the Guru went to the scene of the battle to find out wherefrom had that timely contingent arrived to assist him, he found one of the Sikhs, Mahan Singh by name, still a little conscious. The Guru took him in his lap, wiped his face, and with tears of joy in his eyes, said: "Ask whatever thou may and I grant thee that. Thou hast redeemed thyself both here and in the hereafter." The devotee, his breath choked with emotion, sobbed: "If thou art in mercy, forgive me and my companions our earlier betrayal of thee at Anandpur. Pray tear up the piece of paper on which, to our shame, we wrote: we acknowledge thee not as our Guru. We have tried to wipe our treachery to thee with our blood. Now own us if thou may in thy Mercy and bless us that we die in peace." The Guru blessed him profusely, tore up their collective letter of apostacy and said, "Ye are all saved by God in whose cause ye have laid down your lives. God's Mercy shall be upon ye and upon those who'll choose to follow ye." Mai Bhago who showed signs of life was picked up by the Guru from the battle-field and taken with him for treatment. He got all the dead bodies collected and cremated with due honours.

The Guru now proceeded to Talwandi Sabo (in the erstwhile Patiala state) and now called Damdama Sahib (or the place of the Guru's rest). Here, he stayed for quite sometime dictating the *Adi Granth* to a devout Sikh of his, Bhai Mani Singh, and adding to it his father's hymns and, according to tradition, one verse of his own. He did so because, it is said, the original copy was with his uncle, Dhirmal, who refused to part with it. And, the sikhs wanted an edition certified by the Guru. He also made additions to his own compositions. Here, he was also joined by his wives, Sundri and Sahib Kaur. When they asked the Guru where the young sons were, the Guru replied, pointing to his followers: "For these thousands, I sacrified the other four. So long as these sons of mine are alive, I will not consider the death of my other sons in vain!"

The Guru blessed this part of the land saying instead of coarse grain and shrubbery, it will yield wheat and fruit, which it does now, and scattering his reed-pens in all directions he said, "This will one day be a place of great learning." It is now known as the Guru's Kashi. The Guru, according to trumpp, made 1,20,000 converts during his stay at Damdama. The old glory of Anandpur, it appears, had returned and Sikhs thronged here from far and near. Now, the Guru decided to depart along with five others towards the Deccan via Rajputana, inspite of the beseechings of his devotees. "My message of hope must spread from one corner of this land to the other," he said, "I cannot sit back and relax, when my nation is on fire." It appears, it was now the Guru's wish to integrate his forces with those of the Rajputs and the Marathas to give a decisive battle to the Moghals.

Bahadur Shah's Accession

While The Guru was yet on his way, he heard of the death of Aurangzed. His eldest son, Bahadur Shah, was engaged in a military expedition in Afghanistan at that time. Taking anvantage of his absence, his younger brother, Mohammad Azam, usurped the throne. Bahadur Shah hastened back home to fight his way to his legel heritage. He had often heard of the heroic exploits of Guru Govind Singh, and, also, that being a man of spiritual disposition, he harboured grudge against systems, not men. He, therefore, took a chance and appealed to Guru Govind Singh, through one of his devout Sikhs from Ghazni, Bhai Nand Lal whom he knew personally, to forget the past and help him gain possession of the imperial throne. He promised to look into, and redress, any grievances the Guru might have against his house. (Why Bahadur Shah made, and the Guru accepted, the request for assistance is amply justified by the character of the former as evidenced by historians of the time. Contrary to his father's Sunni creed, Bahadur Shah was a Shia, and a liberal Sufi like his uncle, Dara Shikoh, who too was on the best of terms with the Guru's house and was offered material help and a robe of honour by the seventh Guru, Hari Rai, when Dara was a fugitive after the battle of Samugarh, and which so much annoyed Aurangzeb that he called the Guru to his presence to answer for it. Dara, it may be recalled, was a great votary of Hazrat Mian Mir of Lahore, a renowned Sufi, who had been called upon by the fifth Guru, Arjun, to lay the foundation stone of the now famous Golden Temples at Amritsar. Thus the relations of Sikhism with the Sufi and Shias, both persecuted by Aurangzeb, were of the most cordial.

Bahadur Shah was a generous, munificent and excessively good natured prince. His tolerance and amiability were in great contrast to the bigotry and hypocrisy of his predecessor, Aurangzeb. Brought up in the school of adversity (he was kept in confinement for seven years by his father charging him with softness to, and even hobnobbing with, the Sultans of Bijapur and Golkanda whom he was asked to subdue but with whom he wanted to make a reapproachment of the king-emperor) he had grown up mild and affable to such a degree that the people called him the Saint King.

According to his historian, his gifts in jewels and rich dresses were truly royal. In his dress he was plain like a devotee. He tried at Lahore to introduce the *Khutba,* according to the Shia creed, but on being opposed by the Sunnis abandoned the idea, a singular sign of his liberal outlook. Fond of the society of learned men, he took great delight in discourses on topics of law and divinity. He was most popular in Punjab and one of the gateways of Lahore (Shah-Almi) was named after him...).

Though the Guru wasn't sure of Bahadur Shah keeping his word once victory was his, he had heard of his catholicity of outlook as against the bigotry and one-track mind of his father. So, he decided to give his offer a trial and sent a detachment under one of his trusted disciples, Dharam Singh, to render whatever assistance they could to Bahadur Shah in his hour of crisis. A bloody battle was fought near Dhaulpur for three days in which Mohammad Azam, along with several of his principal officers, was killed, his army scattered and Bahadur Shah proclaimed himself the emperor of India. He was extremely grateful for the assistance that the Sikh detachment had rendered him and sent Dharam Singh, their leader, to express his heartfelt gratitude to the Guru. He also made a request to the Guru to see him, saying he himself would have paid a visit to the Guru, but this gesture might be misconstrued by some of his bigoted followers.

When this invitation was received in the Guru's camp, the Sikhs would not advise the Guru to accept it. They feared there might be some catch in it. The Guru's wives also entreated him likewise. But the Guru said, "Life and death are in the hands of God at all times. Hence, one cannot be too careful in avoiding danger." He accepted the invitation and accompanied by one of his wives, Sahib Kaur, and leaving the other one, Sundri, in Delhi, (the third one had died early), he marched towards Agra where the emperor had encamped himself. On way, he halted at Mathura and Vrindavan and held discourses to the people.

When he reached Agra, the emperor received him with great courtesies, made him costly presents and thanking him profusely for the timely assistance he had rendered him requested him to spend some time with him. The Guru gladly accepted this invitation. He thought it would be a good opportunity to bring to the emperor's notice the tyrannies heaped upon his followers by the proteges of the imperial rule, notably the Nawab of Sirhind, who had ordered his two young sons to be bricked up alive.

This nearness of the emperor to the Guru became an eye-sore to many of his courtiers, and some of them decided to embarrass the Guru. One day, as he was conversing with the king in the presence of some courtiers, one of them, said to be a learned Sayyad from Sirhind, made a request thus: "O Guru, we have heard of the great house of Nanak. You are the tenth in succession to the founder of your religion. We consider only him to be a divine man who can perform miracles. It would give us great satisfaction if you too could allay our doubts in this behalf." The Guru sensed clearly what lay behind this seemingly innocent request. But in order to put his questioner in the wrong, he answered: "Why, the emperor himself is the miracle-maker. He can raise high who's humble and demolish those that are high and mighty." The questioner was, however, persistent: "Sir, what you speak is truth, but I want to know if there's a miracle Your Holiness can perform." The Guru thereupon took out a gold coin and said, "Look, what a miracle is this? It can buy anything in the world, any person, any value. Isn't it?" "Yes, yes, your Honour, but we would be pleased to know what miracles can *you* perform. That is what will allay our doubts." The Guru, thereupon, drew his sword and thundered: "*This* is the miracle I can perform. I can chop off the head of anyone who dares challenge me. Here is the final arbiter for the destinies of men and nations."

The questioner became speechless. The emperor, who was listening to the questions and answers with great interest before, reprimanded the questioner for his impudence. "No, no, Excellency," he said, "You shouldn't mind this impertinence on the part of my courtier." As this news travelled, everyone was amazed at the fearlessness of the Guru even in the presence of the emperor of the land in whose presence it was just not possible for anyone to appear armed, much less to draw the sword.

One day the emperor said to the Guru, "There's no faith better than ours. Why shouldn't those who want to escape hell embrace it." The Guru replied, "O king, it is not the stamp but what is inside it that makes a coin worthwhile. Even when a counterfeit coin has Your Majesty's creed imprinted upon it, no one will exchange it with goods in the market-place. So also in the case of faith. It's not the label, but the content that's pleasing to God, and which determines who's to be consigned to hell, who to heaven. I believe in one God, not two or three, and for me no one is an infidel save one who denies His Presence."

One day, the Guru made known to the emperor the desire he had harboured for some time. This was to deliver up to him the body of Wazir Khan, Subedar of Sirhind, so that he could deal with him as he chose. The emperor was taken aback at this demand, but did not refuse it at the moment. He said, he would consult with his ministers and would tender a reply later, though he expressed his grave doubts if it would not lead to a mutiny in his army if he surrendered a Viceroy's body to the Guru for reprisals. He, therefore, requested the Guru to wait for a year till his rule was firmly established and invited him to accompany him on his march towards Jaipur and other places. The Guru, though annoyed at the emperor's hesitancy, still did not want to break off his relations suddenly and agreed to accompany the emperor on his march, to see if given a further chance, he would meet with his demand which was legitimate and in accordance with the Quranic injunction: life for life.

The Guru, however, waited for some time more at Agra, addressing the holy congregations every morning and evening. Meantime, the emperor marched towards Jaipur. Later, the Guru's camp followed his, and soon overtook the emperor and visited Jodhpur and Chitaur along with him. The Rajput princes of these places paid homage to the Guru, who continued his march southwards along with the emperor till he reached Burhanpur where a devout Sikh had prepared a house for the Guru. The Guru honoured him with his visit and stayed in the house for some time. The emperor in the meantime had left and later wrote to the Guru to join him. The Guru accepted his request and both proceeded to Nanded in the Deccan, on the bank of the river Godavari. This was in the later part of the year 1707 A.D. The Guru had with him some infantry and two to three hundred cavalry equipped with lances.

At Nanded, he visited the house of a Bairagi, Madho Das by name. The Guru had heard that the Bairagi could perform miracles and had such skill in magic that he could overthrow anyone who sat on his couch. The guru thereupon went into his hut, and lay on his couch in his absence. When Madho Das came and saw a stranger occupying his couch, unharmed, he couldn't believe his eyes. The Guru, he was told in advance by one of his followers, had also slain one of his goats and cooked and eaten its meat. This scrilege and affront the Bairagi could not bear, and demanded an explanation from the intruder. The Guru replied that he was too fatigued and having come upon the hut of one who was known for his hospitality, he could not but recline on the couch and eat whatever was available. The Guru also told him that he had come to reclaim him from the life of a recluse. When Madho Das looked into his eyes and at his figure and saw something unusual in his charming, fearless manners, he asked who he was. When told that he was Guru Govind Singh in person, he fell at his feet, and said, "O Master, I'm Thy slave (Banda). You have honoured me by your visit and emancipated me. Pray tell me if there's any command of yours I can carry out. You are the saviour of our race."

The Guru was deeply touched at this homage. When asked, Madho Das narrated his whole story to the Guru. Born in Poonch, near Rajauri (Kashmir), he farmed for sometime, practised fire-arms and went on hunting expeditions. One day, he had killed a she-deer and found, to his utter distress, two young ones in her womb. This shocked him so much that he renounced the world and became a recluse, settling later at Nander and practising austerities. Here he had also learnt the practice of Yoga, and some magic. The Guru liked his sensitive nature, but reminded him that when tyranny had overtaken men, it was the duty of the more sensitive to fight against it and even to lay down their life in the struggle. Madho Das, who now called himself the Master's slave, Banda, offered to do as he was bidden. The Guru thereupon baptised him and named him Gurbakhash Singh (though he continued to be known popularly as Banda Singh Bahadur). The Guru also presented him with a sword and five arrows from his quiver and instructed him to remain chaste, not to turn away from battle, to remain humble in victory, not to found a sect of his own, to look upon his associates in this mission as comrades and equals, as the principles of the Khalsa brotherhood enjoined, and never their superior, and to take counsel with them at all times.

The Guru blest him that so long as he carried out the Guru's mission in the spirit in which it was intended—punishing the evil-doers and raising the poor and the down-trodden-in a spirit of dedication and detachment, with God in the heart, ever and at all times, the Guru's hand will always be at his back. Banda bowed at the Guru's feet and promised to do as he was instructed and never to depart from the path set out for him by the Master.

Thereupon, the Guru gave him detailed instructions to proceed to the Punjab along with three other Sikhs, Binod Singh, Kahan Singh and Baz Singh, and to wait at a point near Buria (in Ambala) for reinforcements which the Guru would get him sent. Thereafter, he was to attack a place nearby, called Sadhaura, where his devout Muslim follower, Budhu Shah, had been executed along with his disciples by his co-religionists for helping the Guru in the battle of Bhangani. Later, he was to march on Sirhind, lay seige to the city and seize and personally execute Wazir Khan, the Subedar, whose head the guru had demanded earlier from the emperor but was disappointed by the latter's evasive replies. Later, he was to settle accounts with the chiefs of the hill states adjoining Punjab some of whom had been inimical, without cause, to the Guru's house and had even joined hands with the Moghal emperor to attack and harass him at a time when he needed and had asked for their help to defeat the common enemy.

Banda left Nander soon after, with a letter from the Guru in the name of the Sikhs to rally to his banner. The Guru stayed here for sometime more.

The Guru after sometime seems to have sent away his wife, Sahib Kaur, who had accompanied him to the Deccan, to Delhi, where his other wife, Sundri, was. She was not willing to part, as she had taken a vow that without seeing the Guru, each day, she would not partake of food. But the Guru prevailed upon her and blessing her with six different weapons told her to look at them whenever she desired to behold him. Bhai Mani Singh, a great divine and learned followers of the Guru, was also made to accompany her.

Death of Guru Gobind Singh

Only three years after death of Shri Gobind Singh, the Sikhs under Banda were the masters of a large portion of territory in central and south-east Panjab and were threatening Delhi. Thirty years after, they were the masters of the Cis-Satluj states, after a life-and-death struggle which, in its heroism and sacrifice, has few parellels in the history of mankind. The Guru had made death for a cause so popular that even when price was put on the head of every Sikh, and the whole community was hounded out of their habitations and lived for years in the woods and hide-outs, not one surrendered or accepted defeat. By the end of the Guru's century, they had established their rule over the entire Panjab, and later also in Kashmir. Ladakh and the Pathanland right upto the Khyber pass. For the first time in a thousand years of India's history, the tide of invasions had turned west-wards. This was nothing short of a miracle.

But, this was not all. He composed poetry that has few peers in the annals of literature: so vast is its canvas and imaginative sweep. The Guru created not merely a community of warriors, but men who would, even during war-time, never forsake God, and whose victories would be for the sake of *Dharma,* not for self-glory or greed. In other words, according to Guru Govind Singh, it was not power, but ethics that must determine the polity of a nation. And a nation must consist of a whole people, not a society broken up by caste, colour, creed or a superior race. This democratic spirit which the Guru infused in the Khalsa brotherhood, in which the highest was equal to the lowest, and where a small, well-knit idea-inspired band of men and women fought and acted in the name, and for the sake, of a whole people has made Arnold Toynbee remark that hc had anticipated Lenin by two centuries. He abolished succession knowing what abuses an office by heredity can lead to. He even proclaimed, as has been pointed out that "whosoever would call me God would be consigned to hell." The Sikhs had to turn in secular matters to the whole Khalsa for a unanimous resolution, or the consensus (the Gurmatta), which was obligatory for everyone to follow. And, though he fought both with the Moghals and their vassals, the Hindu hill chiefs, he inculcated nothing but respect for the other man's faith. "Men are the same all over, though each hath a different appearance," he preached.

For the first time our race was given the message of the whole man. The same person was to be the devotee of God, as much as a warrior, a tiller of the soil as well as the performer of menial duties. *Seva* (Community service), and *Langar* (Community kitchen) have since been the *sine-qua-non* of the Sikh fraternity. The taboos of dress and diet not longer were important for a spiritual life. Nor any profession was forbidden to a Sikh. But, all that he did was to be in the name of God. For, the Guru said, "The Khalsa belongs to God, and so victory also, in every field, is God's." He who only earns but does not share, he who only gathers joys but does not sacrifice, he who runs after the transitory allurements of life but is not dedicated to God forever and at all times, could not claim the Guru as his own. His last prayer was, as it would also be of those who seek to follow him:

> "O God, there's nothing that's mine in me: all that's me belongs to Thee. When I surrender to Thee what's Thine, O what is it, then, that belongs to me?"

4

The New Order

We give below God's Commands to Guru Gobind Singh, before he took birth at Patna City on January 21, 1662:

"When I created this World, I first made the demons, who became enemies and oppressors.
They became intoxicated with the strength of their arms.
And ceased to worship Me, the Supreme Being.
I became angry and at once destroyed them.
In their places I established the gods.
They also busied themselves with receiving sacrifices and worship,
And called themselves supreme beings.
Mahadev called himself the imperishable God.
Vishnu too declared himself to be God.
And nobody though Me to be God.
Then I made the eight Sakhis
Who were appointed to keep watch over creatures.
They told people to worship them,
And said, "There is no God but us."
They did not recognise the Primal Essence,
Worshipped them as God.
How many worshipped the sun and Moon!
How many made burnt offerings! how many worshipped the wind!
Some recognise a stone as God.
How many bathed in the water according to Shastrik rites!
How many, recognizing Dharamraj as their supreme judge,
Performed religious ceremonies through fear!
They whom I appointed to watch over creatures,
On coming into this world called themselves God.
They altogether forgot My orders,
And became absorbed each in his own praise.
When they did not recognise Me, then I created men.
They too fell under the influence of pride,
And made gods out of stones.

Then I created the Sidhs and the Sadhs,
But they too found not the Supreme Being.
Whosoever was clever in the world
Established his own sect,
And no one found the Creator.
Enmity, contention, and pride increased.
Men begin to burn trunk and leaves in their own fires.
(i.e. anarchy was created)
And none of them went My way.
They who obtained a little spiritual powei.
Struck out their own way.
None of them recognised the Supreme Being.
But became mad boasting of themselves.
None of them recognised the Real Essence,
But each became absorbed in himself.
Then I created the Supreme Rikhis
Who afterwards made their own Simritis current.
They who were smitten by the Simritis
Abandoned My worship.
They who attached their hearts to My feet
Did not walk in the way of Simritis.
Brahma made the Four Veds
And caused all to act according to them;
But they whose love was attached to My feet
Renounced the Veds.
They who abandoned the tenets of the Veds and of other religious books,
Became devoted to Me, the Supreme Lord.
They who follow true religion
Shall have their sins of various kinds blotted out.
They who endure bodily suffering
And cease not to love Me,
Shall all to go paradise.
And there shall be no difference between Me and them.
They who shrink from suffering,
And forsaking Me, adopt the way of Veds and Simiritis
Shall fall into the pit of hell,
And continually suffer transmigration.
Afterwards I created Dattatre
Who also struck out his own path.
He pared not his finger nails, decorated his head with matter hair,

And paid no heed to My worship.
Then I created Gorakh
Who made great kings his disciples,
And tearing their ears put rings in them;
But he thought not of the way of My love.
Then I created Ramanand
Who wore the garb of a Bairagi,
Put a wooden necklace on his neck,
And paid no heed to My worship.
They who were created by Me
Struck out their several paths.
I then created Muhammad,
And made him king of Arabia.
He too established a religion of his own,
Cut off the foreskins of all his followers, And made every one repeat his name;
But no one fixed the true Name in man's heart.
All these were wrapped up in themselves,
And none of them recognised Me, the Supreme Being.
I have cherished thee as My son,
And created thee to extend My Religion
Go and spread My religion there,
And restrain the world from senseless acts.
I stood up, clasped my hands, bowed my head, and
Replied: "Thy religion shall prevail in the world
When Thou vouchsafest assistance."

On this account God sent me.
Then I took birth and came into the world.
As He spoke to me, so I spoke unto men;
I bear no enmity to any one.
All who call me the Supreme Being
Shall fall into the pit of hell
Recognise me as God's servant only;
Have no doubt whatever of this.
I am the slave of the Supreme Being.
And have come to behold the wonders of the world.
I tell the world what God told me,
And will not remain silent through fear of mortals.

As God spoke to me I speak,
I pay no regards to any one besides.

I am satisfied with no religious garb;
I sow the seed of the Invisible.
I am not a worshipper of stones,
Nor am I satisfied with any with religious garb.
I will sing the Name of the Infinite,
And will obtain the Supreme Being.
I will not wear matted hair on my head,
Nor will I put on ear-rings;
I will pay no regard to any one but God.
What God told me I will do.
I will repeat the One Name
Which will be every where profitable.
I will not repeat any other name,
Nor establish any other God in my heart.
I will meditate on the name of the Endless One,
and obtain the Supreme light.
I am imbued with Thy Name, O God;
I am not intoxicated with any other honour,
I will meditate on the Supreme,
And thus remove endless sins.
I am enamoured of Thy form;
No other gift hath charms for me.
I will repeat Thy Name,
And avoid endless sorrow.
Sorrow and sin have not approached those
Who have meditated on Thy Name.
They who meditate on any one else
Shall die of arguments and contentions.
The Divine Guru sent me for religion's sake:
On this account I have come into the world—
"Extend the faith everywhere;
Seize and destroy the evil and sinful" (in one self)
Understand this, ye holy men in your mind,
I assumed birth for this purpose
Of spreading the faith, saving the saints,
And extirpating all tyrants. (in one self)
all the first incarnations
Caused men to repeat their names.
They killed no one who had offended against God
(the inner morbid instincts)
And they struck out no path of real religion.

The Muslim Saints and Prophets who existed
Left the world talking of themselves.
None of them recognised the Great Being
Or knew of anything of real religion.
Nothing is to be obtained by putting hopes in others;
Put the hopes of your hearts in One God alone.
Nothing is obtained by hoping in others;
Put the hopes of your hearts in Him.

Some millions read Purans together;
How many silly persons recite the Quran!
But these books shall be of no assistance at last,
And shall save no one from Death's toils.
Why not, O brethern, repeat the Name of Him
Who will aid you at the last moment?
Consider spurious religions as superstition.
No such things will avail you.
On this account God created me;
Having communicated to me the secret,
He sent me into the world.
I shall proclaim to all men what He told me.

I will repeat God's Name,
And all my affairs shall prosper.
I will not close mine eyes,
Or do anything for show.
They who wear a religious garb
Are deemed naught by the saints of God.
Understand this, all men, in your hearts,
That God is not obtained by hypocrisy.
They who act for the sake of display,
Shall not obtain salvation in the next world;
And it is only for life their affairs prosper.
Kings on seeing their acting worship them;
But God is not to be found my mummery.
Yet every one wandereth about this searching for Him.
He who keepeth his heart in subjection
Recognizeth the Supreme Being.

They who by wearing a religious garb keep the people of the world in subjection,
Shall at last be cut with the shears of Death and take up their abode in hell.

They who present appearances to the world,
Experience extreme pleasure in fleecing others.
Spurious, and not worth a penny, is the religion
Of those who practise suspension of breath by stopping their noses.
They who practise spurious religion in the world
Shall fall into the pit of hell.
He who can in no way subdue his heart
Shall not go to heaven by gesticulation.

What God Himself told me I proclaim to the world.
They who meditate on Him shall go to heaven at last.
God and God's servant are both one-deem not that there is any difference between them—
As waves produced from water are again blended with it.
God remaineth apart from those
Who indulge in wrangling and pride.
He is not found in the Veds or in the books of Mussalmans.
Know this in your hearts, O Saints of God.
They who practise hypocrisy by closing their eyes
Should be treated as blind men.
Since road is not seen by closing one's eyes,
How can such persons, my brethern, meet the Infinite?
How far could any one amplify this?
Men would grow weary trying to understand it.
Though one had a million tongues,
Even then he would fail to recount God's praises.

(*Bichitar Natak,* Chapter 6)
"Translation by M.A. Macauliffe"

Guru Gobind Singh's Personality and Teachings

Guru Gobind Singh had an inspiring Personality. He earned laurels in all fields. The Guru gave his life purpose in the following stanza making humble supplication to God to give the boon that he should never shirk from doing virtuous and righteous deeds and that he should leave this world while fighting a righteous cause on the battle-field:

"Give me this power O Almighty that I may never refrain from doing righteous deeds. I should never fear the enemy when I go to battle, but surely go on to victory; I may teach myself that I should have the greed to sing only Thy praises. And when the last days of my life come, I may die fighting in some mighty battle for the righteous cause."

Life is indeed a constant warfare, as repeatedly stated by Guru Gobind Singh in his various writings. Man should not be intimidated or discouraged at the prospect of the combat, but should arm himself with courage and even joy, knowing that he is not alone in the combat, but that God is with him. The spiritual struggle stimulates the constant practice of prayer and is therefore an inexhaustible treasure of precious spiritual benefits. So long man lives he has to attain victory over his passions, even the perfect saints as long as they live are not precluded of all further struggle or combat. This warfare in many never ceases. In saints when the battle for self-love (egotism) ceases, then battle of Divine love begins, for love cannot be idle, but compels the man to serve humanity and to launch himself into the thick of the battle for God's honour or Glory. The Gurus' lives are full of such constant struggles. God Himself gives the strength to fight and to triumph. Guru Gobind Singh taught us:

> "Glory to the noble ones, who on their earthly way, carry upon their lips the Name of the Lord, and ever contemplate deep within their hearts to be ever ready to fight (the evil).
>
> The body is fleeting and shall not abide for ever; man embarking in the ship of singing God's eulogies shall cross the Ocean of the World.
>
> Make this body a house of resignation; light your understanding as a lamp therein.
>
> Take the Sword of Divine Knowledge into your hand, and cut off the curse of timidity within you."

The world itself is a battle-field and the life a struggle. Every moment of our life is full of conflicts in us. We have to take decisions to choose right from wrong. Only those can choose right from wrong, who love Truth (God).

The letter written by the Guru to Emperor Aurangzeb had its effect. He instructed the Prime Minister at Delhi to lift all restrictions on the Guru. He invited the Guru to south India to meet him for a dialogue. The Guru owned no territory, and had never raised any rebellion against the established authority to bring about any change. Nor did he aggress against any one even in retaliation. His fighting was only for self-defence against unprovoked aggressions, which were due to his teaching of equality of all and uplifting of the down-trodden humanity to the status of equality with others. The Guru who was wronged so much by the Emperor at the incitation of the caste and dogma-ridden Hindu Hill rajas, even then on receipt of his invitation to meet with him, set on the long journey in search for peace, with a view to avoiding unnecessary bloodshed of the innocent people. However, he was half way, when he heard the death of the Emperor.

Did he not write to the Emperor that he would have kind words for him to soothe his mind? Do not consider that the Guru was surrendering to the mighty Emperor. In this very letter he admonished him severely for his false oaths on

Quran. The Guru, who had lost both of his parents, all the four sons and countless Sikhs more dear to him than his own sons, was most humane even to those who wronged him most. It is a pity that the Sikhs should have insinuated the Guru most by stating that Banda Bairagi was despatched by the Guru to Punjab to avenge the wrongs done to him and to make military conquests of the lands. The absurdity could not have gone farther, especially when the farthest historical link is wanting. This assertion is the blatant proof of the total lack of understanding of the Teachings and the character of the Guru. This is sheer fanaticism of the Sikhs. The sooner this blunder is corrected the better. Banda Bairagi's misdeeds in Punjab and declaring himself as the Guru, and Mata Sundari Ji's (widow of the Guru) warning to the Sikhs to disassociate from the Bairagi should be examined dispassionately. The Sikhs served the Guru selflessly and there never had been the attraction of any bait of the war booty or promise of any type of luxurious life. How could the question of war booty should arise, when the Guru never aggressed against any one. This phenomenon of Teaching of Equality of all Mankind was unique in the history of Man. *Thus Guru Gobind Singh was a Unique Personality and the Greatest.*

Guru Gobind Singh started his ministry, when he was fourteen years of age after the martyrdom of his father, Guru Tegh Bahadur. Rival claims to the spiritual seat staked by the splinter groups represented by Minas, Dhirmalias and Ramrayas added further to his difficulties by accentuating internal dissensions on the one hand, on the other hand undue interference of Hindu Hill rajas and the Mughal state in the domestic affairs of the community. The integrity of the Faith was further threatened by the corrupt practices of the Masands, acting as in between Guru and the Sikhs and collecting funds from them and misappropriating them. Undaunted by the formidable nature of these difficulties, his own tender age, the paucity of resources at his command and the advice of the sceptics and weak kneed among his own ranks against his decisions, the Guru decided to face the challenge posed by these inimical forces. It was a question of life and death struggle and the Guru had no doubt that it could be ignored only at his own peril. His grasp of the situation was remarkable and the manner in which he was able to reorganise and rejuvenate his people so as to enable them to face grim challenge and to endow them with a definite mission for the future, is amazing. About the transformation brought about in the people by the Guru is described by M.A. Macauliffe, in his book the Sikh Religion, Vol. V, pages 99-100.

> "The Guru's teachings had the magical effect of changing a pariah or outcast through an interminable line of heredity into a brave and staunch solider... The metamorphosis had been accomplished defiance of the hide bound prejudices and conservatism of the old Hindu systems. Prior to the time of the Sikh Gurus no general ever conceived the idea of raising an army from man who believed to be unclean from their birth; but the stimulating precepts of the Tenth Guru altered who had hitherto been deemed to be the dregs of humanity into warriors whose prowess and loyalty never failed their leaders."

What is important to remember here is that these brave soldiers were essentially God fearing and God loving community dedicated to the establishment of a plural, free, open and progressive human society. This evolved was God oriented, non-aggressive, but firm in holding their own and for every aggression, ever ready to combat for self-preservance, through organised resistance and forward looking, yet non-ambitious society, as against the closed, tyrannical, inequitable and an aggressive social order then prevailing. To an atmosphere of gloom and degradation he brought a message of hope and deliverance and a will to die for Truth and Righteous cause. All he could do within the short span of less than 47 years of his life.

Hereunder is given as example of his live for his Divine Father, Whose Son he himself proclaimed. Immediately after losing his two elder sons and his closest disciples at Chamkaur, and was unaware of the fate of his two younger sons and other members of his family, even as he lay, all by himself, being hotly pursued by a ruthless enemy, in the jungles of Machiwara, under a cruel wintry sky, he the Son of God, reiterates his faith in the Will of God, in a glorious Song of hope and re-affirmation:

> "Go, tell the Beloved Lord the condition of His yearning disciple;
> Without Thee, rich coverings are an agony to us,
> And to live in the comforts of our house-holds is like living with snakes!
> Our water-pots have become like pikes on which men are impaled.
> The cup we drink from has an edge like a dagger,
> Beloved, Thy turning away from us is like what a beast endures from the slaughterer!
> With the Beloved a matress of straw would please us,
> Without Him, in rich houses we are burnt alive."

It is reiterated that in the midst of such trials and tribulations, only a Man like him, the Son of God, was at perfect peace with himself, who could have sung such a song.

Time out of number it is stated in Sri Guru Granth Sahib that life is difficult and full of problems—'bhojal sansar.' Those who accept life in this fashion, for them life is no longer difficult. Because once it is accepted that life is difficult, it no longer matters. Such a man comes near God and accepts His Will. Most of us do not fully see that life is difficult. Instead they moan more or less incessantly, noisily about the enormity of their problems, their burdens, and their difficulties in life as if generally everything is easy. They voice their belief, noisily or subtly, that their difficulties represent a unique kind of affliction that should not be and that has some how been especially visited upon them, or else upon their families, their tribe, their class, their nation and so on. There is no doubt about it that a difficult condition we generally moan. The question is do we want to moan or solve the problem?

Discipline is the basic set of tools to require to solve life's problems. Without discipline we can solve nothing. With some discipline we can solve some problems. With total discipline we can solve all problems. Such an understanding comes to man by His Grace. The Khalsa Discipline requires us to attune our will with His Will, as taught by Guru Nanak in the first stanza of Japji Sahib. If we understand this basic thing we can learn much from the life of Sikh Gurus, especially from the life of Guru Gobind Singh Ji. One is amazed to find how the Great Guru in extreme adverse situations remained calm and cheerful and resolved all the problems.

What makes life difficult is that the process of confronting and solving problems is a painful one. Problems depending upon their nature, evoke in us frustration or grief of sadness or loneliness or guilt to regret or anger or fear or anxiety or anguish or despair. Those are uncomfortable feelings, often very uncomfortable, often as painful as any kind of physical pain, sometimes equaling the very worst kind of physical pain. Indeed, because of the pain that events or conflicts engender in us that we call them problems. Since life poses an endless series of problems, life is always difficult and is full of pain as well as joy.

Yet it is this whole process of meeting and solving problems that life has its meaning. Problems are the cutting edge that distinguishes between success and failure. Problems call forth our courage and our wisdom; indeed they create our courage and our wisdom. Guru Nanak taught us that the pain is a remedy to us; while ease and luxury is sickness—dukh daroo sukh rog bhia. It is only because of problems that we grow mentally and spiritually. When we desire to encourage the growth of the human spirit, we accept the challenge and encourage our capacity to solve problems. It is through the pain of confronting and resolving problems that we learn. It is for this reason that wise people learn not to dread but to confront the problems. We should face the problems directly and if necessary to experience the pain involved bodily. There are numerous prayful beseechings to Almighty God made by Guru Gobind Singh to bless him this boon only that he should never be wanting to fight out the problems to serve the righteous cause, and in this process if need be he may lay down his life on the battlefield fighting heroically. These problems take us near God. By living with God the way to their successful solution becomes known. There is then great joy in solving the problems with the aid of God, Who is with in us. Guru Gobind singh lived every moment of his life with God and spent whole of his life in solving the problems for the good of the humanity, notwithstanding the heavy cost he had to pay. There was an unparalleled spiritual growth in the Guru, while those who wanted to lead an easy life by killing him, lost everything in losing their self-respect.

The Guru was the apostle of determination, self-confidence, perseverance and optimism. We do not find an example of any other mortal, who in the circumstances was not disheartened and overwhelmed in the inextricable distress. The whole Mission of the Guru had been positive approach to life and total elimination of 'intro-punitive' and 'extropunitive' techniques to solve the problems, which nullify the spiritual progress completely. The Guru was the Ocean of live and compassion for all and treated all his own. He never aggressed against any one under any circumstances, nor did he ever retaliated to avenge the wrongs done to him. He had to defend himself, when unprovoked armed attacks were made on him by hysterical perverts. In Guru's heart love had completely prevailed over the hate (aggression). This had been the miraculous effect of the unique unparalleled victory of the Guru and the way of life as taught by him. The Self of the Guru was immeasurably strong, and he never lost his presence of mind in extreme difficult situations. Rather he took decisions of paramount importance in such situations, especially at Chamkaur, where he and few Sikhs were besieged by the hundreds of thousand of Mughal and Hindu Hill rajas's troops.

Love experience means freedom at its loftiest. The love is to act freely without compulsion or coercion. In other words to be free means to do one loves to do. Love and true freedom are therefore complementary to each other. Compulsion and coercion are the negative of love. Where there is love, there is no coercion and vice versa. The greater the love, the greater is the freedom. A person, who loves all humanity is truly free in this universe. A person who hates is the greatest of the slaves, subjectively and objectively. The true love gives a feeling of fearlessness and power, as the conscious is free from guilt. Where there is a fear, there is feeling of guilt, cowardice and absence of live. The best and most scientific remedy for the fear is love. A person truly in love with God and his creation cannot be intimidated or bribed. The Sikhs and the Gurus had been bound up on the basis of true love. The Guru gave no allurement of any abode in paradise in the life hereafter, nor any promise of material benefits during their present life. The Sikhs were not the mercenary soldiers in the employ of the Guru, nor had the Guru established an estate of his own to rule over others. The Sikhs had not joined the Guru's army for the lure of the war booty, for the Guru had never aggressed against any one, but had fought only in self-defence. The Guru never tried to acquire an inch of any one's territory despite his victories over his adversaries. There was an injunction by the Guru that in no circumstances the Sikhs would molest women as war booty. These character traits were observed by Sikhs sincerely, not only during the Guru's life time but thereafter as well. The Sikhs on their free volition and love for the Guru rendered matchless services to him and made supreme sacrifices. The extreme love of the Sikhs for the Guru exhibited by them during various battles fought. It is therefore very much incorrect to compare the freedom movement of the Guru with any other movement or uprising for fulfilment of territorial ambitions.

There was also unbounded love in the Guru for the Sikhs and the humanity at large. The Guru declared "The Khalsa is my very form." The Guru merged his Self in the Khalsa in such a way that he hailed it as his own flesh of flesh, blood of his blood. The Guru bowed before the Five Beloved Ones (Punj Piyare) and touched his forehead to the feet of all the Five, one by one. It meant that the Guru had bestowed Guruship to the Five Beloved Ones. He then prepared the 'Amrit' of the Double-Edged Sword and baptised each one of them from the same bowl. Amrit is sipped from the bowl by the persons from one end of the persons to the other end, and then vice versa. Guru Nanak started the programme of caste extinction, and the succeeding Gurus took more steps in this direction. Guru Gobind Singh not only brought to an end this virus in the society by introducing taking of Amrit by all the Sikhs, he made every baptised Sikh as the Guru Khalsa and he himself also took amrit thus becoming Guru Khalsa. Now there was no distinction left between the baptised Sikhs called the Guru Khalsa and Guru Gobind Singh as the Guru Khalsa. Complete Equality of all persons and also the Guru was evolved. Any baptised Sikh had the same status as the Guru had, provided the baptised persons were to lead the Khalsa way of life.

There was the unbounded love in the Guru for the humanity at large. The Guru felt equally pained when the weaker sections of the humanity were oppressed by those in authority. He did every thing to serve the oppressed humanity. The Guru once said: "Service of the people alone delights me; my heart does not like to serve the blood-sucker imperialists or to flatter them. In my house my mind, body and wealth are theirs." This he proved by his own deeds. He wanted and worked for the upliftment of the fallen, low and the Untouchable people and for which he paid heavy cost.

The basic concept of God is that He is Infinite Spirit and His knowledge is Unfathomable. All who take birth are finite beings. God does not take birth and never dies. It is a sin to say that any one is or was an Incarnate of God. Guru Gobind Singh said:

> "All who call me the Supreme Being shall fall into the pit of hell.
> Recognise me as God's servant only.
> Have no doubt whatever of this.
> I am a slave of the Supreme Being, and have come to behold the wonders of the world.
> I tell the world what God told me, and will not remain
> silent through fear of mortals." *(Bichitar Natak)*

Unfortunately after the demise of the Guru, the hands of the clock were reversed by ignorant and self-seeker Sikhs. Their whole attention was for acquisition of the material power and conquest of the lands. All the biographies of the Guru written except that of the contemporary poet Saina Singh, (Gur Sobha) give quite negation of the Sikh Teachings having complete leanings towards Hinduism. Conquests of lands by raising of rebellions was made the sole aim of the Sikhs after Guru Gobind Singh. Many heinous crimes were enacted by them. Even to-day the Sikhs have not understood the Guru and think that he had come to restore temporal power. His life and his Teachings are mininterpretted to suit the evil ends of the opportunists. The Teachings "Cause no fear to any one and accept no awe from any quarter" are completely ignored. The Sikhs do not even to-day know that the Gurus worked for Equality of All Mankind, and for this they gave extreme sacrifices. The Sikhs observe the

Caste System as the Hindus do, though in modified form. There is no talk of Equality of All in the religious discourses in the Gurdwaras. If they are educated to know the Teachings of Equality of All Mankind, then on what basis they would ask for their separate rule to dominate others? In the Gurus' Teachings there is no idea of domination and submission. Then why not work for Equality of All and establishment of Brotherly Rule every where, thus establishing the Kingdom of God on Earth. The emphasis should be on Man, not state. Create the saintly society, it will be all peace, for state is only the reflex of the society. As is the society, so is the state. Good society is governed by good men. The Guru's all emphasis was on raising of the individual character of man.

5

In South India

After attending the coronation ceremony of Emperor Bahadur Shah, the Guru continued to stay at Agra for three months. The reason was that neither the Emperor nor the Guru himself desired that he should go back to Anandpur and settle there under the prevailing conditions. Wazir Khan, who had tortured to death the two younger sons of the Guru, had the guilty conscience, which had made him restless. Ever since the distardy act of killing the two innocent sons of the Guru, he was on the move to eliminate the Guru somehow. Establishment of the cordial relations between Emperor Bahadur Shah and the Guru, was an eye-sore to him. Sikhs were also smarting with rage at this cruel and inhuman act of Wazir Khan and his Hindu minister, Suchananad. This cowardly attack on the infant sons on the Guru inflicted a deep would in the minds of the Sikhs, which could never be healed unless Wazir Khan and his Hindu Minister were brought to the book. It was therefore likely that on the return of the Guru to Punjab there would be general uprising of the Sikhs to deal suitably with Wazir Khan and others. But the Guru did not want this to happen. The Guru during his stay at Agra used to address the holy congregations every morning and evening.

On October 2, 1707, Guru Gobind Singh sent the following letter to the Sikhs of Dhaul. Dhaul is situated about 25 miles south of Agra. The Guru moved to this place and made it as his missionary centre.

> "To the entire congregation of Dhaul, you are my Khalsa. The Guru (God present in all) will protect you. Meditate on the Guru. Your human birth will be redeemed. We were received here by the King Emperor and honoured with a robe (Siropa — that which covers one from head to foot) and jewelled daggar (Dhukhdhukhi) with Rupees sixty thousand. Other tasks also are being accomplished by favour of the Guru. We are also returning to you in a few days. To the entire Commonwealth of the Khalsa my command is: keep unity in your ranks. When we come to Kehloor i.e. Anandpur, the entire Khalsa should come armed into our presence. Send two tolas of gold worth Rupees forty by draft (hundi). If the messenger (Mewra) delays, turn him out of the congregation. Samat 1764 (Vikrami), Katik 1."

From the above quoted letter of the Guru, we can infer:

(1) The Guru had taken up the matter with the emperor for his going

back to Anandpur and creation of the normal conditions there.

(2) Some understanding had been reached with the Emperor for the Guru's move to Anandpur.

The Guru had come to Agra in July 1707, remained there for about three months. He then came to Dhaul on October 19, 1707. He made this place as his headquarters for spread of Sikhism in this part of the country. Hundred of thousands of the people adopted Sikhism as a result of the Guru's preachings.

Emperor Bahadur Shah lived at Agra in peace till November 12, 1707, when he had to go to Rajasthan, as disturbances had broken out there. The emperor reached Amber (Rajasthan) in January 1708. After settling the dispute at Amber, the Emperor then advanced toward Jodhpur. Here also after settling the dispute, the Emperor returned to Ajmer.

Rebellion of Kam Baksh

Before his death, Emperor Aurangzeb had despatched Kam Baksh to Bijapur as the viceroy of the province. Bijapur city is about 250 miles south of Ahmednagar. If Azam had decided to deal with Kam Baksh in the first instance in Bijapur, Bahadur Shah in this way could capture Delhi and Agra easily. Azam at the outset proceeded toward Agra and there lost his life in the battle of Jajau.

Kam Baksh, before he reached Bijapur, had heard the news of his father's death. On his arrival at Bijapur he crowned himself as the successor to his father, Aurangzeb. He spent two months in Bijapur organizing his government and raising an army. He was of childish habits, jealous and obstinate. His clever courtiers made a fool of him in inciting against certain men who counted. He completely ruined his prospects for success. Under delusion of treachery against him, he got many ministers and officials tortured to death and confiscated their property. Many other insane acts of cruelty were done by him. Thus he became notorious in southern India for his cruelty. He had now raised a standard of rebellion against the rule of his older brother, Bahadur Shah. Bahadur Shah received reports of Kam Baksh's activities, while he was in Rajasthan.

Emperor Bahadur Shah began making preparations to go to southern India to settle the affairs with his younger brother Kam Baksh. The Emperor requested Guru Gobind Singh to accompany him. The Emperor did not want that the Guru on any count should visit Punjab.

Emperor Aurangzeb had to go to southern India from Rajasthan as a result of the rebellion raised by his son Akbar. The Prince joined the Marhattas and posed a threat to the Emperor. Thereafter Emperor Aurangzeb inextricably involved himself in perpetual hostilities in southern India for twenty six years till he died in February 1707 at Ahmednagar. The continual fighting brought about sufferings to the people. Now a similar situation had arisen. Emperor Bahadur Shah was going to southern India to subdue his rebel brother Kam Baksh. The Guru after reviewing the situation in which he found himself, accepted the offer of Bahadur Shah to accompany him to visit southern India.

The Guru thought that the Emperor was now proceeding to southern India to quel the rebellion raised by his younger brother, Kam Baksh, and it was likely he might have to deal with Marhattas there. It was not certain when he would return to northern India. Till the Emperor was to come back to northern India, no action in Punjab could be taken to bring the conditions to normal, otherwise there would have been uprising of the Muslim fundamentalists. As such the Guru's going to Punjab or Anandpur was not possible till the return of the Emperor from the southern India. The Guru did appreciate this position.

It may be recollected that during the last four to five years of Emperor Akbar's regime, Sirhind became the centre of a very orthodox revivalism among the Muslims. The head priest Shaikh Ahmad al Faruqi, popularly known as Sirhindi, was extremely a religious fanatic person. He was initiated in the Naqshbandi order at Delhi. He was a youth of about 35 years of age, when he began to boast of having the spiritual power of all the religious orders of orthodox Islam. He claimed that he had been appointed by God to be the supreme leader of the religious and spiritual affairs of Muslims. He was furiously fanatic and worked for enforcement of orthodox Islamic faith in its purity and had the mania to destroy all those who differed from him in any way. Muslims were greatly influenced by his antics. He was particularly against Sikhism, and caused the execution of Guru Arjun Dev, the 5th Guru under a false pretext. This legacy was still persisting at Sirhind. All those fanatics were the great supporters of Wazir Khan. It was not easy for the new Emperor to keep these fanatics under control, if any action was taken against Wazir Khan, more especially when the Emperor would be in southern India.

The Guru anticipated that the same situation would arise, if he settled in northern India outside Punjab, which had arisen earlier, that is, the people of the vested interest would not allow him to live in peace and practice and preach Equality of All Mankind. In that case he would not be living in a fortified town like Anandpur.

Keeping all the above factors in view, the Guru decided that it would be much better to visit southern India along with the Emperor, when he would be free to practice and preach Sikhism, especially the Equality of All people.

Throughout the stay of Guru Gobind Singh at Agra and Dhaulpur, Sikhs in large numbers from Punjab and other areas continued to come to Agra for a glimpse of the Guru. The Guru bade farewell to the people of Agra and Dhaulpur in April 1708, made his way toward Rajasthan and joined

Bahadur Shah at Ajmer. The Guru's camp and Bahadur Shah's camp then proceeded toward southern India. They passed through many towns and reached on the banks of river Narbada. The Guru and the Emperor pitched their respective camps on the banks of the rivers and passed few days there. M.A. Macauliffe states: "They both visited Jodhpur and Chitaur. Each raja sent his envoy to conciliate and do homage to the Guru. At Chitaur there arose a quarrel between the Sikhs and Rajputs on account of some grass the former had taken for their horses. The Guru censured his Sikhs, and ordered them to take nothing for the future without payment."

Dr. Ganda Singh, however states: "When the two camps passed near the town of Chitaur, a Sikh named Zorawar Singh along with some companions went to see the city of Chitaur and the Fort. Two or three Sikhs also went to purchase grass for their horses. There was the beat of the drum, and on hearing the sound of the drum of the people of Chitaur thought that the town had been invaded by the robbers and the dacoits. They all came rushing out, and saw the Sikhs purchasing grass. However, there arose some discussions between them, which turned into fighting. In this fighting Zorawar Singh was killed. Zorawar Singh now being referred to was the son of Bhai Nathu, the carpenter. Nathu's wife, Bhikhi used to help in the Guru's house-hold work. Bhikhi son, Zorawar Singh was of the same age, as was the Guru's son, Zorawar Singh. Once both the Zorawar Singhs had had a wrestling match. In this match Bhikhi's son, Zorawar Singh had come out the winner. Guru Gobind Singh was watching this wrestling match. The Guru patted Bhikhi's Zorawar Singh and said: "This Zorawar Singh is also my son." The Sikhs also began to treat this boy as the Guru's son."

Hari Ram Gupta gives a totally different account of happening at Chitaur. He writes:

> "The contemporary author Abdul Rasul, in his Tarikh-e-Muazzam Shah written in 1708 A.D. narrates an incident which he says took place at Chitaur in April 1708. Emperor Bahadur Shah was halting there on his way to the Deccan. Guru Gobind Singh was with him. There was a lad not yet downy, whom the author calls "Son of Guru Gobind." He was anxious to see the fort, and accompanied by 50 to 60 comrades went up the hill. The guards at the gate obstructed them saying that no body could enter the fortress. A scuffle caused in which the guards were killed. Thereupon another strong contingent of troops (fauj-e-digar) emerged from a place of ambush (kamingah). A fierce fight took place. The Rajputs surrounded the Sikhs on all sides, and destroyed all of them with bullets, arrows and stones. "The son of Guru Gobind like a furious tiger struck down several men with his piercing sword and fell dead by the side of his companions. As the hostility of the Mughal court to the Guru was well-known, the Rajputs seem to have taken such a drastic step without any fear from the Emperor who really took no notice of it... It appears that the Guru had been fascinated by some lad whom he

treated with great love and affection as a foster father and the people looked upon him as the Guru's son. Sainapat calls him Zorawar Singh, while Fauja Singh says that he was the son of a carpenter of Bassi Pathanan near Sirhind."

It is, however, significantly clear that the Guru and the Emperor were moving toward southern India quite separate from each other with their respective security forces. The Guru did not reside in the imperial camp, as intentionally incorrectly stated by Hari Ram Gupta. The Guru was leading 500 to 600 armed Sikhs separately. Khafi Khan, the historian of the time, states that the Guru was proceeding toward southern India with Emperor Bahadur Shah at the "head of two or three hundred horse-men and also infantry men armed with spears."

When the imperial camp halted on the banks of river Narbada, a Muslim trooper killed Bhai Mann Singh, one the surviving heroes of Chamkaur, who had never parted from the Guru.

Macauliffe says: "The quarrel between the Sikhs and the Muhammadans was kept alive by the Emperor's escorts, many of whom were relations of the imperial soldiers slain by the Sikhs at Anandpur. The Guru sent Mann Singh, to adjust the difference between both parties. While on his mission of peace, he was assassinated by a fanatic. The Emperor was much distressed on hearing of his death and ordered that his murderer should be seized and given upto the Guru for punishment. The Guru pardoned him, and thus gained praise from the Muhammadans for his mercy and clemency."

The Guru and Emperor crossed river Narbada on May 17, 1708. During the halts enroute the Guru and the Emperor had their separate camps. They reached Burhanpur after crossing river Tapti. On the beseechings of the Sikhs of Burhanpur, the Guru extended the period of his stay at this place. The place where the Guru stayed in Burhanpur is called "Mandir of Hathi Singh." Yogi Jiwan Das of Burhanpur served the Guru with great devotion. Mahant Jait Ram, the custodian of "Dadoo Dwara", who also happened to be there at that time, came to pay his homage to the Guru.

The Emperor continued his journey, while the Guru remained at Burhanpur. After some days, the Emperor wrote to the Guru to join him. After staying few days at Burhanpur, the Guru joined the Emperor and went to Amravati, situated 80 miles east of Burhanpur. From amravati he went 100 miles southward to Hingoli. This place is 50 miles from Nanded. On reaching Hingoli, the Guru parted company with Bahadur Shah, who with his army headed toward Hyderabad. The Guru took to the road leading to Nanded. He passed through Basmuth and finally reached Nanded. He encamped on the banks of river Godawari on July 19, 1708. This version is according to late Prof. Dr. Sahib Singh, given in his book on the life of Guru Gobind Singh. Justice Pritam Singh Safeer also confirms in his book on Like of Guru Gobind Singh that the Guru reached Nanded on July 19, 1708.

The Guru travelled with Bahadur Shah from Ajmer to Hingoli, which distance was covered between 3-4 months. The Guru's parting with Bahadur Shah at Hingoli was a normal event, as the Guru was not accompanying the Emperor for fighting a war against Kam Baksh. The Guru came to Nanded and settled there.

H.R. Gupta in his book on 'History of Sikh Gurus' has stated that Guru Gobind Singh was killed by Court Conspiracy-Destiny drags the Guru to death trap. About Guru Gobind Singh accompanying Emperor Bahadur Shah to southern India, he writes: "The Guru's residence in the imperial camp was a fatal mistake committed by the Guru. The entire Mughal Court was anti Sikh. The Guru was looked upon as a rebel punishable with death. Wazir Khan was a hero for them, fit to be rewarded rather than punished... Every courtier was alert to see that no harm came to Wazir Khan, while intrigues and mechinations to harm the Guru were set afoot in right earnest... The Guru was no diplomat. While in the Emperor's camp for fifteen months, July 1707 to September 1708, he had told everybody that he was there to secure punishment of Wazir Khan. The Emperor's troops and nobles did not like the presence of the Guru and his Sikhs in their midst. They knew their objective and hated them... The courtiers continuously impressed upon the Emperor not to yield to the Guru's pleadings..."

What Hari Ram Gupta has written is not based on any authority or facts. We have already made abundantly clear at the onset that the Emperor could not make any changes or take any action against any official serving in Punjab, as long as he would be away in southern India to settle the affairs there and then return to north, in the interest of maintenance of peace and the solidarity of the empire. The Guru fully appreciated this position and reconciled to the new requirement. It was the Guru who helped Bahadur Shah to win the throne of Delhi. Surely, the Guru never wished ill of him for his selfish interests. As already explained the Guru has come to southern India with the Emperor for his own interest of personal security. In the north he was not safe, firstly, due to the mad acts of Wazir Khan, secondly, on account of the religious intolerance of Hindu bigots like Hari Ram Gupta. The Guru was All Wise, being always in tune with his Creator, knew it very well where he was to go and what he was to do. The never put his residence in the imperial camp. The Great Guru was God like, never committed any mistake. We have already quoted the famous contemporary Muslim historian, Khafi Khan that the Guru was leading his men separately toward southern India from the Emperor's camp. Further, the Guru and the Sikhs stayed separately at Burhanpur with the Sikh residents of that place and even over-stayed there, the Emperor having left the place earlier.

Hari Ram Gupta also states: "The Emperor (Bahadur Shah) asked the Guru to stay at Agra to give him the pleasure of his company. The real object was not to allow the Guru any occasion to revive his struggle against the Mughal Government."

Dr. Gopal Singh in his book 'History of the Sikh People' states: "the Guru thereupon, left for a tour of the South via Rajputana to see if he could integrate his forces with those of the Rajputs and the Marhattas to forge a common front against the imperial tyranny of the later Mughals. But before he could do so, he was assassinated at Nanded in the Deccan by a Pathan hireling of the Nawab of Sirhind, in October 1708."

We reiterate that none of the Gurus ever raised a standard of rebellion against any established authority, as it is an immature and imbecile act. And the above writers who are made after raising rebellion and cherish extreme hatred against Muslims, are surely not the normal sensible men and are not in a position to analyse anything in its proper perspective.

The question arises, why a few months earlier did the Guru give armed help and his blessings to Bahadur Shah to make him the Emperor of India? If the Guru was against all Muslims, then that was the opportune time to let the Muslim princes fight among themselves and destroy themselves in the civil war that took place, and the Guru should then have consolidated all the Hindu forces and helped them to establish their rule. But this was not to the liking of the Guru. He wanted the most deserving man to be the ruler, who was to do justice to all the sections of the people. Could Gopal Singh let us know what tyranny Bahadur Shah had inflicted on the people?

It is most interesting to note that it is Hari Ram Gupta in his book 'History of the Sikhs' Vol. II, page 36, writes: "Banda aimed at national awakening and liberation of the country from the oppressive government of the Mughals. Guru Hargobind and Guru Gobind Singh had transformed the Sikhs from a peaceful people into a class of warriors. They fought against the government in self-defence. They never took any offensive. They did not acquire any territory, did not take prisoners, and did not seize enemy's property and wealth. The two Gurus never tried to establish their own rule in their own territory, they believed it belonged to the government. The government rules were obeyed, and government coins were used."

GURU GOBIND SINGH'S DEPARTURE FOR HEAVENLY ABODE

Poet Sainapat (Saina Singh) was one of the 52 poets in the Court of Guru Gobind Singh. His is the only version about the life of the Guru that is reliable and true. As regards the later historians and the writers till this day, none of them has been found reliable and without prejudices. The modern Sikhs are so much politically orientated that they wrote everything in terms of powers.

At Burhanpur

In Burhanpur the Guru and the Sikhs stayed at a place called 'Mandir of Hathi Singh.' Yogi Jiwan Das of Burhanpur served the Guru with great devotion. Mahant Jait Ram, the custodian of 'Daddoo Dwara,' who also happened to be there, came to pay his homage to the Guru. The Emperor without waiting for the Guru proceeded onward toward southern India. The Guru was busy in imparting of the Sikh Teachings in that part of the country. Further, the Sikhs of Burhanpur had requested the Guru to stay there with them for few days more. Throughout the journey from Agra to Nanded the Guru utilised this time for propagation of Sikh Teachings. Dr. Ganda Singh writes that at times the Guru was not seen in either of the two camps for days together, even for whole week, and was busy imparting Sikh education to the people. This could not have been possible, had the Guru remained in northern India and had not accompanied the Emperor.

Poet Sainapat writes:

> "The Guru was at Burhanpur, while the Emperor had covered a long distance. The Emperor wrote a letter to the Guru to come soon and give a Glimpse of His Person. When the Guru received the letter of the Emperor full of affection, he also responded with equal affection. Immediately the Guru rushed to meet the Emperor. He did not take the Sikh army with him. The Guru crossed river Tapti, and the Sikhs also hastened to meet with the Guru. The Guru and the Sikhs halted at three or four places. There the Guru selected some of the Sikhs to accompany him farther and asked the remainder to go back to their homes. Then the Guru proceeded to meet with that Emperor. When the Emperor saw the Guru coming towards him, the former was so much pleased that the Royal Drummer began beating the drum. The Guru in best of his form with aigrette in his turban met the Emperor. It gave utmost pleasure to the Emperor as long as the Guru remained with him. The Guru then came back to his camp."

In view of the relations between the Guru and the Emperor as given by Poet Sainapat in the above mentioned account, there is not a semblance of reality in the biased accounts given by Hari Ram Gupta, Dr. Gopal Singh and even M.A. Macauliffe and others that the Emperor cherished hatred against the Guru.

The Guru and the Emperor resumed their journey toward south, and came to a place called Nanded on the banks of Godawari river. The Guru decided to stay at Nanded and made it as his permanent abode. The Emperor after staying here for few days resumed his journey to Hyderabad. The Guru came to Nanded on July 19, 1708.

MURDEROUS ASSAULTS ON THE GURU

Poet Sainapat states: "I heard from the people who came from Nanded that a Pathan came there with a view to killing the Guru. He spent two to three hours there uttering some sweet words. He could not attack the Guru, as there were a large number of people there. He left the place, where the Guru was staying, and swiftly came back to his place of residence. After two or three days he again came to the place where the Guru and Sikhs were staying. He again could not take chance to strike at the Guru. He, however, spent three to four hours there. He continued to attend the religious meetings held every evening. This Pathan was seen in a holy congregation for many days. On all these days he did not get a chance to strike at the Guru, but was successful in thoroughly acquainting himself with the surroundings of the place and the daily routine of the Guru. He fully studied as to when and where he could find the Guru alone and to take him unaware. He observed that the evening service lasted till darkness used to set in, and that the Guru would be alone in his tent. The Pathan considered that the evening time was best suited for his work. On one evening he came to the Guru's place and as usual joined the evening congregation. When the religious service was over, the Sikhs as usual dispersed and the Guru alone went to his place of retreat for rest. The Guru finding the Pathan standing outside his tent, called him in, and gave him seat near his bed. The Guru gave him the Sacramental Food (Parsad). On receiving the 'Parsad' in his hand, he hurriedly put his hand into his mouth and devoured it. The Pathan found that the Guru was alone and no person was to be seen anywhere. However, there was one Sikh outside the Guru's tent, who had gone to sleep. Shortly thereafter the Guru laid himself on his bed for rest. Then the Pathan took out his poniard and thrust it into the Guru's abdomen. Before the Guru could defend himself, this rascal again thrust his poniard in his abdomen. The Guru was on alert and sprang up from his bed to deal with the assassin. The Guru by this time got hold of his sword and with a lightening stroke killed the Pathan. The Guru struck the Pathan once only and there was no necessity for another stroke. Inspite of having received two deadly attacks of the rascal, the Guru did not let him go, but killed him with one stroke of his sword. The Guru then shouted for the sikhs to come immediately. On hearing the call of the Guru the Sikhs rushed from all directions to see him. All the Sikhs came to the Guru's tent running as fast as they could. Hundreds of Sikhs gathered together outside the Guru's tent. The Sikhs saw two confederates of the assassin. These two confederates tried to flee to a safer place, but the Sikhs caught hold of them and during the scuffle that ensued were killed. On hearing that the Guru had been mortally wounded by the attack of a Pathan, there then arose a great commotion as if the Dooms Day had set in. The Sikhs became completely restless and could not be calmed. Those Sikhs who entered the Guru's tent, they saw a Pathan lying on the bed of the Guru. When the Sikhs started beating the Pathan, the Guru told the Sikhs not to beat the Pathan, as he had died long before. The Guru further stated that the body of the Pathan be removed from his bed. The Sikhs after removing the dead body of the Pathan, observed that the Guru's shirt had been dyed dark red on his left side. No one thought that the Guru had been mortally wounded by the Pathan. When the Sikhs touched the Guru's body near his heart, then only the Sikhs could know that he had been mortally wounded. The Sikhs became utterly grief stricken. They began to beat their heads with their both the hands, uttering, "O Great Guru, what a drama you have enacted; You are the Master of the Human Destiny." Seeing this condition of the Sikhs, the Guru consoled them saying: "The Almighty Immortal God has saved me." (In the light of this statement of the Guru, there cannot be any doubt that the Guru did not die by the Pathan's stabbing. The stores given later by the Sikhs that the Guru was trying a heavy bow or when he stretched his body, the wounds gapped open, which became cause of death, are totally baseless. No such bow exists as a relic. The stories apart from being untrue, are derogatory to the Guru. After about passing 50 days as a healthy life, the Guru himself said that he had been summoned in the Divine Presence, having completed his Mission. This all took place on August 18, 1708.

"On hearing such encouraging words uttered by the Guru, the Sikhs were a little consoled. The Sikhs then brought a local surgeon, who washed the wound and also stitched it. The Emperor was immediately informed of the incident, who hastened to send his own British Surgeon, named Cole. The British Surgeon reached Nanded on the following morning, and started his own treatment. He removed the stitches of the wound, washed and cleaned it thoroughly. He then re-stitched the wound and applied some ointment. This Royal British Surgeon stayed at Nanded for about ten days (The Guru used to give this British Surgeon ten gold coins daily as long as he stayed at Nanded. Dr. Ganda Singh mentions this fact on the basis of the book on the title of Guru Gobind Singh, written by Dhian Singh).

The Sikhs passed three to four days and nights with extreme anxiety. They were wailing, crying and praying for the health of the Guru. A large number of Sikhs came to Nanded to pay their respects to the Guru and to have a Glimpse of him. The Sikhs stood on the door of the tent and wistfully begged the Guru for a Glimpse of him. The Guru accepted the desire of the Sikhs. It was his fourth day after his having been mortally stabbed. The Sikhs finding the Guru amidst them gave them immense pleasure." All Sikh chronicles state that the Guru was completely healed in ten days time.

The Guru had come to Nanded on July 19, 1708, and was mortally stabbed on August 18, 1708. He fully recovered his health on August 28, 1708.

Poet Sainapat further states:

"Many days passed in this way. Now it was the days of early October 1708. A few days before his demise, the Guru told the Sikhs that he had been summoned to the Divine Presence. The Sikhs were grief stricken. One day before his demise, some of the Sikhs gathered together and asked Sri Guru Gobind Singh Ji, "what form would you take after giving up this form?" Satguru replied to them: "Khalsa in My Form, I am only concerned with Clean and Pure People (Khalsa). I have passed on My

Light to the Khalsa, who would appear till Eternity." Khalsa is My very Form and I ever live in and with Khalsa. My Light shines in the Khalsa. Only that Man is Khalsa, who is pure hearted, who is not a superstitious and skeptical person. He who does not believe in formalism, rituals, superstitions, he only is verily the Khalsa, and our Master."

Poet Sainapat further clarified the following effect.

God is Infinite Spirit and the Source of All Virtues. It is He alone Who is the Sustainer of all creation. His visible Form is His Word. Right from Guru Nanak Dev, all the Gurus ever made their obeisance to His Word and Guru Granth Sahib, the visible Form of God. Guru Gobind Singh passed on His Light of Personal Guruship to the Khalsa People till eternity. His Word is the very form of God - wah wah bani nirankar hai, tis jai vad avar na koai - Rag Sorath, Guru Amar Das. God is the Supreme Spirit. His Greatness is not subject to any one praising Him. The Holy World is God and He is the Giver and Not the Receiver. Guru Gobind Singh merged his Light in the Khalsa People till Eternity, and the people are called Guru Khalsa. The Guru entrusted the Khalsa to the care of God, verily Guru granth Sahib. The Guru himself bowed before Adi Guru Granth Sahib for the last time in the presence of Holy Congregation, before his demise.

The Poet finally says:

"And now the time came, when he was to return to his Heavenly Abode. The Guru told the Sikhs to eat the dinner early on that day. The Guru also took his meals early. After eating the food, he drank some water also. He assured the Sikhs that death was not an unnatural phenomenon and that they should not fear death. It was now mid night, about four hours before the dawn. He caused the Sikhs to assemble in the assembly hall. The Guru then reduced himself to the Sound only. The Sikhs could listen what he was saying, but could not see his body. - bhai shabad roopi. Now he began talking about his leaving the Earth and merging his Light in the Supreme Light. The Guru greeted the Sikhs with the salutation of `Wah-e-Guru Ji Ka Khalsa, Wah-e-Guru Ji Ki Fateh' for the last time. This left the Sikhs grief stricken and dazed. The Sikhs in their utter grief were heard saying - "we were left dumb and could not ask anything from him. On listening His Message that He was merging His Light with the Infinite Supreme Light, we feel completely lonely and fear stricken."

The Sikhs were grief stricken, that only a short time before, the Guru left them. They were wonder struck as to how in a few moments the things change completely. The Sikhs at that very time considered as to how and when the Body of Sri Guru Gobind Singh Ji was to be disposed. There was the unanimous decision that the Body of the Guru should be cremated at that very time. The Guru's body was cremated at that very time before dawn. It was then October 8, 1708.

Emperor Bahadur Shah did not Visit Nanded

According to the findings of Prof. Dr. Sahib Singh, the two camps after passing Amravati came to the town of Hingoli. From Hingoli there are two roads leading to different places further south, one leading to Hyderabad and the other to Nanded. The Emperor took the road leading to Hyderabad, while the Guru proceeded toward Nanded.

Maintenance of peace in northern India was of paramount importance. There was no talk on any subject between the Guru and the Emperor, which could be said to have broken down. The Emperor acknowledged that the Guru was the Man of God and that he would not do anything which was un-ethical. The Emperor was not at Nanded, when the Guru was attacked by the assassin as per Sainapat's version. A messenger was sent to him to inform him of the incident.

Character of Emperor Bahadur Shah

Bahadur Shah had a mild and calm temper, great dignity of behaviour, and excessive and inconsiderate generosity of disposition. He was learned and pious, without any bigotry, and possessed a power of self-control and profound dissimulation which was styled personal cowardice by his rival brother Azam. He was incapable of saying no to anybody, and his only idea of statesmanship was to let matters drift and patch up a temporary peace by humouring everybody, without facing issues and saying future trouble by making decisions promptly and courageously. Still the tradition of dignity of the empire and of good administration left by Aurangzeb continued through his short reign, as he inherited his father's able officers and treated them with confidence and respect. On his accession, his own weak position and softness of fiber, coupled with advanced age, prevented him from asserting his will in any matter. He had promised the post of minister to Munim Khan, his able deputy and most useful servant of the days of his princehood, and yet he could not resist the demand of Asad Khan (Aurangzeb's minister) to be the first officer of the state. In his usual spirit of compromise, Bahadur Shah tried to please both by creating Munim Khan Vazir or revenue minister and Asad Khan Vakil-i-mutlaq or prime minister. But this division of authority pleased neither of them, while it complicated the administration. He conferred titles with a profusion which made them ridiculous. The Turani nobles (their chiefs being of the family of the Nizam) were kept in the background during his reign. Bahadur Shah addressed a kind letter to his rebel brother Kam Baksh. He wrote: "Our father entrusted you with the government of the two subas of Bijapur, we now relinquish to you the government of the two subas of Bijapur and Hyderabad, and all their subjects and belongings, upon the condition, according to the old rule of the Dakhin, that the coins shall be struck and the Khutba read in our name. The tribute which has hitherto paid by the governors of the two provinces we remit." To this letter Kam Baksh insolently wrote a provoking reply, and persisted in the course of his rebellion. Bahadur Shah gave the orders not to bring on a fight, but to surround Kam Baksh so that he should not be killed. In the fight that ensued, Kam Baksh and his two sons were wounded and were placed near the royal tent. European surgeons were asked to attend them. Kam Baksh rejected all treatment, and refused to take the broth as his food.

In the evening Emperor Bahadur Shah went to see his brother, Kam Baksh. The Emperor sat down by his side, and took the cloak from his own back, and covered him, who lay dejected and despairing, fallen from throne and fortune. The Emperor showed him the greatest kindness, asked him about his state, and said: "I never wished to see you in this condition." Kam Baksh replied: "Neither do I wish that one of he race of Timur should be made prisoner with the imputation of cowardice and want of spirit." The Emperor gave him two or three spoonfuls of broth with his own hands, and then departed with his eyes full of tears. After a little while, Kam Baksh and one of his sons died. Both the corpses were sent to Delhi, to be interred under the Tomb of Emperor Humayun.

The Emperor was a God fearing man, gentle and considerate; and would never harm anybody.

Why Emperor Bahadur Shah could not Take any Action against those, who Committed Heinous Crimes against the Guru and the Sikhs

Bahadur Shah, when he was made Emperor, stayed in the northern India for a period of seven to eight months only. He felt that by that time he could not have full control of the reigns of the power. As already stated Sirhind continued to be the centre of Islamic fundamentalism, since the time of Emperor Akbar. Emperor Aurangzeb zealously subscribed to the way of the thinking of the founder priest Shaikh Ahmad al Faruqi, popularly known as "Sirhindi." His followers were ever more active than before at Sirhind. Aurangzeb himself was the pupil of Sirhindi's grandson, Khwaja Saifuddin. The Muslim fanatics at Sirhind were a great force to be reckoned with. Nawab Wazir Khan of Sirhind enjoyed the full support of these religious fanatics. Emperor Bahadur Shah was apprehensive that even if Wazir Khan was transferred to any other place from Sirhind, there would be uprising of the Muslim fundamentalists against the regime. He wanted to let some more time to pass.

Now the Emperor had come in southern India to settle certain state affairs, there was thus no question for taking an action against any one till he went back to north. Hari Ram Gupta, Dr. Gopal Singh and even Macauliffe, who still made out the false case that the Guru was constantly persisting that the Emperor should take action against all those officers who committed excesses against the Sikhs. According to them this had created animosity between the Guru and the Emperor, and that he wanted to eliminate the Guru from his way. They thus consider that the Emperor had the hand in the assassination of the Guru. All these are baseless charges. The only idea of such writers is their extreme religious bigotry against Muslims, and Hari Rami Gupta's extreme religious bigotry against the Guru as well as the Muslims. The fact is that these fanatics paint the Guru in their own colour.

Views of Indubhusan Banerjee as Expressed in His Book "Evolution of the Khalsa" Vol. II, Pages 150 and 151

After giving the narration of Poet Sainapat, Indubhusan Banerjee writes: "Here at last we have an account which is free from all ambiguities and is perfectly sober and rational. Moreover, it is the account of a contemporary, and an associate, who must have been in the know of things and we think of no reason why it should not be accepted. Sainapat, however, does not say anything with regard to the identity of the Pathan and the motive behind his murderous attack. It has been suggested, however, that the man was a hireling of Wazir Khan of Sirhind, who was the real instigator of the crime. (This view is supported by the Chatur Jugi, an old manuscript written by Bhagwan Singh and discovered by Bhai Vir Singh of Amritsar). The increasing friendliness of the Emperor towards the Guru must have unnerved him because it was not difficult for him to guess the object that the Guru had in view in thus closely associating with the Emperor and even accompanying him to Rajputana and the Deccan. He was the greatest living enemy of the Guru and he must have felt and felt strongly that he was not safe so long as the Guru was alive. His execution of the two younger sons of the Guru was an unforgettable and unforgivable crime and he must have realised this in his heart of hearts. We think, therefore, that there is nothing unbelievable in the story that Wazir Khan was the real instigator of the murderous attack (on the Guru)."

Bairagi Madho Das

Ram Dev Rajput lived at Rajauri in the present Jammu and Kashmir state of India. He begot a son in 1661 A.D., who was named Lachman Dev. When Lachman Dev grew of age, he developed a great aptitude for use of arms and for hunting. Once, when he had gone on a game, he killed a pregnant deer. He was so much moved by the event that he left hunting and became a disciple of a Vaishnav Sadhu, Janki Das. Lachman Das was then re-named as Madho Das. He practised Yogic physical exercises for a long time and attained certain occult powers. As a wandering yogi he came to Nanded. The panoramic beauty of the land-scape and the river fascinated him so much that he built a hut on the river side and began to live there practising Yogic Sadhana.

The Guru meets with Bairagi Madho Das

On his arrival at Nanded, the Guru took rest for four to five days, and thereafter along with few Sikhs went to the abode of Madho Das, which was quite near to the place where the Guru was staying. The Guru saw a couch lying in the hut. He went inside the hut and took his seat on the couch. Madho Das as usual wanted to throw down the occupant of the couch by turning it upside down by his occult powers gained through yogic exercises. Mahant Jait Ram had earlier told the Guru of this character of Madho Das, while the Guru was at Burhanpur. Madho Das this time was not successful in his designs. After having been totally exhausted by such fruitless efforts to turn the couch, Madho Das realised of his uncommon visitor. Madho Das was so much impressed with the dynamic personality of the Guru, that he allowed himself to fall at his feet. On the Guru's enquiry about his antecedents, Madho Das replied that he had become his slave (Banda). In a few days time he became familiar with the Sikhs. Under instruction from the Guru, Madho Das was initiated to the Khalsa Brotherhood by administering to him Baptism of the Double-Edged Sword, and re-named as Gurbakash Singh. Although Madho Das was re-named Gurbaksh Singh, but he was greatly known as Banda Singh, as on his first meeting with the Guru he had told him that he was his slave (Banda). It may be recollected that in Malwa Tract the Guru baptised a Muslim Fakir and had re-named him as Ajmer Singh. He became greatly known as 'Mehma' by the Sikhs, on account of his fame and was as such called Mehma Singh. When Gurbaksh Singh was a Bairagi Sadhu, people used to call him 'Baba Ji.' Now, when he became a member of the Khalsa Brotherhood, he began to be called 'Baba Banda Singh.' Banda Singh had already got good experience in the use of arms.

Wazir Khan Emboldened

Wazir Khan observed that the Emperor had taken no action against him for the excesses committed by him against the Guru and the Sikhs. He was thus very much encouraged and became determined to do away with the Guru.

We have already given the detailed account of the assault made on the life of the Guru according to Poet Sainapat's narration. Three Pathans were despatched by Wazir Khan, who appear to have been shadowing the Guru from Agra.

The two Pathans were killed in an encounter with the Sikhs. The dying Pathans confessed that they had been deputed by Wazir Khan, the Nawab of Sirhind, for the job. One Pathan was killed by the Guru, when he stabbed the latter.

The Emperor had not reached Hyderabad as yet, and was on the way. When the Emperor heard the news of the assault made on the Guru's life, he sent his surgeon to Nanded immediately. He was a British Surgeon, named Cole, who on arrival took over the treatment of the Guru.

It is said that the Emperor on hearing the news of an assault on the

Guru's life by a Pathan, sought to round up about 700 Pathans of the area and punish them for harbouring criminals, but the Guru asked him not punish the innocents. Dr. Gopal Singh as already stated the Guru completely recovered in 10 days' time. This incident has no relation, whatsoever, with the Guru's Final Departure from Earth on October 8, 1708. This incident took place on August 18, 1708, and the Guru was fully recovered on August 28; 1708.

Professor Dr. Sahib Singh in his book on the life of Guru Gobind Singh states that when relatives of the Guru's assassin felt that they might not be harmed, they through certain influentials approached Emperor Bahadur Shah and told him that the assassin was swayed by the passion aroused in him by the disrespectful words uttered by the Guru against the Prophet of Islam during the discourse. We have already stated the mild and weak disposition of the Emperor. The Emperor gave a robe of reverence to the dead, to the relatives of the assassin on October 28, 1708. According to Dr. Ganda Singh, the robe of reverence was given by the Emperor, as he was a government official of Sirhind.

When the Sikhs came to know of this slanderous act against the Guru, they sent a representation to the Emperor bringing out the factual position of the whole affair. The Emperor was then deeply moved and sent the robe of reverence to the Dead to Mata Sundari through the Sikhs on October 30, 1708.

It is said that certain officials advised the Emperor to confiscate the huge property of the Guru, as he had died issueless. The Emperor thereupon said that the state would not be enriched by taking possession of the property of the Holy Man.

Effects on Banda Singh

Far from slurring over harsh and politically embarrassing facts, Bairagi Madho Das (now Banda Singh) heard from Sikhs a long tale of woes of the Guru and Sikhs and also the prevailing uncertain conditions in Punjab. Banda Singh realised that the Guru had undertaken the life of extreme sufferings to uphold the cause of liberation of the suffering humanity from the clutches of Hindu and Muslim rulers. The steadfastness and the tenacity of the Guru in the face of heavy odds made a very deep impression on Banda Singh. Banda Singh and other Sikhs fully realised that there was no hope of receiving any justice from the hands of Emperor Bahadur Shah, who was docility personified. They resolved that Khalsa would award suitable punishment to Wazir Khan.

Banda Singh and about 25 other Sikhs appeared in Hissar (a town in Haryana) in October 1709. The distance between Nanded and Hissar is about 1660 Km or 1,000 miles. There were about 300 horses, when the Guru went to Nanded. As such it can safely be said that Banda Singh and other

Sikhs were travelling toward northern India on horses. Travelling on horse backs the distance could have been covered in less than a month's time i.e. at an average speed of 50 miles per day. It means that Banda and other 25 Sikhs left Nanded after about a year's time from the time Guru Gobind Singh died. Banda appeared in the country north-west of Delhi and sent letters to various Sikh Sangats informing them the evil acts of Wazir Khan and the demise of Guru Gobind Singh at Nanded. He summoned the Sikhs with a view to awarding suitable punishment to Wazir Khan. At Bhiwani, Banda looted the government treasury and distributed the money among his followers. This attracted a large number of young men to join him. Plundering of government treasuries and also the rich people was repeated at many places. The money realised was distributed among his followers and to poor people. He routed the Commandant of Sonipat in November 1709 and plundered a large amount of money and war material. In this way he could gather around him about 40,000 armed Sikhs and a number of robbers and plunderers. Sirhind was attacked and conquered by slaying Wazir Khan and general masacre of Muslim population without regard to age and sex.

Suffice it is to say that Guru Gobind Singh did not depute Banda Singh to go to Punjab and create disturbances there and to avenge the wrongs done to the Guru. There is no mention of Banda in certain earlier old Sikh chronicles. It is most unfortunate that all the modern writers except Prof. Dr. Sahib Singh, wrote that Banda Singh was sent to Punjab by the Guru to cause disturbances there and punish Wazir Khan.

It is most absurd and ridiculous to state that the Guru was in search of a man who could lead the Sikh for the action in Punjab. The Guru always avoided clash of arms and unnecessary shedding of blood of innocent people, never for his personal cause. We have seen from the study of the Guru's life that he never:

(1) attacked any one even in retaliation for taking revenge;
(2) believed in secret diplomacy, and fraudulent ways;
(3) sent Sikhs on expeditions and himself stayed behind; and
(4) sent Banda Singh to Punjab, who was till then playing childish games by the magical powers attained by him.

Taking of revenge creates the chain reactions and leads to perversions. Can the personality of the two younger sons of Guru Gobind Singh be equated with that of Wazir Khan? One is surprised to see such degradation of the Sikhs, who glorify the mad acts of Banda Singh, who after the demise of the Guru stirred up frustration in Sikhs for his selfish motives. Banda Singh did not punish Wazir Khan only, but massacred thousands of innocent Muslims regardless of their sex and age. Can that be called punishment of Wazir Khan only? Could Guru Gobind Singh have given such commands? The rebellion raised by the Sikhs led by Banda Singh was the turning point in the Sikh history. From November 1709 to this day the Sikhs have reversed the hands of the clock and have led to the present situation. Since Banda Singh's time Sikhs started raising rebellions against the established authorities on any count, considering this as the Sacred acts of patriotism, thus have destroyed their character completely. They have not only marred their character, but also have inflicted grave injury to Sikhism. Unless they dispassionately realise their mistakes and mend their ways, the situation cannot improve.

On the basis of Jodh Singh's writings (Sri Kalgi Dhar Hulas), Hari Ram Gupta writes: "The Guru told the Emperor that on a previous occassion Emperor Jehangir had surrendered Chandu Diwan to his grandfather Hargobind. Similarly, the Guru demanded that the following persons might be delivered up to him:

(1) Wazir Khan of Sirhind, (2) Suchanand of Sirhind,

(3) Gangu Brahmin of Kheri, (4) Jani and Mani of Morindah,

(5) Shamas Khan of Rajwara, (6) Mukarram Khan of Jullundur, and

(7) Dilawar Khan of Lahore.

The Emperor expressed his limitations for the time being and promised to do so as soon as possible."

In so far as martyrdom of Guru Arjun Dev is concerned, the Guru was executed under the orders of Emperor Jehangir himself, and not by Chandu Diwan. Guru Hargobind later developed friendly relations with Emperor Jehangir!!

Guru Gobind Singh never cherished any animosity or hatred against any one. The Guru thoroughly understood the behaviour pattern of Wazir Khan and intentionally always tried to avoid issues with him. Had the Guru thought of the retaliatory measures against Wazir Khan and others, he would not in the first place written a letter to Emperor Aurangzeb (Zafarnama) inviting the Emperor to Dina for talks at the earliest so that he could utter some kind words to the Emperor, and later sent himself on the long journey to southern India to meet with him. Again he would not have stayed at Agra and in its neighbourhood for a period of 8 to 9 months. After leaving Anandpur in December 1705, the Guru's following had increased manifold. The Guru was stressing on Emperor Bahadur Shah to create the normal conditions in Punjab so that he could go back to Anandpur and settle there. The normal conditions could have been established in Punjab, had the Emperor transferred Wazir Khan from Sirhind to any other province. The Emperor was afraid of the uprising of the Muslim fundamentalists, if any action was taken against Wazir Khan. Now the Emperor was going to southern India. The Guru could tell the Emperor that he would not be accompanying him. The Guru could teach Wazir Khan a lesson, when there was the civil war for acquisition of power between Bahadur Shah and Azam, and also when the Emperor had gone to southern India to quel the rebellion of Kam Baksh. But raising of rebellions is against the tenets of Sikhism. Such actions lead to many more immoral and corrupt actions. For a man of God, character is of the highest value, not hankering after transitory vanishing power.

There is no end to the absurd writings about the Gurus, both by Sikhs and non-Sikhs, having not understood them. Now how the question of taking any action against any one in the North could arise, when the Emperor had come to southern India? Did the Guru want to create chaos in northern India? Was the Guru a child that he could not understand such things?

Causes of Guru Gobind Singh's Death

M.A. Macauliffe writes:

"The current Sikh account of the Guru's death is that he was stabbed by Gul Khan, a grandson of Painde Khan, in revenge for the death of the latter at the hands of Guru Hargobind. More probable is the account given in one of the recensions of Bahadur Shah's history — The Guru was in the habit of constantly addressing assemblies of worldly persons, religious fanatics, and indeed all varieties of people. One day an Afghan, who frequently attended these meetings, was sitting listening to him, when certain expressions which were disagreeable to the ears of the faithful fell from the Guru's tongue. The Afghan was enraged and, regardless of the Guru's dignity and importance, stabbed him twice or thrice with a poniard.

The Emperor on hearing of the outrage dispatched some of his most skillful surgeons to attend to the Guru's injuries; and so skillfully did they perform their duty that the Guru's wounds were nearly healed in a fortnight, after which the surgeons took their leave as being no longer required. In a short time the Emperor again sent to inquire after the Guru's health and made him several offerings, which included two bows. A discussion arose whether the Guru could bend them. On this he took up one and on bending it burst open his imperfectly healed wounds. Blood began to flow copiously. The wound was bound up by the Guru's attendants, but this time past medicament."

Dr. Gopal Singh correctly gave an account of how the Guru was stabbed, as given by Sainapat in his book 'Gur-sobha.' He was the contemporary poet in the Guru's court. We have already given his version in the beginning. Dr. Gopal Singh also states:

"All evidence now goes to prove that the murderer was a hireling of the Subedar of Sirhind, who fearing reprisals from the Guru for his distardly deeds despatched this hired assassin to put an end to the Guru's life at the first opportunity. According to the Khalsa Namah of Bakht Mal,

Bahadur Shah granted a firman in favour of the Guru upon Wazir Khan for the payment to him of Rupees three hundred a day. It is natural, therefore, that on account of this close association of the Guru with the Emperor, Wazir Khan had got an attempt made earlier also on the life of the Guru, but it had failed.

The wound was treated immediately and stitched up. On the 4th day (according to Bhai Santokh Singh), the Guru appeared in his Darbar and it was considered he was well on the way to recovery. But in the middle of night, when he stretched a little, the wound again gapped open. Some chronicles, like Mehma Parkash (1774 A.D.) suggest that he was trying a heavy bow, when the stitches gave way. The Guru sat up, in pain, and thinking his journey's end to be near, he called some of his immediate followers. By the time they arrived, the Guru was in meditation, but the Sikhs were at once apprehensive that something dreadful was in the offing. His face was serene and calm, as usual, and he betrayed no signs of sinking man, but of one utterly composed and withdrawn in his own inner being, his eyes quietly closed, like petals of lotus at the sundown. As soon as the prayer was over, some of them choked with emotion could not resist expressing their deep anxiety at what they feared was in the womb of the future. But, the Guru, collected as ever, replied in subdue tones: "The one thing men dread most is death. I have always lived in its nearness and looked it in the face. So should every one of you who claims to follow me. I'll ride to my death as a bridegroom does to the house of his bride... So, do not grieve for me. For where so ever are the Five Pure Ones of you dedicated to God, there my presence shall also be."

Dr. Gopal Singh, has not confined himself fully to the account given by Poet Sainapat. The later historians cannot be correct, they mixed their own imaginations. Gopal Singh quotes 'Mehma Parkash' of Saroop Das Bhalla, written in 1774 that the Guru was trying a heavy bow, when his stitches gave way. We do not have that bow as the relic!!!

It will be noted from the above mentioned account of Dr. Gopal Singh that the Guru on the fourth day after the assault appeared in his Darbar and it was considered that he was well on the way to recovery. But in the middle of night, when he stretched a little, the wound again gapped open, Gopal Singh then refers to Mehma Parkash, written in 1774 A.D. that the Guru was trying a heavy bow, when the stiches gave way. The assault on the Guru took place on August 18, 1708. In other words, according to these accounts the Guru's demise should have taken place in the month of August 1708 itself; while the actual date of his death was much later on October 8, 1708. Obviously, the account given by Sainapat can only be relied upon.

Dr. Hari Ram Gupta states:

"Bahadur Shah entered into a conspiracy with the two Pathans deputed by Wazir Khan. Gul Khan alias Jamshed Khan and his brother Ataullah Khan were prevailed upon to put an end to the Guru's life as early as possible. Once in the enemy camp, it was absolutely not possible for the Guru to escape unhurt from court conspiracies, except by the artifice like the one adopted by Shivaji. An undiplomatic opponent of the Mughal government and living in their camp had to pay for his life. There was no other recourse. The two Pathans regularly attended the weekly sermons of the Guru and displayed keen interest in his teachings. They also won the confidence of other Sikhs. One day in the evening the Guru was taking rest in his tent. He was all alone in the tent, while a few Sikhs were loitering here and there. The Guru was half asleep with his back toward the door. Just at this moment the two Pathans came to visit the Guru. No body suspected the treachery. One of them Jamshed Khan by name, a huge and strong fellow quietly entered the tent of the Guru. He thrust his dagger (Jamdhar) into the left side of the Guru near the heart. The Guru seized the hand of the assailant, pulled the dagger out of the body and pierced it into the stomach of the Pathan killing him on the spot. The other Pathan was cut to pieces by the Sikhs. It took place 4 Bhadon Samvat 1765 (September 1708). A Jarrah or surgeon was immediately summoned. He applied ointment and stitched the wound. Under proper care the Guru began to recover. The Emperor daily sent messengers to inquire after the Guru's health. The news that the Guru was speedily recovering dismayed him. He now decided to adopt a cunning device frequently used by his father. He tried to contrive the death of the Guru in such a way as never to allow the Emperor's complicity to come to the surface. He sent rich presents to the Guru as a token of his pleasure at the Guru's speedy convalescence. Knowing the Guru's weakness for bows and arrows, he included two strong and hard bows beautifully bedecked. A clever emissary accompanied by Firoz Khan, the taluqdar of the place, was sent to deliver the gifts. His main duty was to see that the Guru himself tried the bows then and there. He was successful in inveigling the Guru to test the quality of the bows. In doing so the stiches of his wound gave way and blood flowed profusely. The wound was sown again, but it purified."

H.R. Gupta gives the proof of the Emperor's pious fraud as under:

(i) The Emperor halted at Nanded for 7 weeks as long as the Guru was there. He left the place and crossed river Godavari in 4 or 5 hours after the Guru's last breath. The Emperor was not in the Deccan on a picnic. For him every hour was critical. All the way from Ajmer to Nanded he had never stayed anywhere for more than a couple of days. His brother Kam Baksh had set himself up as Emperor at Hyderabad, and was in open revolt against Bahadur Shah. At Nanded the Emperor was not marking any military preparations. They had already been made. He delayed his departure from fear of the Guru. He was not prepared to leave him alone. The Guru had already sent

Banda Bahadur to Punjab to create disturbances there. He had openly defied the Emperor for his failure to punish Wazir Khan. The Emperor was afraid that the Guru might join the Marhattas, when he was involved in fighting with his brother.

(ii) On October 28, the Emperor ordered that a dress of mourning be presented to the son of Jamshed Khan Afghan, who had been killed by Guru Gobind Singh. Gupta says Jamshed Khan was not a mansabdar of the Mughal court or a high dignitary upon whom such high honours were bestowed by the Emperor. He was spy of Wazir Khan in the disguise of a soldier in attendance upon the Sayyad, who was also deputed by the Governor of Sirhind.

(iii) It was 2 days later, on October 30, 1708, that the Emperor ordered for the grant of a robe of mourning to Guru Gobind Singh's family. It means that the Emperor gave not only equality to Jamshed Khan with the Guru in rank and status but also accorded him priority over the Guru.

(iv) On November 11, 1708, it was represented that the deceased Guru Gobind Singh had left a lot of goods. What were the orders about the forfeiture? It was ordered that such chattles would not replete the imperial treasury. This was the property of a darvesh (Saint). There should be no interference with it. Gupta says that the Emperor's refusal to attach the Guru's property against the will of his courtiers shows his diplomacy, a pious fraud.

Our views on Accounts given above

M.A. Macauliffe has written about the Gurus in consultation with the Sikh advisers, whatever occurred to them without any regard to the personality of the Gurus and their Teachings. He states that Gul Khan, a grandson of Painde Khan, who took revenge of his grandfather killed in war by Guru Hargobind, the grand-father of Guru Gobind Singh. The question arises why this man had to come to Nanded, while the Guru remained all his life in northern India. It is all absurd.

The other reason for the murderous assault given is that the Guru in a religious meeting uttered such words against Islamic faith, which were not agreeable to Muslims. In this regard we have already stated that when the relatives of the Pathan feared lest they should be harmed, they through certain influential officials approached the Emperor, to tell him that the assassin was swayed by the passion aroused in him by the disrespectful words alleged to have been uttered by the Guru. The credulous Emperor gave a robe of reverence to the dead of the relatives of the assassin on October 28, 1708. But when the Sikhs came to know of this slanderous act against the Guru, they sent a representation to the Emperor bringing out the factual position of the whole affair. The Emperor was then deeply moved and sent the robe of reverence to the Dead, to Mata Sundari through the Sikhs. It is most surprising that Macauliffe as advised by the Sikhs should include such baseless charges against the Guru. Indeed most of the works of Macauliffe are not historically factual.

Macauliffe further states that the Emperor sent his officials to inquire after the Guru's health and made him several offerings which included two bows. A discussion arose whether the Guru could bend the bows. On this the Guru took up one and on bending it burst open his imperfectly healed wounds. Blood began to flow copiously. This action of the Guru brought him on the verge of death. Certain later Sikh chronicles also give similar story. This credulous act of the Guru was made rife in order to involve the Emperor to this distardy act. These actions of biased Sikhs against all Muslims do not do any harm to the Emperor, but only to the Guru and Sikhism. The Guru was All Wise. We dismiss this charge on the understanding of the Guru as most absurd and childish. Guru Nanak in Jap Ji says, "Men of God are immortal and cannot be guiled." Moreover, we do not find any of the two heavy bows kept as relics!!! As already stated by us, if we accept the story of the Guru trying a heavy bow, then the Guru would have expired in August or at the most in early September 1708, not on October 8, 1708!!! Some old chronicles state that the Guru expired on October 18, 1708. There is a gap of about two months between the dates of murderous assault on the Guru and his final departure from Earth.

As regards Dr. Hari Ram Gupta's assertion that Emperor Bahadur Shah was personally involved in killing Guru Gobind Singh, we may state that none of the four proofs given by him are correct. The new narration of the assassination given by him is not supported by any authority. All these are his funny conjectures to defame the Guru.

The Guru along with 500 to 600 armed Sikhs came to Ajmer from Agra to join the Emperor for journey toward southern India. He travelled with the Emperor from Ajmer to Hingoli. From Hingoli the Guru came to Nanded and reached there on July 19, 1708. The Emperor went to Hyderabad and reached there on January 13, 1709, covering a distance of about 120 miles in about 6 months. Even if the Emperor went to Nanded and stayed there upto October 8, 1708 and then went to Hyderabad, it should not have taken him to cover distance of less than 100 miles to reach Hyderabad, the period of more than three months. When the Guru was stabbed on August 18, 1708, special men were sent to inform the Emperor, who were somewhere between Hingoli and Hyderabad. He immediately sent his British Surgeon, Cole, who reached Nanded next morning only, and started his treatment. This clearly proves that the Emperor was not at Nanded, when the Guru was stabbed. It is also not understood what interest the Emperor had in getting the Guru killed? The Guru as an All Wise Man clearly understood that no changes in administration could be made in northern India, while the Emperor was engaged in hostilities in southern India. Even if the Emperor were to be in northern India, and any action which would have mean creation of the chaotic conditions in the country, the Guru would certainly not have insisted on making the administrative changes.

The Guru had never raised any rebellion against any established authority. Could he as a religious Prophet do this immoral act now in sending Banda to Punjab to cause disturbances there and incite Marhattas to rise in rebellion in southern India? The Emperor had full confidence in him that he would do neither of such immoral acts, only the bigots, who are against Muslims are now defaming the Guru. It was with the blessings of the Guru that Bahadur Shah had become the Emperor. The far-sighted Guru never made mistakes. It does not behove of the Sikhs at least to charge the Guru that he began working against his own creation! This would completely demolish his Personality. When this fact that by stretching the heavy bow the Guru would have harmed himself injuring his newly healed raw wounds can be recognised by every common man, how absurd thinking is that the Guru could not think of this, who was sent by God to teach the world to lead a good life. How childish it is to levy such charges against the All Wise Guru!

We have already clarified why the Emperor on October 28, 1708 gave a dress of mourning to the son of the Guru's assassin, Jamshed Khan. The mourning dress was given to the assassin's son, as the Muslims had widely spread the rumour that the Guru in his religious meetings had spoken ill of the Islamic faith. When the Sikhs came to know of this slanderous act against the Guru, they at once appraised the Emperor of the truth. He was then deeply moved and repented for his earlier action. He then sent the robe of reverence to the Dead of Mata Sundari through the Sikhs. We have already given the nature of Emperor Bahadur Shah. He was too weak to face any opposition, and would easily surrender. He was also afraid of the Muslim fanatics.

The other objection Gupta states is that on November 11, 1708 it was represented that the Guru had left a lot of goods and the officials sought the permission of the Emperor for their forfeiture, as the Guru had died issueless. The emperor ordered that such chattles would not replete the imperial treasury. This was the property of a darvesh (Saint). There should be no interference with it. In Gupta's view the Emperor's refusal to attach the Guru's property against the will of his courtiers shows his diplomacy and a pious fraud. We can hardly understand what Gupta wants to convey!

The Story narrated by Gupta about the assassination attempt of the Guru is sheerly his own imagination, not be substantiated by any written historical record. The only authentic contemporary records are 'Guru-Sobha' by Poet Sainapat to be fully relied upon. Poet Sainapat clearly states in his narration that the Guru after having been stabbed said that God Almighty had saved him. He was fully recovered of the injury in 10 days' time. Then the Poet says that many days passed peacefully, and at last the time for the Guru's Departure from Earth came. All later accounts are biased against Muslims.

The Emperor always cherished utmost love for the Guru. Dr. Ganda Singh supports the view that the Emperor had absolutely no hand in the assassination intrigues. Let this be very much clear that the Guru did not die of the stabbing, but was fully cured. He left this Earth when the Divine Call was received by him, which he announced a few days earlier before his death.

To summarise this important discussion, it may be stated that the Guru came to Nanded on July 19, 1708, and was stabbed by Jamshed Khan, a hireling of Wazir Khan, Nawab of Sirhind, on August 18, 1708. The local surgeons were immediately called, who washed the wounds, got them sewn and applied on ointment. From next morning the Royal British Surgeon, Cole, took over the treatment. The wounds were speedily healing. The Guru on 4th day could come to attend the religious meeting. The stitches were removed in a week or 10 days' time. It can safely be said that the Guru was fully recovered during this time. So the Guru lived the whole month of September in perfect health. His departure for Heavenly Abode on October 8, 1708, was in the normal manner similar to the earlier Sikh Gurus, Nanak Dev, Angad Dev, Amar Das, Ram Das, Hargobind and Har Rai. Guru Arjun Dev and Tegh Bahadur were executed by the rulers and Guru Hari Krishan contacted Small Pox while serving the people and died of the disease. Guru Gobind Singh is stated having said in early October 1708, that he had been summoned to the Divine Presence. The Sikhs were shocked and dismayed. The other six Gurus we have mentioned and also Guru Gobind Singh at the time of their final departure from Earth, never suffered from any disease or there were any other signs of death. The Gurus would sufficient time before their death appoint their respective successor and appoint him as the Guru, before their deaths, it was in the same manner Guru Gobind Singh told the Sikhs on October 7, 1708 that he had bestowed the Gurship to the Khalsa People in Collective Form and his Light had merged in them. He entrusted the Khalsa People to the care of Akal Purkh (God), Whose Visible Form was His Word, as enshrined in Guru Granth Sahib—The Supreme Guru.

6

Views of Scholars

Prof. Abdul Majid Khan

The Spirit of the Khalsa

Prophets and saviours with strong minds and great hearts, who appear time to time have a very vital role to play in the remaking of society. History is eloquent on the fact that Guru Gobind Singh came with a clear message and stood for a definite spirit. Indeed, the be-all and the end-all of his strenuous efforts was to rejuvenate a rotten social order.

Guru Gobind Singh saw that the people of the Punjab, nay, of northern India, were slaves of prejudice, pride and passion, in-as-much as they attached undue importance to theological disputes, metaphysical abstractions, meaningless conventions and customs, with the result that either they were unbalanced and fanatical or they were steeped in sloth. So, the situation was quite hopeless and the atmosphere was very depressing. Political tyranny of the Mughals, shackles of the caste system and vested interests of reactionary religious fraternities, were the odds he had to contend with. The Tenth Master realised that he would have to work ceaselessly to change the psychology of his countrymen. He felt that that was the first desideratum. In the absence of a sense of direction, plan and compass, even when things are done with the best of intentions and for the purest of motives, the result is heavy sorrow, or blank despair. The master-mind, the great genius that he was, he put an end to all hazy indetermination, impotent rage and the idle dreams of the sluggards and the cowards. In other words, he was convinced of the supreme necessity of the work of liberation—political as well social.

New Baptism

Political power was to be seized and a parallel government was to be established in order to draw all the patriotic elements to a rallying point, to a strong centre. The Guru achieved this by introducing a new form of 'baptism' and thenceforward called the initiated Sikhs, "the Khalsa of Wahiguru", the Lord's Own. The Panj Piyaras i.e. the first Five Baptized Ones and their revered Guru formed the nucleus of the band of liberators. The Master aimed at building up a nation of the Purified Ones, who would be completely free from fear as well as selfishness, from hatred and haughtiness and would count no sacrifice too great for emancipating their land from the galling yoke of the rulers, who were intoxicated with the heady wine of power. He was also keen on saving from the cluthces of fanatical priests the gullible folk of rural India. In other words, the Khalsa came into being to uphold righteousness and to uproot oppression. The Guru was bent upon the development of a well-kint, homogeneous class of people, inspired by a common national ideal and jointed together in a common cause—the freedom and the uplift of India and through India he wanted to serve humanity.

Short-sighted historians are wrong when they hold or even imply that the struggle in the days of Guru Gobind Singh was between the Sikhs and the Muslims. As a matter of fact, the armies of the Tenth Master had a considerable number of Hindus and Muslims among them. On the other hand, the Mughal forces had the active support of some of the Hindu rajas of the Hills. Guru Gobind Singh could always count on his faithful friends like Qazi Pir Mohammed. Ghani Khan and Nabi Khan, who saved his life at a critical moment. Pir Budhu Shah of Sadhura sent 500 pathans and his sons, who died fighting under the flag of Guru Gobind Singh. Saed Khan and Maimu Khan, two famous Muslim Generals offered ungrudging help to the Guru. Likewise, numerous liberty-loving Hindus generously supported him.

Nationalism not Enough

The teachings and message of the Tenth Guru are for the whole of the troubled and groaning humanity. As a far-sighted seer and a noble sage, he knew that nationalism was only a passing phase in the evolution of mankind. True, it was a sort of half-way house between tribalism and international unity or global co-operation. In one of his swayyas, the Master says. "The Power of God and Bliss, this is my sole prayer before Thee: Give me the strength to pursue righteous conduct, come what may." And when he emphatically said, "*Recognize all humanity as one*", he implied thereby that no cause could be nobler than the firm conviction that basically and essentially East and West constitute one global brotherhood. Every human being is a spark of the Divine Essence. God, in the final analysis, is the sum total of millions of human souls i.e. there is no Divinity higher than humanity. Compare the Practical Vedanta of Swami Vivekananda with the core of the message of Guru Gobind Singh. Swami Vivekananda held, "The Only God to worship is the human soul in the human body. Of course, all animals are temples too, but man is the highest, the Taj Mahal of temples. If I cannot worship in that, no other temple will be of any advantage."

The tragedy of the present-day civilization is that the conquest of the forces of nature has not been accompanied by the ethical control over the dispositions of mankind. Intellect has done wonders, but it has not yet dispelled inner darkness. The head has grasped a lot but the heart continues to be as diseased as ever, as bad as ever. Guru Gobind singh rightly stresses the over-riding importance of the refinement of human emotions. "May the dispositions of men remain under the control of ethical reason, and the ethical reason of men, under the guidance of God, for ever and ever, Amen", is an excerpt from the daily congregational prayer of the Khalsa—the prayer which Guru Gobind Singh himself used to offer every day.

Talking to Bhai Nand Lal—one of the most cultured and trusted disciple, Guru Gobind Singh remarked "Men should listen to the Guru attentively and with devotion. That what the Guru teaches, they should hear and preach. Men should listen to the words of the Guru with love in their hearts and faith in their minds. *Men should serve each other without pride and without selfishness. Those who serve humanity thus, their service do I recognize as service to my person. Pay attention, O Nand, in this way humanity shall be freed and attain everlasting bliss.*

Day in and day out, we talk of service to mankind. It is impossible to serve others till we believe in the ideals of equality and fraternity. What does that mean? The U.N.O. is now emphasizing the importance of making the world free from fear and free from want. About three hundred years ago, the Tenth Master stood and strove for making this terrestrial globe, this earth i.e. the whole of mankind free from fear and free from want. He was totally opposed to privilege, in the social as well as in the political domain.

The challenge of today is democratic liberalization of religion—religion which under the guidance of guru Gobind Singh influenced lives and conduct of thousands of politically backward and socially disinherited folk and welded them into a strong brotherhood, pledged to the service of mankind, through India. Faith is anything but a dope. Indeed it is a living and vivid belief in the gospel of bringing man nearer to man, of promoting global goodwill and universal peace. This is the spirit which the Tenth Guru infused in the Khalsa. Let us all be worthy of it. Let us all live up to it. May God bless us with "strength to right the wrong, through truth and justice."

GURU GOBIND SINGH—HIS CONTRIBUTION TO NATION BUILDING

(Gurmukh Nihal Singh)

I

Guru Gobind Singh was born at Patna 300 years ago when conditions in India had reached a critical stage. Aurangzeb was then on the Mughal throne and he had determined to make Islam the sole religion in his vast empire. In order to achieve his object he did not hesitate to use all methods, fair or foul, not excluding torture and the sword. He ordered destruction of non-Muslim places of religious worship and in particular the Hindu temples. He denied to the people the freedom of conscience and of Religious

Worship. Guru Tegh Bahadur, the revered father of the boy Gobind, decided to stem this tide of religious persecution and Mughal tyranny by offering himself for sacrifice.

At the time of his revered father's unique martyrdom, his con Gobind was hardly nine years of age, though he was a party to the decision of Guru Tegh Bahadur for making the supreme sacrifice. According to his father's instructions, young son was installed as the Tenth Guru—early in 1676. The responsibilities of this high office were particularly onerous at the time but the young Guru undertook them seriously, with firm determination to uproot tyranny and religious persecution and to restore the Freedom of Conscience to the people.

The contribution which Guru Gobind Singh made, during the brief span of his life (1666-1708), to national life was manifold. He was a great spiritual leader, a poet of distinction, a great litterateur and patron of learning, a great warrior with a commanding and magnetic personality, an eminent statesman and a unique nation-builder. This essay, as the title shows, is primarily devoted to the Guru's contribution to Nation-building, although his contributions to the other spheres of national life were also of no less importance and he shared fully in laying and strengthening the spiritual foundations of his people. His contributions to *Gurbani*, mainly in *Braj Bhasa*, were both voluminous and sublime. His language was direct and expressive and had the rare quality of penetrating the hearts of men, as an arrow, discharged with force from the bow, penetrates the body.

II

Guru Gobind Singh was greatly distressed to watch the deteriorating situation in the country. The morale of the people had suffered greatly everywhere and the non-Muslims had become hopelessly divided, weak and demoralised, unable to withstand, much less combat, the Mughal tyranny and that of the so-called higher-caste Hindus. The *Brahmins* in their caste pride and arrogance looked down upon the Sikhs, many of whom belonged to the so-called lower castes. Even the agents of the Guru, the *Masands*, particularly in more distant parts of the country, taking advantage of the simple minded Sikhs and their great devotion to the Guru, were resorting to evil practices to fill their own pockets at the expense of the Guru. The Mughal Emperor was utilising the Hill-Chiefs to strengthen his political hold and was doing his best to undermining the influence and power of the Guru, whom he regarded as the chief obstacle in the way of achieving his objective and a potential threat to his Empire.

Guru Gobind Singh pondered deeply over the unfortunate situation prevailing in the country. He continued to strengthen the moral and spiritual fibre of his people and their power of physical resistance and suffering. He gave as many of them as practicable training in the art of warfare of their own defence and that of the oppressed people. He came to the conclusion that *Satyagraha* and sacrifice alone were unable to stem the tide of tyranny and the use of force had become inevitable in the circumstances then existing in the country. As he himself put it in his autobiography—*Bachitar Natak* (the Wonderous Drama)— "When no other way was left to me I took the path of war and put my arrow to the bow; when all other means have failed, it is righteous to take to the sword." He, therefore, decided to complete his preparations for *Dharm Yudh*—righteous war or a religious crusade, and to take the final step to achieve the specific purpose of his human sojourn to witness the wonderous drama (*tamasha*), as he has himself explained in *Baethitar Natak*:—

These quotations from the Guru's autobiography indicate clearly the real purpose of his human sojourn and the means he considered necessary to achieve his objective. He had taken birth at Patna Sahib in 1666 with the difficult task of ending the reign of terror and oppression and to uproot evil and evil-doers, protect the helpless, uplift the lowly and bring the holy to the forefront.

III

After prolonged and careful consideration he came to the conclusion that it was necessary to impart a new spirit to his people and build up their spiritual, moral, material and physical fibre. He had been devoting himself to this sacred and uphil task with a rare devotion and thoroughness for a period of some twenty-two years. He reared the new structure of the community on the spiritual, moral and social foundations laid down by the first nine Gurus and strengthened by his own contributions. He gave them also physical stamina and trained them in the art of warfare and prepared them for the struggle ahead in defence of freedom and higher human values—not for self-aggrandisement. When he thought that the time had come for taking the final step, he summoned his people, from far and near to assemble in full strength at Anandpur Sahib on the *Baisakhi Purb*, 1699 with their hair uncut and beards unshaved. He personally supervised all the arrangements for holding the *Diwan* in a huge *Pandal*, screened from outside view by high *Kanats* and got a closed tent pitched near the place of the *Diwan* and five goats tied inside secretly. Uncle Kirpal alone was taken into confidence and entrusted with obtaining the five he-goats (*bakras*) at night and have them tied securely inside and to arrange for guarding the tent so that the secret may not leak out.

On the historic day (*Baisakhi* of 1699) Sikhs in large numbers from all parts of the country, who had come obeying their Guru's order, began to assemble in the *Diwan* from very early hours of the morning. After completion of the usual singing of *Asa Di War* and *Shabd-Kirtan* the audience looked forward to an inspiring discourse from their beloved, peerless Guru. Soon after the Guru came and took up a standing posture on the Dais. He was specially dressed in saffron robes for the great occasion and looked handsome, full of vigour, divine light and earthly splendour. Suddenly he took out his sword from his scabbard and flourishing the naked sword in his right hand, assumed a threatening attitude and spoke in a loud voice, demanding a human sacrifice—Is there a Sikh present who would give his life for the sake of the Guru? The great expectancy turned into distress and consternation. When no one came forward the Guru repeated his call in a still louder and more urgent tone. At last three was some movement and one brave and devoted Sikh came and stood before the Guru with folded hands, begged forgiveness for his tardy response and offered himself for sacrifice. He was Bhai Daya Ram, a *Khatri* from Lahore. The Guru left the *Diwan*, taking Daya Ram to the closed tent, slaughtered one of the give goats, which fell with a loud thud (heard in the *Diwan*), and a strem of blood flowed outside the tent through a narrow shallow drain. Bhai Daya Ram was told to bathe and dress in one of the new uniforms placed inside the tent and the Guru left again for the *Diwan*, with the naked, blood smeared sword held aloft in his right hand, and demanded another human sacrifice. Bhai Dharam Dass, a *Jat* from Rohtak responded immediately, who was also taken by the Guru in the closed tent. The Guru slaughtered the second goat, gave the same instructions to Dharam Dass and, as before, left for the *Diwan* where he repeated his call for another sacrifice and this was done similarly for the fourth and the fifth times as well, thus selecting the *Five Piyaras* (Beloved Ones). They were, (i) Bhai Daya Ram, (ii) Dharm Dais), (iii) Mohkam Chand *Chhimba* (a calico-printer) from Dwarka, (iv) Himmat, a Kahar (water-carrier) from Jagannath Puri, and (vi) Sahib Chand, a *Brahmin* from Bidar.

After the *Panj Piyaras* had bathed and dressed in their new uniforms, the Guru marched them, with himself at the head, in a picturesque procession to the *Diwan*, The Guru was beaming with joy, proud of his five 'Beloved Ones', who had just emerged safe and pure from the crucible of sacrifice. The happy tidings of the rebirth of the five devotees quickly spread outside the *Diwan* all around and those weaklings, who had skulked away in fright earlier, returned quietly and took their seats at the rear of the *Diwan*.

The last Act of the 'Wonderous Drama' enacted by Guru Gobind Singh at Takht Keshgarh Sahib, Anandpur, on the Baisakhi of 1699 was indeed most spectacular and unique in the world history. On the Dais sat the great Warrior-Saint, dressed in saffron-coloured, silken *achkan* and white *chooridar piyjama*, with the priceless, luminous, world famed *Kalgi* on his turban (*dastar*) and his bright sheathed sword resting calmly by his right side from the belt slung from the girdle (*gatra*). The Guru's handsome face was lit with a divine glow and halo, radiating grace, joy, spiritual power, physical prowess, personal magnetism and gratitude and devotion to God. On the side of the dais stood the *Panj Piyaras*, purified by their great sacrifice and devotion to the Guru and God, dressed in bright new uniforms, upright and stalwart with swords hanging by *gatras* on their right side, serene, happy, full of kindness, devotion, strength dignity and humility and pledged to the service of God, the Guru and Mankind. The entire scene was a sight for the gods to see.

The stage was now fully set for the final scene. On a *Choki*, a low, square table, in front of the Guru lay in its middle a *bata*, a large iron bowl, in which there was water and sugar-candy (*Patashas*) and on the right of the bowl a *Khanda* (a double-edged sword). The Guru took up the *Khanda* from the *choki* in his right-hand, assumed an erect posture and after praying to god for guidance and support and asking the five *Piyaras* to concentrate their attention on the bowl on the *choki*, repeating in their hearts fifth Guru's couplet entreating God to forgive the past misdeeds and guide them in future to the right path, began stirring sweet-candy in water in the bowl with the *Khanda* and to receive five *banis* from *Adi Granth* and *Dasam Granth, Japji Sahib, Jap Sahib, Anand Sahib, Chaupai* and *Swayyas* one after the other. He thus prepared the baptismal water, *Amrit*, the nectar or the Elixir of immortality for administering the new 'Baptism of the sword' to the five beloved ones.

The Guru stood up and came forward near the five *Piyaras* with a Sikh holding the *bata* and began to administer the baptism (the *Pahul*) to each one of them by turn.

The Guru gave five *chulus* (handfuls) of the Baptismal Water to the first *Piyara* one after the other, asking him to repeat each time after him, "*Waheguru ji ka Khalsa, Shri Waheguru ji ki Fateh* (The Khalsa is of God and victory be to Him). Then he administered five *chulus* of the *Amrit* (Nectar) in the knot of his long hair in the same manner one after the other, asking to repeat each time after him the new salutation of the Khalsa. Next, the Guru asked the *Piyara* to face him, with his eyes wide open, and dashed five times *chulus* of the Elixir, to sprinkle it over his eyes and face, the *Piyara* repeating each time the new salutation after him as before. In the same manner the Baptism or the *Pahul* was administered to each of the other four Piyaras. All the five were asked to drink directly from the bowl their own share of the remaining baptismal water by passing the bowl from one to the other. The five *Piyaras* also ate together from the same bowl the Parshad (Sweet pudding) known as *Karah or Mahan Parshad.* All distinctions of caste, touch and high and low were thus completely obliterated and the five *Piyaras* became *Gur-Bhai* (Brothers in faith), sons of the Guru and God, the first members of the new order, the *Khalsa*—a community of soldier-saints—(*sant-sipahis*)—or the Sikh Panth—a truly equalitarian society. Their last name was changed and it ended with 'Singh'—(lion, the symbol of majesty, strength and power).

The Guru took another surprising and revolutionary step by requesting the five baptised *Piyaras* to prepare the baptismal water in the same manner as he had done for them and administer the *Pahul* to him and to rename him Gobind Singh—the Sangat (congregation) acclaimed him then as, their 'wonderful Guru', who was himself the Guru as well as the discipl :—

In the *Adi-Granth* there is a couplet by the fifth Guru, which describes God as—"God is himself the Teacher and the Disciple." So did Guru Gobind Singh tell the five *Piyaras* : "I am the son of immortal God. It is by his order I have been born and have established this form of baptism. Those who accept it shall henceforth be known as the *Khalsa*. The *Khalsa* is the Guru and the Guru is the *Khalsa*."

Then the Guru addressed the congregation and explained the significance of the new 'Baptism of the Sword', and the responsibilities and duties of the baptised Sikh and *rehit-meryada*, rules of conduct and the new way of life he was expected to lead. The Guru stated, quoted from *The Sikh Religion*, Vol. V by M.A. Macauliffe, "since the time of Baba Nanak *charan-pahul* hath been customary. Man drank the water in which the Guru's feet (or *toe*) had been washed, a custom which led to great humility; but the *Khalsa* can now only be maintained by bravery and skill in arms." Therefore, I now institute the custom of "Baptism of the Sword" (*Amrit Khandedhar*), and change my followers from Sikhs to Singhs or lions. They who accept the nectar of the *Pahul* shall be changed before your very eyes from jackals into lions (from sparrows into hawks), shall obtain empire in the world and bliss hereafter." The Guru also laid great emphasis on unity and equality. The five *Pyaras* came from all the four corners or parts of the country and belonged to various castes—the so-called 'lower' and 'higher' castes. They were all made equal and welded together in a single entity—the *Khalsa*

IV

The Khalsa *Panth*—this unique community of integrated, devout, brave soldier-saints (*Sant Sipahis*) was established by Guru Gobind Singh on the basis of devotion to their Guru and God, on the principles of service, sacrifice and equality. So far as history records such complete equality was never established by any one either before Guru Gobind Singh or after his passing away from this world. Even the Sikhs did not keep it for very long after him. Of course the communist theory does contemplate the establishment of an equalitarian society sometimes in the remote future but no time limit has been fixed by Marx or those who claim to be true "Marxists" and are not "Revisionists." And it is a fact that even the extreme Left-Communists in their States have so far not succeeded in ending, what is known as the "Dictatorship of the Proletariat" and constitute a truly communist, stateless society—the idealistic society contemplated by Marx, Bakunin, Kropotkin or Tolstoy. It was Guru Gobind Singh alone, who established complete equality in practice in his community of soldier-saints, by raising his disciples to his own level and abolishing the distinction between himself and the five *Piyaras*. He went so far as to describe his Singhs in highly eugolistic terms, to remove any vestige of inferiority in them and to declare to the world their new status and the high esteem in which he held them. He proclaims:

(i) "Khalsa is my special form or image...
Khalsa is my Sat-Guru in his fullness...
It is not possible to tell his greatness or sing his praises...
I am of the Khalsa, Khalsa is mine; the whole is the ocean composed of water-drops, i.e. water-drops make up the ocean.'

(ii) All battles I have won with the loving grace of my people,
Their undying love and faith has been my sole protection,
All the glory, my home and heart enjoys are their precious gifts,
Through their efforts and help I have always acquired knowledge and wisdom,
It was with the help of these people I have always defeated my enemies,
For them I was born, through them I have attained glory and greatness.
What am I without their loving support—There are millions of creatures like me on earth."

(*Translation by:* Dr. Trilochan Singh)

Such generous praise by the Guru gave a new dignity and stature and made them more self-reliant and courageous and more devoted to their Guru, God and Humanity. It made the undying flame lit in their hearts by the 'Elixir of Immortality', the *Pahul*, the 'Baptism of the Sword' stronger and brighter and gave them fresh courage to perform the sacred task for which *Khalsa* was established by the wonderful Guru Gobind Singh.

V

Each member of the new order, the *Khalsa* or the Sikh *Panth* established by Guru Gobind Singh, was required to observe certain 'Rules of Conduct', *Rehit Maryada*,—the 'Do's' and 'Dont's' of life, prescribed by the Guru. The Guru stated :

"Only he who lives by the rules is my Sikh.
He will be my Guru, I his follower."

(*Translation by:* Khushwant Singh)

These Rules have been divided in three categories as follows:

(1) The five Essential Symbols of a Sikh—The five '*Kakkars*', the five 'K's' because their name begins each with the letter 'K' are:

(i) *Kesh*—uncut or unshorn hair—*Jatta-Joot*, the God-given form kept intact, with the long hair of the head tied usually on the top in a knot—*Joora*, the form of *Rishis* and warrior-teachers of yore;

(ii) *Kangha*—a small comb for keeping the hair clean, usually kept behind the knot, which also serves to hold together the hair and keep the knot firm at the top of the head;

(iii) *Kara*—a steel bracelet worn on the wrist of the right arm—a symbol of upright, disciplined life, of self-control;

(iv) *Kachha*— knicker, shorts worn, for sex discipline, a necessary article of the Khalsa's uniform; and

(v) *Kirpan*—the sword, for the protection of the weak and the oppressed and for that of life, honour and property and his hearth and home.

(2) The five 'Do's—functions or activities performance of which was essential to discharge the duties and responsibilities of his membership of the Khalsa and to promote his own welfare—physical, moral, material and spiritual:

(i) To recite daily five Banis, comprising *Nit-nem,* participation in congregational worship, singing of sacred hymns and the reading of *Guru Granth Sahib* and listening to exposition of *Gurbani*—essential for his spiritual development and for the attainment of the ultimate objective of his human sojourn,, merging of his spirit in the All-Soul, the Eternal or the supreme Spirit or Light;

(ii) To look to no one else for favour, support and assistance except the One and only God—the Lord of all so-called *devi, devtas, aulias, paigumbers,*sons and messengers and to pay obeisance only to Him and worship Him alone and no body else;

(iii) To make oneself trained in the use of arms—in the art of war-fare and be ever-ready for *Dharm Yudh* (righteous war) to protect the weak and the oppressed and to defend one's own life, hearth and home and honour;

(iv) To live by the sweat of his own brow and earn his own livelihood—and not to sponge on others and be a parasite on society; and

(v) To give *Daswand,* 1/10th of one's income for good and religious causes or as an offering for the Guru, the maintenance of *Guru's Langer* (free kitchen) for all who come, without distinction of caste, sect or sex in *pangat*—it makes one's earnings more meaningful and of greater usefulness.

(3) The five 'Dont's, renunciations or prohibited acts, which are essential to observe for the preservation and social progresss of the *Khalsa:*

(i) To refrain from cutting or shaving off his hair, which lowers or degrades him and makes him an outcaste in society, among the Khalsa—a *patti,* (apostate);

(ii) To refrain from keeping company or having any dealings or association or relationship with people who have been disloyal to the Guru and the *Panth*, such as the *masands Meenas, Ra-Raiyas,* etc., as it is disloyal and dangerous;

(iii) To refrain from such evil-practices as female infanticide and *Sati*, which were then demoralising society, and from worshipping *Marhis-Masans* (tombs and crematoriums);

(iv) To refrain from keeping company with concubines or to have sex relationship or intercourse with any other woman except his won life—says Guru Gobind Singh; and "Don't even dream of sharing bed of any other woman except your own wife."

(v) To refrain from the use of all intoxicants or narcotics, of including use of opium, *Bhang, Charas, Naswar*, tobacco in any form and liqour—they are injurious to health and morals, they turn a many into a beast and lead him to commit social wrongs and involve him in quarrels, to use foul language, which may lead to *mar peet* i.e. beating, killing and murder. The use of intoxicants has ruined many a home and reduced many to a state of bankruptcy—moral, material and social degeneration.

VI

It is not necessary to comment or give any elaborate explanation or interpretation of the rules of conduct given above or of what are known as the "Sikh Symbols." It is only necessary to draw attention to two of them here—*Kesh* and *Kirpan*.

(1) Guru Gobind Singh attached importance to *Kirpan*, the sword and its use with strength and skill. Sword was then the most useful weapon of defence and protection. It was on the point of the sword that Aurangzb and his officials had destroyed the freedom of conscience and religion. As quoted above, its use was considered by Guru Gobind Singh not only necessary but legitimate as well when all other measures fail to secure redress—as they had proved—and as was reminded by him in his two famous epistles to Aurangzeb (contained in *Zafar Namah*). The keeping of the sword always with him—*ang-sang*—was, therefore, made incumbent on every Sikh.

Guru Gobind Singh addressed God by numerous names (see his composition) but his most favourite Names for Him were *Bhagoti*—and the All-Steel-*Bhagoti*, the Sword is also mentioned as one of God's name in the *Adi-Granth* :

Guru Gobind Singh gave primacy to because of the special needs of his times and because he considered it necessary for the preservation of the *Panth*, established to carry out the mission entrusted to him by God. The Sikh *Ardas* (Prayer) begins by paying first obeisance to *Bhagoti*:—

Guru Gobind Singh has described sword, by various names in *Shastar Namah*:

However, times change and with it comes the use of other improved weapons for defence as well as offence. The people have these days substituted for the sword the pistol as a weapon for defence as it is more convenient and effective and has a higher range of action. It is, therefore, as a mere 'symbol' that it is largely kept today by the vast majority of Sikhs—a tiny *Kirpan* is either attached or tied to the small wooden comb or is inserted in the thicker part of the *Khanda,* which is not even visible from outside. A small number of more orthodox keep a smaller *Kirpan* of 7 to 9 inches, slung from the *gatra* and the full sword is today only carried naked in their hands by the five *Piyaras* in front of shri *Guru Granth Sahib* in processions or laid in front of *Guru Granth Sahib's Prakash* or held in the hand by *Piyaras* standing on two sides at *Diwans.* However, the *Panth* has so far not taken any formal decision on this matter by a *Gurmatta* or issued an Edict from the Akal Takht, the highest seat of religious authority among the Sikhs. It has just become a prevailing convention.

However, the position with regard to *Kesh* is entirely different. It is the distinguishing mark of a Sikh—which marks him out as separate or distinct from all others—he can be spotted from a distance in a crowd. There is no need of dwelling upon the various elaborate interpretations given by certain learned Sikhs. I am afraid, they are both unnecessary and unsatisfying.

The origin of this most prominent 'symbol' by which a Sikh is distinguished from others and he is instantly recognised in India and abroad, is his turbaned head (over the long, knotted hair) and beard, either bound on the sides from the chin in military style or flowing in front, giving, as Dr. Arnold Toynby has remarked recently, the stalward well-built Sikh a dignified, stately appearance. It must be borne in mind that Guru Gobind Singh did not want to make his Sikhs mere soldiers of future but wished to create saint-soldiers (*Sant-sipahis*), devoted to God and the Gurus, ready to sacrifice themselves in the service of the oppressed and for the protection of the weak and the holy. It was for *Dharm Yudh* that the Guru prepared his Sikhs, fired their imagination, trained them in the art of warfare and administered to them the 'Baptism of the Sword'—so that they may become *rishi warriors* like those in ancient India and therefore, gave them a similar form and appearance. The Guru was bent upon driving out weakness and cowardness from the hearts of his men and inspired in them a new, undying spirit and gave them a distinct form and personality—*Niyari* (different), so that they could not skulk away from danger or escape detection. He never engaged in a war of attrition or to acquire territory or possession of others. Guru Gobind Singh had expressly forbidden Banda Singh Bahadur to make any bid for power and his disobedience resulted in the leashing of a reign of terror and to his own martyrdom and that of many of his followers. For a long time a price was placed on the head of a Sikh and Sikhs had to make jungles their homes and spend their time in most cases on horse-back, armed each *Jatha* (organised unit) under the leadership of its *Jathedar.*

Many brave Sikhs suffered martyrdom gladly rather than forsake their faith or part with the sacred hair. There are the noble examples of Bahai Tara Singh who resisted to his last breath the removal of his long hair, which was scraped with *rambi*, a garden implement, with a dull blade and wooden handle from the skull, piece by piece, and Bhai Mani singh, the Head-Priest of Shri Harimandir Ji, Amritsar, who was cut up in small pieces, each joint separated from the other, bit by bit, who was the most learned scholar of his times and the scribe of both the final editions of the *Adi-Granth* (*Damdama Sahib* recension) and the *Dasam Granth* and also the compiler of the existing edition from which *Dasam Granth* was later printed and published. Such were the Sikhs created by Guru Gobind Singh through the 'Baptism of the sword', who faced singly hordes of the enemy and kept them at bay, made them die or run, but in case overwhelmed by the enemy and ambushed, gave their lives in battle like heroes, smilingly. As a bard has picturesquely described it,

The Khalsa has worked wonders in the field of battle ever since its establishment right up to the Indo-Pak conflict in 1965. And yet without engendering hatred for others. There is the noble example of Bhai Kanhaiya, who distributed water without discrimination among the wounded on the battle-field, irrespective of whether they were Sikhs or their invaders.

The explanation by certain scholars and medical experts in recent years that *Kesh* denote power and physical prowess with such instances as of the old Biblical story of Sampson and Delila or by marshalling out the evidence from medical science is besides the point and is far from convincing to our modern, sophisticated and educated young men. It was in January-February 1927, Gyani Sher Singh, a post-graduate student at the Lahore Government College, invited views from prominent Sikh intellecctuals, among whom were Hon. S. Joginder Singh, Professor Teja Singh, Jodh Singh (Bhai Sahib) and Harkishan Singh (Bawa), Sardar Sardul Singh, Mr. S. Partap, I.C.S. and others including myself on a letter received by him from a Sikh student in America, who had asked for guidance on the keeping of "Sikh Symbols" and desiring a clear and rational explanation or justification. The views of these persons published by Gyani Sher Singh from Lahore (27th February, 1927) in book form entitled *Thoughts on Forms and Symbols in Sikhism*, with an introduction by Professor Madan Gopal Singh, I.E.S., later Registrar, Punjab University and murdered in his office by Muslim fanatics, a few months after the partition.

In my article in this booklet (pages 65—79) I stated : "It is hardly possible to exaggerate (the) past utility (of the Sikh Symbols)."...They have kept constantly before our eyes the noble personality of our Saviour and Preceptor, Guru Gobind Singh and those of his inspired Sikhs, and have knit us together as nothing else would have done", I then posed the question, "To what extent are these symbols of ours" a living reality and useful today? I gave instances of high I.M.S., I. Eng. S. and I.C.S. Officers and other highly educated Sikhs, who regarded themselves as good Sikhs inspite of having parted with their long hair and were devoted followers of the Gurus and students of *Gurbani*, some of whom had published translations of *Gurbani*. They gave examples of great *Sehjdhari* Sikhs and Sikh devotees, who were honoured and respected among the Sikhs, among whom may be mentioned the names of Sadhu T.L. Vaswani, Colonel Bawa Jeewan Singh Bedi, I.M.S, and more recently Dr. M.S. Randhawa I.C.S. And asked as to how far it was just to condemn them as 'apostates' and turn them out from our fold. Are we so rich in intellect that we can afford the loss of some of our ablest men?" I added 'that way lies destruction. We must be wise enough to keep men of the type just mentioned, in our fold and adjust our ideas—hard as it is bound to be—to the changed conditions.' I emphasised the necessity of enlarging the definition of a Sikh to include such men and made a suggestion in this connection. However, I pleaded at the same time with my educated brethren not to neglect their duty towards their less educated, brethern and the Sikh masses. "They owe it to the Gurus, *Panth* and God to work among them for their uplift" or it must not be forgotten that they can only serve them if they go amongst them as one of them and in the form and appearance in which they can accept them as their elder brothers and leaders." and I reminded them also that the Sikh Symbols do continue to possess a real meaning for them, who believe that they could be true to their religion only if they do not swerve by even "a hair's breadth from the foot-steps of the Guru and of Sikhs like Bhai Taru Singh, Bhai Mani Singh and others."

VII

Such was then the most important contribution made by Guru Gobind Singh in his short span of life, 1606-1708. By establishing the *Panth*, he knit his people together in a completely equalitarian Society, comprising of devoted brave saintly soldiers, pledged to the service of humanity and dedicated to their Guru and God and the cause of the weak and the oppressed, irrespective of all distinction of caste, sect, sex, region or country—an example in nation-building for others to follow,

Guru Gobind Singh installed, just before his departure from this world, "Guru Granth Sahib" as the permanent Guru of Sikhs:

Since its birth in 1699, the Khalsa has built up glorious traditions of valour, sacrifice and service, unequalled by any other people in this land. It is our sacred duty to maintain undiminished and untarnished, shining bright as ever such high traditions. It is my earnest desire that, while observing the celebrations of the birth anniversary of Guru Gobind Singh Ji, we should take a solemn pledge to discharge the responsibilities of the membership of the Khalsa *Panth* as true followrs of the Guru.

GURU GOBIND SINGH
(Malik Hardit Singh)

I wonder if there has ever been anywhere in the world a personality as remarkable as Shri Guru Gobind Singh Ji.

There have been great sages and saints in many countries who have worked for the spiritual regeneration of humanity, philosophers, literary giants, great military leaders, great artists, but never so far as I know has there been one person gifted with excellence in so many varied fields. A saint, a poet, an inspired leader of men, a warrior; all this was Shri Guru Gobind Singh.

He was born and brought up in a family devoted to the Sikh ideal as propagated by Guru Nanak and the eight Gurus who followed him; the Gospel of love of God, brotherhood of man. and the service of humanity, particularly of those who were suffering, devoted to truth and integrity.

From a very early age he seems to have been conscious of the great tasks that lay ahead of him. This was a time when absolute and unlimited authority in the form of the Moghul Emperor Aurangzeb was being used as the instrument of tyranny, religious bigotry and intolerance, and the population of India was being reduced to a state of demoralisation which threatened to destroy for all time the rich and varied heritage of the great Hindu civilisation.

The foundation of this resistance to this tyranny by the use of arms, if necessary, was laid by Guru Hargobind but it was the martyrdom of Guru Tegh Bahadur that brought the whole issue to a climax and led his son, Guru Gobind Singh to the decision to devote his life and all his energies to the destruction of this tyranny.

The Khalsa has worked wonders in the field of battle ever since its establishment right up to the Indo-Pak conflict in 1965. And yet without engendering hatred for others. There is the noble example of Bhai Kanhaiya, who distributed water without discrimination among the wounded on the battle-field, irrespective of whether they were Sikhs or their invaders.

The explanation by certain scholars and medical experts in recent years that *Kesh* denote power and physical prowess with such instances as of the old Biblical story of Sampson and Delila or by marshalling out the evidence from medical science is besides the point and is far from convincing to our modern, sophisticated and educated young men. It was in January-February 1927, Gyani Sher Singh, a post-graduate student at the Lahore Government College, invited views from prominent Sikh intellectuals, among who were Hon. S. Joginder Singh, Professor Teja Singh, Jodh Singh (Bhai Sahib) and Harkishan Singh (Bawa), Sardar Sardul Singh, Mr. S. Partap, I.C.S. and others including myself on a letter received by him from a Sikh student in

America, who had asked for guidance on the keeping of "Sikh Symbols" and desiring a clear and rational explanation or justification. The views of these persons published by Gyani Sher Singh from Lahore (27th February, 1927) in book form entitled *Thoughts on Forms and Symbols in Sikhism*, with an introduction by Prof. Madan Gopal Singh, I.E.S., later Registrar, Punjab University and murdered in his office by Muslim fanatics, a few months after the partition.

In my article in this booklet (pages 65-79) I stated: "It is hardly possible to exaggerate (the) past utility (of the Sikh Symbols)" ... They have kept constantly before our eyes the noble personality "of our Saviour and Preceptor, Guru Gobind Singh and those of his inspired Sikhs, and have knit us together as nothing else would have done", I then posed the question, "To what extent are these symbols of ours" a living reality and useful today? I gave instances of high I.M.S., I. Eng S. and I.C.S. Officers and other highly educated Sikhs, who regarded themselves as good Sikhs inspite of having parted with their long hair and were devoted followers of the Gurus and students of *Gurbani*, some of whom had published translations of *Gurbani*. They gave examples of great *Sehjdhari* Sikhs and Sikh devotees, who were honoured and respected among the Sikhs, among whom may be mentioned the names of Sadhu T.L. Vaswani, Colonel Bawa Jeewan Singh Bedi, I.M.S., and more recently Dr. M.S. Randhawa I.C.S. And asked as to how far it was just to condemn them as 'apostates' and turn them out from our fold. Are we so rich in intellect that we can afford the loss of some of our ablest men?" I added 'that way lies destruction. We must be wise enough to keep men of the type just mentioned, in our fold and adjust our ideas—hard as it is bound to be—to the changed conditions.' I emphasised the necessity of enlarging the definition of a Sikh to include such men and made a suggestion in this connection. however, I pleaded at the same time with my educated brethern not to neglect their duty towards their less educated brethern and the Sikh masses. "They owe it to the Gurus, *Panth* and God to work among them for their uplift "or it must not be forgotten that they can only serve them if they go amongst them as one of them and in the form and appearance in which they can accept them as their elder brothers and leaders." And I reminded them also that the Sikh Symbols do continue to posses a real meaning for them, who believe that they could be true to their religion only if they do not swerve by even "a hair's breadth from the foot-steps of the Guru and of Sikhs like Bhai Taru Singh, Bhai Mani Singh and others."

VII

Such was then the most important contribution made by Guru Gobind Singh in his short span of life, 1606-1708. By establishing the *Panth*, he knit his people together in a completely equalitarian. Guru Gobind Singh was only nine years of age when his father was killed in Delhi but even at that early age he made himself ready for the struggle that lay ahead and gathered round him people who would in later years be his devoted followers and companions in arms. In waging this holy war, he sacrificed his all, his beloved four sons, thousands of his soldiers whom he loved as his own sons, and eventually his own life, but as a result of this sacrifice his brilliant inspiration and leadership, his creation of a fighting force such as the world has never seen, he succeeded in destroying the tyranny and restoring freedom to our suffering people. Here is what an historian has to say of this achievement. Writing about the situation in 1768, after thirty years of relentless struggle, he says:

> "Thus had the Sikhs emerged triumphant from their deadly struggle of the past thirty years; and the long drawn agony of their subjection came to an end, and the dream of their independence was released. They had admirably succeeded in holding their own and in steadily pursuing their course, not withstanding the hosts of terrors and disasters, that gathered themselves together, not only to check their ardour and to intercept their progress, but also to bring them to the verge of annihilation. Surging floods of opposition rose and increased; the impetuous rains of consternation descended and fell; the rending storms of desperation blew and raged; and all those opposing elements struck and beat upon them; but they could not shake the sturdy Sikhs standing on the steel-like rock of faith and freedom. The internal vigour consisting of their dogged faith in themselves and in the prophecy of Guru Gobind Singh that they would one day become a nation, their determined courage and unconquerable spirit of resistance, not only sustained them against the bloody persecution of a great Government determined to suppress them, but also raised them up again with greater strength after attempt to annihilate them."

And then,

"We now close the narrative of the Sikhs, who placed themselves at the head of the nation; who showed themselves interpreters of the rights of the people; who maintained the struggle between good and evil; between the sovereign will of the people and the divine right of Kings, and the opposition of liberty to despotism; who avenged the insults, the outrages and slavery of many generations past; who delivered their mother country from the yoke of the foreign oppressor; who displayed all that was great and noble; who left to the children of this province a heritage unsullied by the presence of any foreign soldier, who won for the Punjab the envied title of "bulwark of defence against foreign aggression", the tide of which had run its prosperous course for the preceding eight hundred years; and to whom all other people of Northern India, in general, and of the Punjab in particular owe a deep debt of gratitude."

Guru Gobind Singh ralised early in his life that the only way to fight the tyrant was to have an army not only skilled in the use of arms but, because it would always be small in number compared to the enemy, it would have to be an army, every soldier of which possessed not only the highest moral character but was dedicated to the cause of freedom and prepared to make every sacrifice in this cause and to have complete faith in victory, a faith based on the conviction that he could fight successfully against overwhelming odds only if he had the spirit to fight on until victory or death.

This was the spirit inject into the Sikhs on the occasion of that historic ceremony at Anandpur Sahib on Baisakhi day in 1699, when Guru Gobind Singh created the Khalsa and made his Sikhs into Singhs.

The Khalsa proved its mettle when Guru Gobind Singh fought his first major battle at the age of 20 against the neighbouring Hill Chiefs who had become jealous of Guru Gobind Singh and his Khalsa and in many subsequent engagements in which they are victorious against great odds. The achievement of the Khalsa under the inspired leadership of Guru Gobind Singh continued after his death and indeed right up to the time of Maharaja Ranjit Singh. It was only the rivalries among the Sikh Sardars and the corruption and treason of the leaders that followed after the death of that distinguished and wise Ruler that brought about the ultimate disintegration of the Khalsa army.

What kind of army was it ? Here is what a contemporary writer who is no friend of the Sikhs has to say about them:

Qazi Noor Mohammad, the author of the *Jang Namah* who came with Ahmad Shah Abdali in 1764 to fight against the Sikhs, naturally uses most offensive expressions for the Sikhs, their religion and their Gurus but even he says this about them:

> "Do not call the Sikhs "dogs", because they are lions and are brave like lions in a battle-field. How can a hero of the battle who fights like a lion be a dog?"

He goes on to say this about their character :

> "Besides their fighting, listen to one thing more in which they excell all other warriors. They never kill a coward and do not abstruct one who flees from the field. They do not rob a woman of her gold or ornaments, may she be a queen or a slave-girl. Adultery also does not exist among them. None of them is a thief, Woman whether young or old is called by them a "Burhiya" one who has retired from the world. The meaning of "burhiya" in Hindi language is an aged woman. The "dogs" never resort to stealing and no thief exists among them, and they do not keep company with the adulterer and the thief."

This was the creation of Guru Gobind Singh. We Sikhs are naturally very proud of this heritage, looking at it quite dispassionately. Has there ever been a body of men so disciplined, so expert in the use of arms, so valient, so dedicated to a noble cause and at the same time of such high moral character that even a bitter enemy was forced to pay such high tribute?

What about the man who created this remarkable force? He had the complete devotion of his Khalsa and he was the Master in every way but he sought no such mastery and his first act after the creation of the Khalsa was to proclaim them as his equals by making them administer *Pahul*, to him. When we say, therefore, *Wah Wah Guru Gobind Singh ape guru chela*, this is no idle praise. He occupied such a position of eminence, he outshone every one by the sheer splendour of his spirit and his personality; many of the people around him must have been constantly flattering him. A smaller man than Guru Gobind Singh would under these conditions have become a dictator. But he had no such ambition or desire. On the contrary he would always remind his people that he himself was nothing. What he had become and what he had been able to do was by God's Grace and blessings of the Sangat:

And then again he warned his people against making him a God....

How he looked upon his beloved Khalsa is illustrated by the incident when the mother of his four sons, torn with grief, complained to him and his answer was, "Why do you grieve for our four when so many thousands of our children (meaning the Khalsa) are alive." Then about his Khalsa he said:

Here were a great leader who had absolute power over his followers, a power based not on fear of punishment or hope of reward. It was based on mutual love and respect, admiration and esteem. It was indeed a living democracy of the kind that one may dream of. Oh for Guru Gobind Singh and his Khalsa today, when we are with nessing in so many parts of the world such abuse, nay the prostitution of democracy.

So much for Guru Gobind Singh the saint warrior and leader of men. What about Guru Gobind Singh as a writer and a poet? There has been too little research done into the writings of Guru Gobind Singh and this great task of love, dedication and scholarship lies before someone who has the spirit and the capacity to undertake it. I hope that this will be done in real earnest by the Guru Gobind Singh Foundation who have already published some literature on the Guru. I regret to say, however, that what has been prepared so far has been done in such a hurry—why I don't know—that I fear that in most of the cases the admittedly good printing, paper and general get up of the books tends to make one overlook the mediocre quality of the contents.

There is a transcendental quality in the writings of Guru Gobind Singh which, to use a popular expression, simply takes one's breath away. Certainly they strike a cord deep in our inner being which elevates us for the moment almost into the presence of the Almighty Himself. Apart from the obvious erudition and scholarship which are the background of his writings, there is a wealth of language, a flow and a variety of arrangements of the words and expression that leaves the reader in a state of ecstacy and wonder, admiration and love for the writer. One can truly say about it *Dhur toan Bani ai.*

Guru Gobind Singh will live forever in History. His teaching, his life was a blend of the highest spiritual conception and the great human virtues of character and nobility. He has left to us an heritage of which we are only half conscious still. The recent occasion of the celebration of his three hundredth anniversary has made people aware in many parts of the world of the message of Guru Gobind Singh which has a significance for people of all races and faiths everywhere. For the message is simple as all great things are. The message is this: Love God and always remember Him. Forget yourself. Only then can you be conscious of His voice which must be your guide. Only then will you be able to give of your best, to live fearlessly a life devoted to truth and the service of your fellow human beings. This was the message that inspired the Khalsa and this is what the world is in such need of today when Man, because of his great advance in knowledge is tempted to have an inflated idea of his ego and to worship and run after power. Without the necessary correction of character, this power threatens to destroy humanity itself. The world today needs to remember this truly remarkable personality.

BENGAL'S RESPONSE TO SIKHISM

(Dr. R. K. Dasgupta)

In his autobiography Rabindranath speaks of one Lenu—a Punjabi who worked in the Tagore house-hold as a person for whom he had great affection and regard. 'The cordiality of reception he got from us' he says, 'would have been worthy of a Ranjit Singh himself. Not only was he a foreigner, but a Punjabi to boot—what wonder he stole our hearts away?' 'We had the same admiration for the whole Punjabi nation' he continues 'as for Bhima and Arjuna of the *Mahabbharata.* They were warriors; and if they had sometimes fought and lost, that was clearly the enemy's fault. It was glorious to have Lenu, of the Punjab in our home.'

This is more than a juvenile fancy for a person belonging to virile race. When Tagore knew Lenu, Sikh religion and history had already made a profound impression on the higher intelligence of Bengal. The earliest important writing in Bengali on Sikhism is an article entitled 'Nanakpanthi' published in 1850 in *Tattvabodhini Patrika* a Brahmo monthly established in 1843. It is significant that the author speaks of both religious and political achievements of the Sikhs as a great event in Indian history: 'Guru Nanak's followers were first united in faith and then in arms... First they were a sect devoted to their faith, later they showed remarkable prowess in national struggle.' It was, however, the Universality of the Sikh faith which appealed to the Brahmo religious mind. A year after the publication of this article appeared a writer in the *Vividhartha Sangraha* said in a series of three articles that their (Sikh's) country was our country and they inhabit the most important part of Hindusthan.'

In February 1857 Rabindranath's father, Dabendranath Tagore visited the Golden Temple at Amritsar and was deeply moved by the evening *arati,* He was so profoundly touched by the hymn *gaganamai thala ravi chandra dipaka bene* that he resolved to learn the Gurmukhi and read *Adi Granth* in original. In his Bengali autobiography Debendranath reproduces the whole hymn in Bengali script and remarks: 'In Brahmo Samaj we have prayers for two hours in a week only; and in the Sikh temple of Hari there is worship, night and day. This good example should be followed by the Brahmos.'

Rabindranath visited Amritsar in the company of his father in 1872 and the impresion which the prayers at the Golden Temple made upon the boy of eleven is recorded in his autobiography: 'The Golden Temple of Amritsar comes back to me like a dram. Many a morning have I accompanied my father to this *Gurudwara* of the Sikhs in the middle of the lake. There the sacred chanting resounds continually. My father seated among the worshippers, would sometimes add his voice to the hymn of praise, and finding a stranger joining in their devotions they would wax enthusiastically cordial and we would return loaded with the sanctified offerings of sugar crystals and other sweets.'

The poet's biographer syas that the system of vespers and matins and readings from the scriptures in the Brahmo-mandir at Shantiniketan may have been introduced after the example of the *Akhandpath* in the Golden Temple.

When Rabindranath wrote his essay 'Virguru' in 1885, the religious and political history of the Sikhs had already made a profound appeal to the Bengali imagination. In the same year was published *Nanak Prakash* in two volumes including in its appendix short biographies of the nine Gurus after Guru Nanak. Rabindranath's essay on Virguru, that is, Guru Gobind Singh, is a brief but perceptive account of his life and work as a saint and as a statesman and as an excellent summing up of his philosophy of religion. What struck Rabindranath most was the fact that the Guru disclaimed any divinity and warned all his disciples against treating him as anything more than a servant of God.

Later in the same year Rabindranath wrote his essay 'Sikh-svadhinta' to carry on the history of the Sikhs from the death of Guru Gobind Singh to the rise of the Sikh power in the Punjab. He calls it the fulfilment of Guru Gobind Singh's objective.

Three years later in 1888, Rabindranath composed his poem, 'Gurugobinda' which is his well-known composition on the Guru. It is a monologue of the tenth Guru about his spiritual preparation for his great task. The idea was obviously suggested by Cunningham's brief reference to Guru Gobind Singh's secluded life preceding his historic work as the founder of the Khalsa. Cunningham says 'Gobind was placed in retirement amid the lower hills on either side of the Jumna and for a series of years he occupied himself in hunting the tiger and the wild bear, in acquiring a knowledge of the Persian language and storing his mind with those ancient legends which describe the mythic glories of his race.' Rabindranath makes this period of self-education a very important phase in the life of the Guru. This life of thoughts before the life of action will make him an instrument of the Divine Will. Refusing to plunge into action he says that he will wait for the day when after this life of contemplation he would be able to say that he has realized his identity with his people and that they may now find their salvation through is work.

Unfortunately an unsatisfactory Urdu translation of this poem misled the Sikhs of Lyallpur about the poet's idea and a protest meeting was held in that city at which a resolution was passed censuring the poet for what was called his offensive remark on the Guru. The poet wrote a letter to Professor Teja Singh saying that he did not mean any disregard for the Guru and that he had developed his theme from what he had read about the Guru's self-preparation in MacGregor and Cunningham.

The poem 'Nishphal Upahar' (The Useless Gift) was composed almost immediately after the poem 'Gurugobinda.' In the essay 'Vir Guru' Rabindranath gave an anecdote to illustrate the Guru's indifference to wealth. This poem 'Nishphal Upahar' is a short verse tale based on the anecdote. When rich disciple of the Guru gave him as a present a pair of golden bangles he threw one of them into a river. Imaging that it was only an accident a Sikh asked a diver to recover the bangle and promised him a reward of five hundred rupees. When the diver asked the Guru about the spot where the bangle was dropped he threw the bangle towards the direction and this was enough for both the Sikh and the diver to understand that the Guru had really shed the gold deliberately.

In one of his letters dated 28th February 1893 Rabindranath goes back to the idea of the Guru's long period of self-preparation and compares it to the Pandavas living *in cognito* for a year before the great war.

Rabindranath's third and last poem on Guru Gobind Singh is 'Shesh Shiksha' which was composed in 1899. Three years earlier Tinkari Banerjee had published his biography of the Guru based on sources available in Punjabi which he acquired for this research. The account of Guru Gobind Singh's death in this biography is based on Santokh Singh's *Sri Gurupratap Suraj Granth* also known as *Suraj Prakash*. Towards the end of his book Tinkari says that there are various accounts of the death of Guru Gobind

Singh but according to the Sikh scholars the most reliable of them is the one in *Suraj Prakash*. Those who are acquainted with the various accounts of the death of the Guru must have noticed that they have some common features and that the most important of them is that he was assassinated by a Pathan.

Rabindranath's poem on the death of the Guru is a moving story of a heroic act. Rabindranath was not acquainted with Gurmukhi or Persian sources but in the course of his wide reading in Indian history in English and Bengali he came upon the account of the Guru's death given in *Suraj Prakash*.

Rabindranath's essay on 'Sivaji O Guru Gobind Singh' published in 1910 is a critical analysis of the evolution of the Khalsa which he says marks the transformation of a gospel of universal brotherhood into a military and nationalist cult. While he admits that the historical situation demanded this new approach he reflects on the irony of history which forced the use of the sword in defence of the ideal of universal love. What Khushwant Singh has called the martial metamorphosis of the Guru's conception of God is now an important theme for historical research. We know how after the battle of Bhangani in 1686 the Guru said, 'When all avenues have been explored, all means tried, it is rightful to draw the sword out of the scabbard and wield it with your hand. In the prayer he offered to God before the battle he said:

> Eternal God, Thou art our shield,
> The dagger, knife, the sword we wield,
> To us protector there is given
> The timeless, deathless Lord of Heaven,
> To us all—steel's unvanquished might,
> To us all-time's restless flight,
> But chiefly thou, protector brave,
> All steel, wilt Thine own servant save.

(*Akal Ustat*)

In the essay Rabindranath says that this necessity of use of steel in defence of a great faith gave a new direction of Sikh history.

THE ZAFAR-NAMAH

(Gurbachan Singh Talib)

There are two views about the historicity of Zafar-Namah—the Epistle of victory—addressed to Aurangzeb. The traditional view makes it out to be actually and literally the letter which Guru Gobind Singh sent to aurangzeb while the latter was in the Deccan, and as a result of which he was in a manner conscience-stricken and also got better informed about the true state of affairs in the Punjab. This view is widely held, and is part of the Sikh historical heritage. But there are certain aspects of this composition, which raise doubts as to its being actually the document which the Guru sent to the Emperor. These doubts are raised mainly by the content and tune of this Epistle; by the usual style of diplomatic and official correspondence prevalent in Mughal times, and also by the fact that as a result of this letter the Emperor developed a lenient and conciliatory attitude towards the Guru. It is, of course, for historians and such factual evidence as they may be able to adduce in support of the view of this composition being the original Epistle, to determine the truth of the commonly held view. On a study of the Epistle and its internal evidence of style etc. I am rather inclined to concur with the view of Professor Indu Bhushan Bannerji that *Zafar-Namah* is a poetic composition, or 'dramatization' as he puts it, of the Epistle sent to Aurangzeb, and that the communication actually despatched and received by the Emperor was different. I find this view to be sound and historically as well as stylistically more convincing.

First, as to the manner of the diplomatic and official correspondence prevalent in those times: These are extant epistolary collections of Mughal times, the most famous of which is the *Ruqaat* or official despatches of Abul Fazi, Akbar's Chancellor, the greatest Persian stylist of his age, and a man of vast reputation as a scholar. Abul Fazi is a case apart in point of the finish and ornate quality of his style, which is said to have excited the wonder and admiration even of the official secretaries at the Persian court. But the whole point to note is that all such correspondence was in *prose,* and the manner of expression was not only extremely courteous, but decorous. That was the convention and the accepted code. There are other collections of letters extant, such as the *Ruqaat-i-Alamgiri,* letters addressed by Aurangzeb on different occasions. Some of these are personal and intimate, such as those addressed to his sons, while others are official. In these the style is generally free from egregious ornament. These too are in prose, except for the use here and there of an illustrative verse quotations. In other letters of the age also, prose is as a matter of form and convention used in letters, whether personal or official. Verse is used only while *dramatizing* or *reporting* letters written in various contexts, such as definace, supplication, love etc. as these occur in epics and other narrative fictions. Such letters can be read, as composed by the respective poets, in Firdausi's *Shah-Namah,* Nizami's *Sikandar-Namah* and such other works.

It is not easy to believe that *Zafar-Namah* being a serious official communication, addressed to the sovereign on the throne, containing complaint of heinous crimes (the murder of the Sahib-Zadas at Sirhand and breach of safe-conduct given to the Guru at Anandpur) would not be in a style practised at Court for such correspondence. The Guru had in his entourage a number of scholars—among whom was the persian poet. Bhai Nand Lal, who is reputed to have been connected in some capacity with the

Mughal Court. To attribute ignorance of Court procedure to those who waited on the Guru, advised him and carried out his work, is to assume what is manifestly unjustified. It is, therefore, correct only in a loose way to say that *Zafar-Namah* is the Epistle originally sent to the Emperor. All that such a statement means is that it reflects some of the matter contained in the Epistle actually sent, and that its general sentiments, and the faith in God and the moral ideal expressed therein is in accordance with the Guru's teachings. To assert more than this is to take assumption for fact.

Zafar-Namah is in the matre in which all great Masnavis or Epic poems, including the greatest, *Shah-Namah* are composed. It reads, therefore, style apart, like an epistle from one of the Masnavis. In its opening, it contains the usual preamble affirming faith in God—the God of Guru Gobind Singh's conception. In the middle portion, called *Dastan* or *The Tale,* the Guru's charges against the Emperor's functionaries are contained. These relate to breach of faith, which herein is attributed in very severe language to the Emperor himself. Then there is a tone of definance and of determination to wage war, along with the famous couplet (itself a quotation from Saadl's *Gulestan).*

Chu Kar az hama hilate dar guzasht,
Halal ast burdan ba shamshir dast.

(When all other resources are rendered unavailing, it is justified then to unsheathe the sword).

Towards the end is conventional praise of the Emperor, quite out of keeping with the severity of his condemnation in the body or *Dastan*.

There is another fragment recently discovered consisting of twenty complete couplets and one incomplete which has been called *Fatah-Namah*. This is in the same metre as *Zafar-Namah*—only its style is much more forceful and of a higher literary quality than *Zafar-Namah*. This is perhaps a parallel dramatization, by another poet. The existence of this fragment called *Fatah-Namah* only lends further support to the thesis advanced herein, that the original Epistle must have been in prose, of a serious and formal character, of course asserting the Guru's ideals; and from some copy or report thereof, the versions in verse were made.

Translation of a few verses from each is given below:

1. He who is under the shadow of the Huma,
Will not submit to be overshadowed by the impudent crow.
One who pursues the mighty lion,
Will not chase goats, sheep or deer.
What could forty famished men do,
When surprized in assault by thousands?
They came after breaking a solemn oath,

Attacking with swords, arrows and natchlocks.
So forced, I took the field,
And replied with a rain of arrow and shot.
When all other resources are rendered unavailing,
It is justified then to unsheathe the sword.
Strange the way you keep your promises!
One should consider it evil to swerve from the truth.
Wield not the sword in ruthless bloodshed;
Heaven shall one day strike thee too.
Man, be not thou unmindful of the terrible retribution of the Lord,
Who is without desire and needs not man's gratitude.
He is the King of Kings—without fear.
The True King of the universe and All Time.
He is God, the Lord of the earth and the ages,
Creator of the universe and all that is in it.
He has created the little ant as well as the mighty—elephant,
He cherishes the humble and destroys oppressors.
He bears the name—Cherisher of the Humble;
He needs not man's gratitude or his offerings.
What though my four children have been killed—
Living still is the coiled serpent.
What bravery is this that you extinguish sparks of fire,
But raise a vast conflagration:

(*Zafar-Namah*)

2. In the name of the Lord of the Sword and the Axe,
The Lord of the Arrow, the spear and the shield.
In the name of Him who is the God of warrior-men
And of chargers swift as the wind.
He also gave thee Kingship,
Gave to us the wealth of faith in righteousness.
Thine is aggression by guile and deceit;
Mine is to seek redress with truth and sincerity.
By favour of *Akal Purush*,
Such a shower of steel will I scatter
That as thou comest unsuccessful from the Deccan Hills,
And bitter and frustrated from Mewar—
So, if thou turnest thy gaze hitherwards,
That failure of bitterness shall increase manifold.
Such a fire will I light under thy horse's hoofs,

That thou shall not be able to taste the water of Punjab.
What though a jackal by deceit and guile
Has killed two young ones of a lion;
If this fiery lion lives,
For sure, he will avenge this outrage foul.

(Fatah-Namah)

7

Sri Guru Gobind Geeta

CANTO ONE

It is *Baisakhi,*
A day of all days,
For prayers
As also for going gay;
For taking stock of the twelve months gone;
And making resolutions
For the twelve months to come,
Nay, for the many hundreds thereafter;
When challenges are monumental
And long-cherished values are at stake;
Or, for that moment
When nations are in the bloody throes of rebirth.
On this day,
Even time begins to tick
With a new melody.

It is *Baisakhi,*
A day of all days,
And I once again turn a Punjabi
And go back to my roots;
To my rich traditions and noble faith;
To my illustrious seers;
To my venerable Gurus
Who, by words and by deeds
(More by deeds than by words),
Told me always
That each one of us
Is a son of immortality,
A servant of the Timeless,
Despatched hither to participate
In a drama enacted by millions

And directed by One;
The drama without parallel or end—
The drama of life,
And that we would do well
To play our parts
As the Director would want us play.

Time is Existence,
And all relationships
Whether of blood or of love,
Whether of passivity or of hatred,
Are in the ultimate analysis
Existentialist only.
And as long as
We, in innumerable characters
Scripted for the saga of sagas,
Act and evolve,
It is our function
Not merely to serve Time
But to be its master.
For, the real essence of existence
It is the Timeless alone.
Which is what *Sat Sri Akal* means.
And anyone who proclaims it
Is eternally blessed
By the Timeless Himself.
Timeless because it is time alone
Which fashions each particle of existence
From the first cry of life
To the very last breath
And He is beyond and above, it;
Timeless because
He is neither born nor shall He die
Though time
The most profound dimension we experience
Is born and dies like all else.
And in this splendid creation of the Timeless
Man alone has in him
The dimension of the One without dimension,
The timeless operation of the Timeless
That eternal entity,
The *Dharma*.

It is *Baisakhi,*
A day of all days,
And I am at the feet of Guru Gobind,
My Hero, My Saviour
My Saviour and Redeemer,
The Redeemer of my *Dharma;*
The whole saga Of being and becoming—
The discipline of the heartbeat
That sustains everything, everywhere;
The *Dharma*
Which sustains man,
Man of the profound spirit,
Both in his singleness
And in his plurality,
And who in turn sustains it
Through words and deeds,
Through living and serving;
The *Dharma*
Which is sustained by
Each particle intrinsic in
This awesome canvas of the universe
Of the Painter;
By each blade of grass
In the profoundest possible manner—
Through commitment,
Relentless commitment,
With no exit or escape from reality—
Escape
Which is the refuge of most men of God
In this land of God Himself,
The country we call India.

And as I gaze silently
At this canvas by the master Painter
In which man is the central portrait,
I see pictures of men come alive—
Heroes of deathless valour
And skyscraping achievements,
Trendsetters of glorious traditions
And enduring practices,
Builders of unalloyed successes

And unblemished richnesses,
Legends from every race and clime,
By the dozen, if not more.
But the rarest of the rare is,
Verily, the man of *Dharma*.
As were my Gurus,
As was my Gobind.
Men who were born
As beautiful expression
Of the Timeless Himself.
Men who set foot on our soil,
To decipher His code.
As did my Gurus,
As did my Gobind,
For us Punjabis—
The Aryans great,
The valiant race of the *Bharatas*,
Who live in this country called India,
In this land of *Sapta Sindhu*—
My Punjab, my beloved Punjab.

I often talk with Guru Gobind
In the small hours of the night,
Halfawake, halfasleep.
For a man of the world that I am,
This is a peculiar feeling;
Of the unreal in the real.
Or, it is the other way round?
And when it happens,
I turn to him in full supplication,
In total surrender.
In full splendour
He reveals himself:
The king of kings,
The *yogin* of *yogins*,
The warrior of warriors,
A deathless spirit,
A man immortal,
A man of *Karma* and *Dharma*
Who rides his horse
Just as the Timeless rides existence.

Unconquered and unconquerable is he
In body and mind,
For, *Bhawani,* the Goddess Durga,
The last dispenser of justice on earth,
It is sword he wields;
For, Siva, the destroyer,
Who lords over Time,
Casts his invincible armour
Around his frail human form.
And together
The invest him with the divine halo
Of the imperishable.

But on the *Baisakhi,*
A day of all days,
I am sad,
Sad not because anything untoward
Has befallen me personally,
But because some things
Are happening
Which I do not understand.
And I want to hear
His sacred mouth
Explain to me
This strangeness,
And shed light
On this mystifying
And saddening darkness.

In that dawn of the New Year
It is still dark.
But pregnantly.
For, soon a light appears
And increases in intensity
To a blinding brightness.
My eyes do not open,
I cannot see a thing.
But my mind's eye does behold
My hero,
My Saviour and Redeemer,
My Guru.
In the background of that darkness

His brilliant contours suggest
He is not too sad, but not too happy.
Is he thinking
Or meditating?
Yes, he must have been about as reflective,
As thoughtful,
On that fateful *Baisakhi* day
When he created the Khalsa—
The Army of the Pure!
He does not speak
As he used to;
He does not smile
As he used to.
I prostrate and tremble.
I beseech him not to remain silent,
To say what he has to,
What he wants to.
It's a moment longer than eternity,
And then my wish is granted.
Says he: "O my bard!
Today once again
My people are passing through
A period of darkness,
A period of uncertainty.
Men of truth and honour
Have become scare.
Manliness has taken wings.
Where are the heaven-born people
I wonder!
The Aryaman of the Vedas,
The *Gursikhs* of the Nanak's *panth,*
Who mocked at death
Nay, embraced it
Just as one would
The most beautiful woman
On the nuptial bed.
Today I am in search
Of another Banda,
A willing servant of Destiny
Who will carry out my words,
Who will accomplish my mission,

Who will neither waver nor relent,
Until his last brave blood-drop,
Until his last loyal heartbeat."

"O Guru !
What is it you want done?"
I cry.
"Could I be of any use?
If you want me,
I will be your instrument
With all the commitment
I can muster."
"Yes," replies my Guru.
"I have come to you
As you have long been my devotee.
A silent worshipper.
And now is the time
When you will no longer remain silent.
Because you will speak for me.
You are my messenger.
Also benign to you is
Saraswati, the Goddess of speech,
Who gives meanings to words,
As spirit to the flesh.
You will take down my message
For my people,
The people of Punjab,
The message of
What transpired between me
And the Banda.
The whole dialogue
That infused in a recluse
The spirit of the sword.
You are a poet
Of the Punjab soil.
All the five waters flow in your blood.
And I want you to sing this message
To reunite my people
In the cause of their shared destiny,
In the service of this ancient country,
In the service of this most sacred tradition,

This dateless *Dharma,*
The like of which
None exist in this world.
So, I command you my bard!
Recreate my dialogue with the Banda
And sing it everywhere—
Until your throat goes hoarse
And your tongue trembles;
Until your voice falters
And my people once again
Awake and follow
The path of the Timeless,
Steadfast and sure-footed."

Was it all a hallucination
Of a man overwrought?
Or, a vision granted
To one chosen by Destiny?
You may ask, you may wonder!
I cannot tell,
For, I myself ask and wonder!
All I know for sure
Is that such an experience
Comes but once in a life-time.
And is worth a life-time
To be commanded thus
By the Dashmesh himself!
I, therefore, begin
In my own imperfect way,
In total humility,
The dialogue of the Guru
With one who was his own Banda—
A bonded slave.
A dialogue of destiny
Which I verily name
"Sri Guru Gobind Geeta."

CANTO TWO

The sacred Godavari gently meanders by.
It is sacred
Not because sacred is
Every river to us Indians,

But because
On its banks one day
Had written Rama and Sita
An important chapter of their life
In preparation for
Their final battle of *Dharma;*
Sacred because
In the forest groves lush on its banks
Live saints and sages,
Hoary with wisdom,
Performing a thousand austerities
In a thousand ways profound;
Sacred because
Here in a hermitage lives our hero,
Madho Das Bairagi,
A warrior turned a recluse,
In search of peace.
Renounced he has the world,
Having one day killed a pregnant doe
And its undelivered calf
When his arrow
Ripped open its womb.
As the doe tottered to its gory doom
The bloody revelation struck the Bairagi:
The futility of violence
In all its naked horror.
A great battle does he wage
Caught between instinct and
His conscious denial of it.
Yet, nowhere is he near his goal.
All his austerities,
All his yogic practices,
All his resolutions,
Have come to nought
Again and again.
Is the Bairagi like the Godavari?
Deceptively placid, concealing fury,
Content to flow within its banks?
And does he flow as smoothly?
He has damned the flow
Of his wretched instincts,

Unsure of the consequences
Were the dam of restraint ever to burst.
But the conflict within
Has today acquired a new edge.
The consuming fires raging in his heart
Make him twist and toss
With abject restlessness.
Now he looks at the horizon,
Now at the gently lapping waves,
Trying to decode the message
He knows not what!!
He knows not how!

A different day it is;
He has not known the kind before.
Signs and omens flutter and flit by
In a language he cannot decipher.
Paces he now up, now down,
Perches he now on stone, now on wood.
Tries he now to focus his thoughts,
Decides he now to scatter them.
Nothing seems the same,
Nothing has changed either!
After years he has taken out his arms,
Even cleaned and oiled them,
But he knows not why.
O God!
Why is he falling apart like this?

The emperor has set up camp
In the neighbourhood with his armies.
The Guru too is around with his soldiers
The like of which he has never seen.
And lo! There comes a messenger,
Announcing the arrival of the Guru!
Guru Gobind!
The great leader of men,
Men moulded with a new fire,
Men surging with a new destiny,
Men whom the Bairagi has admired,
Even felt jealous of,
Ever since he had met them

Face to face
In the great battle of Bhangani
Where their reckless valour
Carried everything before them,
Against odds so overwhelming.

Such being the greatness of this
Guru and warrior,
The Bairagi comes alive with a start,
And rushes to the gate
To welcome the noble guest.
He helps him dismount,
Keenly admiring the horse and the horseman,
The companions, about fifty in number,
Are simple lot
But oldiers nevertheless
Untired of many a great battle,
Each one dignified in his demeanour,
Each one disciplined to the core,
Each one heroism personified.
The Bairagi, overcome,
Bows to touch the Guru's feet.
But no, a Bairagi is not allowed
Such a supplication.
The Guru himself
Quickly takes him in his arms
And so overwhelmed are both
That they exchange no words
But speak in the language of silence
That could, verily, for them,
Serve as a medium
For a thousand meanings profound.

Soon they retire
To the Bairagi's own quarters.
The soldiers are happy;
They are to have a respite after all!
Respite which they so badly need
To pray and meditate,
The relax and refreshen
And to prepare to fight another day.
As the Guru makes himself

Feel at home,
The Bairagi addresses him:
"Tell me O Guru !
What brings you hither?
One as august as you
To one as insignificant as me,
Sitting miles away from the world of action?

Guru: Strange that you should ask me
What I have come hither for,
To you and your hermitage!
For, the Timeless tells me
That you have been waiting here
For me, only me,
To tell you all about your *Dharma!*

Bairagi: First of all,
Do you know
O Guru!
Who I am!
Where I was born?
What did I do in life
And what I am here for?

Guru: Why not? O Bairagi!
You are and have been my instrument
Always and ever.
To me it appears
That there was never a point
In time or in space
When you were there
And I was not.
Can one hide from one's own destiny?
No. Not.
You are the high-minded recluse
I have been looking for.
You came here not so much in search of peace
As to wait for me—
Your Guru and your deliverer!

Bairagi: No doubt, O Guru!
Some inner voice has always told me
That sooner or later someone will come

To redeem me,
By releasing me
From the talons of ignorance,
So as to embrace my Maker
In body and in spirit—
A goal I have been striving for
All this time.
Yes, I am waiting
For the one
To whom I could surrender;
For the one
To show me light;
To lead me on to my destiny.
But how, O Guru, do I know
Whether that moment in my journey
Has arrived,
And whether it's you
Who is to be my redeemer?

Guru: No Bairagi!
There can be none but me,
The servant of the Timeless.
For, it was not only your quest
To wait for your redeemer,
It has been mine too.
In the din of battles,
In the clash of steel,
In the roar of guns,
Amidst the charge of horses,
When man knows death
To an extent of such intimacy
That he is no less than a sage,
I had always sensed,
I was yet living a part of myself,
Seeking to become a whole.
I have always known
I must ferret out
That bit which has
To complete my puzzle
Before my destiny is fulfilled.
So, O Bairagi!

If you were a fugitive
In body as well as in soul
Seeking to know
What your destiny held in store,
My own task was no less difficult.
You had turned a recluse
Retired from the world of action.
You had taken to a path
You thought would lead to salvation.
But for me it was different.
Destiny had cast me
In a mould of blood and steel.
I was not supposed to
Work for my own salvation
But for human kind,
By defeating the forces of *Adharma*,
By defending the forces of *Dharma*,
In a grand upsurge of the spirit,
Capable of uplifting the whole society,
An upsurge so engulfing
That its conflaggerating fires
Consume all the dead wood,
All the palpable falsehood,
All the base instincts
All the mean practices—
That lie buried under
The shaky foundations of *Adharma*.
And it is this mould of blood and steel
That's your destiny.

Bairagi: That you should be so emphatic
Amazes me no end.
I have gone too far
On the path of my quest;
I have moved too far away
From purposeless acts of killing,
The path you so vehemently uphold.

Guru: But what can you do
If that's what the Timeless wills you to.
Remember, you are born to destroy falsehood.
You have to fight the forces of *Adharma*

In fierce battles,
In raging fires
So that truth ultimately prevails.

Bairagi: O Guru!
If such are the fires
I am destined to release,
Then where is the guarantee
That they would not,
At the same time,
Engulf truth and destroy it
Just as they would
All the falsehood?
Why not presume
The forest fire so sparked off,
By whatever means,
Would be an all-consuming one?
Can't we say with equal emphasis
That when masses join hands
In total unification to act,
Muted are all questions of
Right and wrong.
Blindfolded are all eyes to
Reason and justice.
For, the fury so unleashed,
Mass and unintelligent,
Can never distinguish
Truth from untruth.
The goal of total salvation
Is indeed fascinating!
Fascinating enough, perhaps,
To end up in total slavery!
Is it not wiser to work for
One soul, one salvation?
Through independent action?
Through individual paths?
To me, it appears that
Collective journeys are meaningless
As, in fact, no collective path exists.

Guru: Yes, O Bairagi!
That's your way of looking at things,

The way of all runaways-From life!
Since they find the going too tough,
Since they cannot stand up to it,
They cross over to the path
Where least resistance do they encounter
And glorify it as though
Theirs is the only true path.
There are, in fact, many such paths!
For example, tell me
If the path you follow
Is the true path of God,
Then what sanctity adorns life?
Why did God create man and woman
And imbue them with desire,
Desire that is creativity itself,
Creativity that is
The only evidence of spirituality?
And why in supplication
To this spirituality,
Built they this
Whole edifice of civilisation?
So sublimely beautiful
That God is thereby remembered?
Why do you saints, *Sanyasins* and *Bairagis,*
Sit on the fringe of that civilisation
And suck away its milk?
Does it behove a man like you,
A born lion!
To eat the flesh
That jackals should bring to you?
No. Never.
In fact, so different are you
That your are not like any one of them.
That's why,
You are the chosen one of His will.
Know I
The people around are docile and servile,
Ignorant of the underlying truth of things—
They need refugee and protection,
For, they fear the nemesis of
Their sins of omission and commission.

And the so-called men of God—
And, I must say, you are one such—
Parade themselves as their protectors.
For they have acquired some powers
Which unquestioning minds accept as godly.
And thus is man so thoroughly debased
That he is divested of all spirit,
All spirituality.
My question is: Why?
Why can't you, yes you, participate in life
And render it a meaning
Ever more beautiful.
Let me inform you:
Life is polluted
Only when men like you,
Men who have a better grasp of reality,
Men who have powers to charm and protect,
Do not-perform their function.
Such men alone can skim off the scum
That then gathers over the seas of life.
It is by churning without let,
By agitation without respite
That life, acquires its true purpose.
Doubt me, do you?
Come along and I shall show you
How but for men like you,
Dauntless and fearless,
And born to fight injustice
And protect the oppressed,
The world has become
Too ugly a place to live in.
Today, neither the weak can with dignity breathe,
Nor the strong with honour live.
Because men of your ilk seek
Escape in individual salvation.

Bairagi: No Guru !
You talk in terms too general,
In phrases too simplistic.
You are eulogizing a path
Your yourself could not but traverse,

A path thrust upon you!
What's wrong in trying to know
What one is?
And what one must be
In body and in spirit
In relation to
Not only the world transient
But the value permanent,
The maker of this world,
The Transcendant Self,
The One that ever wants to make us equally transcendental.
For aught I know,
Relationships
We experience and bind us,
Are all sordid.
I hope that you too realize
That every man is alone.
And as to the world that we think is ours,
That's but our ego manifested!
Because relationships exist
Or the world itself exists
As long as we live.
Life tastes sweet or bitter
In relation to
Our own experience of it.
And as all experience is singular
All men have different perceptions of it,
So, tell me, O Guru!
What's the harm
If one wants to end pain
And seek release
In bliss and ecstacy,
The highest *Ananda* attainable,
On the dissolution of duality,
By choosing a path of individual salvation?

Guru: It's all very... well said,
But tell me, O Bairagi!
All that you have been saying,
Is it your own experience
Or the experience of some other?

Or, is it something more profound?
That which you have gleaned
From some pages wearing
The mantle of indisputable wisdom
In their yellowed, moth-eaten appearance?
Or, have you heard and stored
This seemingly elevating thought
From some deluded minds
Nurtured on *hashish* and opium
And such other beguiling drugs
That induce trances
And lend a pleasant appearance to escape?
I am inclined
To dismiss all this
As a feat of intellectual sophistry,
Illusions of realisation
Seldom realised.
Tell me, O Saint of Nanded!
Is it not a mirage
That you pursue?
A mirage that recedes
As far as you advance?

Bairagi: No, O Guru!
I am nowhere near the goal,
I admit,
Of being one with the Maker.
But then, I do realize,
If I cannot achieve that destination
Here and now,
It is because the path I have chosen
Is harder and lonelier than any other,
Where even you and your Maker
Do not appear to go together,
Even though all that exist between the two
Is sheer ignorance!
Born of the relationships of this world,
Of attachments and desires,
Of *Mahamaya* only.
All which is transient,
Still to be known,
Still to be sought,

Is a quest of several, several births,
One upon the other.
I, therefore, am clear in my mind
That on my path I have to cover
Several stages of transcendence
Before I proclaim: "I have arrived!"

Guru: O Bairagi!
You do make a very profound person!
But tell me:
Have you come across anyone
Who fits in with your description?
Anyone who can proclaim: "I am arrived?"
Do you find a single self,
Clad in human form
Who is without ego, desire, lust, greed, or anger?
Well, if ever there be any
I would like to meet him.

CANTO THREE

Bairagi: You ask for the moon, O Guru!
Know you too well
That those who have reached anywhere
Do not trumpet about their accomplishment.
Even if they wish
They cannot!
It's a language that is never spoken.
If someone does speak it,
He has not arrived!
As to your query
If I have seen one,
Well, I have seen one,
Well, I have not.
But does that by itself
Prove there is none?
Or, there was none
And will be none?
I am clear by now
About my path of gradual transcendence.
I have worked on this path;
I have attained considerable success,

I have awakened my spiritual self.
My serpent of knowledge
Which is *Kundalini*
Rises from the base of my spine
To the highest plexus,
The *Brahm Randhra*
The gateway to *Brahman*.
And I can also help you do the same
(If ever you wish, that is!).
On my part, I am willing to demonstrate
What I can do,
And shall deem it a privilege
If you agree to reciprocate,
And show me what you can do.

Guru: I know not, O Bairagi!
Whether to laught at
Or weep for
Your great profundity.
You seem to want me reduced to
A street urchin,
A braggart
Whose bravado it is
To swear at anything and everything!
Is this the manner all
Such spiritually awakened
Settle such questions?
Yet, I will accept your challenge
And in doing so
Will like you to demonstrate
What miracles you can perform
And then I shall let you know
What I can.

Bairagi: You must have seen many *Yogins,* O Guru!
Men of great spiritual powers.
Still, pray tell me,
Have you witnessed
Walking on water,
Flying in air,
Stepping through a jungle of fire,
Becoming invisible in a wink,

Diminishing to a size smaller than an ant,
Or growing to be taller than a mountain?
Well, I can do all that.
I can converse with spirits in the nether regions,
I can even tell
What you ate before you arrived here,
Or which route you followed
And what happened to one of your soldiers en route.
Not just that.
I can hold my breath for days on end
Swimming in the milky seas of my awakened consciousness.
Are not these abilities extraordinary
In the truest sense of the word?
Has not one to live many lives to attain these?
Call your soldiers
And I will also gather men from my hermitage,
So that what happens here between us
Is not only witnessed
But also is attested to.

Guru: No, Bairagi!
You need not perform
Any of these miracles.
I concede I have never seen
Yogins performing all that you describe
Though... some rope-dancers may have!
But do not take umbrage at my remarks.
I regard you as a very special man,
A chosen one of the Timeless,
A man of iron will,
Born to perform much mightier deeds
Than what you presently claim.
So, permit me
To elaborate on my mission
And what I am going to do with you.
Well, I shall transform you,
To make you fight the battle of *Dharma*
No furiously raging in Punjab.
You will have all my men,
Men whose legends precede them,
Men who have shaken

The Moghul tyranny to its very roots.
I shall make you their commander,
The leader of my mission,
That will treat the path of Guru Nanak,
The path of One God,
The path of all humanity,
And the path of your destiny as well.
And as long as
The heavenly bodies
Shine in their firmament,
Your deeds will also shine as bright.
And wherever, whenever I am remembered,
Your image too shall spring to the mind
As my chosen one,
The one who lived and died for me.
Now, tell me O Bairagi!
Are you willing to let me
Transform you in this manner?

Bairagi: I am grateful to you, O Guru!
For your honeyed words.
But you have first to convince me
That your path alone is right for me.
When I see the irrefutable evidence,
You shall have this Bairagi
Surrender to you
Of his own volition.
And then you shall not have to ask for permission;
You will order
And I shall do.

Guru: I accept your invitation, O bairagi!
I shall satisfy
All your curiosities,
Set at rest
All you doubts and queries,
And shall convince you
That this path of mine
Is indeed the only correct one for you.
At this point of time.
What happens here and now
At your little hermitage

Will affect all seekers of truth
In that bigger hermitage, the world.
It's verily a challenge of history
That must be met.

Bairagi: Even though, O Guru!
Your reply is very clever,
I consider it fair enough.
I throw myself open to you.
I do not deny I have been a fugitive
For some time now.
I have been trying to determine
What I should and should not do.
Doubts have invaded me
Time and again,
For I am at a point in my quest
Where only purposelessness seems
To be in waiting.
I want purposefulness restored to me.
What am I here for?
Is the question that baffles.
The *Shastras* and their rigmarole tire me.
My equation with myself eludes me.
My destiny I see only as a blur.
So, if you can really help,
I am your slave
Of my own free will.

Guru: Agreed.
I know I have the answer.
Yet, the way you have asked me
To restore purpose in your life
I concede the first round to you!
Because to be a true Guru
Is perhaps easy,
But to be a true seeker
Is infinitely more difficult.
The true measure of the Guru's stature
Is dependent on the seeker's stature.
The true seeker is a mortal
Who's beyond even immortality.
There is no mystery

That mystifies him;
No destination
Which he does not reach.
He makes a niche for himself
In the very soul of the Timeless.
He is a star
Whose light guides the pathless
In the long nights of pathlessness
On the choppy seas of life.
So, before I accept to do
What you want me to do,
Let me surrender my ego
To my Guru and the Timeless Himself
So that I approach you as a
Pure and luminous spirit,
For being able to communicate
With one who is
So pure and luminous as you:
Behold me in your mind's eye,
Arresting your breath
And your thoughts
And sliding into a *Samadhi*.
And tell me:
Can you cast away your ego?
Can you surrender yourself to me?
Do I hold you ?
Can you merge into me?

Bairagi: No, O Guru Not yet.
At this point
I shall just say that
For a long time now
I have felt the futility of my quest;
Just as you pointed out
That the path I have chosen
Is not the one for me
Despite my attainments.
But what instead should be my path
Has never been clear to me.
My spiritual hankering has not ceased,
Rather, it has heightened.
And I know that

If God were ever so kind
Then someone must appear on the scene
To guide me through these blind alleys
Where I am utterly lost.
When such a person does appear on the scene
I will find anchorage
Firm and strong,
To be able to launch upon
The high seas of my quest
All over again with renewed vigour.
But that it would be you
Is yet to be determined.
Let my doubts be stilled,
let peace once more reign in my heart,
Before I address you as my Guru,
My preceptor, my pathfinder, my redeemer.
And once I do so
Then you shall see that
I follow you with a faith
More firm than the Himalayas
If, for some inexplicable reason,
You ask me
To hop into the fire and be roasted,
I will do so without question.
So, O Guru! First establish yourself
To stand in such a relationship with me.

CANTO FOUR

Guru: You have, O Bairagi!
Placed me in a great predicament.
It looks as though you want me to declare
Here and now
That the path of Nanak,
The path I extol,
Is the truest spiritual path,
The only path all must journey on
To experience the greatest spiritual bliss;
To obtain on themselves
The grace of God in unbounded measure;
To cover themselves
With His most resplendent glory;

To bring about
The greatest good of the greatest number
By awakening the social conscience of man.
So, even if it is egotistical
To so proclaim,
For, all paths leading to God
Are inherently the same,
I shall not refrain from making this statement.
And if doubts arise in your mind
I don't blame you
As it seems to run counter
To the Indian mind and thought—
The profound spiritual tradition of this land.
Yet, this spiritual thought of India
Is so vast and complex,
As is apt to confuse
The best of minds
For, anyone who smears his body with ash
And practises
Or even feigns to practise
A few austerities
Is most likely to become a demi-God
Worshipped by a multitude of people.
And when it happens thus,
It is apt to become the vested interest
Of such demi-Gods
To keep them ignorant and unenlightened,
Quite often destroying in them
Even the most basic virtues of righteousness.
Now add to it
O Bairagi!
The ritual,
The tyranny of Brahmins,
The learned and the repository of all knowledge,
And the picture that emerges
Is a sordid one
Because it makes people totally helpless,
Grovelling in backwardness,
Devoid of faith in themselves
And in exalted Indian traditions.
The resultant man

Is but a mere form sans content.
In fact, he has seldom known the content.
And so he is
Greedy or callous or resigned.
He lacks the sensibility to react
To misery, superstition, disease, and death.
He just vegetates
No longer does he live!
Now this happened in this very hand
Where Krishna taught
To man
The primacy of action;
Action as the will of God;
Action that is unbounded freedom.
Krishna had also invoked the seeker,
A man like Arjuna.
To know God
As the total existentialist Truth
Through knowledge,
Through full spiritual awakening,
Through the total operation of *Karma*
As a part of the life spiritual.
Do you then know why all this happened?
It happened because
We as a race
Had suspended our thinking and judgement,
Our capacity to doubt and inquire,
Our urge to seek the truth,
Our manliness to defend it when necessary.
In fact, in this land of faith,
We had seen to it that
Faith alone became the casualty!
For, can you imagine,
We had forgotten,
That in this existence
The sole proof of God is creation,
Only creation?
And that man's glory it is, therefore,
To create,
To be creative.
But what we created was

The function of instinct—
A mere biological necessity.
We did not create as a means of His Will,
We did not even respect our womenfolk
Verily, God's own instrument of creation
The source and fount of everything beautiful,
Divine and spiritual,
In this entire existence!

Bairagi: Let us now, O Guru!
Not talk in terms too general
Let us talk in concrete, specific terms
For, I know not what you talk,
Or what I hear.
You, therefore, relate yourself
To my limitations of knowledge and experience,
And then tell me what you mean.

Guru: Yes, O Bairagi!
I anticipated what you have said.
In a nutshell, if I may so say,
Indians have a basic dread
Of encountering Reality.
We are content to vegetate
In the world of here and now
And concern ourselves only with
Our small, small worlds
Of achievement and action.
We do not want to shape it
As we ought to.
We have lost the very concept
That we belong to a race,
That we are part of vast, living society,
That we are in daily contact with
Men, women, and children
Whose total life is our concern.
You want me to be more concrete?
So shall I be.
But it requires a heart
And you shall need to have one
To let me treat you great Bairagi!
As a specific case is point.

Bairagi: O Guru!
Your are laying the honey
Certainly thick!
You call me
A seeker, an evolved man,
A man of vision and achievement,
A man of destiny as well,
And then you want to discuss
Me as a case in point.
Well, even if I know not
What precisely you mean,
I am prepared to submit to your surgery.
Dissect me with all your scalpel-sharp skills,
Analyse me with all the ruthlessness
You can muster,
For I am groping for light,
And if ever the rays strike me,
I shall be grateful beyond measure.

Guru: You are a blessed one, O Bairagi!
In giving me the fiat of destiny,
In laying open to criticism
Your chosen path.
One does not extend such an invitation.
You are a reservoir of courage,
To be so supremely confident,
And candid about your quest.
Now, coming to the point:
How are you meritorious
By attaining all your great *Siddhis?*
You say, you can walk on water,
Fly in the air,
Become invisible when you wish.
Yes these are miracles all
Against the laws of nature as they are.
But have you conquered nature in any way?
If not, then your claims are futile.
They are all gimmicks
Of no real consequence,
Mere artefacts
Which afford you to project your ego.

A child flaunting his new toy
Thinking that he has what no one else has,
Is a happiness short lived.
Have you conquered your hunger or thirst?
Do you not need to wash yourself every day?
Do you not feel helpless
When anger overpowers you?
What happens
When your profundity is challenged?
When a woman is all alone with you
Don't you desire her?
It is naive of me
To ask answers of you for these.
These are the laws of nature,
The nature of our being;
Conditions of existence and
We are helpless,
Utterly helpless before them.
Even if one can really perform
The miracles you claim,
Should people bow before him
As a man of God?
No, not at all!
Because, life itself is the greatest miracle.
A miracle shines in its every turn.
Each day that dawns
Is a wonder unrivalled,
And we do not know what will happen
During the next twentyfour hours.
Myriad are the things
That may materialise during this
Short span of time,
A mere day
By which we measure
Our life processes.
In the course of this one day
A great king may be reduced to a pauper,
A man hale and hearty may crop off,
An army heaped with victories may be vanquished,
A whole bustling city may be razed to the ground,
Whole new valleys may form,

New rivers may take birth,
New mountains may raise to touch the sky!
These are all miracles
Much bigger than you ever hope to perform!
For instance,
With all your powers,
Do you know how the day will end?
Or will end at all?
No One can never predict this.
You may reveal what I ate this morning
Or what befell one of my men
En route to your hermitage.
But how much more can you say?
There is a limit to occult practices.
Even a clairvoyant can go thus far and no more.
Therefore, it is well to remember, O Bairagi!
All human affairs are miracles *per se*.
There is no miracle
You can perform
Which is yet in the realm of the unknown.
Let us recall a classic example:
Ramchandra, they say, was God
descended on earth.
His coronation had been fixed
And everything worked out
To the minutest detail.
But who could know
What destiny carried in her womb?
On the very day he was to be anointed,
Destiny had him banished!
Dashratha, his father, had thought
He would be lavished with the greatest of praises
When Rama put on the mantle
Of the heir apparent.
But he was damned by everyone, all the way!
And the moment he had chosen
To return to the jungle
To sit with God,
Was exactly the moment
When he died in all ignominy.
If the events of that most well worked-out day

Could not be foretold
Even by a sage like Vashishtha
Whose eyes could scan
All the three dimensions of time,
Then who could tell
What might happen to ordinary mortals
In ordinary times!
There are six things,
None can predict:
Life and death;
Honour and disgrace;
And profit and loss.
Destiny is there only to the extent
That these six things
Are still not in control of the mortal.
Were it otherwise
All charm would vanish from life.
Life would then be
A mere mathematical formulation
Whose solution
We know in advance
Or can possibly work out
With some effort.

Bairagi: Your oration is powerful enough, O Guru!
To pierce the veil of my ignorance,
Albeit my ego
Which covers the eyes of my being.
Each word you have just spoken
Is worth golden tonnes.
For, from my experience, I know
That not I, but the people at large,
Made me into what I am today—
A miracle man!
Several times,
People approached me with impossible demands
And as I was their Godman,
I blessed them.
I do not know how many of these got fulfilled.
But I know this much:
Many a time
I prayed to my God for hours together

To honour my words!
And gradually it came to be
That I myself started believing
That my word had the power of being fulfilled
And that the eharlatan of a man,
This humble self before you,
Was, in fact, a man of God!

Guru: No Bairagi!
You should not think
Of yourself in such derogatory terms.
You are truly a man of God
In that you have the humility
To admit the reality
However unpalatable it be.
You have a transparent mind.
You are honest enough to feel and respond.
Now I have no doubt that
You are really the man
I have been looking for.

CANTO FIVE

Bairagi: O Guru!
With all my failings
Can I still be redeemed?

Guru: (*Laughing*) Yes, why not?
Not only are you redeemable,
You are already redeemed!
You are the one
I have chosen to redeem myself!
What do you say to that?

Bairagi: I know you have no reason to flatter me.
Yet, I am overwhelmed.
You are the real Guru
I feel and even know.
But do tell me:
What exactly means the epithet Guru?
How do you justify the various roles
You have assumed as a Guru?
What do our traditions say?

Why do you feel that
Violence and bloodshed
Are admissible in a situation like this?
Or, in what situation
Can or must the Guru
Permit or ask for all this?

Guru: O Bairagi!
You have in a single breath
Raised more questions
Than one can possibly handle
In a life-time!
Even so, I will endeavour to
Satisfy your curiosity
As best as I can,
Combining with things concrete
Matters of general interest,
Where necessary.

Bairagi: O Guru!
Your words ring in my ears!
I want to listen to you
Till the end of my life;
A more profound encounter
I have not had before!
Kindly continue your discourse
Till I am fully satiated,
Fully soaked in your lore!

Guru: At the outset,
Let me tell you
The point most profound I know;
Most profound because
It runs into the warp and woof of
Life Indian.
It is so exclusive to our culture
And yet eludes all explanation.
It is the corner-stone
Of our great Indian tradition.
Universalised it becomes
The culture for the world,
Nay, the mother of all cultures,

The path eternal of all transcendental minds.
Dharma—
Dharma holds everything,
Fire, water, sky, air,
And all that.
It is a mystical discipline
Which governs
Reality at all possible levels,
Natural, physical, psychic, mental,
And spiritual.
Within the society, within the family,
It has several forms.
Each one more profound than the other,
Not only sustained by it
But supporting it.
How is this sustenance mutual?
When Rama had been banished
And was preparing to go to the forest,
His mother, invoking *Dharma*, blessed him thus:
"Son, may the same *Dharma* sustain you
Which you were to sustain as king!"
Could she explain it?
Not at all.
Yet, Rama must have understood.

They say Ram Rajya was a model society
Because in it *Dharma* ruled supreme,
Which means everything was in the right place.
Now, no one need define it,
Yet, we,
The sons and daughters of Mother India,
Understand it fully,
From our instinct perhaps.
It is not one man alone,
It has to be the totality of creation,
Each thing affecting us
And, in turn, being affected by us.
One is apt to be confused
About one's *Dharma*
At each step,
Even at the highest level.

As for instance,
Arjuna was when he needed it the most.
In fact, even logic
Does not help one
Determine one's *Dharma*.
Sometimes it merely confounds
Or beguiles.
Why logic?
Every instrument perfected to improve life
May take us along paths
Leading to *Adharma*!
Hence, men of *Dharma* have been few,
And men of *Adharma* always many!
The advance of civilisation itself
Has this process intricately woven into it,
And leads to a dialectical conflict
Which is that of *Dharma* and *Adharma*
Going on in this world all the time.

Understand, O Bairagi!
That in our individual Dharmas,
There are so many individual lives
Yet, collectively called *Dharma* only.
Dharma alone destroys,
Dharma alone renews,
Dharma alone protects,
And we are at different points in between.
Therefore, O Bairagi!
To know what *Dharma* is
Is extremely difficult,
To precise it
Is infinitely more difficult!
You have to have a model before you
Who by precept and example becomes
The model practitioner of *Dharma*,
Above ego, above vanity, above falsehood.
It is this man
Who is the Guru,
Who has the right to lead others
In the moral conflict of
Dharma and *Adharma*.

What the Guru upholds is *Dharma,*
What he discards is *Adharma.*
He assumes complete responsibility
Of the life spiritual
Of the thousands who follow him,
The Sikhs who would otherwise be confused
About what to do.
To be or not to be
Is the fundamental process of becoming,
Leading to the ultimate being.
One falters at every step
And hence has to be led by someone,
Whom we in the language
spiritual call
The *Satguru.*

Bairagi: You confuse me, O Guru!
More than you enlighten me.
Tell me how to know the true Guru?
What are the tests of being one?
And can Guruship be institutionalised?
Can Guruship pass on from father to son?
Or from Guru to Guru?
Is it the leadership qualities
That single him out
And make him the Guru?
Or is it something more?

Guru: Frankly, O Bairagi!
Such questions cannot be resolved
Much less answered
Without faith,
Faith that moves mountains.
But this faith is not an external attribute.
It is a surrender of
The heart, the mind, the intellect,
Nay, the total conscience,
Nay, the whole spirit.
And since it is so
It should not be enforced.
It should be left to grow from within.
It happens at specific points in history.

Let me bring before you an epic situation.
The question is:
What makes Rama
The total upholder of *Dharma*?
It is the fact that
He is born a prince
And a king has a *Dharma* unto the people?
Or is it that he is led by a man like Vashishtha?
Or is it again
That Vishnu had blessed Dashratha
That He would be born to him?
And that
All the signs of appearance of God
Would attend His birth?
In fact, nothing of the sort
Makes him the upholder of *Dharma*
Unless and until he marries Sita.
Because it is she
Who in her person
Represents the dividing line
Between *Dharma* and *Adharma!*
You may be confused about it,
That I am detracting from the greatness of Rama.
But not at all,
Yet, he was the Lord God come to rid
Humanity of *Adharma*
As only the husband of Sita,
Sita, who was the embodiment of the oppressed.
Just recall how she was born
And whole thing will become crystal clear.
How?
There was a king named Ravana
Who had become the oppressor.
He had asked his tax-collectors
To collect taxes
From a bunch of sages.
These Godmen had nothing to pay
Either in cash or in kind.
But the king's tax must be collected!
So they paid it
In their own blood.

But what to do with that blood
It was state property
Duly entered into inventories.
But no treasury would keep it!
Hence that pot of blood was ordered
To be entombed somewhere,
And lo and behold!
That blood of sages
So oppressively extracted
Assumed the form of Sita,
The fond wife of Rama
Who came to be regarded as
The mother of us all Indians.
It was her being
That irrevocably divided Rama and Ravana—
One upholding *Dharma*
And the other bent on destroying it.
Now, whether myth or fact or whatever,
It has aeons of meaning underlying it.
People who stood by Rama
Knew that they were on the side of *Dharma*.
Otherwise, why should the down and out
Of the ages,
Living away from the pale of civilisation
And labelled no more than monkeys
All of a sudden take up arms
To defend *Dharma*
And become the greatest heroes of India?
It is something unheard of!
It is these down and out, O Bairagi!
These exploited of the ages,
These so-called dumb cattle,
Who ultimately determine
When *Dharma* hearkens them,
To shake them out of their slumbers,
To stand up and fight.
The call of *Dharma* in essence
Brings about a qualitative change.
It leaves nothing the same again.
It speaks through five tongues,
The *Panch Janya* of Krishna

Or the *Panj Piyaras* of the Khalsa,
The voice of the age,
Verily, the voice of *Dharma*.

Now I come to the path of Nanak,
The path that I follow,
The path that I want you to follow.
Why is this the path of *Dhurma*?
Because it hearkens men
To be men again—
Self-respecting, noble, and spirited men.
It wants them to know
What Indra in the Rigveda says:
"I am Indra, I cannot be defeated."
During the long centuries
Men have lost the very urge to be men,
Men who ought to be free and equal,
Men who ought to be masters of their destiny,
Individual as well as collective.

Bairagi: When man, O Guru!
Acts as an individual,
The fruits of his actions
Also constitute individual *Dharma* only,
Whether in family or in society.
What is this collective destiny?
What *Dharma* is that?
Why should work for it?

Guru: O Bairagi!
You think
You have raised a profound point,
Which, in essence, is merely academic.
Can the spirit
Work for its salvation without the body?
Why talk in abstractions?
Can you tell me of a person
You may have met,
Who was so weak and ill
And yet whose spirit continued to soar high.
No. It does not happen.
A person in physical trauma

Simply cannot think of
What we know are tasks spiritual,
For which reason the ancients said:
"Body is verily the first instrument of *Dharma!*"
Why body alone,
Which is the home of the spirit,
Even external factors,
Events and situations
Or even perceptions of
Happiness and unhappiness,
Affect it.
A soul in the body
And a man in the world
Are, in essence, the same.
A man always short of money
Thinks of acquiring money only,
Sometimes at the cost of principles,
Many a time
By means so palpably unfair,
Which he thinks are strokes of his genius!
Similarly, most crimes,
Most sinful acts,
Are but the results of
Society denying
What individuals need.
Now, tell me
What spirituality do they have?
It is only in a social environment
That spirituality grows.
Janaka, the father of Sita
Was absolutely right
In refusing to go to heaven
Because his mere presence in hell
Was so much a solace
To its countless inmates,
Being roasted alive in the inferno.

Then, O Bairagi!
The world we live in
Is an important to us spiritually
As our own inner development.

Because all inner enlightenment
Takes place through the medium of
External factors
Or objective reality,
That we know of.
Hence the first task
Before Nanak as Guru was
To restore to men,
The greatness that is man's;
Above all religions,
Above all paths of worship,
To make men protest against
Tyranny and injustice,
Wherever, whatever.
Religion of protest,
The religion of aroused social conscience,
It the first spiritual principle
Enunciated by Nanak.
For, what is the use of practising austerities
If the man next door is dying of hunger?
What is that world
Where the able-bodied are given no work,
Or the old and infirm condemned to inhuman drudgery?

So, O Bairagi!
The Timeless is not a were deity.
It is the Transcendent Self
Living and illuminating
Each particle of this creation.
Nay, the countless creations
Beyond and yonder,
In the endless vistas of space
Or even countless spaces!
Guru Nanak did not divide God.
He invoked *Ek Omkar*
The formless One who above all has the apparatus
Of becoming many
When He in His Grace so desires
As the Lord of *Nada Brahm*.
This is how Nanak sought to integrate humanity
Divided so badly in different castes and creeds
And even numberless paths of worship.

O Bairagi!
It is this supreme Formless
Who does not fear anyone,
Nor wants anyone to fear Him;
Who bears enmity to none
And none bears enmity to Him;
It is His boundless grace alone
That can defeat
The empirical cycle of birth and death
So ruthlessly determined by the Karmic Law
And lead each one of us to salvation
Our final merging with Him.
Now how to achieve it?
There may be many paths to do so,
But Nanak enjoined remembering Him
Always and ever.

So, the right to work.
And the will to share,
Are to Nanak's path as important
As the right to protest,
And the will to fight injustice.
Nanak also knew
That even if all this is realised
A society
Where everyone is equal and free
And there is no suffering, no privation,
Shall, sooner or later,
Breed egocentricity in man,
The worst enemy of the man spiritual.
He therefore asked man
To be the instrument of the Timeless only,
In total surrender, total supplication,
Through the constant repetition of His name
Which is verily another form of *Yoga*,
And which awakens inner powers,
And thereby not only makes the man omniscient
But also an heir to the total fund of creativity
That is there in the whole world.
Such a man is Indra, the immortal,
Whom all oppressors,

All the men of *Adharma* dread.
Sikhism or the religion of Nanak
Is the congregation of such invincible Indras only.
Such men alone can scale the Himalayas.
Now, no wonder, we see
Such men persecuted,
Such men driven from pillar to post
By the so-called established order—
The State—
Which then starts decaying from within
To a state
In which none can perform his *Dharma*.

Bairagi: Tell me, O Guru!
Is it the gospel of revolt
Or is it the path spiritual
That you speak of?
Tell me also: How is revolt compatible with
The man's ultimate destiny,
The life spiritual,
The quest of the Timeless?
I want to understand all this
At greater length,
Because it appears
To be something new,
Something different,
Something fundamental.

CANTO SIX

Guru: No Bairagi!
It is not new.
It is the rebirth of the ancient,
A rediscovery of what had been forgotten,
A rediscovery of *Dharma* and *Dharma* alone,
The law eternal
That sustains *Samsara*,
The reality in flux.
No one can crete *Dharma* afresh.
It is the only existentialist reality known,
Between us, the mortals, and the Timeless
All we can do is to restate it

For, the regeneration of the life spiritual.
This has happened all the time.
And we, the sons and daughters of this ancient land,
Know more than anyone else,
The validity of this principle.
Rama did it before,
Krishna did it before,
The Buddha too did it before.
But there is one important difference
Which must be understood:
They were God themselves,
God descended on earth!
They fought the forces of *Adharma*
And restored the Kingdom of *Dharma* on earth.
And now comes Nanak,
A different kind of man,
The man spiritual,
Mind you, not God on earth!
But the Guru—the saviour and servant of men.
And *Dharma* is instantly resurrected.
The fight for its defence rages all anew.
Now Nanak does not retire to the forest
Like the Buddha,
Nor like Rama or Krishna
Has he kingly titles
For the legitimisation of their roles
As the heroes of Ramayana and Mahabharata,
To wage wars,
The lead armies,
To be automatically blessed by saints and sages,
As it was known well beforehand
That they were incarnations of God.
And people rendered fugitive
Were waiting for them.
But Nanak, the Guru, had no such claim.
Nobody had ever proclaimed his birth.
No one knew how to legitimise his status.
He appeared on the stage of the world unheralded
And started life like any other mortal.
No special signs betokened his birth,
Nor did the wise come from afar to worship him.

But soon he was known as Guru,
The bestower of God's grace
Through words and deeds,
On the suffering and the exploited,
For the redemption of mankind.
Now I must explain to you
Something which has caused much confusion:

Who is a Guru in the sense Nanak is?
Nanak is neither the Prophet like Mohammad
Through whom speaks out Allah,
Nor is he the son of God as Christ,
The chosen one of God to lead the flock.
He is a man,
Just a simple mortal,
Who is engaged in his spiritual evolution
Through his own cognitive apparatus and experience.
He is a man reaching out to God
In the shape of his fellow humans
As a spiritual entity,
Talking to fellow men
As one superior among equals—
A Guru, a friend, a teacher or a preceptor,
A pathfinder, a saviour or a redeemer!
Yes, a man can at best be one,
But so multi-dimensional is Nanak
That he is all-rolled-in-one,
A superior man,
A Guru,
The like of whom
There is none even in the Indian tradition.
For instance,
The Buddha was preceded by twenty four *Bodhi-Sattvas*,
And was the inheritor of
The total spiritual evolution of them all.
Almost similar was Mahavira
The heir to all the *Tirthankaras*.
Supposing they were men and not incarnations of God,
Even then,
They were the last of a tradition,
Followed by a church

Embodying their injunctions.
But this is not so with Nanak!
He appears as the first
In a chain of ten Gurus,
Building one upon the other,
Each one perfecting his message
And giving practical shape to his ideas
So that the quest for spiritual evolution,
The fight for justice and fair play,
Albeit the return of the rule of *Dharma*
Should become a movement.
He is the first one to see it clearly
That social justice is
At the centre of spiritual regeneration,
And without one
The other has no meaning.
Nonetheless, it should be understood
That it was no revolt against tradition
The difference in the message occurred
Because an alien social order
Was the oppressor.
Islam as religion,
Or any form of worship,
Could have been worthwhile in India,
But how could we Indians
Accept a proselytising creed
And a whole society patterned on it
As superior to ours?
How could we concede
That their's was the only true path
For all men in the world
Always and ever
Even if force was to be used
To promote it?
Guru Nanak revolted at the idea
Which remains ever abhorent to all Indians.
Nothing could be more refined than
The concept of *Dharma*
Embedded in our social consciousness,
In our personal lives,
In our total cycle of births and deaths,

In our cause-and-effect relationship with *Karma*
Moving in the vehicle of matter
And carrying the soul on to
Its final transcendental journey !

Tyranny and oppression
In the name of God
Cannot be an acceptable proposition
In India.
Even if the oppressor is none other than a Hindu.
There are umpteen instances
When kings had to be thrown out
Because they had become megalomaniacs.
Prahlad had to be born
To Hiranya Kashipu himself
So that the victory of God alone
Could be proclaimed by the men of spirit.
But now there was no king in India
To stand up to this strange tyranny,
Calculated to demolish Indian society.
Instead, there were sycophants all around.
The Brahmins proclaimed from house-tops:
"The master of Delhi is the master of the world,"
Implying that
It was sedition not to abide by his command.
There was no character left in the people.
Spineless like jelly fish,
They had allowed
Knowledge to become subservient to power.
Administering of Islam
As a spiritual medicine,
Was changing the very pathology
Of the Indians as a race!

It was, therefore, natural for Nanak
To create an instrument of popular will,
Where temporal and spiritual could work together.
The Guru himself had to lead the two spheres
Till the Sikh fraternity itself,
The fraternity of *Dharma,*
Threw up its own king
And established a kingdom

Of freedom, peace, and progress,
Removing all shackles of religious oppression.
This was verily a renaissance.
Never had the Indian thought
Shaped in this manner.
It was a combination of
Dadhichi and Indra
The aliens were now facing.
In the land of the five rivers.
The gateway to India,
The Kurukshetra of India's destiny,
Nanak was the man
Who feared none,
For he was a man of God.
He stood before the armies of Babur
And denounced them
As "a bridal procession of sin
Descended from Kabul."
Why did he do it?
He was a man of God
And everyone,
King or pauper, Indian or alien,
Was equal in his eyes.
But no!
He was a man with an aroused social conscience as well.
To him sainthood did not mean
He could be immune to social injustice,
In whatever the shape or form,
Whether Hindu or Muslim.
Yet, it was no revolt.
It was the spiritual regeneration,
Of a whole people,
Of which social justice became an essential part.
But why did people begin hailing him
As Guru?
It is a subtle question.
A Guru would mean
A hermitage
Where he taught and discoursed.
Or, a few people
Who derived spiritual solace from him

And had left their destiny in his hands.
Or, he held the exalted office of the wise counsellor
To a great king or kingdom.
No.
Nanak did not fall in any such category.
He could not have belonged to tradition either,
For he was not a Brahmin
But a Kshatriya,
A State functionary,
As Ordinary as any other.
Nanak is amongst those realisers and thinkers
Who are also men of action,
Men who do not tread beaten tracks
But make enduring paths of their own
In the footprints they leave,
So that those who come after them
Are not befuddled and led astray.
Being ritualistic and priestly,
Brahmins could not be interested in problems
Of soul and *Brahm*.
This knowledge known as *Brahm Vidya*
Was the repository of the Kshatriyas,
Kings, princes, generals, and leaders.
Like Janaka, Bhishma, Krishna, the Buddha, Mahavira,
And now Nanak!
This fact alone explains
Where he stands in the whole tradition.
He would not bow to anybody
Who was not evolved in thinking,
Who had not been aroused in social consciousness.
Which is why Nanak
Rejected the rich food of Malik Bhago
And rejoiced in the hard bread of Bhai Lalo.
When questioned about it
Nanak demonstrated:
How the rich food of the parasite
Was full of the blood of the poor,
While the hard-earned bread of Lalo
Was overflowing with the life-giving nectar.
A man who explained the Indian tradition
In such earthy terms

Was certainly a preacher,
But with a difference.
He was not talking of the outward form
But of real essence—
The essence
Which pervades the form but is not bound by it.
And thereby Nanak acquired a following
Both among the Hindus and the Muslims
As a man of God
The like of whom
They had not known before.
It is this man Nanak
The Hindus called the Guru,
And the Muslims, the Pir.
He was common to all
Because he had joined them
In thc commonwealth of suffering,
To restore man
Not so much to the kingdom of God.
As to his (man's) own kingdom.

Now, if this be not enough proof
That he was the true Guru,
Let us look at the whole story
From another angle.
It is cardinal to Indian tradition
That at the apex of all spiritual inquiry
Stand the Vedas,
The finest incarnation of the *Nada Brahm*.
The repetition of which
Awakens the *Kundalini*—
The key to higher knowledge,
Through his *Japuji,*
The great prayer to be repeated constantly.
Guru Nanak was himself knowledge incarnate,
The Veda.
He awakened the *Kundalini* of his Sikhs
And thus opened the flood-gates
Of all knowledge and wisdom to them.
Now can there be a greater Guru?
A greater imparter of knowledge?

He was the first in the long tradition of Gurus
Who demonstrated
That every man had the complete knowledge,
The Veda within him.
All that he required
To tap that knowledge
Was the word of the Guru.
Who, even unknowingly,
Through repetition of the name alone,
Guides the seeker
To the seat of knowledge
And the fount of creativity!
Thus every Sikh of the Guru
Is the highest *Yogin,*
The knower of all knowledge.
That is why his *Grantha*
Is the Veda itself,
The *"Gurmukh Vedam"!*
The Veda emanated from the Guru's mouth.
And *Adi Grantha,*
The *Grantha* of the Guru,
Is patterned on the Veda itself.
It has the same simplicity,
The same spontaneity,
The same uplifting spirituality,
And the same *Chhandas*—
The power of the rhythm of creativity—
The same overflowing of divine music
That is so characteristic of
The first book of creation,
The Rigveda of our forefathers,
The spirit of India
Was reborn in Nanak,
Heralding the regeneration of this ancient country,
In the restatement of *Dharma* which
People had forgotten how to practise.
So, O Bairagi!
Nanak was the Guru *par excellence!*

Bairagi: My Guru!
All this while you spoke

As a man with a halo,
The one recepient of the Light Divine.
I have no doubt now
That Guru Nanak was the real Guru,
The true saviour
Who brought about the ressurection
Of the splendid heritage of India,
The spiritual India.
And you too are to true Guru
In the same immortal lineage,
A man dedicated to the great mission
Of regenerating a spiritual society.
Certainly I shall follow you.
But before I do so
Kindly show me
What divine men
The Guru had moulded.
Men, who through the alchemy of the Name,
Performed miracles
No other man of God had performed.

Guru: I am happy that
You have resolved
To take up my mission.
Let us, therefore, thank the Timeless
That you have agreed to become
The instrument of His will,
The existentialist will,
In the operation of which
Dharma alone endures and
All else perishes.
Now, this is the miracle of spirit
I had mentioned
A man of God can perform.
This is the transformation
The message of Nanak has performed.
Can you imagine
People weak in body and mind,
People gutlets and spineless,
Vying with one another
To become the *Sant-Sepahis*—

The soldiers of Nanak?
Or, can you imagine
The down and out of the ages
Who had withdrawn totally,
Shunning the realities of life,
Trying to be the first in the race
To give off their heads
So that others,
Whom they did not even know,
Lived without coercion
With the fullest expression of their beings?
After all
What can the Guru promise
But an honourable life on this earth?
Or, alternatively,
A much more honourable death,
Because it is in the service of mankind;
Because even as the physical body perishes
The human spirit as enshrited in *Dharma*
Shines ever more.
The law of *Karma* makes death
A necessary stage of evolution
On the gradual journey of transcendence.
But death when courted
As an instrument of *Dharma*
Is life eternal.
For such men
There is no world to be conquered,
No riches to be looted,
No slaves and concubines to be enjoyed.
Wine, wealth, and women
Are perfect taboos to a Sikh.
The only compensation is
The strength of denial,
Not of resignation,
Accepted voluntarily;
The *ananda* of submission
Not the pleasures of ego and assertion.

It is really a hard drill, O Bairagi!
To be living on hourseback
With sword and spear in hand

And His name on the lips!
It is this miracle,
The miracle of spirit,
No man of God had performed before
Nanank came upon the scene!
Those who live are blessed.
But those who die are simply divine.
Because *Dharma,*
The most elusive Indian entity
Embedded so deep in our culture
Cannot be defended without embracing death
In the highest tradition of martyrdom.

A question arises here:
If Islam as a religion is fine
Then why this strife?
Why not we become Mohammedans
And live happily ever after?
No. This is not done;
It is the way
The weak and cowards would behave.
Those who disown their God,
Their symbols, their martyrs,
Fathers, forefathers,
Such people deny the very path of spirit.
While we love Mohammed
And his path of worship,
We cannot belong to it.
All paths may be spiritual.
But there is no substitute for
One's own faith and traditions,
Hallowed by memories of the forefathers,
Ennobled by the lay of the land.
Think!
Can we ever think
Of bartering away
Our mountains, our valleys, our rivers,
Our trees, our flowers, our birds, our animals,
Our food, our dress,
Our dances, our music?
Can we agree
To give away the Ganga

For any river that we know?
Every child born
Grows in the sweetness of the milk of his culture.
We love our traditions.
We are sustained by our *Dharma*.
"Better to die in one's own *Dharma*
Than to try to follow someone else's,"
Says Lord Krishna in the Geeta.
No, Bairagi! No!
We cannot follow any other path
However good it be.
We are the most moral people;
We are the most spiritual race.
All we need to do is reform ourselves
And then learn to live
Firmly anchored in the soil of
Our own *Dharma*,
That is why in India
Nobody gets converted
Of his own volition.
And the few who do so,
Do not love their traditions
As well as they ought to.
It is not a clash of religions.
It is a clash of two traditions,
Two mutually exclusive social organisations.
And when the issues are as well articulated
By a man like Nanak,
Embracing death to defend such subjectivities
Becomes the only honourably way—
A martyrdom *par excellence!*

CANTO SEVEN

Bairagi: I am becoming clear, O Guru!
About your great mission
And its objectives.
What use are my arms
And my skill in wielding them
When my *Dharma*,
The most sacred nutrient
In the milk of the Mother India,

Lies in such great peril?
I am prepared to do my duty and,
Should you so desire,
Lay down my life
On the altar of your noble mission.
Yet I wish
Your fiery invocations
Temper further
The steel of my will,
As also your narratives
Of the glorious deeds
Of the legendary Sikhs
In the land of Five Rivers,
In defence of *Dharma*.

Guru: I have already related to you,
O Bairagi!
About how Dadhichi and Indra
Act in unison in Punjab;
How saints have turned soldiers
And soldiers, saints of the highest order!
The path of Nanak is that of *Bhakti*.
It releases man from the captivity of
Involuted thought,
Mechanical rituals,
Lifeless words,
Immobility of castes and professions,
Scriptures far removed from reality;
In fact, it releases from the whole world
Of hypocricy
Where man and his spirit
Have remained imprisoned
In the intricacies of convoluted truth
None could accept or reject !
The *Bhaktas* burst forth into singing
The praises of the Lord.
In clusters, in congregations,
In the temples, in the open,
With a new environment of
Spontaneous freedom of expression.
Yet the great force that *Bhakti* generated

Did not somehow release the soul of India.
Rather, it put into chains
The *Bhaktas*
Who, far from being
The free men of God,
Suffered from egos expressed in humility.
Well, *Bhakti* might have been the force
Of love and freedom
India needed,
If only
Its leaders had also
Combined social purpose with it.
Bhakti became another escape route
Of all those who lacked the will to act.
Go to Braj—
The land of Krishna, the *Karma Yogin,*
And see for yourself
How the great *Vaishnavas*
In their *Dasa Bhava,*
Moods of subserviency to the deity,
Lie prostrate,
Worse than jelly fish.
If, therefore, that is *Bhakti,*
Nanak's path is certainly not !
He merely accepted and included
The chorus singing of the congregation
And the constant repetition of the Name.
But beyond that
He harnessed and channelled
The social forces thus released
Into a mighty tidal wave
That assumed the form of Sikhism,
With this difference:
He did not believe in the incarnations of Vishnu;
But sang praises of the Timeless, Formless One
Who permeates every living being,
Even lifeless matter.
What is the use of shedding
Tears before the deity
And swooning and doing things of the sort
When *Dharma* is in wilderness,

Crying for protection,
Not from the deity
But from men of flesh and blood?
So, Nanak's message spread
Like a flood of unremitting fury
Of ideas, metaphors, and parables
That came wave upon wave
In the language of the people
And drenched each one to his very soul.
It was verily a storm of beautiful poetry
Suffused in divine music,
Singing the spiritual anguish of the people
And made them into a different kind of men—
Men no longer resigned to their fate
But out to carve out a new destiny,
Not for themselves alone,
But for all men of spirit.
Death in the cause of the Guru
Was to these people
As much joy
As life itself.
Even more.
Because while death kills a worn-out body
It simultaneously renews the spirit
That comes to reside in a brand new body,
As an appropriate instrument of *Dharma,*
The religion of the soul.

The fires of the *Yagna*
That Nanak kindled
Were fuelled by oblations of spirit
Day after day,
Generation after generation,
Nanak himself being reborn
In each generation
As a new Guru,
Responding to the social situation,
The call of the time,
In the battle of *Dharma.*
In the traditions of saints,
Stoics may have come

One following the other,
But seldom have come men of spirit and action
As in the mission of Nanak,
Each one informed with a new sense of destiny,
Growing and evolving itself
In the dialectical,
Nay, the existentialist,
Battle of *Dharma* and *Adharma*
That rages incessantly.
Tell me, O Bairagi!
Where else do men of God
Wear swords
Except in the path of Nanak?
Like Drona, the Gurus
Taught their followers the use of arms,
Like Bhishma
Led them in battles,
Like Parshurama
Killed the terrible foes of *Dharma*
To demonstrate
That nothing exists more powerful than *Dharma*—
The existentialist essence of life;
That men do not live by bread alone.
They have a spirit
Far above the constraints of the flesh.
For the first time it was
In the long Indian tradition
That men of God wielded arms
To defend themselves.
Even a sage like Vishwamitra
Who was adept in the use of arms
And was himself a Kshatriya prince
Born to fight,
Did not himself kill the demons
To become a defender of *Dharma*.
Rather, he had them killed by Rama,
God's instrument to sustain *Dharma*.
The Guruship in the path of Nanak
Deviated from this tradition
In a remarkable way
In that the Gurus themselves became

Instruments of sustaining *Dharma*.
It created a throne of the Guru,
Not just the seat of the Guru,
Right up to me.
Because for *Dharma* to be sustained
The battle had to be long drawn out
And could not be abandoned
For want of a defender
In case the Guru died.
Causes cannot be defended by men.
They need institutions.
Also understand, O Bairagi!
The calibre of leadership
So gloriously manifested by the Gurus:
The way Guru Arjan was a willing martyr;
The way my revered father agreed to give his head;
The way his companions embraced death;
The way my five Sikhs gave themselves unto me
To become the immortal *Panj Piyaras;*
The way my two young sons
Had themselves buried alive in a brick wall—
All these gems of the Guru leadership
Amply signify the fact
That when such challenges emerge
To defend *Dharma*.
The human spirit is so steeled
That the body is rendered totally insensate
To the pain of death.

Listen, O Bairagi!
It is their spirit
That death can never conquer,
And which makes people believe
That the world of spirit
Is much above the world of death.
It is death that dies
While the spirit lives!
Now, it is this message of immortality
Perfected over the past two hundred years
That transformed sheep and cattle into lions
And sparrows to kill falcons

And one Sikh to equal
An army of a lakh and quarter.
Today in Punjab,
The land of the first *Aryaman,*
The land of the Rigvedic sages,
The land of Nanak,
The land of his matchless followers,
The Sikhs,
The land of my true sons,
The Khalsa,
No fear of death exists anywhere.
None seeks escape to become a recluse.
All are soldiers on the battle-field
With souls of steel.
They ride emaciated horses,
Live on frugal rations,
And are so scantily armed,
You will wonder:
What manner of army is this?
But they are so much filled with
The message of the spirit
That the mightiest armies dread them.
They are all *Akalis,*
Followers of the Timeless.
They salute with *Sat Sri Akal*—
Invoking unfading glory to the Timeless
Who alone is the essence of the Immortal,
When all else is subject to change
And shall perish.

So, O Bairagi!
O You, the wielder of arms!
The conqueror of your body,
It is in Punjab
That you are needed.
It is there that destiny awaits you!

CANTO EIGHT

Bairagi: O Guru!
Pray, don't call me Bairagi,
I am not one any more.

I am your *Banda,*
A bonded slave of yours.
I concede
You are the true miracle-man.
The so-called miracles
I claimed I could perform,
Pale into insignificance
Before your resplendent powers.
You have changed me
So radically, so thoroughly!
Something is happening to me,
Something has happened to me,
In the true spirit of a *Bhakta*.
I would remain sitting at your feet,
Listening to you speak
The same blissful fiery, divine speech,
As a lover would his truly beloved.
Your poetry sublime
Can without doubt
Bring forth tears from stones
And inspire mountains to action.
You are the master of *Durga,*
The master of *Saraswati,*
As equally in command
Of words as of sword.
Would you humour some more
This persistent questioner
And tell him all about
How you acquired this power?
How you became the man of the moment,
The messenger of the Timeless?

Guru: Yes, you are my Banda!
The one whom
Destiny has chosen to carry out
The will of the Timeless.
By being my Banda you know that
You are called upon to do
What remains still undone.
However, there is no need to praise me
That much out of proportion.

I am no more than
A slave of the Timeless,
Occupying the stage of the world
For as long as my role lasts.
I am no exception.
I am like everybody else.
The only difference is
That I have realised my role
Through the blessings of my Guru,
Guru Nanak,
And his mission
Of restoring *Dharma* to men
So that they be free.
And this great mission:
By constantly repeating the Name,
By constantly remembering the Timeless,
By constantly working for the success of the mission,
Has not allowed me even a minute's respite.
I have reached a stage
That is seldom reached
Even by the *Siddhas*.
If I have mastered
The sword and the word
It is because I am Nanak's servant.
No mortal is Siva or Brahma.
And I am much less.
An ordinary mortal.
So, O Banda!
Even if you want me, your Guru
To be lauded,
Do not invest me with the supernatural,
With what I am not,
For that would be mere sycophancy.
I am no God.
Nor was Nanak.
We are mortals working with mortals
At the bidding of the Timeless only.

Banda: Don't frown so, my Guru;
I had merely indulged in poetic exaggeration.
Otherwise, going by existentialist logic

In the world of matter
Nothing is good or bad,
It happens because it has to.
Else, why should we presume
That while we are engaged in defending *Dharma*,
Others are out to destroy it?

Guru: It is now, O Banda!
That you are coming out with the real problem.
I know
In the existentialist situation
Rama and Ravana are equals,
Peers of each other.
And what they did was
Only perform a drama.
Call it divine if you may.
But in the larger context
Nothing actually is divine.
Everything is existentialist.
Yet, why do we hail Rama as
The protector of *Dharma?*
And Ravana
The destroyer?
Even in this existentialist reality
Supposing the world is a river,
It has to have two banks.
Now what flows in the river
Is life or the world in flux,
The existentialist water,
Whose flow is regulated by *Dharma*.
One bank of the river
Is the forces of the deprived, Rama,
And the other bank is
The forces of the deprived, Ravana,
The two peers caught eternally
In a dialectical conflict.
We join the battle
On Rama's side
Because the forces of spirit
Should never be vanquished.
The forces of Ravana grow automatically,

For *Adharma* has that apparatus
In which not convictions
But interests reign supreme.
The forces of Rama have to be strengthened.
You have to join them
Without any selfish motive,
With pure conviction.
Nothing else.
It is the will of the Timeless
That goads us to do such things—
The only purpose in
The world of blind action.
Hence, there can be no two opinions about it.
Now, let us see why
People flock to Nanak's mission.
Because it is a mission of light and spirit,
The only flickering brightness
In these raging storms of darkness.
This light has to be kept alive
At all cost,
Even at the cost of lives,
Yours, mine, others.
That is what the Khalsa is now engaged in.
That it too must not
Suffer the same fate,
The ravages of time,
Has been my deep concern.
You can invoke great fury
But how to channel it
Is the challenge
A true leader will meet.
Successfully.

Banda: I am more than convinced that
You are the messenger of the Timeless
And you stand for *Dharma*.
But to what use
If tomorrow
It has to degenerate into *Adharma?*

Guru: Despite what you assured me
I suspect you are still groping for an escape route!

Well, every intelligent man has this problem.
But remember!
Action comes from conviction only.
And you have committed yourself
To the path of ruthless action,
A path which does not admit
An iota of doubt!
One cannot lay down one's life
In the spirit of martyrdom,
One cannot chop off heads
In the spirit of giving oblations
As in a divine *yagna*,
If one were not to surrender to faith.
And you are required to do both.
Hence your faith as being
The instrument of *Dharma*
In the service of the Timeless,
Has to be unbounded.

There are no heaven-born people
In the scheme of things.
If a people stand at the top today
They may touch rock bottom tomorrow.
The Hindus,
The wisest and noblest,
What has happened to them?
Now, no more than
Hewers of wood,
Drawers of water,
Even in their own land!
Egypt, Rome, Greece, Mexico,
Mesopotamia,
Great civilisations all,
All vanished in the vicissitudes of time!
Even Islam,
The Path of Mohammed,
The last Prophet and Redeemer of mankind,
Has lost its thrust.
Today Aurangzebs and Wazir Khans
Are its hopeless champions,
Smeared with the blood of the innocent,
Denying even natural justice to their people.

Even sages are being asked
To contribute their share of taxes,
What if in blood!
Such is the state of affairs!
All around humanity wails
"Save me, save me!"
The cry only rebounds
In several eerie echoes,
Filling the pitiable souls with ever more fear!
Fortunately our *Dharma* is self-renewing.
It responds to the forces of tyranny
By giving birth to a saviour.
Hence Nanak.
And again. And again. And again—
Nine rebirths,
All of us form but one body of Nanak.
His spirit is enshrined in his Veda,
The *Guru Grantha,*
The light of man's spirit.

But I had to take some very hard decisions
To ensure Nanak's path
Would not degenerate in its purpose
And its self-renewing spirit
Remained sensitive to the forces of injustice
By reacting manfully.
The hereditary Guruship has,
Like all hereditary institutions,
An inherent weakness in that
It could degenerate into one man's tyranny.
So I decided
That after me
The Guruship would end.
Yet the ten Gurus would remain living,
Always and ever.
In the body of the *Grantha,*
In the purity of the message,
In the greatness of *Nada Brahm,*
In the music celestial.
No book has ever been elevated
Too such a status.

And more important
Than the perpetuation of Guruship
In the *Grantha,*
Was the creation of internal democracy
In the total body of the Khalsa
So that
In the absence of written commandments
Paths could be determined by the collective will
As embodied in the person of *Panj Piyaras,*
The Five Beloveds
Whom I had to place
Even above myself,
The living Guru.
When the battle was on
In Chamkaur
And my two sons had died fighting,
And the odds were overwhelming,
And my instinct and even *Dharma* was
To die fighting sword in hand facing the enemy
In the highest traditions of a Kshatriya,
I had to, alas, bow to the command of my
Panj Piyaras!
So that the fight could continue
And even if battles were lost
The war could be won.
Now has such a democracy
Ever existed in any spiritual path?
It is this democracy that ensures
New social forces,
New spiritual ideas,
New emerging technologies,
To constantly agitate from within
For acceptance
And form part of Nanak's spiritual path.
Does such an apparatus exist
In any religio-spiritual tradition?

And who are my *Panj Piyaras?*
Not men chosen for popularity,
But men of sterling worth and character,
More firm in their steadfastness

Then the unshakeable Himalayas.
Men of faith and devotion
Who stand by unwavering principles.
Guided by truth
And not mere stratagems!
Men mellowed with wisdom
And tempered with experience.
Men who accept the Timeless
As the ultimate reality,
Yet not shunning the world of affairs.
Men of *Dharma*
But above the shackles of caste and creed.
For, the battle between *Dharma* and *Adharma*
Is always total
And has to be fought
In all its ferocity.
By the total society.
Men of superhuman yogic powers
Whose higher mind is fully awakened
By the constant *jap*
Of the *Japuji* and the *Sukhmani*.

Thus, O Banda!
Living within the larger fold
Of the Indian tradition,
The path of Nanak
Has been perfected in such a way
That it becomes
The most potent arm of *Dharma*—
A package of mystical values,
Divine but more real than life itself
Which society had forgotten how to defend.
And even if we,
The followers of Nanak,
Believe in the efficacy of prayer
And repetition of the Name
As also the grace of the Guru,
Without which we would grope in Darkness,
We believe in the primacy of *Karma*
And the cyclical concept of rebirth.
We do not live for here and now.

We also live for the hereafter.
For *Dharma* is the net product of *Karmas* only
And it alone forms the basis of
How we shall act.
That is why we believe in
The purity of body and mind,
Speech and actions,
Means and ends,
Faith and devotion.
It is a path
Only the best of men can follow,
For, every Sikh of Nanak,
Every Khalsa of mine,
Is an Arjuna in the battlefield of life,
Fighting out the Mahabharata—
The final battle of *Dharma* and *Adharma*.
We ring the death-knell of all tyranny,
We pull down the curtain on all injustice,
We are the harbingers of a new age,
In which all men will live with peace and honour
In this land of *Karma*,
In this country of *Dharma*.

Banda : Is this why we are fighting Islam, O master?
And when we win
And *Dharma* is restored,
Will the fight be over?

Guru : No Banda!
This is not the true mission
Of the path of Nanak.
We are not at war
With Islam or Muslims.
We refuse to be inspired
By the spirit that informed
The crusades in Europe.
We are at war against everything
Which cripples the spirit of man
And tempts him onto the path of *Adharma*.
We are fighting for the resuscitation of
The spirit of man,

Which is the only projection of the Timeless.
Ours is a path of love and affirmation,
Not condemnation.
All paths leading to the Timeless
Are sacred to us,
But our affirmation is in action,
Absolutely positive.
We are not arm-chair sophists,
Nor even saints and sages
Proclaiming from forests
And unwittingly becoming
Instruments of *Adharma*.
If we have removed fear,
Then we have shown the world
That no terror can subdue the spirit.
And that in any war of *Adharma*
It only behoves the saintly people
To first offer their heads,
Mocking at the phenomenon called death—
Because at the worst
It is a rebirth into this world
To once again take up the noble fight,
And at the best
It is merging with the Timeless.

CANTO NINE

Banda: Bravo, my Mentor !
The exposition of your mission of *Dharma*
Is simply superb !
Still pray, tell me :
If your mission is really that meritorious
And makes no distinction whatsoever
Between a Hindu and a Muslim
Then, did any Muslims take up your causes ?
Did any of them defend them at the cost of his life ?
Did anyone dare the Moghuls
Against their tyranny
In persecuting you or your Sikhs,
In the way they did ?
Why I ask this question is
Because as your chosen slave

I shall have to deal with situations
Involving any number of Muslims.
I should, therefore, know
How to make a distination
Between the one who stands for *Dharma*
And the one who does not.

Guru : I am glad
That you raised this question.
These are umpteen number of Muslims
Who stood by me
In my hour of need
As they believed my cause was
One of righteousness.
Let me tell you
I would not have been living
If Nabi Khan and Ghani Khan
Had not taken me out of mortal danger
In a palanquin,
Disguised as there own venerable Pir.
Not just that.
Remember, how Pir Buddhu Shah of Sadhaura
Came to my help
In the raging battle
When he came to know
That his Pathans had deserted me
And sacrificed his own sons.
As also his followers.
Then, how can I forget
The noble Sher Mohmmed Khan of Malerkotla
Who lodged his moral protest
Against the kind of justice
Wazir Khan handed down to my young sons,
In full view of the court of Sirhind.

Therefore, O Banda !
Do not ever think
That our struggle is a partisan one:
We are sacrificing everything
Only because *Dharma* has to be defended
And there are numerous Musalmans
Whom it is as dear as their own *Din*.

Banda : Yes my Master !
The issues are clear cut.
And denominations are irrelevant
In this war
That does not distinguish between anything
But *Dharma* and *Adharma*.
And I am itching to confront
All those ranged against *Dharma*.
Yet a few minor curiosities
Bother me, O Guru !
Not because these are any more material to my resolve
But because I want to partake
Of more and more
That comes from your sacred mouth.
Tell me, O my Mentor !
When the path of Nanak
Is so dead set against superstition
And you are his chosen one
To spread his message,
Then why did you choose to be superstitious ?
Why did you worship the Goddess ?
Whey did you recreate mythology ?
Why did you talk of your previous birth
As a sage or whatever ?
Don't these things obscure the vision ?
Don't these things weaken the resolve?

Guru : I find, O Banda !
That your perception of things
Is still that of a sophisticated man
And if anything weakens the resolve
It is such thinking !
Take, for example, a man caught in duality.
He may be the best of men
With an aroused social conscience,
But what can he do?
For, his intellectual sophistication
Always gets the better of him !
So cast away your intellectual conceit
And take up the resolve
"To do or die"

The resolve that pervades
Everyone in Punjab,
Each blade of grass I know.
This epic
It born of my those acts only,
Which you call superstitions.
Acts that arouse heroism,
Heroism of an order
Never before attained.
Certainly I spoke of my previous birth.
We not only believe but also know
That the soul transmigrates after every birth
Until it transcends
And merges with the Timeless,
Never to return to the earthly coils of birth and death.
If this were not so
Dharma would be meaningless.
We know that *Dharma* exists
And when it so exists.
The cycle of births and deaths also exists !
The only superstition I practised,
If you wish to term that so,
Was that God Himself ordained
A *Rishi* undergoing penances,
To take another birth
And do as I have been doing
All these years !
You may exclaim
That a believer in the Timeless
Should not say so!
For, the Formless, Timeless
Can only be felt
And not seen face to face.
But pause and reflect
And you will know
That I did not overstate.
The mind in meditation
Is in tune with the Timeless.
It does receive messages
From the Timeless.
To be able to hear the innermost voice,

Your *Antahkarana,*
Is like knowing the highest truth.
And one is to act accordingly,
In supplication to the Timeless.
Review my whole life
And see if I ever wavered
From my service to the Timeless.
I have done
Just what the Timeless has bid me do
Through the voice of my *Antahkarana*.
Else, how does a child of nine
Want his father to give his head
In the cause of *Dharma?*
Being in tune with the Timeless
I have always been guided by Him.
And you are the first to know it.
My life has been "A Resplendent Drama"
And when you hear it all
You may perhaps wonder
If it is not a mild description!
All my four sons died,
Two of them at the most innocent ages
But with a courage
Seen only in lion cubs.
That was their destiny!
Neither son, without martyrdom,
Could help me fulfill myself
And my followers' exceptations
In this cause of *Dharma*.
Today, the Punjab is so different
Each heart, each hearth, each hamlet
Is afire with heroism.
Even the worst of cowards
Now mocks at death,
For, that dreaded word
Now symbolises the highest attainment
On the path of spiritual journey.
It is the essence of nature—
Existentialist and ruthless!

And as for me, the father,

I would have broken down
With grief and remorse.
My young sons were denied
The most precious right,
The very right to live.
And I, none but I,
Was responsible.
But it was the last necessary oblation
I had to perform in the *Yagna* of *Dharma*.
Pride,
Pride that no father must have experienced
At the performance of his sons,
Was my only consolation.
And, as if this loss was not enough,
I lost my literature too—
Cartloads—
Only a poet would know
The terrible anguish on such a loss.
If Brahma were given the choice of
Losing his creation or losing his Vedas,
What would he choose?
Surely he would opt to save the Vedas;
He is not only their father,
But their mother too!
He contributed not only the seed
But also nurtured them through gestation.
The Timeless probably did not will
I should leave behind anything
Other than my life.
I had prayed each moment of my life,
Urging myself never to feel down and out,
To always keep my chin up
Which is becoming of a saint-soldier—
A true follower of the path of Nanak.
Which is why
When Aurangzeb tried to humiliate me
By his assuaging words of hypocricy,
I wrote back
My *Zafar Namah*,
The Epistle of Victory—
The undiminished lustre of my spirit—

In that otherwise darkest hour of my life.
I am confiding all this in you
Because you have surrendered yourself to me
In body as well as in spirit.

You can accuse me of
Something more—
My worship of *Shakti*
In the form of the sword.
It would seem to be
My final propitiation of the cult of violence
That could degenerate society into
Primitive tribalism
Where prevails rough and ready justice
And where the strong rule the weak.
But to me
It is as clear as day that
In the total Indian ethos,
In all the deep layers of our racial memory,
Nay, the sub-consciousness of mankind,
There lies embedded
An invisible image of the primal Mother.
The energy Principle of Matter,
The Consort of Lord Siva,
The female partner of *Purusa*.
While it explains many things
Like the divine image of *Ardh Nariswara,*
And even the man-woman relationship,
It also represents
One thing more,
And as a Rajput,
The son of the sword,
You know it as well.
That it is the Mother
Who is the final upholder of *Dharma,*
The last arbitrator of justice and injustice.
When in this eternal conflict
The forces of *adharma* score victory after victory
Over the forces of *Dharma,*
And the gods run helter-skelter,
When even

Brahma, Vishnu, and Mahesha
Cannot give them any quarter,
Then they turn to the Mother
And worship that primal energy
That infuses meaning to all that exists.
She is their last resort.
Once the Mother is so propitiated,
The sword of *Dharma* flashes
And She crushes *Adharma,*
And all the evils that it stands for
In bloody battles.
Having smitten *Adharma* down thus
With incomparable ruthlessness,
She dances uninhibited
With garlands of skulls adorning her neck.
The whole creation trembles.
So bewitching is the sight
That gods go down on their knees
And pray in utter supplication
And beg her
To return to her benign self.
Thus, she banishes all fear of death
As also all love of life
To render the soul clean and pure.
The effect:
The warriors give off their best
And poets rival Brahma in creativity.

Now soaked is my place of actions
With these traditions of *Shakti-*
If the Mother were ever real
It is evident
She must have performed her great deeds only there!
Rajputs all around worship her
As the ruling deity of their kingdoms,
Propitiating her to seek valour and victory
In their many battles.
Now picture yourself
As having been blessed
By Durga, the demon killer,
Riding her lion,

And Kali drunk with human blood,
Thirsting for more
As she dances possessed
With her protruding tongue dripping blood,
Close on your heels
As you speed to the battle-field
To measure your performance.
So, as a poet of valour,
As one steeped in the Mother tradition,
As a man with a mission
To fight tyranny and injustice,
Sworn to uphold *Dharma*,
I wanted my men to relive
The saga of the Mother—
Not as a piece of fascinating mythology,
But as a part of a much higher reality,
The reality of the sword,
Where She herself becomes the protector.
I wanted to register on my men
That in the final arbitration of right and wrong,
When all pros and cons have been mouthed,
It is the sword
That decides the issue.
The sword is used by both the opponents.
But while the sword of the tyrant
Is no more than a piece of iron,
The sword of the man of *Dharma*
Is the Mother herself!

It is no superstition, O Banda!
The sword is the highest *Dharma*
Of the man aroused
To the existentialist issues of the age.
This vision of the Mother
Made me as good a soldier
As a poet.
By immortalising the sword
As Goddess in verse,
I not only immortalised myself
But also all the followers of the Timeless.
My message, therefore, is:
When the social and moral order is in danger,

When tyranny reigns supreme,
It is no use slipping rosary beads
Through your fingers
And meditating over issues
Of soul and *Brahm*
In a remote forest grove.
Every saint must wield the sword
And transmute the issue into
A *Dharma Yuddha!*

So arise, O Banda!
And go with your sword in hand
To where you really belong—
Your own field
Not of action
But salvation!
Become the instrument of the Timeless
Because He hearkens you
Through me.
Shed off all your doubts
And all your cultivated sophistry.
Release yourself
Form the coils of your intellectual conflict
And carry fire and sword
Wherever you go
So that the tyrants tremble
As the nemesis of their deeds
Catches up with them.

(Banda in utter supplication, falls at the lotus feet of the Guru, kissing them again and again and washing them with his tears. The Guru tries to lift him up and take him in his arms. But Banda refuses to relent, remaining in that very worshipful posture for long time.)

CANTO TEN

Guru: Arise, O Banda!
It's the time to respond
Rather than be overwhelmed.
It's the time to be cool
Rather than be emotional.

It's the time to be a man of *Dharma*
Rather than be a man of God!

Banda: Let me for a while, O guru!
Sit at your lotus feet
And allow your pure blessings to shower upon me.
Let me be rid of my ego and conceit.
Let me forget that I was a Bairagi,
A runaway from my *Dharma*.
Let me take rebirth
As your bonded slave
And, therefore,
Of the Timeless.
Let me remember my sword
Which must now flash and strike
And wipe out root and branch
All those deservedly dead
Of their own actions.
Let me in these few moments
Steel my will
So that it never wavers
Whatever crops up to bar my way.
Let my tears
Not only bathe your divine feet
But also bleed out of me
Any cowardice
Still resident in some hidden corners.
Let me, O Guru!
Know what it is like
To unite in faith and spirit
With one chosen of the Timeless.
Let me swear by your immense solicitude
That I shall not allow
Any snares, any provocations
To get the better of me.
Let me be baptised by you
And blessed in all these resolutions
As I sit at your feet.

Guru: You have reached a point, O Banda!
And I am happy to see it,
In time and space,

Where the disciple is as good as the Master.
Were it merely the world of spiritual attainment,
I would have accepted you as such.
But alas! My path is one of supreme
Sacrifice.
The path of life's blood and warring steel.
All that I can bestow on you is
Death in a noble cause
In the battlefield.
I cannot even promise you victory
And the rule of
All the three worlds
As Krishna did to Arjuna!
For, I know that it will not be so!
But you have to kiss martyrdom
As none before in history,
As a saint-soldier
Of the noblest spirit,
Of the highest order.
I shower the glory of my mission
Upon you
By accepting you
As my Banda.
Now arise,
Come into my arms,
Be mine as I am yours.

Banda: Yes, My Guru!
I am fulfilled.
I have found
What I could not find,
In all penances, in all my *yoga*.
Today no quality bothers me.
Even as a speck of this dust
I am the universe.
For me, death in your cause
Is life eternal.
Let me not speak a word more now!
Let my actions,
The actions of a recluse,
Speak for themselves

Through earth-shaking deeds
That will make even the Himalayas
Tremble to their foundations.

Guru: Agreed, O Banda!
Let us not waste time.
For the time with you and me
Is short.
You are to immerse in action,
Relentless, unremitting action,
And I am to prepare myself
To join my Maker.
I am in a hurry
For, the Timeless calls me!
My only great quest was to find you out.
And I am happy that I have.
What more is there left to do?
But, O Banda!
Let me tell you something
You must be indeed dying to hear
Just as the whole world:
The fight to the finish
Will commence
As soon as you reach Punjab.
You will see
Every soldier of mine
Itching for action,
Deathless heroism informing each one's spirit.
Indeed you will never have seen
Such soldiers.
You will be a great general
Of a great army.
The army of *Dharma*.
The army ever victorious.
Each soldier vying with the other
To fight till the last,
Very last drop of blood.
The are soldiers unimpressed by numbers.
Undaunted by impediments,
Unaffected by adversities.
Soldiers who by sheer will,

Endurance and faith,
Conquer even the unconquerable—
Death.
For years on end, O Banda!
They have not known their women and children,
Their hearths and homes.
Most of them snatch moments of sleep
On horse-backs only.
Indeed when such men are born
Tyranny should only be a fleeting nightmare!
Certainly you are the most honoured one
To lead them into fierce battles,
The battles which will decide
Whether the Khalsa or the Moghuls
Are going to rule the country,
Whether the sunshine of *Dharma* will prevail
Or the darkness of *Adharma* will envelop.

You will find, O Banda!
That the praise of my men is
Not at all misplaced.
But still a question remains:
Why did I not lead my men myself?
Why did I not square my own quarrels?
All I can say is:
It was not willed in that manner.
For, if I were to kill the tyrants
I could be accused of two things:
That I was smitten with revenge,
Irrespective of the men
Who were to die on either side;
And secondly,
Camouflaged in the garb of *Dharma Yuddha*
Was my desire to establish my own rule.
I am the Guru, a man of God,
Never to be motivated by such things.
My function it is to sensitize the ground
For the army of the Khalsa to move in.
I am an instrument fashioned by the Timeless,
To handpick the issues
For which the righteous and the pure will battle.

And lastly,
I had to determine the one
Who was to fight the battle
As my chosen general,
As the general of the Khalsa.
In fact, the Timeless so wills
That I should be dead
Before the first victory of the Khalsa
So that no one could ever say
I was a coward,
Sitting far away from the field of action!
I have done my duty:
Now you will do yours!

Banda: But before I begin my mission, O Guru!
Baptise me into your Panth
As you did thousands of your sons, The Khalsa
So that I be one of your very own,
One of the Khalsa only,
So that I do not waver
Or err, or falter,
In carrying out your exalted mission.

Guru: You are my very special man, O Banda!
Talked we have
So much between us.
You alone have been given
Explanations by me
For each act of mine.
You alone know
Why I did what.
I have convinced you so long and hard
That baptised you already are
In spirit!
Yet, a formal baptismal is necessary
And I administer you one
With full ceremony
Because when in power
You act as the Khalsa would want you.
The Khalsa should be able to judge you
On your acts
And not as my viceroy among them,

Not answerable to anyone but me.

(The Guru then duly administers 'Amrit' to Banda).
Now, the final act:
Let me do you the greatest honour,
The honour you so richly deserve.
Let me confer upon you
The order of the Khalsa,
Which means Fearless as the Lion!
And bequeath to you
My own arrows
As a token of that.
So henceforth, O Banda!
People shall forget you as a Bairagi.
Hereafter, they will remember you
As Banda Bahadur,
Or Banda Singh Bahadur,
Or Banda, the Lion,
Or Banda, the Fearless.

Banda: O Sodhi Sultan!
O the best of the great race of Raghus!
From today onwards
You are my father,
Not as you are
To your countless, sons, the Khalsa
But my own father,
My real father,
Whose name and lineage
My own sons shall carry in the world.
Today I disown my own proud lineage of
The great *Agnikula* Rajputs.
Today I become a Sodhi and a Raghu
Born of you from the seed of your mind,
The nectar of immortality that I've sipped
From your sacred hands
Has made me to be reborn
In you and to you.

Guru: Blessed are you, O my son!
Not you,
I too am fulfilled.

But no more talking,
No more display of emotions,
No more wasting of time.
I, therefore, Order you
To go and prepare yourself
For your journey tomorrow—
The journey of destiny!
You shall report to me in the morning
When my *firmans* and my men,
Your companions,
And the *Panj Piyaras*
Will all be ready
To join you.
May you be victorious!
May the Khalsa be victorious!
Ever, ever victorious!!

—Sat Sri Akal—

Appendices

APPENDIX I

GURU GOBIND SINGH — TENTH GURU OF THE SIKHS 1666 - 1708 (42 YEARS)

Father—Guru Teg Bahadur

Mother — Mata Gujri

GURU GOBIND SINGH

Place of Birth — Patna

Date of Birth — 22nd Dec. 1666

Name before Guruship - Gobind Rai

Religion - Sikh

MARRIED TO

1. **Mata Jito in 1677 (11 years) Died 1700)**
2. **Mata Sundri in 1684 - Died 1747**
3. **Mata Sahib Devan in 1780 - Died 1745**

Son - (Mother-Sundri)	Son - (Mother - Jito)	Son - (Mother-Jito)	Son - (Mother—Jito)
Ajit Singh	Jujar Singh	Zorawar Singh	Fateh Singh
1687	1690	1696	1699

EDUCATION

Place - Patna, Anandpur

Subjects - Punjabi, Religions, Sanskrit, Arithmetic, Horse Riding, Weaponry

MISSION

1. Heir of a religious throne
2. To complete the mission of Guru Nanak
3. To uproot evil and administer justice
4. To create an army of immortal God

BATTLES (42)

Before the creation of Khalsa — 9
After the creation of Khalsa — 33
Time Period - 1684-1706

THE GURU PERIOD

Place of residence — Patna,
Period of Guruship — 1675-1708
Anandpur, Paonta, Damdama,
(33 Yrs)
Nanded

TEACHINGS

1. Belief in—One God, Guru, Guru Granth Sahib, Freedom and Democracy.
2. Vow not to; Cut Body Hair, Eat Kosher Meat, Smoke, Worship Images, Commit Adultery.

CONTRIBUTION TO SIKHISM

1. Five Symbols — Kesh, Kanga, Kara, Kucch, Kirpan;
2. Five Rules of Conduct — Life of: Honesty, Truth, Restraint, House holder, Religious

RELATED GURDWARAS

Total = 64
Location = Hem Kunt(1), Patna(4), U.P.(2), Himachal(5), Punjab(37), Delhi(3), Nanded-Andhra Pradesh(9), Haryana(3)

HYMNS

Recording in Guru Granth Sahib — one sloak (Page 1427)
Dasam Granth (Compiled 26 Years after Guru Gobind Singh's death),
Sarab Lo Granth
Language/s Used — Braj Bhasha, Persian, Punjabi

SAKHIS/SOURCE

1. Janam Sakhis of Guru Gobind Singh
2. Var Bhai Gurdas II
3. Works of Bhai Nand Lal
4. Works of Sonapat
5. Dasam Granth

6. Bachitar Natak

IMPORTANT NAMES

1. Aurangzeb, 2. Bahadur Shah, 3. Budh Shah, 4. Nabi Khan & Gani Khan, 5. Nawab of Malerkotla, 6. Chandu, 7. Wazir Khan.

THE DEPARTURE

Place of Death — Nanded
Date/Year - 1708

APPENDIX II

GURU GOBIND SINGH — THE TENTH GURU OF THE SIKHS

		Guru's Age
1666	Born at Patna Godfather—Raja Maini	
1670	Moved to Anandpur	4
1675	Martyrdom of Guru Tegh Bahadur Anointment of Gobind Rai as the tenth Guru of Sikhs	9
1677	Marriage with Mata Jito who died in 1700	11
1685	Marriage with Mata Sundri,who died in 1747	19
	1699—marriage with Mata Sahib Devan, Who died in 1745	
1686	Birth of Ajit Singh (at Paonta from Mata Sundri) died 1704 (age 18)	20
1687	Went to Dehra Dun to help Punjab Kaur and to punish the masands	21
1690	Birth of Jujar Singh (from Mata Jito) died 1704 (age 14)	24
1696	Birth of Zorawar Singh (from Mata Jito) died 1704) (age 8)	30
1699	Birth of Fateh Singh (from Mata Jito) died 1704 (age 5)	33

1699	Birth of Khalsa at Takhat Kesgarh, Anandpur	33
1706	Compilation of Second version of Guru Granth Sahib at Damdama Sahib	40
1707-20th Feb.	Death of Aurangzeb 20th Feb.	41
1707-June	Bahadur Shah coronated as the emperor of india	41
1707 2nd August	Visited Bahadur Shah at Agra	41
1708-Sept 15	Reached Nanded	42
1708-2nd October	Sent Banda Bahadur to Punjab; Mata Sahib Devan was also asked to go with Banda	42
1708	Death at Nanded	42

APPENDIX III

IMPORTANT BATTLES

Before Khalsa Period

		Guru's Age
1682	First war of Anandpur with Raja Bhim Chand of Kahlur	16
1685	Second war of Anandpur with Rajas of Kahlur, Kangra and Guler	19
1688	War of Bhangani, with Rajas of Garhwal, Bilaspur, Kangra, Mandi, Guler, Hindur, Kotgarh, Nurpur, and others	22
1690	Battle of Nadaun	24
1691	Third war of Anandpur	25
1693	Fourth war of Anandpur	27
1694	Fifth war of Anandpur	28

1696	Sixth war of Anandpur	30

Post Khalsa Period

1699	First war of Anandpur with Mughals	33
1700	Battle of Nirmogarh with Mughals	34
1700	Battle of Bharsali with Wazir Khan	34
1702	Second and Third war of Anandpur with Mughals	36
1703	Fourth and Fifth war of Anandpur with Hill Rajas	37
1704	War of Kiratpur with Mughals and Hill Rajas	38
1704	Sixth and last war of Anandpur with Mughals and Hill Rajas	38
1704	Battle of Chamkaur	38
1705	Battle of Khidrana	39

APPENDIX IV

The Guru	*Age at Death*	*Age at Meeting the Guru*	*Age at Guruship*	*Period of Guruship*	*Age at Marriage*
Nanak Dev	70	NA	38	32	18
Angad	48	28	35	13	15
Amardas	95	61	73	22	23
Ramdas	47	12	40	7	19
Arjan Dev	43	NA	18	25	16
Hargobind	49	NA	11	38	12,18,20
Har Rai	31	NA	14	17	10
Harkrishen	8	NA	5	3	NA
Tegh Bahadur	54	NA	43	11	11
Gobind Singh	42	NA	9	32	11,18,34